The world pharmaceutical industry

James Taggart

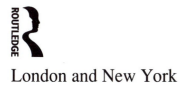

London and New York

The world pharmaceutical industry

James Taggart

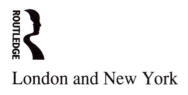

London and New York

First published 1993 by
Routledge
11 New Fetter Lane, London EC4P 4EE

Simultaneously published in the USA and Canada
by Routledge
a division of Routledge, Chapman and Hall, Inc.
29 West 35th Street, New York, NY 10001

© 1993 James Taggart

Typeset in 10/12pt Times by
Ponting-Green Publishing Services, Berkshire
Printed and bound in Great Britain by
T.J. Press (Padstow) Ltd, Padstow, Cornwall

British Library Cataloguing-in-Publication Data

A catalogue record for this book is available from the British Library

ISBN 0–415–02500–1

Library of Congress Cataloging-in-Publication Data has been applied for

ISBN 0–415–02500–1

For Jenny
with love and appreciation

Contents

Figures

Tables

Preface

Even during the final weeks when the last draft of this book was in preparation, despite the long hours I spent working on the text, I could not help noticing how often the pharmaceutical industry made the news. A television exposé on Myodil, an oil-based dye used in myelography, purported to demonstrate wrong use of the substance. Myodil was designed to be injected into the spine to increase the definition of X-rays in that area of the body. Unfortunately, because it is an oil-based preparation, it is retained in the spine for long periods after the injection. In some patients this seems to have led to arachnoiditis; that is, the spinal nerve becomes irritated, causing the formation of scar tissue, which is thought to be the source of severe and prolonged pain for the sufferers. The television programme claimed that warnings about arachnoiditis linked to the use of Myodil began to appear in 1973. The UK supplier, Glaxo, disclaimed negligence, pointing out that warnings of side effects had always been given and that one of the recommendations for use of the product was that it should be removed from the spine subsequent to radiography. As often happens in these cases, disagreements between health care professionals do nothing to alleviate the sufferings of the admittedly small proportion of patients who developed acute arachnoiditis.

Another television documentary covered the problem of Halcion, a best-selling sleeping pill manufactured by Upjohn, the US drugs multinational. Halcion and its generic equivalent, triazolam, belong to the benzodiazepine group of drugs. Benzodiazepines are the subject of a large number of legal actions in several countries. In the UK, for instance, over 10,000 individuals have applied for legal aid to pursue actions involving benzodiazepine addiction. The problem for Halcion is more specific. It is reportedly associated with a much higher frequency of side effects, particularly memory loss, than other similar drugs. Having reviewed the available data, the UK Committee on the

Safety of Medicines (CSM) requested that Upjohn and the five generic suppliers voluntarily stop selling the drug in Britain. Only Upjohn refused, whereupon the CSM suspended (subject to appeal) the firm's licence to sell Halcion in the UK from 2 October 1991. This represents the biggest withdrawal since the 1982 Opren shock, and it is the first time in nine years that the CSM has imposed such a ban. It represents a severe difficulty for Upjohn, not because of the annual £5 million of sales in the UK, but because of the possible cascade effect on the firm's worldwide market of $240 million per annum. Not only is Halcion the second best seller in the Upjohn drugs portfolio, but the contretemps with the CSM may assist the legal claims against the company initiated by 140 individuals in the UK alone. Upjohn's perspective on the affair was different, and it clearly intended to fight the ban. Chairman and Chief Executive Theodore Cooper was quoted as saying: 'There is absolutely no scientific or medical evidence that warrants the withdrawal of Halcion tablets in the UK or any other country.'

Coincidentally, as Upjohn was confronting its Halcion problem, another benzodiazepine manufacturer was fighting its way out of the doldrums. The Swiss multinational Hoffmann La Roche rose to become the world's biggest drugs firm in the 1960s on the back of its tranquilliser Valium, the pharmaceutical industry's first global blockbuster. By the end of the following decade, patents had expired worldwide and Roche went into a period of decline. A new management team was installed in the early 1980s; it developed a strategy of increasing the efficiency and productivity of operations and diversifying out of the pharmaceutical industry into other high value-added product areas like flavours, fragrances, vitamins and diagnostics. However, the acquisition of the pioneering US biotechnology firm, Genentech, for $2.1 billion in 1989 perhaps indicated a re-focusing on the drugs industry. From being world leader, Roche had sunk to around fifteenth place in the pecking order at its 1979 nadir. In 1990, it had fought its way back to No. 11 and has ambitions to rejoin the top five in the medium term.

Of the three problem areas outlined above, the third exercises most intellectual attraction on me. The ethical and moral dilemmas faced by the world pharmaceutical industry are critical to society as a whole; the questions posed by Animal Rights, Oxfam, the environmentalist movement, and by a host of other special interest and pressure groups are questions that must be addressed and answered by drug firms and their manufacturers' associations. However, important as they are, these matters are not the primary focus of this book. Instead, I have concentrated on the strategy perspective; I have examined where the pharmaceutical industry and its firms have come from, where they are now, and where they might be headed as the twenty-first century beckons. I have leaned heavily on the standard analytical tools of business strategy and depended on my knowledge of the industry, such as it is, for synthesis, interpretation and prediction.

The first three chapters provide the historical and conceptual framework within which the pharmaceutical industry operates, with particular stress on the critically important element of managing the technology. Chapter 4 examines the impact of the single European market (EC, 1992) legislation, possibly the most far-reaching set of regulations to impinge upon the pharmaceutical industry. These will obviously affect companies based in Europe, or foreign affiliates operating in Europe; but they will also be important strategy determinants for other firms seeking to become major pan-European players. Chapter 5 analyses the immediate operating environment of the drugs industry, using the framework developed by Michael Porter. The following four chapters look at four major market areas in turn, including a strategic assessment of three drug multinationals based in each area. The final chapter summarises the arguments, and provides my outlook for the industry to the turn of the century.

This book has been in preparation for seven years and consequently the term West Germany is used consistently throughout the text. During this time I have many people to thank, though the errors of fact and judgement are all mine. My friend and colleague, Steve Young, guided and encouraged me throughout the project. Another friend and colleague, Michael McDermott, helped with constructive criticism at a key juncture. Contacts with pharmaceutical company executives across the globe were invaluable, but I would make special mention of the personal kindness of Dr Paul Worrall of Bristol-Myers. Many colleagues helped unstintingly with the background research; in particular I am grateful to Bernard Ayton (for Chapter 4) and Vicky Alme (for Chapter 5); I must also acknowledge the assistance of Charles Tosh, Willie French, Nick Stranks, Freddie McKean, John Kelly, Bernard Dyer, Terje Dengerud, David Williams, Mike Cuthbert, Michael Pretious, John Gemmill, Anthony Keating, Gareth Gadd, Tim Blaxter and Tor Minsaas. Finally, the book (and its author) owes a great deal to the efforts of Sheila McLean who deciphered my hieroglyphics and typed, and retyped, and retyped....

Inevitably, the burden of writing a heavily researched book falls principally on the author's immediate family. Nothing is possible without a wife and friend like Jenny. I can also promise Joe, Alan, Mairi, Fiona and Gill that crabbit old Dad will (temporarily) revert to smiling, conversation and other humanoid traits.

J.H.T.
Glasgow, November 1991

1 The development of the world pharmaceutical industry

HISTORY

At the turn of the present century doctors were, by and large, unable to treat the cause of disease; at best, they could make some attempt to alleviate the symptoms or encourage the body's natural defence mechanisms into action. Thus, the general practitioner had an armoury of only four specific disease-fighting drugs: digitalis for certain heart conditions; quinine for malaria; pecacuanha for dysentery; mercury for the treatment of syphilis. Many of the other crude drugs which were used to lessen disease symptoms dated back to (or even pre-dated) Galen, who was the personal physician to Marcus Aurelius.[1]

The brilliant theoretical work of Pasteur on the causes of infection, including the subsequent practical development of the theory by himself and Lister, was one of the two signposts to the modern pharmaceutical industry which were erected in the late nineteenth century. The other stemmed from earlier attempts by William Perkins to manufacture synthetic quinine from aniline. He actually succeeded in producing the first artificial dye, aniline purple. German and Swiss companies were quick to take up this discovery and began to synthesise a wide range of dyes. As a by-product of this activity, these firms were also able to synthesise a range of compounds which were therapeutically useful. Thus the Bayer company in Germany developed aspirin in 1899. Another German company (Hoechst) actively supported Paul Erlich's work in developing his concept of the 'magic bullet'; this involved using synthetic dyes, which were able to stain animal tissue differentially, as a delivery system to carry drugs to particular parts or organs of the body. Eventually, after over 600 molecular manipulations, he produced Salvarsan, which was highly effective against syphilis.

While Erlich's work stimulated further drug research in his own and other countries, very few new drugs were discovered in the next twenty-five years. However, in 1935, Dr Gerhard Domagk of the Bayer company discovered the powerful anti-streptococcal effects of injecting Prontosil, a red dye derived from coal tar. Bayer's patent on Prontosil proved to be worthless when scientists at the Pasteur Institute discovered that the dye breaks down in the body, and that the therapeutically active substance is sulphanilamide. Unfortunately for Bayer, this substance had first been prepared many years earlier by Paul Gelmo at the Vienna Institute of Technology. The therapeutic properties of the preparation had not been recognised, the patent had expired, and the drug was in the public domain. However, Domagk's discovery gave tremendous impetus to the search for new drugs, and within a few years a large number of sulpha drugs – derivatives of sulphanilamide – had been produced, patented and marketed. Thus, the value of patents in this industry was demonstrated at an early stage.

The Second World War was the stimulus for the development of penicillin, the first really safe antibiotic, on a commercial scale. Fleming had first discovered its antimicrobial qualities in 1928, but it was a further nine years before Florey and Chain developed it as a potentially useful therapeutic agent. Even then, it required major development by Pfizer in the US in order to produce the drug in commercial quantities. Again, however, penicillin was non-patentable.

By this time, many of the current industry leaders were now active in pharmaceutical manufacturing; as well as Bayer and Hoechst in Germany (mentioned above), the Swiss firms Roche and (the forerunners of) Ciba-Geigy had entered the industry, as had US firms Pfizer, Eli Lilly, Merck and Abbott Laboratories. UK representatives included Glaxo, Beecham and the Wellcome Foundation.

The hunt for new drugs now became very intense, and fresh discoveries followed on rapidly. Dr Selman Waksman of Rutgers University discovered the anti-tuberculosis agent streptomycin in 1943. This was followed by a rising tide of new products emanating from industrial laboratories, beginning with chloramphenicol – the first broad-spectrum antibiotic – in 1947; the tetracycline range of products, beginning in 1948; and, during the 1950s, the development of corticosteroids, oral contraceptives, antihistamines, antidepressants, diuretics, semi-synthetic penicillins, and many more – all patented. Thus, within the space of about twenty years, the pharmaceutical industry was transformed from a commodity business, where each company manufactured the full range of medicaments for pharmacists to compound, into a research- and marketing-intensive business, heavily dependent on patents and brand names.

Recent years have seen the evolution of the new science of biotechnology, in which much of the innovative effort has gone into producing new drugs for human consumption. By 1984 it was estimated[2] that there were some 200 biotechnology companies worldwide. While the figure had almost certainly grown by the order of 100 per cent by 1990, this masks the very large number of firms, including pharmaceutical companies, involved in the research stage of biotechnology. For example, a MITI survey in 1982 indicated that 157 companies out of 200 surveyed already had a biotechnology research programme under way.[3] Many of the biotechnology firms have formed close working relationships – and even financial linkages – with the major pharmaceutical companies. Thus, the companies involved in the modern pharmaceutical industry derive from a number of different backgrounds, and operate in different sectors of the industry. Pradhan[4] has classified them as follows:

1 *Medicinal chemical manufacturers.* Medicinal chemical organisations produce the active ingredients used in pharmaceutical preparations; they produce bulk organic and inorganic chemicals and their derivatives, prepare drugs from animal sources, synthesise or isolate products into pure form, and extract active principles from botanical drugs and herbs (such as alkaloids).
2 *Biological products manufacturers.* These firms produce vaccines, serums, toxoids, and analogous products such as allergenic extracts, normal blood serums, and blood plasma for human or veterinary use, and products for diagnostic use.
3 *Ethical pharmaceutical manufacturers.* Ethical pharmaceutical companies formulate drugs into suitable dosage forms such as tablets, capsules, injectables, elixirs, syrups, and ointments; the products are called ethical because they are promoted to health care professionals and are available to individuals through hospitals, pharmacies, chemist shops and – in some countries – through physicians, on written or oral prescription by the prescriber.
4 *Proprietary product manufacturers.* These firms produce preparations that are common general home remedies used for the relief of minor temporary ailments. These are promoted to the general public and can be purchased without prescription.
5 *Private formula or brand manufacturers.* These companies manufacture products for distributors, or make generic and home remedies for themselves; if the products are produced for the distributors, then they use the distributors' brand name or the generic name, and the distributor is responsible for marketing these products.

Since the research-intensive pharmaceutical firms which serve international markets are concentrated in the third category, it is on the 'ethical pharmaceutical manufacturers' classification that attention will be focused in this book.

CHARACTERISTICS OF THE WORLD PHARMACEUTICAL INDUSTRY

The purpose of this section is to describe in some detail the characteristics, particularly elements of structure and morphology, which so clearly differentiate the ethical drugs industry from any other. The most obvious feature of this industry is that it is characterised by a very large number of small sellers, and a relatively small number of large companies which tend to be international in outlook and operation.

These large firms are concentrated in the highly industrialised OECD countries. Tables 1.1–2 show the industry structure in the six largest drug consumption nations. Of a total of 2,757 firms in 1986, 10 per cent (270) are classified as large. This varies from a high of 20 per cent in the case of Japan to only 6 per cent for the US (see Figure 1.1). The level of foreign penetration of these six major markets is shown in Figure 1.2 in terms of both numbers of foreign-owned firms and sales of foreign-owned firms. By either measure, foreign penetration is very low in Japan, and is also low in the US. However, the differential in the two measures for the US indicates that the average sales level of foreign firms which have established a foothold in the US is still significantly lower than that of domestic firms. The opposite applies in the case of the UK.

Table 1.1 The structure of the pharmaceutical industry in each of six large nations, 1983

Country	No. of companies	No. of large companies	% Ownership				
			Domestic	European	USA	Japan	Other
West Germany	530	38	57	24	18	–	1
France	320	40	57	20	22	–	1
Italy	345	30	47	47	6	–	–
Japan	400	81	83	9	8	–	–
UK	212	24	46	21	33	–	–
US	950	57	70	30	–	–	–
Totals	2,757	270					

Source: R. Chew, G. Teeling-Smith and N. Wells, *Pharmaceuticals in Seven Nations*, Office of Health Economics, London (1985)
Note: – indicates nil or negligible.

Table 1.2 Share of national pharmaceutical markets attributable to companies originating from each of six large nations, 1983 (%)

Country	Home Base of Companies					
	US	*German*	*UK*	*French*	*Italian*	*Japanese*
France	20	11	5	53	<1	<1
West Germany	18	56	4	3	1	<1
Italy	17	15	7	3	46	–
Japan	8	4	1	–	–	85
US	82	4	5	–	<1	–
UK	38	9	36	3	<1	–

Source: Chew *et al.* (1985)

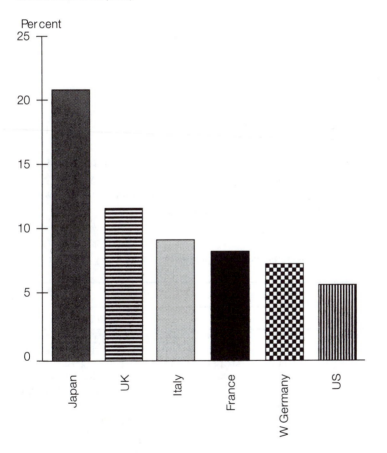

Figure 1.1 The structure of the pharmaceutical industry: large companies as a percentage of all companies *Source*: Office of Health Economics (1986)

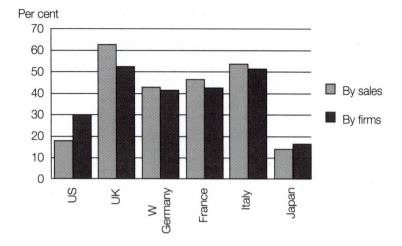

Figure 1.2 The structure of the pharmaceutical industry: penetration of domestic markets *Source*: Office of Health Economics (1986)

Table 1.3 shows the employment in the industry for the six target countries for various years from 1970 to 1988. Generally, West Germany, France and the UK show fairly stable employment performance, though rising in the most recent period; Italy, the US and Japan between them accounted for most of the employment growth of some 219,000 jobs over these eighteen years.

Table 1.3 Number of employees in the pharmaceutical industry in the six target nations

| Country | Total employed | | | | |
	1970	*1975*	*1980*	*1982*	*1988*
West Germany	76,000	72,000	69,806	73,166	76,000
France	60,500	64,257	64,363	65,000	69,000
Italy	51,436	59,482	60,801	61,328	69,000
Japan	103,912	129,663	155,415	170,500	214,000
UK	71,000	76,000	72,000	72,000	78,000
US	148,900	166,600	189,866	199,200	225,000
TOTAL	511,748	568,002	612,251	641,194	731,000

Source: Derived from Chew *et al.* (1985). 1988: author's estimates

Manufacturing

The manufacturing process in the pharmaceutical industry consists of four stages: the acquisition of raw materials, the production of pharmaceutical chemicals, the production of final dosage forms, and quality control. These four stages have varying requirements in terms of capital intensity and technological intensity. The general position is shown in Figure 1.3.

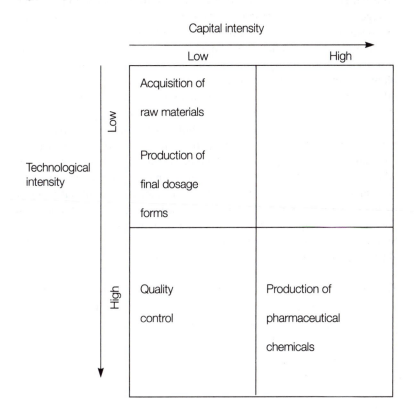

Figure 1.3 Manufacturing requirements *Source*: Author

The acquisition of raw materials   The particular properties of the raw materials have a bearing on manufacturing methods and scale of production. It was indicated earlier how the industry has swung away from dependence on natural materials to the utilisation of synthetics. A similar change may now be in progress with the advent of biotechnological production of raw materials. However, no matter the source of the raw materials, the quality requirements of the industry are such that supplier involvement in the industry is not insignificant, and this has been a factor in encouraging vertical integration.

The production of pharmaceutical chemicals   is the second stage of manufacturing, and could be considered as part of the fine chemicals industry; indeed, many pharmaceutical multinationals are involved in both fields. These chemicals are the active ingredients used in the final dosage forms, and are produced from animal or plant resources, or are synthesised by the same multiple-stage batch processes as are used in the fine chemicals industry. For many pharmaceutical chemicals, e.g. antibiotics produced by fermentation, it is possible to utilise the same plant for several different manufactured end products. However, for others – e.g. synthetic hormones – highly specialised plant and expertise are required. Whilst it would be possible for a major pharmaceutical multinational to concentrate all its bulk production for a particular active ingredient in a single plant, for strategic reasons most of these companies maintain one such plant in North America and one elsewhere – usually in Europe. Production of pharmaceutical chemicals is normally undertaken only by the large pharmaceutical multinationals or by manufacturers in the standard fine chemicals industry. This does, of course, provide an entry point into either market, from either direction. Small pharmaceutical companies will buy most, if not all, of their active ingredients from the primary producers.

The production of final dosage forms   is the third stage, and size of company is less important. What is involved here is the physical operation required to prepare the active ingredient for final marketing. This will include any or all of:

1 Compounding of ingredients.
2 Dispersion of ingredients.
3 Granulation.
4 Drying.
5 Coating.
6 Tableting.
7 Encapsulation.
8 Packaging.

These processes have little in common with the skills required for the production of pharmaceutical chemicals; in fact, they share many common facets with the formulation of certain other chemical-based products such as toiletries and cosmetics. This commonality of processes has allowed entry into any one of toiletries, cosmetics and pharmaceuticals from either of the other two.

As with pharmaceutical chemicals, it is often possible to produce many different products on the same manufacturing equipment, subject, of course, to necessary limitations like the complete segregation of antibiotics and hormones. However, the essential flexibility of this .stage of manufacturing means that wide geographical dispersion is economically possible. As this is also politically desirable, it is normally found that the drug multinationals produce pharmaceutical preparations in all the major markets in which they are involved.

This stage of manufacturing is significantly less capital-intensive than the production of pharmaceutical chemicals. The labour content is normally fairly high and, for the most part, does not require a particularly high level of skill. However, where required, capital can normally be substituted for labour.

Quality control   at all stages of manufacturing is of paramount importance, owing to the nature of the end-use market. Standards of manufacturing practice have improved with the passage of time, but legal requirements in most countries are a constant spur to the improvement of quality; these requirements are also the guarantee of purity and lack of contamination. This is particularly so in highly quality-conscious markets like the US, UK, Japan and West Germany. In recent years, increasingly stringent legal requirements have pushed up the relative cost of quality control, and also the absolute degree of expertise required to implement a satisfactory system. Large firms will, increasingly, be in a better position to capitalise on this trend.

Marketing of pharmaceuticals

Pharmaceuticals marketing differs from almost all other consumer goods in that the buying decision is not made by the final consumer; the drug is prescribed by the general practitioner (usually) and paid for by the patient, with the state making a varying contribution to the cost of treatment. In addition, ethical pharmaceuticals may be advertised only to medical practitioners. The most effective way in which a manufacturer may influence the prescribing behaviour of the general practitioner is generally agreed to be face-to-face contact involving the firm's salesman. These salesmen must be highly knowledgeable about diseases and their treatment, and about the side effects and other problems involved in using his firm's products. The training cost of such a sales representative is high, as it probably takes up to a full year before a new recruit becomes fully effective.

In order to make this face-to-face contact with each doctor sufficiently frequently (say three or four times a year) to have some influence on his prescribing behaviour, firms must maintain a large sales force in each market where they have a presence. For example, in the UK, with a population of some 55 million, and around 21,500 medical practices, an ethical drugs firm wishing to maintain regular contact with doctors will require to maintain a sales force of some forty to a hundred.[5]

As well as direct representation, firms also use other methods of communicating with medical practitioners, including advertising in the medical journals, direct mail, and the organisation of medical conferences and other meetings. However, no matter what particular method of communication is chosen, the success of the marketing function rests on the concept of brand names. According to the Office of Health Economics,[6] modern competition depends on differentiating new products from those already on the market, and then promoting the sales of these new brands. Brand names and sales promotion, by this perspective, are just as important a part of the overall innovation process as is the product discovery and development stage. This leads to new pharmaceutical products being continually developed and marketed, which makes earlier innovative products obsolete. This, in turn, leads to the development of progressively safer and more effective medicines to replace those already in use. The brand name, in conjunction with patent protection, is an essential part of the commercial aspect of a new drug. As effective patent life is being gradually reduced in most developed countries, there is increasing pressure on innovating firms to recoup past research expenditures quickly before the sharp decline stage of the product life cycle is reached.

It is at this point that the research-intensive firms run up against a number of problem areas. The fact is that many governments have imposed restrictions on the amount that firms are allowed to spend on sales promotion. For example, in the UK, allowable sales promotional expenditure was cut from 14 per cent of sales to 10 per cent in 1978. Any overspending on this figure was to be added back to profits for purposes of price negotiation. In 1985 this figure was further reduced to 9 per cent; additionally, all overspending above this figure must now be paid back direct to the government as well as being added back to profits. This kind of restriction causes especial difficulties for smaller firms, who find it progressively more difficult to finance a large enough sales force to give adequate coverage of all doctors.

For the research-intensive firms, the whole area of patents and patent practice is fraught with problems. The firm's basic reason for patenting a new drug is to guarantee the exclusive legal right to profit from its innovation for a specified number of years. In the view of the pharmaceutical industry, patents are the essential means by which a firm accumulates funds for future research rather than compensation for past efforts.

Generally, two types of patent exist. The 'product patent' covers the chemical substance itself, while a 'process patent' covers the method of processing or manufacture. Of the two, the process patent offers much less protection, owing to the comparative ease of modifying an organic chemical manufacturing process to evade the patent. It is also very difficult to provide legally binding proof that a patented process has been used to manufacture a product identical to that of a competitor. Most countries relied only on process patents to regulate the pharmaceutical industry until the mid-1950s. Since then, however, many countries have recognised the product patent in law. The question of patent protection is further elaborated later in this chapter.

Another difficulty, which follows the expiry of a patent, is the appearance of generic competitive products. These contain the same active ingredient as the original patented brand, but rely on price competition alone to gain a share of the market. This has the effect of depressing the sales of the innovating firm's product. The situation can be exacerbated by pressure to introduce generic substitution into the prescribing context. Thus, even where a doctor had prescribed a specific brand of drug, the pharmacist may be obliged to substitute a generic form of the drug if it is cheaper. Generic substitution was under active consideration for a time by the UK government, but in 1983 it was decided to reject the concept, recognising the economic importance of the brand name to the research-intensive pharmaceutical industry. In the US, however, the growth of the government-funded Medicare and Medicaid schemes has led to 'maximum allowable cost' schemes for public-sector prescriptions, and these are implemented by allowing the pharmacist to substitute cheaper generic drugs for prescribed brand names. Nevertheless, brand name prescriptions in the private sector continue to dominate the US industry.

Cost pressure on publicly funded health schemes has also led to other forms of prescribing controls. One principal method is the introduction of 'positive' lists of prescribed drugs which may be reimbursed under social security schemes. This approach is used by France, Italy and Switzerland. The 'negative' list sets out the drugs which will not be reimbursed by social security systems and is in use in the UK, the

Netherlands, West Germany, and in the US in some states under Medicare and Medicaid. Only Japan is completely free of this type of control on prescribing. However, in most countries doctors are subject to some form of pressure to encourage them to prescribe economically.

With the exception of the US, all the major OECD countries have some form of price control for ethical pharmaceuticals. In the UK, the principal price control mechanism is the pharmaceutical price regulation scheme (PPRS), which has two prime objectives:[7]

1 To secure the supply of high-quality medicines to the National Health Service on fair and reasonable terms.
2 To promote a strong, efficient and profitable UK-based pharmaceutical industry capable of sustained research effort, leading to new or improved medicines for the NHS and world markets.

The government uses the PPRS to satisfy itself that reasonable profits are earned by the industry and reasonable costs are incurred by the Department of Health. Each participating company is notified of its target return on capital, and price-setting by negotiation with the DHSS takes place within this overall target. Up to 1983, the target returns were in the range of 16–25 per cent, but were formally reduced in 1984 to 15–20.5 per cent, and again in 1985 to 15–17 per cent. It is widely held that the past effectiveness of the PPRS has been due to the maintenance of good relations between all the interested parties. The large reduction in target profitability arrived at by 1985 seems to have had the effect of disturbing the good relationships, because in late 1986 the target range was increased to 16–18.5 per cent, with a possible further increase to be implemented at a later date. Restrictive price controls have also been a problem for the industry in France, Italy, Greece, Spain, Austria, Australia and Canada. Since 1984 the Japanese government has imposed a series of price reductions which have reduced the profitability of pharmaceutical firms in that market; but, since 1984 prices were high, profitability has not fallen below the level of acceptability.

One of the most acute problems arising for price differentials between countries for the same drug has been the growth of 'parallel imports' within the European Community. Currency fluctuations often magnify the price differentials and opportunities arise for dealers to move large quantities of medicines from one country to another within the EC. Restriction of these parallel imports is held to be a contravention of certain provisions of the Treaty of Rome. Paradoxically, the EC Commission is also carrying out an investigation into the drug price control systems of certain countries which give rise to the price differentials, as these are also held to be in contravention of the Treaty of Rome. In the case of the UK, for example, parallel imports were thought to have reached some £75 million per annum by 1984;[8] by 1990 this figure had probably doubled. The reduced prices of these imports have, by and large, been of no benefit to the public purse, as the dispensing pharmacist is normally reimbursed for a cheap parallel-import on the basis of the official UK price. Parallel importing is held to have a depressive effect on the profitability of the research-intensive drug firms, and so reduces the funds available for pharmaceutical-innovation.

INNOVATION

The pharmaceutical industry is critically reliant on continuing flows of new products, which are the fruits of research and development. The profitability, and ultimately the survival, of the major firms in the industry depends on the maintenance of competitive position; in turn, the competitive position is determined by the rate of innovation. Thus, among the major firms in the industry, there are few recorded cases where a company has cut back on research and development expenditure, even during periods of falling profits.

As the importance of innovation has increased, so have the costs of innovative effort. In part, this is due to increasingly strict regulation by governments; in part, it is due to the new directions of innovative effort. With growing frequency, research projects are not being aimed at the production of a new or modified drug, but at understanding the cause of a particular disease and towards the specific actions and side effects of drugs on the human body and its individual tissues and organs. Furthermore, increasing research effort is now being put into the more complex diseases for which no easy solution is forthcoming, e.g. cancer, arthritis, multiple sclerosis. This train of research requires a degree of sophistication in methodology and scientific knowledge that is without precedent in the pharmaceutical industry. Add to that the huge complexity and cost of the industry's move into biotechnology, and it can be clearly understood that pharmaceutical innovation is becoming a considerably more risky investment. Nevertheless, levels of spending suggest that the pharmaceutical multinationals continue to see suitable future returns being made from the huge and growing investments in research and development. If this were not so, the logic behind the continuing high expenditures on research and development would be difficult to follow.

Conceptual factors relating to innovation

In the context used here, pharmaceutical innovation is taken to mean the whole process involved in bringing a new product to market, whether it be a new chemical entity or a molecular manipulation of a previously known drug which yields significant benefits. Innovation is conceptually limited to the first company which produces a particular new drug; any other firm which produces a 'me too' product with no inherent advantage over the innovative drug would properly be called an 'imitator'.

In a major pharmaceuticals company, research requires a wide range of scientific activity, including:[9]

1 Chemical or biological research, aimed at discovering new chemical or biological entities for use in the treatment or prevention of disease.
2 Biochemical research, to elucidate the action of drugs at the molecular level.
3 Pharmacology, the study of the effects of drugs upon disease in living beings.
4 Toxicology, the study of harmful side effects of drugs.

Pharmaceuticals development is taken to mean all other activities subsequent to or overlapping the research phase leading to the production of new pharmaceutical products in saleable form. These activities may involve new or existing drugs. The two main activities involved in pharmaceuticals development are product development and process development. Product development involves the determination of the optimum method of presenting either a new drug or an improved version of an existing one as a finished product. Important factors here are the need for chemical stability, the bio-availability of the active ingredient, and the suitability of administration to the patient. The third of these factors shows wide geographical variations, depending on differing national tastes.

Process development is the study of the most economical method of manufacturing the product at an acceptable level of purity and economic yield. For example, a ten-stage chemical production process (by no means uncommon) with a 90 per cent effective yield at each stage would have an overall yield of only 35 per cent. Thus, long-term process development is often financially worthwhile, but the achievement of this objective may be partially frustrated by shortening product life cycles.

Most of the major pharmaceutical multinationals have historically regarded innovation primarily from the aspect of product technology.

This has led to a high degree of specialisation in the individual therapeutic sub-markets, as will be seen in a later section. Japanese firms – and some in West Germany – however, lay considerable stress on process technology; this expertise may be of very considerable strategic benefit in the long run.

Finally, it should be noted that the increasing risk involved in pharmaceuticals innovation, already referred to, is motivating some large research-based companies to direct an increasing proportion of resources away from the discovery of new chemical entities towards the improvement and development of existing products. This is done primarily in an attempt to increase the product life cycle, maximise the rent from the original investment in R & D, and provide the cash flows necessary to finance current and future research programmes.

Expenditure on research and development

Expenditure on R & D is an important component within the overall cost structure of the industry. Figure 1.4 shows, for the six large OECD nations, total pharmaceutical expenditures on R & D as a proportion of output. Overall, these six nations allocate 8.4 per cent of total value of output to the search for new and improved medicines. The individual nations' allocations vary from 13.1 per cent for West Germany to 6 per cent for Japan.

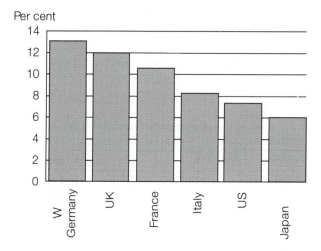

Figure 1.4 Pharmaceutical industry R & D: national expenditures as a percentage of output *Source*: Office of Health Economics (1986)

16   *The world pharmaceutical industry*

Table 1.4 Expenditure on research and development by the pharmaceutical industry ($ million)

Country	1970	1975	1982	1988
US	550	900	1,818	4,900
UK	68	185	626	1,250
West Germany	162	455	902	2,590
France	80	240	545	1,900
Italy	52	114	265	870
Japan	103	323	958	3,310
Total	1,015	2,217	5,114	14,820

Source: Derived from Chew *et al.* (1985); 1988: author's estimates

Table 1.4 shows dollar expenditures on pharmaceutical R & D by the six nations in 1975, 1980, 1982, and 1988. The Office of Health Economics[10] estimated that the 1982 total of $5,114 million represented over 70 per cent of the world total R & D expenditure on pharmaceuticals. Also, while the largest proportion (33 per cent) of this total was accounted for by the US, this country showed the lowest compound rate of growth (13.9 per cent per annum) over the period 1975–88. Highest growth rate was achieved by Japan (19.6 per cent). However, the figures in this table may show a distorted picture of the inputs to pharmaceutical R & D, as they are calculated at current prices and are subject to currency conversions. Table 1.5 shows the total pharmaceutical industry expenditures on R & D in each of the six nations, based on constant prices in local currencies and indexed to 1970. The pre-eminence of the UK position is evident, with a 1982 index number of 232. The Japanese performance (137) now falls below that of West Germany (140) and France (140).

Table 1.5 Pharmaceutical industry expenditures on research and development (index numbers based on constant prices in local currencies, 1970 = 100)

Country	1970	1975	1980	1982
US	100	111	127	129
UK	100	135	204	232
West Germany	100	116	140	155
France	100	111	128	140
Italy	100	97	98	125
Japan	100	110	149	137

Source: Derived from Chew *et al.* (1985)

The outputs of innovation

There are a number of problems involved in measuring the outputs of innovation. The many researchers in this field have used various methods of quantifying the productivity and profitability of the innovative efforts of the pharmaceutical industry, but there is no general agreement on this aspect.

Reekie[11] made an intensive study of patents granted to pharmaceutical companies at the London Patent Office, and drew several conclusions, including:

1 Patents obtained are a function of R & D effort.
2 Most patents and most major discoveries are the products of the R & D efforts of about twenty large firms.

The use of patents as a measure of innovative output may lack reliability, however, as no weight is given to the importance of each discovery. Other researchers have used the number of new chemical entities introduced as a measure of R & D productivity, but it is important when using this method to attempt to evaluate both therapeutic and commercial significance. A study commissioned by NEDO[12] made this attempt in a fairly rigorous fashion, and produced results which have been widely accepted. This study examined every new pharmaceutical chemical introduced between 1958 and 1970; 466 such compounds were identified. Weightings were applied for market shares achieved in the four major country markets, and therapeutic weightings were obtained from a panel of UK medical experts. This study concluded that, pound for pound, the weighted productivity of pharmaceutical innovation in the UK was between two and two and a half times that in the US.

Every analysis of innovative output shows a slowing down in the number of new chemical entities introduced in the years following the boom period of the 1950s. Figure 1.5, derived from Mund,[13] clearly shows the downward trend. This is supported by the data in Table 1.6, which also shows that the US was responsible for just under a quarter of all new pharmaceutical agents introduced during the period 1961–77; and that the UK, West Germany, France and Italy were responsible for 47 per cent.

Mund concluded that, when the cash flows due to innovative efforts are discounted, the return from R & D is generally less than pharmaceutical multinationals could make from alternative investments. Schwartzmann[14] came to a similar conclusion, using a different methodology. He calculated that the expected rate of return to a

Number

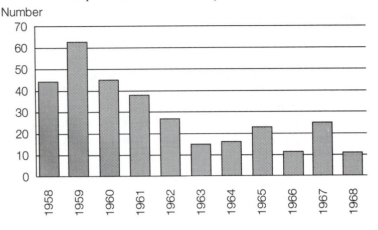

Figure 1.5 New single chemical entities: introduction to the US
Source: Mund (1986)

Table 1.6 New pharmaceutical agents by country of origin

Country	1961–64	1965–68	1969–72	1973–77	1978–80
Austria	6	7	2	3	0
Benelux	12	8	8	6	2
France	60	69	68	57	18
Germany	55	37	27	49	23
Italy	17	20	24	31	20
Japan	31	35	31	32	25
Scandinavia	16	10	8	12	5
Switzerland	32	23	17	26	8
UK	22	17	10	20	4
US	86	72	77	74	39
Total	337	298	272	310	144

Source: OECD (1981) to 1977; Chew *et al.* (1985), 1978–80

pharmaceutical company from investment in R & D was of the order of 3.3 per cent in 1973, having fallen from 11.4 per cent in 1960. However, his assumptions were rather conservative, and, as was noted in the previous section, drug companies have continued to increase expenditures on pharmaceutical R & D.

The absolute cost of developing a new drug has been increasing rapidly, at least in the US, where most research on this topic has been done. Schnee[15] estimates that the pre-1962 cost for one marketed product was $1.1 million. Clymer[16] put the figure at $10.5 million in

1969 (for his company – SmithKline). Schwartzmann[17] had raised this estimate to $24.4 million by 1973. Some of these estimates, particularly Schwartzmann's, may be based on conservative assumptions, but there is no mistaking the strong upward trend.

The most recent confirmation of this trend is in a recent report from NEDO,[18] indicating that the average cost of bringing a new medicine to the market is now over £100 million. As a straight conversion, this represents $130 million (at the time of publishing the report); however, when differential labour costs are considered, a US figure comparable to those above is probably of the order of $150 million to $200 million.

The efficiency of innovation

Clearly, the efficiency of the innovative process will play a large part in determining the relative performance of national pharmaceutical industries and the individual drug companies that work within them. OECD[19] suggests that analysis is best carried out at two levels – productivity differences between companies and productivity differences between countries. As noted in the previous section, patents awarded to companies can be used as a measure of innovative efficiency. Other measures used include the number of new products launched, and the number of journal articles published by the research scientists of any particular firm. Whatever measure is used, there seems to be a clear division in the conclusions drawn, which may be explained by the period considered in any particular study. Those studies, for example by Comanor, Grabowski, Reekie and Monopolies Commission,[20] which used data for the late 1950s, generally concluded that diseconomies of scale in R & D began in companies substantially below the largest size. Later studies, e.g. Angilly and Schwartzmann,[21] used data from the 1960s and reported constant or large and increasing returns to scale in expenditure on R & D. This may well have been due to the effect of the US government's increased regulatory activity since 1962.

For whatever reason, it now appears that the large pharmaceutical multinationals have a decisive advantage in R & D. They spend more, produce more innovative products, and reap the large rewards which follow.

NEDO[22] suggested as early as 1972 that a threshold level of R & D expenditure may exist for pharmaceutical firms, below which it is not possible to undertake a comprehensive range of R & D activities, from exploratory research through to final development. The smallest feasible unit was based on at least three research projects, and was estimated to cost £0.5 million in 1970 terms; this would be around £23 million at 1988 prices – allowing for the vastly increased complexity of equipment. The high-risk nature of expenditure on R & D has already been highlighted, so it is not surprising that intensive pharmaceutical research is confined to a small number of large multinational drug companies.

A final aspect of the efficiency of innovation is the locus of the R & D facility. A central hypothesis of current work by Dunning *et al.*[23] is that R & D in an MNC will orient towards the location which has the best research reputation. The argument is that this situation will be perpetuated across a wide range of research-intensive industries, resulting in a replication of the 'Silicon Valley' syndrome.

The patent system

A very full description of the purpose of patent protection was given by the Swan Committee:[24]

> the theory upon which the patent system is based is that the opportunity of acquiring exclusive rights in an invention stimulates technical progress, mainly in four ways: first, that it encourages research and invention; second, that it induces an inventor to disclose his discoveries, instead of keeping them as a trade secret; third, that it offers a reward for the expense of developing inventions to the stage at which they are commercially practicable; and fourth, that it provides an inducement to invest capital in new lines of production which might not appear profitable if many competing producers embarked on them simultaneously.

Schwartzmann[25] has a more commercially oriented definition: 'A patent is a deed reserving the collectable fruits of investment for the investor.' This definition, rather than the first, more closely touches the heart of the matter so far as the pharmaceutical industry is concerned. Patent protection is normally reserved for new chemical entities, from which will come the industry's biggest profit earners (e.g. Valium, Tagamet, Zantac).

According to UNCTC,[26] there are four forms of patent protection in the pharmaceutical industry:

1 Patents on the composition of matter.
2 Product patents which are granted for a specific product.
3 Process patents which relate to the production process rather than to the finished product.

4 Application or use patents, confined to a small number of countries, e.g. France.

Product and process patents are by far the most widely used. Most countries give some sort of patent protection. However, it is confined to process patents in Austria, Denmark, Greece, the Netherlands, Spain, Sweden, Argentina, Chile, Colombia, Egypt, India, Uruguay and Venezuela. This approach excludes product patents, and is assumed to promote further research into new and more efficient processes. This is thought to be a relatively weak form of protection, as it is comparatively easy to modify a pharmaceutical production process in some small way, thus evading the terms of the patent.

The product patent system is generally recognised to be more effective in protecting the innovator from competition, and this is the system used in the UK, Belgium, West Germany, France, Italy, Japan, Switzerland, Ireland, and the US (these countries also allow process patents). Some countries – including Brazil, Iran, the Republic of Korea, and Turkey – grant no form of patent protection for pharmaceuticals.

In a study in 1967, Walker[27] concluded that pharmaceutical patents were a highly significant resource control, and thus a very important source of market power to the drug firms holding them. Many writers have since suggested that this source of market power has been somewhat eroded by the reduction in 'effective patent life' (i.e. the patent life remaining after the drug has been introduced to the market) brought about by government regulation of new drugs. In most developed countries, nominal patent life (from patent grant to end of patent life) is in excess of fifteen years; but many studies have shown that the effective life (from product introduction to end of patent period) is declining. Schwartzmann[28] studied the average effective patent life of new chemical entities introduced in the US during the years 1966–73, and produced the following estimates:

Period	Effective Life
1966–69	13.9 years
1970–73	12.4 years

A recent paper by the Office of Health Economics produced the estimates shown in Table 1.7 The problems of drug companies are further exacerbated by the probability that the 'pay-back' period of a new drug is even shorter than the effective patent life.[29] This is due to the fact that a patent ensures monopoly profits only so long as the drug is not superseded by some new discovery. The innovator, therefore,

Table 1.7 Estimated life of new chemical entities (years), by country

Country	Nominal Life	Effective Life
West Germany	20	6.4
France	20	13.0
Italy	20	8–10
Japan	15	7–8
Switzerland	20	11.0
UK	20	8.7
US	17	9.7

Source: Chew *et al.* (1985)

cannot count on the full effective patent life to recoup the full costs of developing and marketing the product, together with the profit level necessary to meet the level of risk involved.

SUPPLY AND DEMAND

Demand for pharmaceuticals

The pharmaceutical industry in its present form is less than fifty years old, and so is relatively young by most standards. However, according to Wilkinson[30] this may suggest that the industry is at a critical phase in its development. Wilkinson considered the possibility that the market economies of the world are now in the down-phase of a fifty-year long-wave 'Kondratieff' economic cycle. Reviewing the evidence, he suggests a possibility that major industries will, at best, survive one full cycle, with the virtual inevitability of decline in the next. Reflecting this view on the pharmaceutical industry, it may be that the only firms who will move against the forecast industry decline will be those who recognise the scenario early enough in the down-phase to develop new technologies for the next expansion phase.

Regardless of the movements of the world economy over the last fifty years, the industry growth rate has been consistently high over that period, and consumption of pharmaceuticals now amounts to between 0.5 and 1 per cent of the gross domestic product of most countries, developed and developing. Table 1.8 shows pharmaceuticals growth statistics for the period 1960–85. Over the three time periods shown, the global pharmaceutical market has consistently grown faster than global gross national product, although the differential has fallen over the period. Thus, the growth rate of the global pharmaceutical market declined from 7.1 per cent per annum to 3.9, while global GNP declined much less, from 4.9 per cent per annum to 3.3.

Table 1.8 Average annual growth rates in the non-Communist world pharmaceutical market (%)

	1960–72	1972–82	1960–82	1982–85
Pharmaceutical market (current $)	10.2	12.7	11.3	–
Pharmaceutical market (1982 $)	7.1	3.6	5.5	3.9
GNP (constant prices)	4.9	2.8	4.0	3.3

Source: NEDO, *A New Focus on Pharmaceuticals*, HMSO, London (1986)

Table 1.9 Domestic consumption as percentage of the world pharmaceutical consumption

Country	1960	1972	1977	1982	1985	1985 Rank
US	45.4	31.8	24.2	27.1	33.1	1
Japan	6.6	9.5	12.9	17.5	17.6	2
West Germany	17.5	8.4	10.0	8.0	7.5	3
France	7.3	6.9	7.6	6.3	5.6	4
Italy	5.1	7.0	4.8	4.6	4.6	5
UK	4.9	3.5	3.3	4.2	2.9	6
Spain	1.5	3.5	3.3	2.4	1.8	10
Switzerland	0.5	n.a.	0.9	0.8	0.8	16
Netherlands	0.7	0.9	1.0	0.7	0.6	19
Sweden	0.8	n.a.	1.1	0.6	0.6	20

Total world market in current prices (£ million)

Non-Communist countries	2,320	8,410	21,940	39,260	62,141	
Including Communist countries	n.a.	n.a.	27,520	46,630	73,277	

Source: NEDO (1986)

Table 1.9 indicates that the total market (non-Communist world) has grown from £2,320 million in 1960 to £62,141 million in 1985, a compound growth rate of 14 per cent. Over the period 1977–85 the growth rate of pharmaceuticals consumption in the Communist world was 9 per cent, compared with just under 14 per cent in the non-Communist world for the same period. This table also shows changes in the home market share of world pharmaceutical consumption over the period 1960–85. The total share of the six largest countries fell from

86.8 per cent to 71.3 per cent over the period. Of these, only Japan gained share (6.6 per cent to 17.6 per cent); of the others, the largest losses were shown by the US and West Germany. Nevertheless, the US remains the dominant consumption market, with Japan now firmly established in second place. NEDO[31] suggests that the performance of the Japanese market has been due to the strength of the yen and the rapid increase among the elderly in the Japanese population. A low rate of new product introduction is advanced as the most significant factor in the comparative reduction in importance of the US market.

Supply of pharmaceuticals

The consistently high rate of growth of the pharmaceutical industry can be largely explained (on the supply side) by the observation that it is one of the world's most successful high-technology industries. Since the end of the Second World War, the industry has produced new and useful drugs in very large numbers; and while the rate of innovation seems to be slowing down (see above), it must also be observed that the industry is continuing to plough back increasing sums into research and development in an attempt to maintain the flow of new products.

However, not all the new investment is going into pharmaceutical plant and research. The industry has gone through a period of increasing diversification, which can be classified as follows:

1 Into technologically related industries :

   (a) Proprietary and over-the-counter drug products (e.g. Johnson & Johnson).
   (b) Cosmetics and toiletries (e.g. American Home Products).
   (c) Biologicals and diagnostics (e.g. Abbott).
   (d) Animal health products, mainly vet-prescribed drugs (e.g. Wellcome).
   (e) Specialised chemicals (e.g. Merck).

2 Into technologically unrelated industries – health care products and services (e.g. Warner Lambert, Searle).
3 Into conglomerate diversification – consumer products and services, for example, radio stations (Schering-Plough); motion picture production (Bristol-Myers); sporting goods and leisure articles (Astra); health clubs (Sandoz); restaurants, gift shops, airline catering services (Squibb).
4 Industrial components, for example ultrasonics, liquid crystals (E. Merck).

Even in view of this impressive list of diversification out of drugs, it must still be observed that most – if not all – of the major pharmaceutical companies continue to see their future very much bound up with the ethical drug industry. Indeed, the re-concentration on pharmaceuticals as the core business (almost as the only business) can be seen in the recent strategic divestments of non-drug interests by Glaxo and Upjohn.

International trade

It has already been observed that the consumption of pharmaceuticals is strongly concentrated in a small number of countries, namely the large OECD countries. The position is more diffuse with regard to international trade performance. Table 1.10 shows imports of medicinal products (including pharmaceuticals) for a number of countries, and indicates that total world imports have increased at the rate of 25.2 per cent per annum over the period 1984–88, to reach a figure of $18.5 billion. Of this, 45.2 per cent was accounted for by the six largest OECD countries, while the rest of the world (mainly developing countries) accounted for only 25.2 per cent. This group of developing countries increased their imports over the period by only 9.8 per cent per annum, less than half the rate of the world as a whole. All the six largest OECD countries showed higher growth than the global rate, with Italy and France showing best at 34.7 and 34 per cent per annum respectively.

Over the same period, world pharmaceutical exports grew by a compound 18.9 per cent per annum to a total of some $17.3 billion, as shown in Table 1.11. Of this total, exports from the developing countries accounted for only 5.9 per cent against a total of 59 per cent for the six largest OECD countries. In terms of average annual growth rates of exports, Japan (38.9 per cent per annum) and West Germany (22.9 per cent per annum) show the best performance among the large OECD countries. Remarkably, the overall growth figure for the developing world is 15.4 per cent per annum. Japan has a very low share of 1988 world total exports (1.7 per cent) compared to its share of total consumption (17.6 per cent in 1985, Table 1.9).

Taking these last two sets of statistics together, Table 1.12 shows the balance of trade in pharmaceuticals over the period 1984–88. Over the period, the negative balance of all developing countries grew from $2.6 billion to $3.6 billion. Among the six largest OECD countries, Japan and Italy had significant negative balances. Japan's was a very large one ($1.6 billion) in 1988; while the US was in a position of virtual balance in that year. The total positive balance of the remaining three

Table 1.10 World trade in medicinal products (SITC 5417): imports (current prices, $ million)

Country	1984	1985	1986	1987	1988	Average annual growth %	Share of world total %
Austria	192	195	293	401	451	23.8	2.4
Belgium	359	377	535	688	716	18.8	3.9
Denmark	125	135	204	242	235	17.1	1.3
Finland	93	111	147	199	197	20.6	1.1
France	199	236	356	496	641	34.0	3.5
West Germany	696	790	1,067	1,346	1,710	25.2	9.2
Ireland	119	126	158	174	504	43.5	2.7
Italy	337	400	590	725	1,109	34.7	6.0
Netherlands	348	409	577	710	813	23.6	4.4
Norway	115	114	154	203	145	6.0	0.8
Portugal	75	73	95	109	119	12.2	0.6
Spain	40	54	71	123	178	45.2	1.0
Sweden	239	253	327	408	498	20.1	2.7
Switzerland	231	269	398	484	608	27.4	3.3
UK	491	486	685	915	1,179	24.5	6.4
US	764	816	1,069	1,278	1,787	23.7	9.7
Canada	215	192	226	280	382	15.5	2.1
Australia	116	133	184	252	326	29.5	1.8
New Zealand	86	87	123	142	119	8.5	0.6
South Africa	90	78	134	117	189	20.4	1.0
Japan	670	727	961	1,169	1,928	30.2	10.4
Rest of world	3,199	3,505	3,712	4,349	4,656	9.8	25.2
World Total	8,799	9,566	12,066	14,810	18,490	20.4	100.00

Source: U.N. Trade Statistics Yearbook (1986)

large OECD countries ($4 billion) was significantly higher than the negative balance of the developing countries. Note the high positive balance of Switzerland ($1.6 billion), the highest in the world after the UK, which is due to the presence in that country of three of the world's largest pharmaceutical firms.

In concluding, two points must be borne in mind, which to some extent qualify the observations made above:

1 Increasing exports from a country may be accounted for by a strategic decision to concentrate on direct exports of pharmaceuticals rather than on the establishment of foreign manufacturing subsidiaries or on licensing arrangements. Alternatively, falling exports may mean that alternative strategic decisions regarding foreign

Table 1.11 World trade in medicinal products (SITC 5417): exports (current prices, $ million)

Country	1984	1985	1986	1987	1988	Average annual growth %	Share of world total %
Austria	108	141	203	241	238	21.8	1.4
Belgium	547	560	734	842	860	12.0	5.0
Denmark	306	344	476	609	675	21.9	3.9
Finland	38	51	53	60	53	8.7	0.3
France	1,020	1,143	1,522	1,811	1,914	17.0	11.1
West Germany	1,327	1,426	1,964	2,475	3,030	22.9	17.5
Ireland	107	112	156	237	409	39.8	2.4
Italy	365	427	501	538	594	12.9	3.4
Netherlands	361	382	515	677	766	20.7	4.4
Norway	15	15	24	31	34	22.7	0.2
Portugal	12	15	13	19	7	−12.6	0.0
Spain	94	115	133	173	184	18.3	1.1
Sweden	269	292	412	495	634	23.9	3.7
Switzerland	978	1,044	1,557	2,044	2,003	19.6	11.6
UK	1,182	1,320	1,571	1,893	2,608	21.9	15.1
US	1,135	1,143	1,241	1,313	1,770	11.7	10.2
Canada	65	59	77	90	72	2.6	0.4
Australia	48	42	42	46	122	26.3	0.7
New Zealand	12	11	13	14	12	0.0	0.1
South Africa	10	9	7	9	10	0.0	0.1
Japan	79	93	134	141	294	38.9	1.7
Rest of World	576	554	883	460	1,021	15.4	5.9
World Total	8,654	9,298	12,231	14,218	17,310	18.9	100.0

Source: U.N. Trade Statistics Yearbook (1986)

production have been successfully implemented. The US is a good example of the latter, in that most major US pharmaceutical firms have foreign production facilities; West Germany may be an example of the former, as many of its major pharmaceutical concerns export from the domestic base.

2 The visible trade balances shown in Table 1.12 do not necessarily give the complete picture of trade flows associated with the pharmaceutical industry. Other items which must be taken into account are cash flows like royalties, service fees, management fees, and repatriation of profits; reverse flows would include new investments, purchase of patent rights, etc. Transfer pricing may also be a major factor here, which can operate in either direction.

Table 1.12 World trade in medicinal products (SITC 5417): balance of trade (current prices, $ million)

Country	1984	1985	1986	1987	1988
Austria	−84	−54	−90	−160	−213
Belgium	188	183	199	154	144
Denmark	181	209	272	367	440
Finland	−55	−60	−94	−139	−144
France	821	907	1,166	1,315	1,273
West Germany	631	636	897	1,129	1,320
Ireland	−12	−14	−2	63	−95
Italy	28	27	−89	−187	−515
Netherlands	13	−27	−62	−33	−47
Norway	−100	−99	−130	−172	−111
Portugal	−63	−58	−82	−90	−112
Spain	54	61	62	50	6
Sweden	30	39	85	87	136
Switzerland	747	775	1,159	1,560	1,395
UK	691	834	886	978	1,429
US	371	327	172	35	−17
Canada	−150	−133	−149	−190	−310
Australia	−68	−91	−142	−206	−204
New Zealand	−74	−76	−110	−128	−107
South Africa	−80	−69	−127	−108	−179
Japan	−591	−634	−827	−1.028	−1,634
Rest of World	−2,623	−2,951	−2,829	−3,889	−3,635
World Total	−145	−268	165	−592	−1,180

Source: Derived from Tables 1.10, 1.11

INTERNATIONALISATION OF THE PHARMACEUTICAL INDUSTRY

Accompanying the rapid growth in consumption of drugs over the last thirty years has come the equally swift process of internationalisation of the industry. The theoretical explanations of this development are explored in Chapter 2, but some observations can be made here in the context of an empirical examination of the industry.

The industry is not so obviously oligopolistic as some other high-technology industries, e.g. computers or microelectronics. However, at the level of the therapeutic sub-markets, the pharmaceutical industry shows many more signs of classical oligopoly, e.g. high concentration, low cross-elasticity of demand between sub-markets, lack of price competition. The question of international variations in production costs was addressed above, and it was seen that some advantage may lie in locating the final stages of manufacturing in low-cost areas. Similarly, there may be some advantage in locating research and development in low-wage developed countries.

There is another factor which has a considerable bearing on the nature and extent of internationalisation of investment within the pharmaceutical industry. The high and rising cost of pharmaceutical research and development is a prime characteristic of this industry. There is a clear incentive for innovating companies to maximise the economic rent from these investments by moving into foreign markets. It is becoming increasingly necessary for such innovating pharmaceutical companies to plan in terms of the global market in order to amortise the huge investments required to produce new drugs.

Gereffi[32] considers that there are more than 10,000 companies now trading that could claim to be pharmaceutical manufacturers. Of these, only about 100 have any significance in the international arena, and they supply around 90 per cent of the total world shipments of ethical pharmaceuticals. It will be seen below that the large European and US pharmaceutical companies are highly internationalised, with upwards of 40 per cent of global sales coming from overseas operations.

Table 1.13 shows the pattern of overseas expansion of manufacturing subsidiaries by the twenty-five largest US pharmaceutical companies. The data for the EC refer to the original six member countries: West Germany, France, Italy, Belgium, the Netherlands and Luxembourg. Before 1950 there were only twenty-eight foreign subsidiaries in total, all but six in other English-speaking countries. During the 1950s there was a great surge of further development of subsidiaries in those countries, with Latin America also sharing in the activity. During the 1960s the rate of expansion in Europe increased, while Latin America fell back. This was more than compensated for by an acceleration of the pace in Asia and the Middle East, and the beginnings of substantial interest in Africa. Thus it can be seen that, over the period 1950–70, there was a very high degree of internationalisation taking place within the US pharmaceutical industry, primarily in developed countries, but with many manufacturing subsidiaries (albeit small) being set up in developing countries in the latter part of the period.

There has also been a high degree of internationalisation in research and development within the pharmaceutical industry. Of thirty major multinationals considered below, no fewer than twenty-four conducted substantial foreign research and development operations. The United States, the United Kingdom and West Germany are currently the preferred locations for foreign research activities, with increasing attention being focused on Japan. France and Italy are less important

Table 1.13 Manufacturing subsidiaries established by the twenty-five largest US pharamaceutical multinationals (by time period and geographical region)

Host country	Establishment of first manufacturing plant			Total
	Before 1950	*1950–59*	*1960–70*	
Canada	10	6	4	20
Europe	7	41	64	112
European Common Market	0	25	35	60
UK	7	8	3	18
Other	0	8	26	34
Australia and New Zealand	3	12	7	22
Latin America	6	65	55	126
Argentina	1	11	4	16
Brazil	0	11	3	14
Mexico	4	12	5	21
Other	1	31	43	75
Asia and the Middle East	0	21	38	59
Philippines	0	8	3	11
Other	0	13	35	48
Africa	2	7	13	22
South Africa	2	7	7	16
Other	0	0	6	6
Total	28	152	181	361

Source: Katz (1981)

locations. There is very little foreign research and development activity in developing countries; almost alone in this category, India is the location for a number of multinational research and development units.

The international pharmaceutical companies

As noted earlier, there are over ten thousand companies operating within the pharmaceutical industry, but the vast majority of them are very small. Table 1.14, although dated, gives some indication of the degree of fragmentation in the industry. Thus, typically, the largest four firms are responsible for 20–25 per cent of sales, the top twenty companies for 50–60 per cent of sales, and the fifty largest firms account for 65–75 per cent of sales. In terms of oligopoly theory, this does not represent a particularly high degree of concentration; in other parts of the chemical industry, or in automobiles, the four or five largest manufacturers usually account for in excess of 90 per cent of output. However, the position in therapeutic sub-markets within the pharmaceutical industry is radically different, and very high degrees of concentration are frequently found.

Table 1.14 Degree of concentration of pharmaceutical sales by company size

| Country | Date | Number of firms | Four largest | Percentage of national sales accounted for by: | | | |
				Eight largest	Twelve largest	Twenty largest	Fifty largest
Belgium	1973	70	42	60	72	82	
Canada	1970	136	14	22			
Denmark	1984	137	16	22			
France	1972	434	20	34	44	60	
West Germany	1972	600	29	43		60	77
Italy		500	12	21	28	38	65
Netherlands	1973	50	37	57	69	85	
Norway	1983	113	24	40			
UK	1972	295	62	77			
Japan	1983	400	20	29	37	45	
US	1984	950	10	17			
World (a)	1976	>1,000	11	20	27	37	57

Source: OECD (1981)
Note: (a) UNCTC (1979)

UNCTC[33] has suggested that most of the pharmaceutical multinationals either entered the field through technologically related industries, or evolved from traditional drug supply houses. Many mainland European pharmaceutical multinationals entered by the first of these paths, principally from the manufacture of dyestuffs and organic chemicals. The US drug giants, on the other hand, are largely descended from drug supply houses, and ethical pharmaceuticals still remain an important part of their business.

Table 1.15 lists the world's thirty largest pharmaceutical firms, ranked in order of drug sales in 1984. For comparison, 1977 sales are also shown. In some cases, the sales figure given also includes revenues from one or more of: proprietary medicines, veterinary products, vitamins and fine chemicals, nutritional products, agrochemicals, hospital and laboratory supplies and equipment. Nevertheless, these statistics yield a valuable insight into the pharmaceutical industry. It

Table 1.15 The world's thirty largest pharmaceutical firms, ranked by 1984 sales (£ million)

Firm	Domicile	Ranking 1977	Ranking 1984	Sales (£ million) 1977	Sales (£ million) 1984	Annual average growth % 1977–84
American Home Products	American	2	1	875	2,251	14.45
Merck Inc	American	4	2	831	2,178	14.76
Pfizer	American	9	3	634	1,778	15.87
Warner Lambert	American	5	4	831	1,719	10.94
Hoechst	W. German	1	5	888	1,601	8.78
SmithKline	American	22	6	325	1,581	25.36
Lilly	American	11	7	515	1,514	16.65
Bayer	W. German	3	8	818	1,477	8.81
Ciba-Geigy	Swiss	7	9	673	1,452	11.61
Abbott	American	34	10	206	1,273	29.72
Bristol-Myers	American	6	11	677	1,184	8.31
Glaxo	British	16	12	388	1,159	16.92
Upjohn	American	15	13	414	1,081	14.70
Roche	Swiss	8	14	670	995	5.81
Sandoz	Swiss	10	15	546	991	8.89
Johnson & Johnson	American	24	16	298	967	18.31
Takeda	Japanese	14	17	419	918	11.86
Rhône-Poulenc	French	12	18	441	877	10.32
Boehringer-Ingelheim	W. German	13	19	429	833	9.94
Squibb	American	17	20	384	813	11.31
Cyanamid	American	25	21	278	789	16.07
Schering-Plough	American	19	22	348	788	12.38
Wellcome	British	20	23	342	788	12.66
Sterling	American	18	24	362	770	11.38
Sankyo	Japanese	30	25	241	725	17.04
ICI	British	28	26	250	697	15.77
Beecham	British	23	27	310	612	10.20
Fujisawa	Japanese	29	28	244	610	13.99
Sanofi	French	–	29	122	574	24.76
Shionogi	Japanese	31	30	241	551	12.54

Source: NEDO (1986)

can be seen from this table that the sales of the top thirty firms amounted to £33,546 million in 1984, or some 63 per cent of the non-Communist world total. The fourteen US companies accounted for £18,686 million; the three West German companies accounted for £3,911 million; the three Swiss companies accounted for £3,438 million; the four UK firms accounted for £3,256 million; the four Japanese firms accounted for £2,804 million; and the two French companies accounted for £1,451 million. This information is shown in

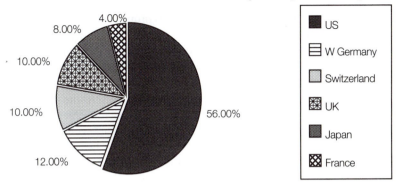

Figure 1.6 The sales of the top thirty firms: proportion by home country (%)
Source: NEDO (1986)

Figure 1.6 in the form of a pie chart. Table 1.15 also shows the growth rate of sales since 1977, the overall average being just over 13 per cent per annum. Of the fourteen companies which have performed above this growth rate, nine are US firms, two are British, two Japanese, and one French. The average rate of growth of the US firms is the highest (15 per cent), and lowest for West German and Swiss firms (9 per cent).

Internationalisation of the pharmaceutical industry, as in other sectors, has been driven by the need to maximise profit through increased sales, by introducing new products and by moving into new geographical markets. However, there are also a combination of reasons specific to the industry which account (in fact) for the rapid degree of internationalisation:

1 Development costs for a marketable new drug are very high and growing rapidly. These large costs have to be spread over the widest possible market.
2 Product life cycles are fairly short, leading to a need to maximise global sales as quickly as possible.
3 The bulk of profits comes from patented products, again providing a motive to move overseas wherever patent protection can be had in order to maximise sales.

Internationalisation began at an early stage, with the US firm Eli Lilly recording its first overseas sales only eight years after its inception in 1876. E. Merck (no relationship to Merck Inc since 1918) of Germany first exported to the US in 1887.

Early access strategies included licensing foreign companies to manufacture a patented drug in particular countries, market agreements which excluded foreign firms from access to proprietary knowledge but allowed them to market patented drugs in their own countries, and joint ventures which established a jointly owned subsidiary for purposes of R & D, manufacturing or sales (possibly all three).

The process of internationalisation was largely confined to these measures until after the Second World War, when the pharmaceutical industry participated in the general outward movement, first of US firms, later of European companies, into world markets by means of wholly owned subsidiaries. However, this was not a fast or universal process. It was only as late as 1968 that Schering-Plough began to convert its dealerships in European countries into owned subsidiaries.

Table 1.13 has indicated the vast increase in overseas manufacturing subsidiaries, which accelerated through the 1950s and 1960s. Today, most of the top thirty firms noted in Table 1.15 operate subsidiaries in over 100 countries around the world.

Strategic groups of firms within the international pharmaceutical industry

Taking the world's thirty largest pharmaceutical firms (listed in Table 1.15) as a working sample, some basic performance figures and ratios are listed in Table 1.16 for the years 1979 and 1984, viz:

1 Total company sales.
2 Total foreign sales.
3 Total R & D expenditure.
4 Foreign sales as a percentage of company sales.
5 R & D expenditure as a percentage of sales.

Note: to avoid problems of changing exchange rates, the sales and expenditure figures are given in the domestic currency of each firm.

Some interesting features emerge from an examination of these statistics:

1 Total company sales have increased for all firms over the five-year period, although the average annual growth rate varies from a low of 0.2 per cent per annum (Warner Lambert) to a high of 19.9 per cent per annum (Beecham)
2 Total foreign sales have increased for almost all firms, with the average annual growth rate varying from a low of 0.3 per cent per annum (Sterling) to a high of 22.7 per cent per annum (Beecham). The two exceptions to this trend were American Home Products

Table 1.16 The world's thirty largest pharmaceutical firms: R & D, foreign sales (local currency)

Firm	Total company sales		Foreign sales		R & D expenditure		Foreign sales as % of total sales		R & D exp as % of total sales	
	1979	1984	1979	1984	1979	1984	1979	1984	1979	1984
American Home Products	3,650	4,486	1,246	1,050	90	184	34.1	23.4	2.5	4.1
Merck Inc	2,385	3,560	1,121	1,531	188	393	47.0	43.0	7.9	11.0
Pfizer	2,746	3,855	1,549	1,704	138	252	56.4	44.2	5.0	6.5
Warner Lambert	3,217	3,249	1,416	1,299	94	195	44.0	40.0	2.9	6.0
Hoechst	27,080	41,457	18,159	31,208	1,142	1,818	67.1	75.3	4.2	4.4
SmithKline	1,380	2,949	632	942	139	279	45.8	31.9	10.1	9.5
Lilly	2,206	3,109	879	995	175	341	39.8	32.0	7.9	11.0
Bayer	26,002	43,032	18,305	33,823	1,104	1,956	70.4	78.6	4.2	4.5
Ciba-Geigy	9,891	17,474	9,450	17,165	824	1,456	97.6	98.2	8.3	8.3
Abbott	1,683	3,104	607	917	85	219	36.1	29.5	5.1	7.1
Bristol-Myers	2,753	4,189	900	1,200	103	212	32.7	28.6	3.7	5.1
Glaxo	539	1,200	287	680	33	76	53.2	56.7	6.1	6.3
Upjohn	1,514	2,188	604	746	129	258	39.9	34.1	8.5	11.8
Roche	5,191	8,267	4,988	8,011	646	1,143	96.1	96.9	12.4	13.8
Sandoz	4,444	7,434	4,177	7,094	386	634	94.0	95.4	8.7	8.5
Johnson & Johnson	4,278	6,247	1,839	2,389	193	421	43.0	38.2	4.5	6.7
Takeda	388,676	530,932	21,526	34,819	17,823	29,785	5.5	6.6	4.6	5.6
Rhone-Poulenc	33,781	51,207	18,039	35,333	1,241	2,467	53.4	69.0	3.7	4.8
Boehringer-Ingelheim	2,583	4,126	1,782	3,218	252	561	69.0	78.0	9.8	13.6
Squibb	1,476	1,886	635	754	69	151	43.0	40.0	4.7	8.0
Cynamid	3,187	3,857	1,115	1,170	124	237	35.0	30.3	3.9	6.1
Schering-Plough	1,454	1,874	674	799	75	164	46.4	42.6	5.2	8.8
Wellcome	412	806	349	707	39	97	84.8	87.7	9.5	12.0
Sterling	1,501	1,827	680	691	49	88	45.3	37.8	3.3	4.8
Sankyo	159,925	232,421	1,600	2,450	6,994	14,500	1.0	1.1	4.4	6.2
ICI	5,368	9,909	3,136	6,474	185	299	58.4	65.3	3.4	3.0
Beecham	923	2,289	614	1,711	31	78	66.5	74.7	3.4	3.4
Fujisawa	130,210	210,302	6,500	10,392	9,710	17,969	5.0	4.9	7.5	8.5
Sanofi	2,941	11,241	1,781	5,659	116	885	60.6	50.3	3.9	7.9
Shionogi	119,469	177,302	12,000	18,000	8,500*	13,500	10.0	10.2	7.1	7.6

Source: Company annual reports
* Author's estimate

(average reduction of 3.4 per cent per annum) and Warner Lambert (average reduction of 1.7 per cent per annum).

3 R & D expenditure has increased in all cases; the low end of the average growth rate is represented by Shionogi (8.2 per cent per annum), while the high is represented by Abbott (20.7 per cent per annum).

In order to examine the industry from the perspective of strategic groupings of firms, it is necessary to construct a matrix, as shown in Figures 1.7 and 1.8. The horizontal axis represents the degree of internationalisation as measured by the foreign sales percentage (taken from Table 1.16); similarly, the vertical axis represents R & D intensity, as measured by the R & D percentage (also taken from Table 1.16). The break points between the classifications are chosen (arbitrarily) as follows:

1 Low degree of internationalisation – foreign sales under 33.3 per cent.
2 Medium degree of internationalisation – foreign sales over 33.3 per cent and under 66.7 per cent.
3 High degree of internationalisation – foreign sales over 66.7 per cent.
4 Low degree of research intensity – R & D under 6 per cent.
5 Medium degree of research intensity – R & D over 6 per cent and under 9 per cent.
6 High degree of research intensity – R & D over 9 per cent.

The strategic groupings for the year 1979 are shown in Figure 1.7. The strategic group characterised by the low internationalisation/low research intensity profile contains one US and two Japanese firms; the other two Japanese firms are in the low internationalisation/medium R & D intensity grouping. In the strategic grouping characterised by medium internationalisation/low R & D intensity, there is a concentration of twelve firms, of which nine are US companies. These three strategic groupings together comprise that section of the matrix which could be termed the 'low competitiveness' sector, i.e. where neither R & D intensity nor degree of internationalisation was sufficiently developed to take full advantage of the globalisation of the industry.

In the high internationalisation/low research intensity strategic grouping are found two West German chemical giants, while the symmetrical 'medium' grouping contains four firms – three US and one UK. There are no firms in the bottom left-hand strategic grouping. The three strategic groupings on this diagonal together comprise the

Degree of internationalisation

	Low	Medium	High
Low	Bristol-Myers Takeda Sankyo	American Home Products Pfizer Warner Lambert Abbott Johnson & Johnson Rhône-Poulenc Squibb Cynamid Schering-Plough Sterling ICI Beecham	Hoechst Bayer
Medium	Fujisawa Shionogi	Merck Inc Lilly Glaxo Upjohn	Ciba-Geigy Sandoz
High		SmithKline	Roche Boehringer- Ingelheim Wellcome

R & D intensity (vertical axis: Low, Medium, High)

Figure 1.7 The world's thirty largest pharmaceutical firms: strategic groupings in 1979 *Source*: Company annual reports

'medium competitiveness' sector of the industry, i.e. where either high R & D intensity or a high degree of internationalisation or, alternatively, a combination of a median level of both, allows the firms in the sector to take considerable advantage of globalisation. Similarly, the bottom right-hand corner of the matrix comprises the 'high competitiveness' sector of three strategic groupings, giving high potential competitive advantage to the six constituent firms as industry globalisation evolves. These six firms include all three of the Swiss companies, and one each from the UK, the US, and West Germany.

Figure 1.8 shows the comparative position in 1984. Over the five-year period, there have been some significant changes. In terms of the degree of internationalisation, five US firms have suffered a decrease in position from medium to low, while two European firms have increased from medium to high. With regard to research intensity, only three US firms failed to improve their positions on the matrix. Overall, comparing Figure 1.8 with Figure 1.7, there is an increase of one firm in the high competitiveness sector and six firms in the medium competitiveness sector; there is a corresponding decrease of seven firms in the low competitiveness sector.

In conclusion, it can be seen that while there has been some diminution in the degree of internationalisation – particularly among

Degree of internationalisation

		Low	Medium	High
R & D intensity	Low	American Home Products Bristol-Myers Takeda	Sterling ICI	Hoechst Bayer Rhône- Poulenc Beecham
	Medium	Abbott Cynamid Sankyo Fujisana Shionogi	Pfizer Warner Lambert Glaxo Johnson & Johnson Squibb Schering-Plough	Ciba-Geigy Sandoz
	High	SmithKline Lilly	Merck Inc Upjohn	Roche Boehringer- Ingelheim Wellcome

Figure 1.8 The world's thirty largest pharmaceutical firms: strategic groupings in 1984 *Source*: Company annual reports

US firms (1979 foreign sales median, 45.8 per cent; 1984, 40.0 per cent), there has been a counter-movement in research intensity (1979 R & D median, 5.0 per cent; 1984, 6.7 per cent). Thus, over the five-year period there has been a significant degree of movement from less to more competitive strategic groups within the industry, indicating an overall improvement in the ability of the top thirty firms to take advantage of industry globalisation opportunities. In Chapters 6–10 we shall examine whether this trend has been maintained over the years since 1984.

SUMMARY

Drawing together the discussion of this chapter, it can be seen that the world pharmaceutical industry can be viewed as the interaction of three principal characteristics which, when taken together, serve to differentiate this industry from all others. First, in its present form of dependence on advanced technology, the industry is relatively young. It has developed by forward integration from the manufacture of dye-stuffs and other organic chemicals, and by backward integration from druggist-supply houses. Its growth has been very rapid, aided by increasing worldwide incomes and a universal demand for better health care. Entry barriers are high and there have been very few significant new players in the last quarter of a century. On the other hand, many major pharmaceutical firms have used the high cash flows from successful patented drugs to diversify into related and non-related industries.

Second, there are some particular distinguishing features at operational level. Manufacturing is characterised by highly centralised bulk production of active ingredients, coupled with the ability to decentralise the dosage form manufacture and packaging to suit particular market needs. Marketing is characterised by the unusual split between the prescriber (the general practitioner), the paying customer (usually the government), and the consumer (the patient). Other notable features are concentration within therapeutic sub-markets, very low cross-elasticity of demand between them, and a correspondingly high and stable level of prices.

Third, to a quite remarkable extent, the profitability of the modern pharmaceutical industry is highly dependent on the successful product innovator, whose costs have climbed very rapidly in the last twenty years as governments have evolved more and more stringent regulations regarding product safety and new product introduction. As the costs have climbed, so have the risk factors involved. Companies which discover major new drugs can look forward to a prolonged period of growth in sales and profits. Companies with a less successful innovative record either have to diversify, license new products from other firms, or be acquired. There is enormous pressure on firms to continually increase R & D expenditure, even in the face of sluggish growth in sales and profits. It is notable that, of the thirty firms described above, twenty-five had higher growth in R & D expenditures over the period 1979–84 than in sales or profits or both.

The principal result of all these influences is a remorseless pressure to internationalise operations in order to spread high fixed costs (particularly the cost of R & D) and maximise revenues from patented products. The thirty major firms are either already highly international-ised or (in the case of Japan) have laid the basis of an international strategy. Note the interesting divergence of the different nationalities of the drug firms in terms of the overall proportion of international business; all the US firms show a decreasing dependence on inter-national markets over the period 1979–84 (partially explained by the weakness of the dollar); all the European-based firms show an increase in foreign business, in some cases a substantial increase; Japanese firms all have low current penetration of international markets.

2 Applying multinational theory to the world pharmaceutical industry

REVIEW OF INTERNATIONAL COMMERCE

From earliest times, mercantilism was the central philosophy governing international trade; it held that the only way for a country to gain wealth and grow powerful was at the expense of other countries (in effect, a zero-sum game). This implied static world resources, and the doctrine disintegrated with the onset of the industrial revolution, which greatly increased world trade through a prolonged period of innovation.

By the mid-nineteenth century, two US companies (Colt Industries and the Singer company) and a Scottish firm (J. & P. Coats) were operating in some ways as multinational corporations (MNCs) do today. By the early twentieth century, several companies – including Ingersoll Rand, General Electric, International Harvester and H.J. Heinz – were functioning as recognisable multinationals.[1]

Before World War I, capital movements were associated with large-scale population movements out of Europe. The majority were portfolio investments, with the United Kingdom becoming the largest creditor nation because of domestic prosperity, the need to secure sources of raw materials, and a highly developed institutional framework which successfully channelled available funds overseas.

In the inter-war period, the relative wealth of European nations decreased and the US became a major creditor nation, increasingly because of direct investment by US corporations in overseas subsidiaries. An additional factor was the global financial crisis of the 1930s, which heralded a considerable fall in international portfolio investment.

Since 1945, there have been three distinct phases in the spread of multinationals. Firms from the US and the UK were dominant until about 1960, and these were concentrated in the extraction of petroleum and other raw materials. During the next decade, firms from continental

Europe and Japan entered the field, and the dominance of the US and the UK decreased. During the third period (the 1970s and 1980s), firms from Europe (followed by Japan) have become an increasingly important source of foreign direct investment. The US is still an important source, but has increasingly become a major recipient of foreign investment from other nations.

Worldwide foreign direct investment is now so vast that patterns of investment, technology and trade among nations (especially the developed nations) are decisively shaped by the principal agent of foreign direct investment – the multinationals. The largest of these companies, operating on a global scale and with global horizons, are beyond the jurisdiction of any one nation to the extent that many governments now view them as a political – rather than merely economic – threat.

Size and multinationality are not mutually conditional, but there is a correlation. The need for strong growth coupled with an oligopolistic position in the home market is a powerful motive to internationalise functions. As with sources of foreign direct investment, the host country distribution of multinational investment shows a dominant position for the industrialised nations.

Foreign direct investment is a dynamic process, and also includes divestment – whole or partial, actual or threatened – in particular locations. This makes divestment a particularly sensitive issue, especially for developing countries, which tend to be recipients of (rather than sources of) foreign direct investment. From the multinational's viewpoint, divestment may bring short-run financial gain, but the long-run cost can be disrupted relationships with host governments – often spreading well beyond those countries directly affected by disinvestment.

Another area of conflict between the multinational corporation and host government lies in the method of entry and ownership patterns. Host governments are generally in favour of greenfield ventures; they tend to be suspicious of entry by acquisition, owing to the fear of consequent loss of host country technology. In addition, and possibly consequentially, the proportion of wholly owned affiliates has declined, while joint ventures have become increasingly frequent. This requirement for more flexibility of approach seems to have been historically more suited to the temperament of Japanese and European multinationals. US multinationals were relatively hostile to the joint venture concept, but in recent years they seem to have become reconciled to joint ventures within the overall development of the concept of globalisation.

Perhaps a less static way of classifying forms and methods of foreign direct investment is by type of diversification strategy; there are three broad classifications. First, horizontal diversification is essentially a form of international replication of operations, and tends to be a stable organisational form. In this context, concentric diversification is a sub-set, where the product range is extended by marketing or production developments, and the new products are sold to new customer groups. Second, vertical integration involves the multinational corporation in extending the stages of production or marketing located in various countries; this is often a somewhat defensive strategy brought about by product market complexities, and may be inherently less stable over the long term than horizontal diversification. The third form, conglomerate diversification, may be the least stable form, especially where it involves many non-related markets. Conversely, it can be a stable and highly successful strategy if applied to markets closely related by technology or end use, e.g. from food into cosmetics into toiletries into proprietary medicines.

The industrial policy of all developed countries and most developing countries allows for, and generally encourages, inward investment. It is therefore to be expected that multinational operations' penetration of most host country industries is increasing, and is often the source of increased friction between the multinational and the host government. This may seem irrational to the multinational, which is not generally subject to the direct political pressure on jobs, wages and prices which affects governments in all countries.

THEORIES OF INTERNATIONAL TRADE

Classical trade theory was originally based on the concept of absolute advantage, later modified to the postulate that comparative advantage is a sufficient condition for mutually beneficial trade to occur between nations. Thus international trade was regarded as being dependent on differences in nations' comparative costs of production. The contribution of the neoclassicists concerned the explanation of these cost differences.

The Heckscher–Ohlin[2] *theorem* attempted to answer this question by postulating that differences among countries in factor endowments (capital or labour) caused the difference in comparative costs. Thus a country will export things whose production makes intensive use of its abundant factor endowment(s), and import products which utilise its poorly endowed factors(s). The theorem argues, for example, that a country which is well endowed with labour will have comparatively lower labour costs, and thus possess an international competitive edge in labour-intensive manufactured goods. It will therefore export these goods, and import relatively capital-intensive manufactures. The assumptions of the Heckscher–Ohlin theorem included:

1 Production functions are the same everywhere .
2 Information about technology is freely and simultaneously available in all markets.
3 Capital and labour are completely immobile across national frontiers.

Relaxing the assumptions of factor immobility between nations makes the Heckscher–Ohlin theorem better able to explain international investment. Heckscher–Ohlin would then suggest, for example, that capital-rich countries would invest in countries where there was a relative shortage of capital, to take advantage of the necessarily higher returns to capital which would exist in these countries. This process, of course, would tend to increase the cost of capital in the investing country and reduce it in the host country, thus contributing to the equalisation of factor prices. In this process, however, the Heckscher–Ohlin theorem does not differentiate between foreign direct investment and portfolio investment.

In 1953, Leontief[3] attempted to justify the Heckscher–Ohlin theorem empirically by an input–output study of data for the US economy for 1947. He expected to find that US exports were relatively capital intensive and that import-competing goods were relatively labour-intensive. The results showed the opposite, and in terms of the then current development of the Heckscher–Ohlin theorem, this implied that the US was a relatively capital-deficient country. The main effect of this 'Leontief paradox' was to stimulate a great amount of theoretical and empirical work on the 'neo-factor' theories of trade, which are extensions of the basic Heckscher–Ohlin theorem.

Neo-factor theories. The 'human capital' aspect of neo-factor trade theories argues that a country may derive comparative advantage from investment in managerial, professional and highly skilled labour. The two-factor approach (labour and capital) must be modified to take account of human capital, and the ensuing model may have greater predictive powers in distinguishing between the possibilities of trade, foreign direct investment and licensing. For example, in some cases trade may be seen as the transfer of skill-intensive goods, foreign direct investment as the transfer of human capital, and licensing as the industrial property rights derived from comparative advantage in human capital.

While the neo-factor theories of trade suffer from the disadvantage that they assume perfectly competitive markets, they nevertheless go some way to clarifying links between international trade and inter-national investment, and increasing the relevance of the basic Hecscher–Ohlin theorem.

'*Neo-technology*' *theories* of trade are based on the classical model, and attempt to differentiate degrees of comparative advantage in world trade by examining economies of scale and the role of technology. These theories specifically allow for imperfections in markets, and their effects on production functions. By including the role of R & D in product innovation (and therefore creating technological comparative advantage), this approach allows an important development of the basic theory. Posner[4] argued that this type of 'technological gap' allows international trade to take place while the knowledge incorporated in an innovation diffuses to all markets. (Cf. Vernon's product life cycle model, discussed later, which explains why innovations occur in particular countries.)

Linder[5] adopted a different approach, postulating that increasing economies of scale in a large home market allow companies to expand quickly to meet this demand, then use the derived comparative advantage to export to markets with a similar pattern of income levels and preferences. Similarly, Dreze[6] argued that product differentiation to allow for home market preferences led to comparative advantage in exporting to markets with similar preferences.

Trade barriers. Classical trade theory postulates that, given perfect competition and free trade, world output will be maximised and shared between nations through the gains from trade. However, in the absence of perfect competition, governments may attempt to manipulate the free-trade assumption in order to increase gains from trade. This is done by establishing a range of barriers to trade in order to protect domestic industry from foreign competition. The barriers are most often imposed against imports, but may also be used to control the entry of foreign firms into the domestic market. The impact of these barriers on multinational corporations is to encourage the location of manu-facturing facilities within the appropriate markets. Trade barriers can be broadly classified into two types: tariff barriers, where the tariff is a revenue-raising tax imposed by the government on foreign goods crossing the country's borders, and is designed to protect domestic industries; and non-tariff barriers, which normally fall beyond the rules of trade agreements but are widely used by governments to restrict imports.

Johnston[7] indicated that there are a further two types of trade barriers, not normally involving government action, which should be considered in developing comparative advantage trade theories: transport costs, which are important when the unit cost is of the same order as the price differential obtaining between the markets; and information costs, which originate in international cultural, political and environmental differences.

Trade theory is limited in its applicability to international business mainly through its assumptions. Multinational corporations do not regard (and do not treat) factors of production as being immobile, markets as being perfect, or information as being freely available. In addition, trade theory is concerned primarily with the movement of goods, and cannot readily explain other forms of international business activity. Certainly, the neo-factor and neo-technology approaches have attempted to develop more accurate predictive tools by modifying and extending the basic theory, but the result has been to produce models which are significantly less robust than the Heckscher–Ohlin theorem.

To make further progress in explaining and predicting the international business system as it applies to multinationals, it is necessary to move away from the simple import–export mechanisms of trade theory and consider alternative ways of securing foreign goods and supplying foreign markets.

Applying trade theory to the world pharmaceutical industry   As for multinational corporations in general, classical trade theories of absolute and comparative advantage have very little descriptive and less predictive power in the case of the international pharmaceutical industry; therefore, no further consideration will be given to this approach.

Similarly, the basic Heckscher–Ohlin theorem has very little bearing, as all three of its assumptions are untenable in this industry. However, certain of the 'neo-factor' approaches are interesting and more pertinent. In particular, the 'human capital' aspect of these approaches has particular significance in the drug industry, owing to the prediction that host countries may derive some comparative advantage from investing in the development of managerial and technological skills. This is a theme which will be returned to many times in the course of this book. This particular variation of the neo-factor model would suggest, for example, that international trade in ethical pharmaceuticals is a clear case of transfer of skill-intensive goods; it would view the mushrooming product licensing activity as a skill-based comparative advantage leading to trading of industrial property. However, the 'human capital' neo-factor model would also view foreign direct investment as the international transfer of human capital; while this may be true in some respects for foreign direct investment in drug manufacturing, it is a much less accurate description of a determinant of foreign direct investment in R & D. Indeed, there is a strong argument, referred to again below, that foreign direct investment in pharmaceutical R & D takes place in order to gain the benefit of host-country skills rather than as a vehicle for exporting home-country skills. The basic failing of the neo-factor models, however, is that they assume perfectly competitive markets, an assumption which does not remotely correspond to the description of multiple market imperfections in the international pharmaceutical industry, recorded in Chapter 1.

The 'neo-technology' trade theories specifically allow for market imperfections, and highlight Posner's useful suggestion that the resultant technology gaps between countries allow trade to occur during the diffusion period of the new knowledge incorporated in a (pharmaceutical) innovation. Linder's approach is not particularly helpful, as exports of drugs to foreign countries are generally driven by 'need pull' rather than by comparative cost advantages generated by home country economies of scale. Also, the proposal by Dreze that exports are helped by the home market imperative towards product differentiation has no useful contribution to make to the foreign R & D discussion, though it may have some measure of descriptive utility to international drug marketing.

In general, the discussion of trade barriers throws no specific light on the drug industry, though it should be noted that non-tariff barriers have been raised increasingly by many countries, possibly to compensate for the lowering of pharmaceutical tariff barriers. Of particular interest in this section was Johnston's indication that information costs are an important consideration in developing trade theories; this is highly pertinent to the pharmaceutical industry, and the whole area of information will be examined below.

However, all the general reasons given above regarding the limitations of trade theory as a predictor of multinational activity refer in particular to the world pharmaceutical industry, as the assumptions of trade theory do not mirror accurately (or even approximately) the real world within which drug multinationals have to operate.

THE THEORY OF FOREIGN DIRECT INVESTMENT

As indicated earlier, foreign direct investment is an activity which is specific to multinational corporations. By locating in a foreign country, the multinational corporation extends itself to the new location in ways which go well beyond the mere transfer of capital. In addition, technological and managerial skills are transferred to the host country and integrated with local factors of production. This often produces international trade flows within the multinational corporation and external to it.

Root[8] suggests that any theory of foreign direct investment should address itself to three fundamental questions:

1 Why do firms go abroad as direct investors?
2 How can direct-investing firms compete successfully with local firms, given the inherent advantage of local firms operating in a familiar business environment?
3 Why do firms choose to enter foreign countries as producers rather than as exporters or licensers?

In addition, a robust theory which is able to encompass these phenomena should also have considerable explanatory power in relation to consequent topics such as: why is foreign direct investment concentrated in some particular industries, and dominated by large firms in oligopolistic markets; why are only a few countries the source of most of the world's foreign direct investment, and why do they make investments in one another, often within the same industries?

Clearly, with such a number of perspectives to cover, there will be various complementary theoretical approaches, each laying differing stress on each topic. The approach used here to assess the current body of theory begins with an examination of the market imperfections approach to foreign direct investment, with a summary of the sources of advantage to multinational corporations. Theoretical approaches based on firm-specific and location-specific advantages are then examined separately. Finally, there is a consideration of the question of a generalised theory of international production, encapsulating the most important of the concepts examined beforehand.

The market imperfections theory of foreign direct investment

In his doctoral thesis, written in 1960 and published in 1976, Hymer[9] suggested that the decision of a multinational corporation to invest in an overseas market can only be explained if the company has, and can utilise, certain advantages not possessed by its local competitors. These advantages may derive from skills in the fields of management, marketing, production, finance or technology; they may refer to exclusive or preferential access to raw materials or other inputs. Whatever the source, the market for the sale of these advantages would have to be imperfect. Kindleberger[10] extended this reasoning to suggest that market imperfections themselves are the reason for foreign direct investment.

Another requirement is that the specific advantages possessed by the multinational corporation must be easily transferred within the firm, sometimes over long distances. However, the fact that such firm-specific advantages exist, are transferable, and cannot be efficiently marketed, is not in itself a sufficient explanation for the firm's decision to locate manufacturing facilities overseas rather than produce at home and export, or license production to an overseas partner. Other location-specific advantages – including input prices, transport and communication availability and costs, existence of trade barriers, sophistication of infrastructure – have to be included in order to evolve necessary and sufficient conditions for the decision to locate production in foreign countries. All the theories of foreign direct investment examined here follow from this premise.

Notwithstanding this second condition, it is certainly true that if firms attempt to exploit such market imperfections across international frontiers, then multinationality will occur. Market imperfections may be created by:

1 The existence of internal or external economies of scale. This may be the basis of many of the oligopolistic markets within which multinational corporations operate. It may arise, for example, by privileged access to raw materials or to final markets; it may arise from the exploitation of firm-specific knowledge assets, making each successive foreign investment less costly than the initial one; it may simply arise from increases in physical production. Certainly, the oligopolies which result do not react as would firms in perfectly competitive markets. For example, Knickerbocker[11] has indicated that oligopolistic competitors show a tendency to follow one another into individual foreign markets, behaviour which is not always justified by profit potential. He suggested that this behaviour might be explained by the motivation of the followers to cancel out any market advantage obtained by the pioneer multination corporation.

   Other oligopolistic factors include the incidence of high research and development intensity and the aggressive use of patents, the importance of economies of scale yielding substantial market power to multinational corporations and very large initial capital investment as a barrier to entry.

2 Factors dependent on, and flowing from, product differentiation. These technology advantages refer not only to products and processes, but to the marketing and organisational skills which lie

behind them. The market for this kind of knowledge may be very imperfect indeed. Multinational corporations which have special advantages in this area use foreign licensees very infrequently, as such advantages are incorporated in human skills. As indicated above, successive utilisation of this type of factor lowers the unit cost, and makes it progressively more difficult for local producers to compete.

3 The impact of government policies on fiscal and monetary matters, trade barriers, etc. According to Aliber,[12] multinational corporations are often able to utilise currency variation patterns to borrow investment capital at a lower rate than indigenous firms. In addition, owing to their stronger and widely accepted credit ratings, multinational corporations can often borrow investment capital in international markets at favourable rates when host government policies make domestic capital expensive or unavailable to indigenous firms. Finally, the multinational corporation is able to build up an efficient portfolio of international direct investments, thus reducing the risk factor involved in any one government's fiscal and monetary policies; this approach is not open to the domestic company.

4 Factor market idiosyncracies like industrial property rights, differential management skills, superior knowledge and technology. Since many of these factors come in discrete quantities, any or all may be underutilised at any one time. Overseas expansion is one way of using this spare capacity efficiently, but not the only way; domestic expansion would have the same result.

Applying market imperfections theory to the world pharmaceutical industry The Hymer and Kindleberger concept has considerable descriptive power for the international pharmaceutical industry. Foreign subsidiaries do possess certain advantages which cannot be utilised by domestic competitors. Clearly, there may be skills in the various facets of production (fine chemical production, bulk process and formulation technology, dosage form manufacture) which are not possessed to the same extent – if at all – by indigenous competitors. Also, there may be marketing skills which have been developed at home and which may be exportable, e.g. particularly successful advertising themes, forms of drug promotion, specific contact and communication skills in respect of the general practitioner community. Finally, and most important, there are obvious technology skills in the form of industrial property rights and innovatory drugs which, as explained in Chapter 1, belong almost entirely to the pharmaceutical multinationals. All these advantages meet the condition of transferability, as they can be moved about by a drug multinational with relative ease to any of the firm's international locations.

Market imperfections arising from economies of scale are generally not of first importance in this industry, though they can be a crucial factor in the decision to decentralise pharmaceutical R & D.

Product differentiation can be an important source of market imperfection, as discussed above. It requires a great deal of marketing and organisational skill to communicate with and motivate effectively the large number of primary (prescribers) and secondary (dispensers) customers in any host country. Increasing product differentiation makes it progressively more difficult for indigenous pharmaceutical firms to compete.

For the international drug industry, the most important market imperfections are almost certainly brought about by particular factor market idiosyncracies, prominent among which is the question of industrial property rights. As outlined in Chapter 1, the cost of developing a new drug has become very high. It is seldom possible to amortise this cost either by concentrating on the home market (because even the largest market – the US – may not be large enough) or by licensing (because there are serious market inefficiencies involved in striking a selling price).

Thus, the market imperfections approach has a great deal of utility in describing and predicting the general directions of pharmaceutical multinational activity. For more specificity, especially in the area of R & D, it is necessary to look at some of the alternative theories of foreign direct investment.

Foreign direct investment theory based on firm-specific advantages

The market imperfections approach helps to identify those industries and firms where internationalisation is most likely to occur. The industry-specific advantages described above suggest what form of internationalisation may be adopted, but a further condition is necessary before valid explanations and predictions can be made. This concerns the non-marketability of certain types of company-specific advantage; that is, the market mechanism is not sufficiently efficient to return the full economic rent to the firm if the advantage is licensed or sold. This is normally because the potential licenser or buyer has no way of evaluating fully the precise market value of the knowledge under consideration.

Thus, a key question in the theory of foreign direct investment is why the external market proves to be an imperfect mechanism for transferring knowledge with the full rent being captured by the owner. Coase[13] produced a hypothesis which he originally applied to the multiplant indigenous firm, but which can be extended to apply to specific aspects of multinational activity. He suggested that the external market mechanism inflicts high transaction costs in areas such as defining and accepting contractual obligations, fixing the contract price, taxes to be paid on market transactions, etc. He argued that these activities will be internalised by the firm wherever this is more cost-efficient than using the external market mechanism.

Buckley and Casson[14] developed this approach into a systematic theory of multinational business activity. They argued for the influence of market imperfections as a causative factor leading to internationalisation, and suggested that four groups of factors are important in this respect:

1 Industry-specific factors, such as product and structure factors.
2 Region-specific factors, such as cultural aspects.
3 Nation-specific factors, such as political aspects.
4 Firm-specific factors, such as management and technical knowledge.

Rugman,[15] who has been active in extending this theoretical direction, stresses the importance of Hymer's original work (already described) in the development of the internalisation approach. He quotes some fundamental statements from Hymer which, he says, have led to the theoretical exposition of the internalisation approach:

the multinational corporation is a practical institutional device which substitutes for the market.

the [imperfect market] leads the possessor of the advantage to choose to supersede the market for his advantage.

many of the reasons for choosing not to license arose from the imperfect nature of the market for the advantage. These imperfections prevented the appropriation of all the returns to this advantage.

The Buckley and Casson approach develops these points with particular regard to the market for the knowledge which the multinational acquires through intensive, long-term research and development. The multinational corporation acquires its unique advantage by internalising its knowledge (or any other advantages) rather than by attempting to sell it through an inefficient market mechanism to a foreign manufacturer.

Giddy[16] has summarised the cost savings which a multinational corporation can realise by the process of internalisation; these savings may arise through by-passing:

1 Concentrated markets for raw materials and arm's-length supply that is expensive and risky;
2 Imperfect markets for the firm's resources (such as management or a brand name), because they are inseparable from the firm itself.
3 Imperfect markets for outputs because of monopolistic control over the distribution outlets, particularly in small countries.
4 Imperfect markets for product resources because of government-imposed barriers to market entry, such as tariffs.
5 Markets for intangibles (such as knowledge or patents) of a 'public goods' nature – once sold, the intangibles are free and can produce no more revenues.

Internalising markets through foreign direct investment also imposes additional costs, which include:

1 Additional communication costs (a function of geographical and cultural distance).
2 The cost of operating in unfamiliar environments.
3 The cost of overcoming the political and social stigmas against foreign-owned firms.
4 The administrative cost of managing an internal market.

Thus, the importance of the work of Buckley and Casson (and others who have developed the internalisation approach) is that it greatly extends and deepens the market imperfections analysis by focusing on the important intermediate product markets (such as skills and knowledge), rather than on final product markets. It sets up the simple hypothesis that when the costs of internalisation are outweighed by the benefits, then foreign direct investment is the preferred strategy.

The approach of Magee[17] to the theory of foreign direct investment closely resembles that of Buckley and Casson, and strongly echoes Hymer's work as previously quoted: 'many of the reasons for choosing not to license arose from the imperfect nature of the market for the advantage. These imperfections prevented the appropriation of all the returns to the advantage.'

Magee focuses on the multinational corporation's ability to appropriate to itself the returns on its investment in R & D. Appropriability is seen as being facilitated by the firm's ability to internalise firm-specific knowledge. This approach lays much stress on its derivation from the theory of information and the public goods nature of new knowledge.

Magee notes that 'Information is a durable good in that present resources must be devoted to its creation, and its existence results in a stream of benefits.' However, information also has the nature of a public good in that, once created, it can be used by parties other than the creator. This secondary use diminishes the private return available to the creator of the information. The degree to which active measures taken by the creator to monopolise the returns flowing from the use of the information is a measure of the appropriability of the information.

Magee notes from his empirical work a 'nearly significant relationship' between monopoly profits and R & D expenditure for nineteen US industries; he argues that monopoly profits earned in innovating industries do not necessarily reflect distortions in the use of economic resources, as they merely reflect the additional returns on past investment in new information. He does, however, accept that such distortion of resource use may occur in concentrated industries with high investments in barriers to entry. These, he argues, are unrelated to appropriability and reflect elements of waste and redistribution in the prices of technology.

Magee recognises five distinct types of information which require investment during the product development cycle:

1 Investments to discover new products. Much of this information is generated by non-corporate inventors. The locus of multinational R & D expenditures is innovation, which is covered by (2) to (5) below.

2 Investments in product development. These investments may take place over a protracted period of time, frequently five to ten years; they consist of applied research, product and process specification, etc. Magee suggests that multinational corporations grow larger because they can transmit more efficiently product development information from product to product within the firm, rather than using the less efficient market mechanism.

3 Investments to create the production function. The production function for any product is determined by the supply and demand for information, for any given price structure of inputs. Magee notes that when a capital-intensive production function is taken from a developed to a developing country, the multinational corporation substitutes relatively cheap, unskilled labour for other factors. This process is limited by the past investment of the firm in developing production techniques which intensively utilise unskilled labour.

4 Investments in information to create product markets. Multinational corporations may be regarded conceptually as sellers of new information and new technologies. They build their reputations by estab-

lishing a high and predictable level of quality in the technology they produce for consumers of new information. Such product markets must be continuously created, maintained and expanded.

5 Investments in appropriability. Magee argues that this is a necessary prerequisite for the multinational corporation in a product development phase. This can be done in a variety of ways, including patents, trademarks, trade secrets, quasi-contractual control over employees, and other methods of protecting industrial property rights. This, in turn, may lead to high costs for establishing and protecting industrial property rights. Colluding oligopolies may be able to evolve a mechanism for sharing these costs. According to this argument, lack of appropriability leads to lack of R & D in highly competitive industries; it may also be a factor in social investment by multinational corporations in technologies utilising unskilled labour.

Magee concludes that the structure of an industry and the creation of technology are jointly determined endogenous variables. Other things being equal, R & D and other investments in innovation are encouraged by the presence of a monopoly or an oligopoly because appropriability costs are lower for these industry structures. Consequently, a major innovation will encourage an increase in optimum firm size, so that the structure of the industry becomes more concentrated.

As an extension of the appropriability theory, Magee notes that his conclusion implies a 'technology cycle' at the industry level, which has some parallels with Vernon's product life cycle theory described below. Thus, while the industry technology cycle is a part of the firm-specific approach, it will be examined below in counterpoint to the product life cycle theory of foreign direct investment.

Applying the theory of firm-specific advantages to the world pharmaceutical industry The previous section indicates quite clearly that internationalisation is likely to take place in the ethical pharmaceutical industry, and suggests that it is more likely to occur among larger firms with well developed domestic markets. For predictions about where and how internationalisation will take place in this industry, it is necessary to turn to the specific theories of foreign direct investment.

Internalisation theory is useful in including resources like the firm's management and its brand names for consideration, but its principal predictive power lies in its consideration of imperfections in the market for knowledge created by the pharmaceutical multinationals' intensive, long-term R & D programmes. Buckley and Casson emphasised the importance of internalising such knowledge; drug multinationals unquestionably derive major competitive advantage by internalising this R & D output rather than by trying to sell it in an international market which cannot accurately or fully evaluate it. In any case, even if an acceptable price was struck for the sale of an innovation, the intrinsic knowledge then becomes a 'public good' and can produce no more revenues for the innovatory firm.

For the pharmaceutical industry, then, the general prediction made by internalisation theory is that foreign direct investment will take place if the benefits of internalising market imperfections outweigh the costs. In terms of drug R & D, the prediction is that foreign direct investment may take place primarily if the knowledge market imperfections give an internalisation net benefit. This is not a sufficient condition, as the cost balance of decentralisation must also be examined.

The question of market imperfections for proprietary knowledge, as developed by Magee, carries important implications for the international drug industry. In his terminology, the industry clearly makes massive investments in appropriability:

1 New molecules emerging from the R & D process are invariably patented at the earliest possible moment, and certainly long before they have been biologically evaluated.
2 Patents, trademarks and trade secrets are jealously guarded; legal action is resorted to promptly if any of these is even vaguely threatened.
3 A very wide range of quasi contractual controls over employees is practised, especially for those involved in R & D; this includes formal employment agreements, loyalty bonus schemes, share option schemes, retirement rewards, freedom of publication, and informal (occasionally formal) undertakings of scientific freedom in research.

However, it should be noted that drug firms also make other large investments in information, according to Magee's classification:

1 Investments to discover new products.
2 Investments in product development. As well as initial investments, drug firms also incur major expenditures in international markets to tailor products for individual markets in terms of acceptable local dosage forms, physiology of users, local climate, etc.
3 Investments in information to create product markets. This is especially important when a new type of drug is produced. For example, when SmithKline introduced Tagamet, the firm made very large investments to educate prescribers that it was not an antacid product, but a new active agent which inhibited the production of certain

stomach acids, thereby making possible a cure for stomach ulcers, not just a palliative. The firm's reward for this investment in information was Tagamet's rapid advance to become (for a time) the world's top-selling drug.

Thus, according to Magee's approach, the oligopolistic nature of many therapeutic sub-markets encourages large investments in innovation because appropriability costs tend to be lower with this type of industry structure.

Foreign direct investment theory based on location-specific advantages

Early work in this field was carried out by Southard[18] in 1932. His book *American Industry in Europe* was directed at US firms' decisions to locate in one foreign country as opposed to others. Later work, mainly case studies of inward investment in particular countries, pursued the same question – for example, Dunning's[19] study in 1958 of inward investment in the United Kingdom by US multinational corporations.

According to Hood and Young,[20] there are four factors which are pertinent to the location-specific theory of foreign direct investment:

1 *Labour costs.* Real wages costs vary significantly, not only between developing and industrialised countries, but also within these groupings. Other things being equal, this leads to the well-known phenomenon of low-technology international industries being located in low-wage economies, with a similar movement being observed in other industries as the technology becomes standardised.

2 *Marketing factors.* Foreign direct investment decisions will obviously be affected by host-country characteristics like market size, market growth, stage of development, and the presence of local competition. The first three of these are clearly tied up with economies of scale, while the degree of local competition will shape many aspects of local marketing strategy.

3 *Trade barriers.* These are used as an element of policy by many host countries trying to encourage inward investment. In theory, and often in practice, multinationals will set up local production facilities to protect an already developed export market if trade barriers are erected.

4 *Government policy.* This has a significant effect on the 'investment climate' in any particular host country, either directly through fiscal and monetary policies and the regulatory regime, or indirectly through the general sociological environment.

This analysis is stated mainly in terms of cost advantages, but recent research into the international location of R & D facilities by Ronstadt[21] and Lall[22] has indicated that non-price benefits can arise from foreign dispersal of research and development.

None of this, of course, represents a theory of location which explains foreign direct investment. Perhaps the best-known theory depending on location-specific advantages (and also making predictions about the timing of foreign direct investment) was developed by Vernon,[23] and extended by Wells.[24]

The product life cycle theory is based on four main sets of assumptions, which set it apart from traditional trade theory. These may be summarised as:

1 Tastes differ in different countries.
2 The production process is characterised by economies of scale.
3 The flow of information across national borders is restricted.
4 Products undergo changes in production techniques and marketing characteristics over time; the pattern of these changes is broadly predictable.

Many of the individual assumptions derive from the debate on the 'Leontief paradox', and the main thrust of the product life cycle theory has been to make practical predictions about the development of international trade in certain manufactured products.

Wells has been a prolific writer on the product life cycle theory, in terms of both theory and empiricism. For example, he sees assumption (3) above as leading to three important conclusions:

1 Innovation of new products and processes is more likely to occur near a market where there is a strong demand for them than in a country with little demand.
2 A businessman is more likely to supply risk capital for the production of the new product if demand is likely to exist in his home market than if he has to turn to a foreign market.
3 A producer located close to a market has a lower cost in transferring market knowledge into product design changes than one located far from the market.

At the time the product life cycle theory was being developed, it was clear that the US market was the one which pre-eminently fulfilled the requirements for manufactured product innovations applying to high-income consumers or which were labour-saving for the user.

In the first phase of the cycle (see Figure 2.1), manufacture takes place in the US because of the relative price inelasticity, so costs are

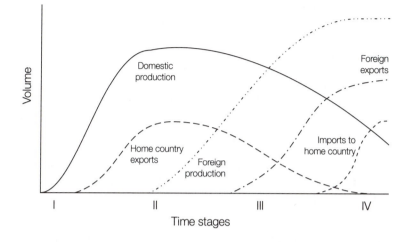

Figure 2.1 The product life cycle *Source*: J. Fayerweather, *International Business Management*, McGraw-Hill, New York (1969)

relatively unimportant. However, quick and accurate communication between the market and the production facilities is vital, so that rapid product changes can be instigated where necessary. During this phase, US manufacturers are likely to have a product monopoly, and exports to other developed markets (e.g. Western Europe) are likely to commence as manufacturing capacity builds up.

As foreign incomes grow, and as potential foreign producers acquire the necessary information to enter the market, then either US firms invest abroad to preclude competition and to protect established export sales, or local producers will do so in direct competition. US exports to the new producing countries (probably European) will cease to grow as quickly in this second phase as formerly, but they will continue to expand by penetrating new export markets – possibly in developing countries.

In phase three, European exports to developing countries begin to displace US exports, and US exports thus begin to fall. Note that European exports and European production for domestic consumption may be manufactured largely – or even wholly – by US affiliates. Also, in this phase of the cycle, as the product matures, manufacturing costs become more important and price elasticity begins to rise.

In the fourth phase, economies of scale in European production have grown to such an extent that exports to the US market become possible, and may grow rapidly. In addition, the increasing importance of low labour costs means that production facilities may be set up in developing countries, thus reducing the growth of European exports to that sector and possibly halting US exports altogether. Thus, in the fourth phase, the US may become a net importer.

In an extension of phase four, which so far has been observed only in products such as standardised plastics, textiles and electronic components, the developing country production facilities may grow to such an extent that exports to Europe and the US become feasible.

As previously noted, Wells has carried out a considerable number of empirical studies which he sees as supporting, refining and extending the product life cycle theory. In particular, one of these carries a conclusion which is pertinent to the pharmaceutical industry, in that it suggests higher prices will be charged in international markets than might be expected:

> Thus, in an industry where the barriers to entry to international markets are high, where co-operation is practised by the firms which are multinational, where economies of scale are important, and where arbitrage is difficult, one might expect to find prices in individual markets which are close to what prices would have been without international trade.

Root[25] considers that the product life cycle theory is most relevant to a manufacturer's initial foreign direct investment, but is less relevant to multinational corporations that already have production and marketing facilities in existence. The explanatory power of the product life cycle theory has diminished as the expertise of multinational corporations has increased; the theory does not address the strategy issue of why multinational corporations undertake foreign direct investment instead of exporting or licensing; nor does it explain foreign direct investment in supply-oriented raw materials industries. Thus, the model is principally useful in focusing on the interaction between the factors which influence the location of production, but does not by itself explain the source of multinational corporations' ownership-specific advantages.

Rugman[26] notes that the model was initially developed to explain the growth of US multinational corporations during the period 1945–65, but that it is less applicable now that multinational corporations have changed their character – particularly in regard to the growth of European and Japanese multinational corporations.

Vernon[27] himself has modified the original model, categorising multinationals at various stages of the development cycle thus:

1 *Innovation-based oligopolies.* Barriers to entry are created through continuous introduction of new products and aggressive differ-

entiation of existing ones, both at home and abroad. These firms exhibit a high ratio of R & D expenditure, and a low ratio of operative employees. Firms in this category behave most nearly in accord with the product life cycle theory, though often the most aggressive firms will exploit foreign markets without waiting for the product life cycle to take its course.

2 *Mature oligopolies.* These firms are able to share markets in the traditional oligopolistic sense long after the products have become standardised, through the maintenance of entry barriers such as the economies of the experience curve, or economies of scale in marketing, production or transport. These oligopolies also depend on high fixed costs as a barrier to entry, and thus adopt stabilising strategies such as:

(a) Follow-the-leader behaviour in entering new countries or product lines.
(b) Pricing conventions.
(c) Mutual alliances (jointly producing subsidiaries, long-term contracts, etc.).
(d) Mutual hostages (affiliates in each other's countries tolerated).

3 *Senescent oligopolies.* These tend to occur when existing barriers to entry erode, and multinational corporations either drop out of the particular market to concentrate on newer products, or move production to low-cost locations.

Wells has summarised the usefulness of the product life cycle theory to foreign direct investment, noting that the developed model has been validated by empirical work, and that it helps in understanding the international flows of manufactured goods. He suggests that the model has the following particular uses:

1 It assists the businessman in scanning for products that are likely to be good performers in the export market, or in predicting imports of standardised products where foreign markets are large enough to allow large-scale production techniques to be used.
2 It can assist governments in predicting thresholds beyond which certain products may be exported in quantity from developing countries.

However, the product life cycle theory is still not fully accepted by the theoretical economist, as it is not rigorously defined in all its aspects. Some writers see it as a concept which has outgrown its usefulness. Perhaps the best-known criticism of this nature is by

Giddy,[28] who feels that the product life cycle theory itself has experienced growth, maturity and decline as a central concept in explaining international trade and investment patterns. Echoing some of the criticisms above, he points out some of the shortcomings of the model:

1 It is unable to predict correctly international patterns in many manufactured goods, for example in new products such as digital watches and disposable razors, and in mature products such as processed foods and toiletries.
2 Raw materials trade cannot be predicted by the model.
3 The model does not address properly the question why multinational corporations do not license or export, but instead prefer to invest in their own foreign production facilities.
4 The model does not examine what systematic advantages foreign firms have that enable them to overcome their inherent disadvantages *vis-à-vis* local firms.

Giddy recognises that the product life cycle theory still has a degree of explanatory power in some cases, but believes that it is now only one facet of a number of survival strategies multinational corporates have developed for foreign direct investment.

The product life cycle theory is, of course, based on country-specific advantages. But, as indicated earlier, it does have some structural similarities to Magee's[29] concept of an 'industry technology cycle', developed from his appropriability theory of foreign direct investment. Magee notes that this parallel concept of an industry cycle originates in Nelson's[30] conclusion that the cumulative number of patents granted to any particular industry tends to follow an S curve over long periods of time, i.e. after a period of rapid growth the number of new patents granted per year diminishes over time. He argues that this implies eventually diminishing marginal returns on the stock of information created by an industry. His appropriability theory suggests that industry structure itself is an endogenous variable which varies systematically over time; this implies, for example, that young industries are concentrated and have high R & D, while older industries are more competitive and invest less in R & D.

Magee puts forward five reasons why technologies are transferred within firms:

1 Appropriability. Innovating firms expand to internalise the externality brought about by new information, i.e. the public goods aspect.
2 New products tend to be those which the prospective consumer cannot evaluate merely by visual inspection (experience goods). Just

as standardised goods are more likely to lead to a licensing operation, so the development of experience goods is more likely to cause multinational subsidiaries to be set up in order to maximise the private returns from the new knowledge.

3 Service information is a vital provision with sales of high technology; the establishment of service subsidiaries leads to growth in the firm's optimum size.

4 Because of product complementarities within development information, production information, marketing information, and appropriability information, there is a tendency for information-producing multinational corporations to maximise the product range.

5 The spread between the buyer's and the seller's valuation of new information is lower in standardised than in experience products; this suggests that market transaction costs are relatively lower later in the cycle, so that the optimum firm size will tend to fall through the industry cycle.

Magee argues that these five points are the key to the industry technology cycle, and that they explain why:

1 Size of multinational corporations is positively correlated with information creation.

2 Concentrated industry structure is correlated with new technologies.

3 International trade in technology occurs within large multinational corporations rather than through licensing agreements.

4 Older industries are more competitive and less innovative.

The three stages of the industry technology cycle are somewhat different from the phases of the product life cycle theory:

1 *Invention*, which precedes the product life cycle theory first stage, and which occurs before any attempt is made to evolve a commercial product.

2 *Innovation*, which includes the product life cycle theory first and second phases. This includes the development of the invention into a commercially attractive product, and the further product development required as the product is introduced into new markets.

3 *Standardisation*, which coincides with the product life cycle theory phases three and four.

Applying the theory of location-specific advantages to the world pharmaceutical industry Having observed in the foregoing sections the forms that internationalisation is likely to take in the pharmaceutical industry, and having noted circumstances in which particular firms might look to foreign markets, the question of possible locations for foreign direct investment now comes under scrutiny. The set of models based on the product life cycle theory would seem initially to have a degree of descriptive power with respect to the international drug industry. The four main sets of assumptions on which the theory is based seem to hold, at least in a modified form, for pharmaceuticals, viz:

1 Therapeutic needs and requirements differ according to the economic and social development of different countries.
2 There are economies of scale which can be achieved, both in bulk production of fine chemicals, and in formulation and dosage form manufacturing.
3 The flow of information across national borders is restricted in direct proportion to the strictness of patent law.
4 Drugs undergo changes in production techniques and marketing characteristics over time as physiological and biological reactions and side effects become better known, and as the drug becomes useful for a wider range of indications.

In addition to this close fit of assumptions, the three broad conclusions arrived at by Wells also hold good for the drugs industry:

1 Drug innovation is more likely to occur in or near highly developed markets than where sales *per capita* are low.
2 A drug firm is more likely to invest in the development and production of a new pharmaceutical product if there is likely to be a substantial demand in its home market.
3 Feedback from the home market is more easily transferred to the R & D unit, and at a lower cost, than information from foreign markets.

However, when the predictive power of the model is examined with respect to pharmaceutical multinationals, many of the defects indicated by Giddy are evident:

1 The model does not predict correctly the international patterns of foreign direct investment, either in manufacturing or in R & D, of the drug multinationals.
2 In particular, it does not predict correctly the relatively high degree of international production carried out by European drug multinationals.
3 It also fails to predict why firms set up foreign R & D facilities in the first place, why they select the locations they do, why these locations are mainly in developed countries, and why less developed countries are used at all.

Before discarding the product life cycle theory as a useful tool, however, it will be helpful to examine Vernon's modifications of the original model. By this classification, pharmaceutical multinationals undoubtedly display the key characteristics of innovation-based oligopolies:

1 High barriers to entry are raised by the constant stream of new drugs, by improvement of existing drugs, and by their use for an expanded range of indications.
2 Drug multinational corporations exhibit a large and growing ratio of R & D expenditure to sales (see Chapter 1).

Vernon suggests that firms in this category behave in a manner closest to the product life cycle theory, but allows that the most aggressive firms will exploit foreign markets without waiting for the product life cycle to take its course. This conclusion and qualification hardly apply to the drug industry, at least to the R & D-intensive sector of it. Instead, it has been argued in Chapter 1 that the internationalisation process of a new drug is very rapid indeed, mainly driven by the need to amortise the large R & D expenditures. Where Vernon's suggestion may have some validity in this industry is in the consideration of those firms which have a poor record of new drug discovery, whether their R & D expenditures are high or low. It may be argued that these firms generally exhibit the following characteristics:

1 Follow-the-leader behaviour in entering product lines developed from out-of-patent drugs.
2 Mutual alliances, including jointly producing subsidiaries; this has become a more frequently used strategy of some US firms in coming to terms with the approach of Japanese drug companies to international markets.

These, of course, are two of the main characteristics of another of Vernon's classifications – mature oligopolies. Thus, an important facet of the product life cycle theory may be its ability to detect the early moves of the pharmaceutical industry away from its 'sunrise' status, rather than any ability to predict locational strategies.

THE GENERAL THEORY OF INTERNATIONAL PRODUCTION

In 1973 Dunning[31] published a paper in which he hypothesised that a proper evaluation of UK membership of the European Economic Community could be arrived at only by considering trade and foreign production as alternative forms of international involvement in terms of ownership-specific and location-specific advantages. By drawing together elements of trade theory and foreign direct investment theory, he aimed to derive a comprehensive theory of international production.

Hirsch[32] formulated these concepts into a model which clearly specified the conditions under which foreign markets would be serviced in various ways. He defined three groups of variables which affect the foreign investment decision:

1 Comparative input costs.
2 Firm-specific revenue-producing factors.
3 Information, communication and transaction costs which increase with economic distance.

Using these variables in his model, Hirsch demonstrated that the consideration of only the comparative costs of production was the main weakness of conventional trade theory. He was also able to demonstrate that joint production of several goods and multi-stage production had considerable consequences for the predictions of his model.

Further work by Dunning[33] led to his 'eclectic theory' of international production, which drew on three of the fundamental economic approaches which were discussed above: the theory of property rights and markets, a combination of location and trade theories, and the Hymer–Kindleberger industrial organisation approach which stressed firm-specific advantages. He classified the comparative advantages possessed by multinational corporations into three groups:

1 *Firm-specific advantages.* The multinational corporation must possess ownership advantages which can be at least temporarily held exclusively, and which yield a net superiority over competitors in foreign markets. Firm-specific advantages most often are intangible assets like expertise or technology-based utilities. In a conceptual link with the product life cycle theory, Dunning suggested that – to some degree – many of these advantages originate in country characteristics such as market size, management education, and government support of technology. However, firm-specific advantages may also be derived from the multinationality of the firm, as for example in the access to parent company expertise, financial capacity, and environmental scanning ability.
2 *Location-specific factors.* These are factors which have specificity of origin to a particular place and have to be used in that place. They include trade barriers which restrict imports, most types of labour, natural resources, proximity to final markets, conditions of transport

and communication, degree of government intervention, and cultural distance factors.

3 *Internalisation advantages.* These are advantages a company gains by using its ownership factors internally instead of trying to sell them on the market to third parties, e.g. foreign production as opposed to licensing. These factors are highly relevant to ownership strategy and include the ability to cross-subsidise products or operations, the ability to avoid costs of transaction and negotiation, buyer uncertainty about the value of the technology being sold, the ability to control supplies of inputs and their conditions of sale, etc. In terms of the analysis of methods of servicing foreign markets given previously, clearly only wholly owned subsidiaries and possibly joint ventures give the multinational corporation the capacity to appropriate fully the returns on these advantages.

Dunning formulated these three groups of comparative advantages into his principal hypothesis thus: given the possession of net ownership advantages over the local firms, the most beneficial development is for the multinational corporation to internalise them by extending its own activities; it must then be more profitable for the multinational corporation to combine these internalised advantages with some factor inputs in some foreign countries, otherwise foreign markets would be served entirely by exports and home markets by home production.

Applying the eclectic theory to the world pharmaceutical industry
Dunning's principal hypothesis can be easily and logically interpreted with respect to the pharmaceutical industry:

1 Drug multinationals possess significant net ownership advantages over local firms; these advantages include intensive innovation infrastructure, possession of patents, superior skills in channel management, and excellent internal control and communication systems.
2 Clearly, the best strategy for drug multinationals is to internalise these important ownership advantages by extending their own activities, both nationally and internationally.
3 Therefore, it will be more profitable for international pharmaceutical firms to combine these internalised ownership advantages with selected factor inputs in selected foreign countries.

While the eclectic theory was originally evolved as a model of international production (and, as such, has significant descriptive and predictive power for the pharmaceutical industry), it also has a great deal of relevance in respect of pharmaceutical R & D, in that it outlines the broad strategic direction which pharmaceutical firms follow as they internationalise R & D facilities.

SUMMARY

This chapter has described the economics of multinational theory, and indicated how this has developed from early trade theory and empirical considerations of methods of developing foreign markets. The three main divisions of foreign direct investment theory were examined, viz approaches based on market imperfections, firm-specific advantages, and location-specific advantages. Finally, the general theory of international production was reviewed, not only for its intrinsic predictive power in terms of foreign direct investment, but also because of its utility in emphasising the interdependent nature of the three specific approaches detailed above.

At each stage, the linkages of each theory with the world pharmaceutical industry were examined. Thus, it appears that trade theory (which relies on a range of perfect market assumptions) is not helpful in understanding the international drug industry; approaches based on market imperfections are generally more useful. Internalisation models have some utility in describing the industry and in predicting the circumstances under which internationalisation will take place. It is much less useful, however, for predicting where foreign facilities will be established. This, obviously, will be a facet of some form of locational model. The product life cycle model is not helpful here, particularly in terms of foreign R & D facilities. The locational aspects of the eclectic model are more apposite, especially when considering the internationalisation of R & D.

3 Applying technology theory to the world pharmaceutical industry

DEFINITION OF TERMS

The literature covering linkages between technology and the growth of multinational corporations covers less than a thirty-year time span, which perhaps explains why there is no comprehensive agreement on the definition of such terms as technical change, technological change, technique, technology, research, development, invention, and innovation – as they apply to this field. Some working definitions are set out below which seem to have a measure of acceptability, and these meanings will be used in all that follows.

Green and Morphet[1] define technology as '. . . the systematic knowledge of technique . . .' and technique as '. . . the interaction of person/tool/machine/object which defines a "way of doing" a particular task'. The explicit emphasis on technology as a knowledge system recalls the appropriability theory of foreign direct investment set out by Magee, which was covered in Chapter 2. As noted there, appropriability theory has some useful predictive powers in respect of the pharmaceutical industry.

Green and Morphet describe their approach to technology in economic terms, noting that the production function for a technique is the boundary of technically efficient production possibilities, and that a set of techniques will give rise to a range of production functions. Technical change can therefore be regarded as the effect of a manufacturer moving from one production function (technique) to another within the known range; it may also involve a move along any particular production function. Thus, recent developments in Japanese antibiotics process technology represent a move to a new production function.

Extending this approach, technological change takes place when a completely new technique is added to the existing set, involving new knowledge and requiring the creation of a new production function. Invention can then be regarded as[2] '. . . the process by which technology is changed, or the new technique generated by the process' and innovation as[3] 'the first use (which is rarely immediate) of an invention or the embodiment of an invention in actual productive processes'.

This line of analysis is continued by Green and Morphet to consider research as[4] '. . . a process of scientific enquiry which may be research in technology or research in pure sciences'; and development as[5] 'the activity involved in transforming a theoretical technological advance into concrete operational hardware . . . the whole process by which innovation takes place'.

The (US) National Science Foundation has evolved a more detailed and possibly more widely accepted definition of research and development:[6] '. . . basic and applied research in the sciences and engineering, and the design and development of prototypes and processes'.

According to the National Science Foundation, there are three types of research and development:[7]

1 *Basic research*: '. . . original investigations for the advancement of scientific knowledge not having specific commercial objectives, although such investigations may be in fields of present or potential interest to the reporting company.'
2 *Applied research*: '. . . investigations directed to the discovery of new scientific knowledge having specific commercial objectives with respect to products or processes. This definition differs from that of basic research chiefly in terms of the objectives of the reporting company.'
3 *Development*: '. . . technical activities of a non-routine nature concerned with translating resource findings or other scientific knowledge into products or processes. It does not include technical services or other activities excluded from the above definition of research and development.'

Finally, Schmookler[8] defines technology transfer as:

the process by which science and technology are diffused throughout human activity . . . This can be either transfer from more basic scientific knowledge into technology, or adaptation of existing technology to a new line . . . Vertical transfer refers to the transfer of technology along the line from the more general to the more specific. Horizontal transfer occurs through the adaptation of a technology from one application to another, possibly wholly unrelated to the first.

Technology can be transferred from one country to another or within a country, from one industry to another or within an industry, from one firm to another or within a firm, from one product line to another or within a product line. Efficient technology transfer is seen as one of the principal benefits of multinationality.

Applying the definitions to the world pharmaceutical industry Perhaps this is best illustrated by means of the examples set out in Table 3.1.

Table 3.1 The terms defined

Term	Example
Technology	Computer design of molecules likely to have a beneficial biological effect on disease indications
Technique	Highly developed Japanese expertise in methods of scanning soil samples for new biologically active organisms
Technical change	The recent developments in Japanese anti-biotics process technology represent a move to a new production function
Invention	Domagk revelation of the specific anti-microbial properties of Prontosil, the original 'magic bullet' (see Chapter 2)
Basic research	Discovery of the precise biological significance of H_2-receptors in the human alimentary canal
Applied research	The creation of Tagamet by scientists at SmithKline to effectively and safely inhibit the action of H_2-receptors
Development	The evolution of convenient and efficacious once-daily dosage forms of Tagamet
Technology transfer	The diffusion of scientific knowledge of corticosteroid synthesis, developed by co-operative investigation under the aegis of the National Research Council, into the pharmaceutical company Merck (one of the contributors to the cooperative effort). As a result of this diffusion of knowledge, Merck quickly produced commercial quantities of cortisone which provided dramatic relief to arthritic patients

Source: Author

INDUSTRY STRUCTURE AND TECHNOLOGY

There is a well established body of literature covering the link between industry structure and technology, between market structure and a firm's ability and capability to innovate. Schumpeter's[9] seminal hypothesis predicted that technological innovations are less likely to come from smaller firms than from larger firms. This is an important hypothesis for those concerned with the monopoly or anti-trust aspects of industry, as it argues that there may be a factor at work which increases social returns from innovation with increasing market concentration, due to economies of scale in production and marketing.

There have been many empirical tests of various aspects of the basic relationship, not all of which confirm the elemental Schumpeterian view. In 1964, Hamberg,[10] in a statistical analysis of 340 large US firms, found little support for the hypothesis that the intensity of R & D employment increased with firm size. In a reply, Scherer[11] (1965) criticised aspects of Hamberg's methodology; but he agreed that, in many cases, innovation may be stifled by the sheer size of a company. His analysis showed that, while R & D employment intensity increased with size up to a sales level of $500 million (1955 prices), beyond this point declining research intensity prevailed. Important exceptions to this were the chemical industry as a whole, and the giant firms in automobiles and steel.

Johannison and Lindstrom[12] studied a group of 181 Swedish industrial firms, covering twelve sectors, each firm having a minimum of 500 employees, in a two-year period 1965–66. They measured the variation of firm size (as expressed in total employment) and inventive activity (as expressed by the number of patent applications), and found little support for the hypothesis that large firms are responsible for a larger share of inventions than their market share would suggest. However, like Scherer, they found the chemical industry to be an exception.

Comanor and Scherer,[13] using 1955–60 data, found a significant positive relationship between R & D employment and patents issued to the firm, or sales of new products in the first two years for companies in the pharmaceutical industry.

Rosenberg[14] tested the Schumpeter hypothesis on a sample of 100 firms from the *Fortune 500 Directory*, using data from the period 1958–64, divided almost equally between high and low technological opportunity industries. He found a significant negative relationship between research intensity (as measured by the percentage of total employment allocated to professional R & D) and the firm's market share. This conclusion casts some doubt on the validity of the

Schumpeterian approach. Rosenberg suggests a company behavioural mechanism to explain his results. The medium-size firm which increases market share following increased R & D activity grows into a large firm. It then relaxes and wishes to preserve the *status quo* thereby inducing imitation rather than innovation.

Another test of Schumpeter's hypothesis was carried out by Shrieves,[15] who investigated the 'market power' aspect. He surveyed a sample of 411 firms, over the period 1965–70, using R & D employment as a measure of innovative effort, and sales revenues to measure size. The firms were classified into fifty-six three-digit SIC industries. He found that:

1 Concentration levels were significantly directly associated with R & D performance for 'producers of material inputs and consumer goods'.
2 Producers of non-specialised producer goods showed a positive but statistically weak relationship.
3 A marginally significant inverse relationship was found among producers of specialised durable equipment.

Shrieves concluded that the relationship between concentration and innovative activity depends upon the types of products sold and the kinds of markets served by an industry.

A study by Soete (1979)[16] showed a somewhat different conclusion. His paper reviews previous work in this field, especially the studies carried out by Hamberg, Scherer and Shrieves discussed above. He observes that there is little theoretical justification for empirical studies which cast doubt on the Schumpeter hypothesis. On the question of reliability of data, he points out that Scherer used 1955 R & D employment and 1959 patent data, while even Shrieves's much more recent analysis was based on 1965 data. He indicates that since that period there have been great advances in the range and depth of inventive activity, and great changes in the upper strata of firm size. He argues strongly that both R & D employment and patent information exaggerate the contribution small firms make to overall inventive output, and that this introduces bias against the Schumpeterian hypothesis. As an alternative measure of inventive activity, Soete used R & D expenditure data, which, he considers, are more neutral in relation to firm size. Using an analytical methodology similar to that employed by Hamberg and Scherer for a sample of 730 large US firms during 1975–76, with a much finer classification of size than was possible in earlier studies, Soete draws several interesting conclusions:

1 Innovational effort, as measured by company-financed R & D expenditure, tends to increase more than proportionately with firm size.

2 At the industry level, results were very mixed, but for the drug industry the analysis suggested diminishing returns for all firms, no matter the size; that is, large firms carry out proportionately less R & D than small firms.

3 On a global or industry level, no evidence exists in favour of the Scherer assumption that large size stifles inventive activity, that is, that inventive activity increases less than proportionately with increases in firm size.

In a recent study, Anglemar[17] analysed data drawn from the PIMS Data Base for 160 business units during 1978. All business units in the sample were in industries which had recently experienced major technological changes. This was taken as a measure of high technological opportunity. R & D intensity was measured by company-financed research expenditures calculated as a percentage of sales. On the global level, he concluded that concentration has a negligible, possibly slightly negative, overall impact on R & D investment in industries with a high level of technological opportunity. When individual industries are considered, and when R & D cost and the speed of imitation of inventions are brought into consideration, a wide spectrum of outcomes is seen. Where an industry has low cost and low uncertainty in R & D and strong protection against imitation, then even in the absence of concentration there exist sufficient incentives for innovation. In these industries, high concentration seems to reduce the motive to exploit technological innovations. Conversely, increases in concentration accompany significant increases in R & D investment in industries with no barriers to imitation and with high cost and high uncertainty of research. The high levels of concentration appear to act as an incentive to innovative activity.

Applying the link between industry structure and technology to the world pharmaceutical industry Schumpeter's hypothesis clearly has some validity for the pharmaceutical industry. The research of Hamberg, as complemented by Scherer, confirms the Schumpeterian view for the special case of the chemical industry, of which pharmaceuticals is a sub-set. Both Shrieves and Soete also lend support to this view, though Soete advances the qualification for the pharmaceutical industry that there may be a tendency towards diminishing returns. Anglemar also suggests that concentration may have a slightly negative overall impact on R & D investment.

A synthesis of these views would suggest that small firms in the pharmaceutical industry experience problems in spreading R & D activity and investment over a wide range of activities. However, beyond a certain point, a situation of increasing returns holds, which implies a minimum critical mass of R & D investment and facilities. Below this critical mass, it is difficult to achieve satisfactory returns from R & D investment and facilities. Similarly, the suggestion of diminishing returns at higher concentrations implies an upper level of R & D investment beyond which returns to R & D investment increase less than proportionately. This may be due to reasons of increasing bureaucracy and problems of management control.

The research intensity of the large ethical pharmaceutical firms is certainly one of the industry's most distinctive economic characteristics. In developed countries, all but a very small proportion of these large R & D expenditures are provided by the firms themselves, with very little contribution from government funds. The economies of scale, referred to above, which appear beyond the minimum critical mass show up principally in the utilisation of expensive items of specialised research equipment. The cost of these items can be better spread across a number of projects in the large firm. This trend has been exacerbated in recent years with the advent of information technology for analysis and control. However, it seems to be a generally accepted view within the major firms interviewed in the fieldwork stage of this book that the maximum efficient scale is around 1,000 R & D personnel in one facility. Beyond this size, problems of communication, co-ordination and control tend to become increasingly serious. Of course, many of the largest firms have overcome this difficulty by establishing more than one research facility.

TECHNOLOGY IN THE CORPORATE ENVIRONMENT

A number of economic and econometric studies have indicated the importance of the profit motive in a firm's decision to invest, and how much to invest, in research and development. Without the likelihood of an economic return, there would be little incentive for firms to engage in innovation. The degree of uncertainty associated with innovation also has to be balanced against the forecast returns. Investing in new technology is generally a risky business, but the degree of risk varies systematically with the cycle of activities involved in producing new knowledge. Uncertainty is highest at the basic research stage, and generally much lower in the development part of the cycle. The costs involved show the opposite pattern, with development being the most expensive stage of the cycle. The balancing of costs, risks and returns is a critical skill for the innovating firm. There is clearly a learning curve associated with this process, and the intuitive conclusion would be that a large firm and/or one with long experience of new knowledge production would be better placed to generate effective corporate innovation.

In a survey of the subject, Roberts[18] identified four critical areas:

1 The staffing of technical organisations must provide for the several key functions necessary to achieve successful innovation. These are: the creative scientist or engineer who is the source of innovation within the firm; the entrepreneur who pushes the technical idea towards commercialisation; the project manager who holds overall profit responsibility and who coordinates the commercialisation process; the sponsor, normally a member of senior management, who provides the necessary organisational back-up, funds, and protection from internal pressures; and the 'gate-keeper', whose specialised role is to funnel essential technical information into the organisation.

2 The organisation must be structured to enhance the flow of technical and market information into R & D. The need is to ensure a flow of appropriate technical information into and around the R & D facility, to ensure its correct use within the facility, and to ensure the movement of the results of technical programmes to other parts of the organisation.

3 The organisation's structure must also assure strong links with marketing, to ensure that innovations effectively move forward into commercial success. This can be done by the traditional method, using the marketing and sales departments as a conduit to the market place. However, increasing stress is now being put upon the 'venture management' approach for commercialisation of technological advances.

4 The company must adopt strategic planning methods that improve integration of top management's technical plans with other dimensions of overall corporate strategy. Many firms limit strategic planning to financial, production, marketing and personnel strategies, ignoring R & D as a major variable in the process. By omitting technology from the environment-scanning process there is a danger of being oblivious to opportunities of technological advance or, even worse, of being ignorant of the threats engendered by competitors' technological advances.

In a more recent study of the management of innovation in Japan, Gerstenfeld and Sumiyoshi[19] also emphasise the importance of the organisation structure, particularly at the R & D–marketing interface. In addition, they also note another five determinants of Japanese innovative success:

1 The group structure of the Japanese approach to personnel organ-isation encourages the sharing of risk, and the attitude to large rewards for success via bonus payments is much more progressive than in the US or Europe.
2 Unions are often anti-innovation, particularly in Europe. Japanese unions, which are company-based, have a much more flexible atti-tude to the introduction of new technology.
3 The Japanese decision-making and problem-solving processes are also generally based on a group structure. This high degree of participation greatly assists the introduction of innovations.
4 In Japan there is a high degree of co-operation at the industry/government/bank level. This tends to reduce the intensity of competi-tion in the domestic market, and assists the evolution of an economic environment which encourages innovation.
5 Innovation in Japan is also encouraged by the traditional culture, which stresses collectiveness, homogeneity, enthusiasm and respect for authority, and eschews individuality and inter-personal competi-tiveness.

In contrast to the strong position of Japan, Bartell[20] has recently examined Canada's poor record of industrial innovation. He argues that the lack of innovation and perceived lack of confidence in aggressively undertaking innovation are due to Canada's position as a minor partner in the North American market, and its essential conservatism regarding technological advance and its effects on the stability of society.

In a wider comparative analysis, Chakrabarti *et al.*[21] examined data on 500 technologically significant innovations introduced in the period 1953–73, which showed a marked differential in performance by various countries. The innovations were classified as 'radical', 'major technological shift', 'improvement', or unclassified. They concluded that, since international technological competitiveness is increasing, the apparently uniform position maintained by the US in number of innovations masks a relative weakening in its position. Japan's commit-ment to productivity was illustrated by its high rate of innovation for internal utilisation, about twice as much as other countries at 25 per cent of its total. It was also observed that only about a quarter of all the innovations could be described as 'radical', while about one-third involved major technical shifts. The UK showed the highest proportion of radical innovations, with Japan showing the least. France and Japan both had a significant proportion of innovations involving major technological shifts. US innovations were mostly of the improvement type. Analysis by market structure showed that concentration was significantly associated with the total number of innovations, a conclusion which is in line with the Schumpeterian view. Also, while large firms were shown to account for the majority of innovations, smaller firms were not insignificant in the innovation process. Last, the product line diversity of the innovating firms was shown to be highly significant for their innovative activity.

Finally, it should be remembered that the role of technological innovation is at least as important to the economic growth of the Third World as it is to firms in developed countries. Ferdows and Rosenbloom[22] examined prospects in the five most rapidly industrialising Asian nations (Singapore, Hong Kong, Japan, Korea, Taiwan), and laid great emphasis on the need for formal planning for the continued introduction of technological advance. Shrivastava[23] came to a similar conclusion in a wide-ranging survey of technological innovations in developing countries. He further suggested that transformative technological innovations could lead to the opening up of massive new markets in developing countries, but a precondition would be a reassessment of the corporate role in the Third World.

Applying corporate technology theory to the world pharmaceutical industry   The role of the corporate environment was stressed in the previous section in terms of the links between industry structure and technology. This role was also emphasised above, and the research results quoted are mirrored in the pharmaceutical industry, where control and communication structures are vital to success in the R & D activities within the multinational pharmaceutical firm.

Implicit in much of the research quoted above is a diminution in comparative performance by US firms in terms of returns to R & D investments. This concern is certainly expressed clearly and often within the US pharmaceutical industry. The generally declining rate of pharmaceutical innovation in recent years, noted in Chapter 1, has been accompanied by sharp increases in the cost, duration and risk of new product development. These large increases in the cost and length of pharmaceutical R & D and the accompanying decline in new product introductions have combined to decrease the rates of return on R & D investment.

Yet, in recent years, all the major US pharmaceutical firms have consistently increased annual expenditures on R & D. This apparent inconsistency may be explained by the hypothesis that firms are now undertaking fewer projects than formerly. Also, projects are selected more carefully now, with the accent being on those with relatively higher expected returns. The result is a smaller number of projects, though total R & D expenditure rises because each individual project has become much more expensive.

TECHNOLOGY AND THE MULTINATIONAL CORPORATION

Technological advance is inextricably entwined with the concept of multinational enterprise, in that the main impact of multinational corporations on host countries through international operations relates to technological advantage, and in that the ability to create and use new knowledge is one of the foremost determinants of multinationality.

Franko[24] points out that the huge technology gap in favour of US multinational corporations which existed following the Second World War (though this may be confusing cause and effect), and which contributed to the vast US lead in multinationality, has been much reduced by European and Japanese multinational corporations in recent years. The advance in the abilities of multinational corporations from these countries to innovate in product and process, with the consequent increases in productivity, has been the main engine of growth in multinationality in Europe and Japan. The overall importance of multinational corporations in technological advance can be judged from Mansefield's data, which are summarised in Table 3.2.[25]

Table 3.2 Percentage of innovations introduced in the US by firms with productive facilities outside the US

Industry	Time Interval	%
Iron and Steel	1950–58	51
Bituminous Coal Preparation	1950–58	33
Petroleum	1950–58	85
Pharmaceutical	1950–62	94
Chemicals	1960–69	100

Source: Mansefield (1974)

These figures must be interpreted cautiously, bearing in mind the preponderance of multinational corporations within these industries, the link between size and innovation, and the link between size and multinationality. However, they do indicate that multinationals were responsible for between one-third and all important innovations in these industries over the periods indicated. In addition, there is a clear connection between size and innovative performance and industry structure, as discussed in Chapter 2.

The relationship between multinational corporations and technology has been widely discussed for many years, concentrating at first on host-country imports; but more recently there has been concern expressed (particularly in the US) at the impact on the home country of its multinational corporations and their treatment of technology. Mansefield,[26] Hood and Young,[27] and Caves[28] have discussed host-country perspectives, and the following points have emerged:

1 The acquisition of innovative domestic firms by foreign multinational corporations may lead to subsequent technological advances accruing to the multinational's global operations and/or the home country, without any of the rents accruing to the domestic economy. Whether this will happen depends largely on the government's regulatory procedures and on the bargaining process preceding acquisition.

2 Concern is expressed that host-country R & D facilities may be reduced in scope or eliminated altogether following acquisition of an innovating domestic company by a multinational corporation. However, while centralisation of R & D at multinational corporation headquarters does often take place, this is not an invariable occurrence.

3 Fears are expressed that the economic dependence of the host country will be increased if the concentration of multinational corporation innovation efforts in advanced technological industries limits or removes the possibility of a degree of domestic technological independence in rapidly growing sectors of the global economy.

4 A related concern to this is that future domestic innovation is reduced because centralised multinational R & D reduces the demand for domestic scientists and engineers, and this tends to limit future national capacity in these skills. However, an opposite argument is also put: that multinational corporation subsidiary demand for scientists and engineers limits the current supply to domestic firms, and therefore curtails domestic innovation.

5 A related argument, although mainly confined to Japan, is that foreign-subsidiary R & D constitutes a 'brain drain' in respect of domestically controlled innovation, even though the host-country scientists and engineers do not move abroad.

6 A particular concern of developing countries is that multinational corporations, in line with the product life cycle theory of foreign

direct investment (see Chapter 2) transfer only outmoded or mature technology from the home base, to be replaced there by 'state of the art' and futuristic technology. While the product life cycle model has had significantly reduced explanatory power in recent times, perceptions of the applicability of the model do, nevertheless, have a life cycle of their own; this perceived problem is a source of real concern to newly industrialising countries in particular.

7 The question of protection of industrial property rights is a vexed one. Host countries are particularly sensitive about patents which are taken out then never used by multinational corporations. This is particularly true in relation to the pharmaceutical industry. As well as the obvious social losses, it is claimed that this acts as a brake on domestic technological advance.

The impact of multinational corporation technology on national scientific and technological capacities was taken up in a recent OECD report.[29] *Inter alia*, this suggested that multinational corporation investment in innovation activities generally benefited developing countries with weak economic resources and a small national infrastructure for science and technology. The usual effect of such investment will be to deepen this infrastructure over a long period. The same effect, though much magnified, was also discernible in home (developed) countries, though the precise extent was very much dependent on explicit government policies on cooperating with and supporting multinational corporation investments in technological advances. The case of multinational corporation technology investments in host developed countries occupies the intermediate position in terms of impact on the national infrastructure of science and technology. However, the point was strongly made that any such beneficial effects on national capacities and infrastructures resulting from multinational corporation technological investment were, from the multinational perspective, in the nature of spin-offs. In every case, the explicit policy of the knowledge-creating multinational corporation is to make its technology investments a closely controlled and generally closed system, and thus a major instrument of competition in world markets

Applying multinational technology theory to the world pharmaceutical industry The home and host country pressures relating to multinational R & D outlined above will clearly be important influences on the pharmaceutical industry, owing to the highly political nature of health expenditure in so many countries. These external influences will react with forces within pharmaceutical multinationals in adjusting the point of equilibrium between the desirability of concentrating R & D in the home country and the necessity of developing foreign R & D units.

The specific nature of applied research and drug development within the pharmaceutical industry, and the wide variety of support services required, are probably the most important influences in attempting to centralise R & D. No multinational begins as a multinational, and the high levels of R & D skills required are always found initially in the home country, indeed close to corporate headquarters. The management of highly complex, matrix-organised project teams is also an activity that demands close attention from top management. Applied research is highly skill-intensive, while drug development has become extremely costly. Substantial and diverse back-up services are needed, including specialised information technology facilities, animal laboratories and farms for testing new molecules and a wide range of particular skills ranging from biochemistry and biology, through toxicology and clinical research, to pilot process development and quality control.

Governments attempt to influence the centrifugal forces acting on pharmaceutical innovative capacity, employing measures which range from persuasion and cajolery, through increased patent protection, to attractive price regimes for new products. However, these are often more than offset by regulation of other parts of the activity of the pharmaceutical multinationals, including price controls on existing products, encouraging competition from generic products, and increasing the stringency of drug safety regulations. The problem for the potential host nation is always to maximise the net benefit to the community. On the one hand, it sees improved employment and access to high-tech skills and knowledge as attractive and positive aspects. The down-side risk encompasses dilution of control over local innovative capacity and harm to indigenous companies.

TECHNOLOGY TRANSFER

Of all the resource transfer effects of multinational corporations, transfer of technology is certainly the most important. Diffusion of technology, more than any other factor of production, will act as a prime stimulus to economic growth. As such, considerations of technology transfer will therefore extend well beyond the area of international business, as there will clearly be important political and social factors to be considered. However, the effort is made here to keep the focus on the commercial and economic factors as much as possible; home and host government constraints and incentives are, nevertheless, important determinants of technology transfer, and cannot be avoided in the treatment below.

Technology transfer can serve many purposes, among them the strengthening of local capabilities, closing of the technological gap between nations, providing information and training, advancing local production systems, improving competitive position in global or regional markets, serving as a vehicle to integrate knowledge, and improving the long-run quality of life. Transfers may be either horizontal or vertical, or some combination of the two. Horizontal transfer is the movement of established knowledge or techniques from one operating environment to another, a method in which multinational corporations excel. Vertical transfer is a movement of new knowledge from basic research through development to production and market development. During the transfer process, necessary alterations or modifications call for linkages between the two types as a precondition of successful implementation.

Transfers may take place within or between disciplines, organisations, industries, and governments. Communication problems arise when transfers take placing involving several different levels of diffusion. However, as Contractor and Sagafi-Nejad[30] indicate, technology transfer is not generally a once-only or short-lived act, except in turnkey contracts. It is more often a continuing relationship between two enterprises over an extended period of time.

Technology can be distinguished in four dichotomous classes: hard and soft: proprietary and non-proprietary; front-end and obsolete; bundled and unbundled. Thus, depending on the type of technology being transferred, different emphases will include product, facilities design, personnel training, engineering for quality control, technical support to local suppliers, and so on. Consequently, there are a number of methods of technology transfer, ranging from arm's-length deals to equity affiliation, among which the more important are:

1 *Soft, non-proprietary, front-end, unbundled*

   (a) The free flow of non-proprietary information via books, specialised newsletters, technical and professional journals, and trade magazines.
   (b) Personnel interactions are a potent means of technology transfer whether this be by internal or external training, internal or external seminars, geographical transfer of personnel, inter-firm movement of skilled staff, or employment of foreign technicians or employment of nationals by foreign firms.
   (c) Consultancy services are a widely used method, but one which is

as yet poorly understood. This is a very effective intra-firm method, but it is also widely used by non-profit international organisations as a conduit of technology to developing countries.

2 *Soft, proprietary, front-end, unbundled*

(a) In some cases, international cooperative arrangements can also facilitate technology transfer. This includes: the licensing of patents, trademarks, copyrights, trade names and know-how; franchising of operations and services. Co-production and technical consortia could be considered as special cases of this classification.

(b) Industrial espionage certainly exists as a method, but it is not possible even to estimate the incidence of effectiveness as the whole process is, necessarily, shrouded in mystery. However, the active measures taken by many governments and multinational corporations to minimise technology leakage through this channel may be an indirect measure of its effectiveness as a conduit.

(c) R & D facilities are a prime factor in technology transfer, whether the mechanism is through location in foreign countries; through joint R & D projects with other firms, governments or institutions; through the contracting out of R & D work; or through the subdivision of research and development facilities within the firm. This mechanism is of such vital importance that it is dealt with in much greater detail in the following section.

3 *Soft, non-proprietary, obsolete, bundled*

(a) Contracts and agreements, such as management contracts for equipment maintenance and service facilities, often serve as a vehicle for technology transfer.

(b) Educational institutes are wholly involved in the transfer of information; though not formally recognised as a channel of technology transfer, they are an obvious and effective means, whether it is done formally and explicitly, or by casual diffusion.

4 *Hard, proprietary, front-end, bundled*

(a) Foreign direct investment; establishing a wholly owned subsidiary or joint venture overseas is sometimes done with the subsidiary reason of encouraging technology transfer, in either or both directions. As has already been indicated, the multinational corporation is uniquely suited to the task of technology transfer by nature of the size and scope of its operations, and the geographical dispersal of its activities.

(b) Turnkey projects, where, for an inclusive price, a bundled package is provided which includes all the necessary elements for building, commissioning, and running a plant.

(c) Trade in goods and services, including equipment sales, provision of materials, tools and end products, is possibly the longest established method of technology transfer.

As noted above, all these alternatives may be fitted into the arm's-length equity-affiliation continuum (see Figure 3.1). According to Baranson,[31] the precise choice of locus on this continuum depends upon four sets of interrelated factors:

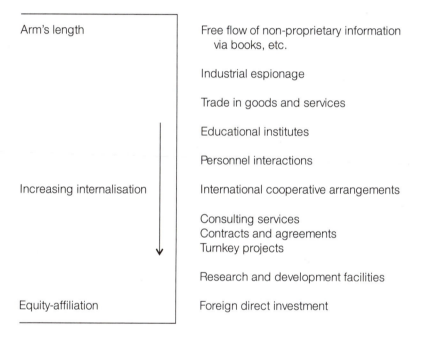

Arm's length	Free flow of non-proprietary information via books, etc.
	Industrial espionage
	Trade in goods and services
	Educational institutes
	Personnel interactions
Increasing internalisation	International cooperative arrangements
	Consulting services
	Contracts and agreements
	Turnkey projects
	Research and development facilities
Equity-affiliation	Foreign direct investment

Figure 3.1 The continuum of technology transfer methods *Source*: Author

1 The nature of the transferred technology, including aspects such as the relative sophistication of production techniques and characteristics of product design. With new or sophisticated technologies, where the R & D investment is large and where companies hold a technological lead, licensing is fairly unlikely. Even so, if the product cycle is short, firms may be willing to license in residual markets which they are unable to exploit through direct investment.

2 Donor firm characteristics, including transfer capability, financial

position and corporate philosophy. Of particular importance is the firm's view of technology in the context of its marketing/manufacturing package, and the desire for control.

3 Recipient firm characteristics such as absorptive capability (referring to licensed technology) and its potential competitiveness. Baranson argues that licensing arrangements may be preferred with developed-country partners because of ease of transfer and possibilities of cross-licensing.

4 Transfer environments in donor and recipient countries, including legal restraints such as exchange controls, insistence on national ownership and staffing, and so on.

In most cases, the direct price paid for transferred technology will be reflected in the licence fees and/or royalties paid by foreign firms (subsidiaries or associates) to multinational corporations.

Finally, a paper by Jeannet and Liander[32] throws some light on technology transfer patterns within multinational corporations. Data for a sample of 40 New England-based multinational corporations was analysed over maturity of multinational involvement and international dispersal of activity. The results of the analysis were not wholly in line with the generally accepted view of multinational corporation technology transfer; this was put down to the differential analysis by maturity of multinationality, rather than to treating all multinational corporations as a homogeneous group. They found that emerging and growing multinational corporations are heavy net technology exporters. Eventually, the level of technology exports stabilises. Within this overall stable level, the proportion of engineering transfers decreases, with a concomitant increase in the proportion of development transfers. Perhaps the most important conclusion flowing from this research was that mature multinational corporations will turn heavily to foreign subsidiaries as sources of new technologies, and thus they change from net exporters of technology to a pattern of balance over time. This is interpreted as indicating that, over time, the US operation will no longer be the leader in all aspects of a multinational corporation's business. However, the writers warn that the conclusions must be treated circumspectly, as the sample was small and possibly not representative.

Applying technology transfer theory to the world pharmaceutical industry   The importance of technology transfer within multinational corporations, outlined above, and the subsequent diffusion of technology within host nations is a particularly strong determinant of attitudes to pharmaceutical technology. Also, Jeannet and Liander's suggestion that mature multinationals will come increasingly to view a foreign affiliate as a source of new technology is particularly apposite in this industry, and yields yet another dimension to the range of centrifugal effects operating on pharmaceutical R & D.

At the macro level, the importance of technology transfer within the drug multinationals is clearly evidenced by the extremely close links between industry members and university researchers in many developed countries. Relations between universities and industry tend to be very close in all countries, and eminent academic scientists are retained as advisers and consultants to pharmaceutical research departments; foreign subsidiaries are particularly active in this field. The net result of this close contact is a flow of technology into the drug multinationals; where a foreign affiliate is concerned, this national technology can be very easily and efficiently transferred to the home country for the benefit of the corporate parent. Once this international transfer is made, of course, similar academic contacts promote the leakage of the transferred technology into the domestic economy.

At the micro level, a large number of pharmaceutical foreign R & D subsidiaries were originally set up to transfer technology overseas, usually process and dosage form technology. Equally, it is clear that, in many cases, the flow of technology has – at least partially – reversed. For example:

1 Upjohn buys all foreign research from its overseas subsidiaries, allowing foreign laboratories to make a profit on research, so that ownership of the proprietary knowledge is clearly in the US.
2 Warner Lambert has set up a research laboratory at Cambridge, England, in association with the university there; again, promising leads on new molecules are funnelled back to the US for further development and global exploitation.
3 Merck's decision in 1984 to establish a major new neuroscience unit at Cambridge, England, to carry out primary research into Alzheimer's disease was guided by the local availability of a foremost scientist in the CNS (central nervous system) field, by the close proximity to the university, and by the easy availability of CNS professionals in the UK. The output from the unit is transferred back to Rahway, New Jersey, for commercial development. Cambridge is Merck's only site for CNS research, a field where it sees major opportunities in the next twenty years.

RESEARCH AND DEVELOPMENT

As defined in the first section of this chapter, R & D represents the set of processes which firms use to discover and transform new knowledge into marketable products and services. As firms and governments have come to realise that technological advance is among the most important determinants of economic growth, so the pressure has grown for increasing investment in R & D. Gold[33] suggests that the benefits of these investments are:

1 Realising competitive advantages through new and often better products and processes.
2 Obtaining know-how and knowledge which can subsequently be sold.
3 Maintaining competitive position.
4 Portraying images of innovative and progressive management.
5 Minimising the disadvantages of input factors.

For these investments in technological innovation to continue at a high rate – and increase – both the current and the expected rate of return must be attractive. Mansefield *et al.*[34] carried out a rigorous analysis of the returns from seventeen industrial innovations introduced by US firms, spread over a variety of industries. Most were average or routine innovations, not major breakthroughs. Benefits flowing from these innovations were strictly classified to allow calculation of social and private rates of return. The private rate of return is, of course, the normally calculated rate of profit as return on invested capital, which is appropriated by the firm and its shareholders. The social rate of return is a wider concept; it encompasses the investment made by society in the shape of opportunity cost, environmental cost, etc.; it also includes net social benefits like better services and infrastructure, and improved quality of life.

Four main conclusions were presented. First, social rates of return on the seventeen innovations were high, the median being 56 per cent. Second, the private rates of return were much lower, the pre-tax median being 25 per cent; however, the risk factor here was large, with six of the innovations having a private rate of return of less than 10 per cent, and five showing more than 40 per cent. Third, in about a third of the cases the private rate of return was so low that, with hindsight, the respective firms would not have made the investment; however, in each case, the social rate of return was so high that the technological investment was very valuable from society's point of view. Fourth, detailed examination of the seventeen innovations suggested that competition plays a key role in preventing the innovator from monopolising the social returns as well as the private returns in cases where competitors were able, legally, to copy the innovation. These results must be viewed with some caution owing to the small size of the sample, but they suggest that social returns from technological investment are high, and (tentatively) that government incentives to encourage private R & D spending have at least some empirical basis.

While Yaprak[35] has indicated that a degree of convergence may now be occurring in global R & D flows among Western European countries, the US and Japan, the historical situation has been a massive preponderance of US R & D expenditure at home, US technology exports in general, and foreign R & D expenditure by US multinational corporation subsidiaries. However, there is now an acute perception that the large technological gap opened up by the US during the period following the Second World War up to the mid-1960s is being whittled away (Nason[36] gives a good summary), mainly owing to conservative business investment practices and excessive government regulation. Mansefield *et al*,[37] throw interesting light on these concerns in a study of thirty US multinational corporations. There firms were asked two questions concerning foreign subsidiary technology:

1 How would your R & D expenditure change (in 1974) if you could not utilise any new technology abroad in foreign subsidiaries?
2 How would your R & D expenditure change if you could not utilise any new technology abroad in foreign subsidiaries, or by licensing the technology abroad, or by exporting new products or processes based on the technology, or by any other means?

While caution must be exercised regarding the answers to hypothetical questions, the responses indicate that R & D expenditure would fall by between 12 per cent and 15 per cent under the first set of circumstances, and by between 16 per cent and 26 per cent under the second. Of course, there was no suggestion in this paper that the US government had ever seriously considered so severe a limitation on the transfer of technology. Indeed, the incoming Reagan administration of 1981 almost immediately announced a major shift in the government's role in US R & D. First, the funding of research was to be increased, particularly in physical sciences, engineering and life sciences; in contrast, funding of development was to be cut back, except for products primarily for government use. Second, the effort to restore the R & D budget of the Defense Department – commenced under the Carter administration – was to be continued. Third, the government would help to stimulate private-sector funding of commercial R & D through such indirect means as tax incentives, regulatory changes, and reform of patent and anti-trust laws, in order to expedite the commercial exploitation of technology. Though this was no more than a statement of intent, at least it accepted the need for action in view of the growing emphasis on technological innovation in Western Europe and Japan.

Yaprak[38] has described the Japanese system as having one of the most organised R & D policies of any industrialised country. The Ministry of International Trade and Investment is responsible for coordinating R & D policy. R & D expenditure is tax-exempt, as is income from technology exports. Joint R & D projects are encouraged among companies in the same industry, and low-interest loans are available to companies for investment in innovation. Most of Japan's R & D is development work carried out on the large imports of foreign technology.

In Western Europe, there is a tendency in small countries to consolidate responsibility for state aid to industrial R & D within a single agency. In Sweden and Belgium, for example, the central agency's responsibility is to disburse funds to other research bodies, while in the Netherlands and Norway the central agency operates its own research establishments. In the larger European countries the approach is more varied. In Germany there are over sixty research associations, each financed partly by member firms, partly by government grants, and partly by contract research income. In France, the central government agency operates various research establishments, and in addition there are about forty research associations serving particular trades and industries. These associations receive some income from contracted research, but are mainly funded by the government.

The UK system is even more complicated. Research aid to industry comes mainly from the Department of Trade and Industry, with a much smaller proportion arising from the Department of the Environment. There are forty three research associations belonging to the various industries, which are jointly funded by industry and government in the ratio 2:1. These associations are non-profit-making bodies and they run their own research establishments. Contract and sponsored work for member firms or groups of members is becoming an increasingly important aspect of their work.

As a special case the evolution of R & D in biotechnology is of interest; it is a very new, high-technology industry and its development – mainly confined to R & D so far – has tended to be global in nature. It has, therefore, avoided some of the problems associated with the various national approaches to technology advance noted above, though it may also have suffered somewhat from a degree of rigid organisation and formalisation. The products of gene splicing have been developed largely by new, research-based organisations – sometimes with the assistance of development seed money from existing high-technology companies in associated fields. Industry sales have been mainly in products for the pharmaceutical, specialist chemical, and agricultural markets. Licensing and joint ventures have rapidly become common-place, e.g. Genentech licensed its human insulin to Eli Lilly & Co., and set up a joint venture with Baxter Travenol Laboratories to develop diagnostic tests.[39]

From the beginning, this technology has been dominated by the US, but that position is now seen to be under serious threat. Japan has made vast strides recently, and it has been suggested that Japanese basic research in this area may be on a par with that of the US by 1995. European effort in this field has also been very large, with particular success in agricultural products. The US government has aided the private sector by the usual mix of low capital gains tax rates, R & D tax credits, etc. The Japanese and European governments, unlike their approaches to R & D in general, have provided the private sector with direct public financing. Additionally, the generally recognised Japanese skill in converting basic research into marketable products is held to be a factor which will become critically important as this new industry develops.

Applying R & D theory to the world pharmaceutical industry   The important part that governments play in the general stimulation and encouragement of national R & D capacities can be seen in some form in pharmaceuticals. While government-financed R & D is a rarity in this industry, nevertheless governments can have a part to play by creating (or failing to create) a national climate sympathetic to the risks and investments involved in innovation, and appreciative of the need for commercial returns for successful innovation.

The role of governments in encouraging R & D in the pharmaceutical industry is perhaps most clearly seen in three areas. First, strong product patent protection, as is offered by the governments of most major drug-consuming countries, is a prime means of supporting the innovative efforts of drug firms. Second is recognition by governments of the key role played by brand names and sales promotion in appropriating the returns to pharmaceutical innovation. Third, controls on prescribing and pricing must be implemented in such a way as to provide the necessary protection to society, but they must also be framed to minimise the disincentives for innovating drug firms.

Some examples confirm that these points of government attitude are often crucially important to foreign R & D location decisions in the pharmaceutical industry:

1 In 1985, Warner Lambert had made a decision to locate an R & D facility in Canada, taking advantage of various government financial incentives. However, because of corporate management's perception of changes in the attitude of the Canadian government towards the industry, the development was cancelled at a very late stage and relocated in Michigan, US.
2 Sterling originally (1981) sited a major new R & D facility at Alnwick, England, because of the very attractive tax credits which were available at that time. Legislation has since removed these valuable cash flows and Sterling is now considering a move out of the UK, or at the very least a considerable trimming back of future development.
3 The establishment of a limited list of drugs available for prescription in the UK in 1985 led A.H. Robins to freeze a planned R & D facility at an advanced stage; the firm's experience with the limited list also led directly to divestment of the firm's UK manufacturing facility to Glaxo.

SUMMARY

This chapter has reviewed the relationship between technology and the corporate development of multinational corporations, specifically within the pharmaceutical industry. Several significant conclusions were arrived at. First, recent research seems to confirm that the Schumpeterian hypothesis holds good for innovation within this industry, but that limiting cases may have significance for the maximum efficient scale of a research facility. Second, the role of control and communication structures was emphasised, together with related evidence concerning diminishing returns on R & D investment which may affect the pharmaceutical industry, though there may be a cyclical effect at work here. Third, the centrifugal and centripetal forces acting on the internationalisation of a drug firm's R & D capacity are never wholly in balance, with potential host governments using policy and other measures to tilt the balance towards decentralisation. Fourth, the importance of technology transfer within the drug multinational, and particularly the possibility of accessing host country technologies and skills, is a further significant centrifugal force acting on the international R & D location decision.

4 The single European market and the pharmaceutical industry

THE 1985 WHITE PAPER

The White Paper[1] entitled *Completing the Internal Market* which was published by the European Community (EC) in 1985 had as its objective the establishment of a single integrated European market consisting of the 12 member states. However, it was not a radical idea, as the original Treaty of Rome had envisaged such a development from the outset. Articles 30–5 and 100 of the Treaty were intended to be the legal basis for establishing this integrated market in which goods, persons, services and capital would be free to move to areas of greatest economic advantage, and where all barriers to the creation and maintenance of such a market would be removed.

Initially the EC saw tariff barriers as the principal obstacle to the creation of the single European market, and aimed at establishing a customs union over the period 1957–70. However, the momentum slowed down owing to economic recession in the 1970s, and had come to a complete standstill by 1978/79. The commitment to achieving the objectives of the Treaty of Rome was restated by heads of state at the European Council meeting in Copenhagen in 1982. This culminated in the 1985 White Paper, which had three overall targets:

1 The welding together of the individual markets of the member states into one single market of 320 million people.
2 Ensuring that this single market was also an expanding market.
3 Ensuring that the market was flexible, so that human, physical and financial resources could move freely into the areas of greatest economic advantage.

The White Paper also identified four types of barriers which needed to be removed in order to create the single market:

1 Differences in technical regulations between countries which impose extra costs on intra-EC trade;
2 Delays at frontiers for customs purposes, and related administrative burdens for companies and public administrations, which impose further costs on trade;
3 Restrictions on competition for public purchases through excluding bids from other Community suppliers, which often result in excessive costs of purchase;
4 Restrictions on freedom to engage in certain service transactions, or to become established in certain service activities in other Community countries.

To this end, the White Paper contained proposals for 300 directives which, if implemented, would allow any product lawfully manufactured and marketed within one member state to be freely sold throughout the single market. This would establish a more competitive environment, resulting in:

1 A significant reduction in costs due to a better exploitation of several economies of scale associated with the size of production units and enterprises.
2 Improved efficiency in firms, rationalisation of industrial structures, and setting prices closer to the costs of production.
3 Flows of innovations, new processes and new products stimulated by the dynamics of the single European market.

BARRIERS TO A SINGLE EUROPEAN MARKET FOR PHARMACEUTICALS

Each of the twelve member states within the EC has its own regulatory body for the pharmaceutical industry, and prices are set at a national level. Thus, there is no single market for this industry. The general function of each national regulatory authority is to determine the risk/benefit ratio for every medicinal product and to grant marketing authorisation if the ratio is favourable. Up to 1988, some twenty directives concerned with ethical pharmaceuticals had been issued by the Commission, aimed at harmonising the data requirements for a product licence application and the manner in which such data are interpreted. Despite this, considerable differences still exist in the manner in which these regulatory bodies interpret their statutory obligations.

According to both the pharmaceutical industry[2] and the Commission[3] the major barriers to the creation of a single European market in pharmaceuticals are:

1 Technical barriers.
2 Pricing/reimbursement.
3 Patent protection.

With regard to technical barriers, serious problems exist at the certification and registration stages which often result in costly time delays. This is because a drug which is to be admitted to a particular national market must be first approved by the national registration authority. In spite of the harmonisation of approval criteria laid down in Community legislation, national authorities still impose specific requirements. Adjusting to country-specific certification procedures causes extra administrative costs and time delays that can go on up to three years, shortening the effective life of patents. Problems still persist even when marketing authorisation is obtained in that each of the national governments has its own formula for determining both the price at which the medicinal product may be sold and for admittance to a reimbursement scheme. This has resulted in considerable variation in prices for pharmaceutical products between the various national markets within the EC.

The industry takes the view that a prerequisite for the establishment of a single pharmaceutical market is a single marketing authorisation which is valid throughout the Community. This means that a pharmaceutical product might be sourced from anywhere within the EC and sold anywhere else within the single European market, regardless of national pricing and reimbursement policies, or the national patent position of that product. Thus the economic parameters and the intellectual property rights relating to a drug cannot be divided from the regulation of medicines. These two issues are interdependent and the future viability of the research-based European pharmaceutical industry may be irreparably damaged unless they are addressed in parallel. This, in turn, would impair the industry's capacity to produce essential new products and to compete internationally. Thus, the industry sees three important issues which need to be tackled:

1 Medicines regulation and the marketing approval machinery.
2 Patent period erosion and the need for patent period extension.
3 Freedom for the manufacturer to determine a common price for new and innovative products to avoid the distortion of trade within the EC caused by the various and incompatible pricing and reimbursement schemes.

There appears to be some sympathy within the Commission for this stance, as one of the objectives of the White Paper is to ensure that the single market should be an expanding market. In addition, the initial directive concerning pharmaceuticals (65/65/EEC), which forms the basis for all subsequent drug-related directives, specifically states that measures taken to regulate the pharmaceutical industry should not be the cause of undue hindrance.

THE DIRECTIVES

The White Paper contained thirteen proposals for directives relevant to ethical pharmaceuticals. These directives have been concerned with reducing the level of disparity in the assessment of product licence applications, the inclusion of previously excluded products, and issues relating to pricing, reimbursement, and the patent protection period. They are, as noted earlier, mainly extensions of previous directives concerned with ethical pharmaceuticals.

These directives and guidelines cover all areas of the pharmaceutical industry, from production, quality control, drug evaluation procedures and requirements, certification requirements and procedures, pricing, reimbursement, patent period, packaging, sales and distribution outlets, to post-marketing surveillance requirements and procedures. Thus, the pharmaceutical industry is probably subject to a greater level of regulation and control than any other industrial sector. The consequence of all of this previous activity has been the development of five basic directives[4] which have five important consequences for the free movement of drugs within the EC:

1 The sole criteria which may be taken into consideration by the member states during an examination of an application for authorisation are the quality, safety and efficacy of the product concerned. These criteria have been progressively harmonised, as have certain aspects of the procedures for granting marketing authorisation (time limits, giving of reasons, publication of decisions, etc.) and for granting manufacturing authorisation (quality control, inspections, etc.).
2 Analytical pharmaco-toxicological tests and clinical trials which have been conducted in accordance with EC rules no longer need to be repeated within the Community.
3 The batch control reports of the manufacturer are accepted by the other member states without repetition of the individual control tests.
4 The general requirements regarding labelling and packaging inserts have been harmonised.
5 A common list of colouring matters approved for use throughout the EC has been adopted.

Directives have recently been issued which extend these requirements to generic medicinal products, immunological medicinal products, and products derived from human blood or plasma and radio-pharmaceuticals.

The EC's evolving regulatory system

The initial directive (65/65/EEC), issued after the Thalidomide tragedy, established the basic requirements and stipulated that each member state must have its own regulatory body. In accordance with the current provisions of the Community legislation, the member states are still responsible for deciding whether or not to grant authorisation to market individual medicinal products within their own territories.

Despite considerable harmonisation in the 1970s, there were still differences in the decisions being reached by member states in respect of individual pharmaceutical products. There was a view that a single European regulatory body was a necessary prerequisite of a single pharmaceuticals market. This body, like the US Food and Drug Administration (FDA), would be able to issue a pan-European marketing approval. However, some elements of the industry[5] did not favour this idea because:

1 The FDA precedent did not suggest increased efficiency in dealing with marketing authorisation in a timely manner.
2 A pan-European regulatory body would, in all probability, contain a combination of the most severe requirements of each member state.

In addition, the small-scale experiment in setting up such a body (the Benelux experiment, 1973–83), failed, for several reasons, including sovereignty issues, insufficient funding, and excessive workloads leading to delays.

Mutual recognition was the pharmaceutical industry's preferred solution. In 1975, Directive 75/319/EEC established a framework through which the process of mutual recognition might work. This directive set up the first pan-European framework for approvals; it was the first successful trial of mutual recognition, and resulted in the establishment of the Committee on Proprietary Medicinal Products (CPMP) in 1977. This allowed a firm to request a marketing authorisation in five or more member states after having first obtained one authorisation within the Community. According to this procedure, the member states which receive an application are obliged to take the original authorisation into due consideration, and should normally grant a marketing authorisation – valid within their territories – within

120 days of receipt of the application. The CPMP was set up to act as a central facilitator for the individual authorities discussing such a submission.

This procedure came to be regarded unfavourably by the pharmaceutical industry, as all that was achieved was an extra delay occasioned by having to wait until the first approval was given prior to submitting applications to individual authorities.[6] As a result, the multi-state procedure was not widely used, as it was felt that the incremental cost of submitting applications to several national authorities was less than that caused by the delay in gaining market approval. In 1985, the cost of this delay was estimated to be between 370 million ECU and 650 million ECU, or 1.1 per cent – 1.9 per cent of total costs. The actual cost to individual drug firms would be greater or less depending on the nature of the chemical entity for which approval was being sought.

The Pharmaceutical Committee was established under Directive 75/320/EEC at the same time as the CPMP. Its function was to examine problems arising as a result of the approximation and harmonisation of laws relating to proprietary medicinal products in the EC. The committee was to advise the Commission on general policy matters relating to pharmaceutical products and on problems which individual member states might have in implementing directives concerned with pharmaceutical products.

Recognising the problems with mutual recognition, the Commission amended the original multi-state procedure with Directive 83/570/EEC, which became operational in 1985. In addition to reducing from five to two the number of member states to which a dossier must be submitted, the applying company could now communicate direct with national authorities after obtaining initial approval. Previously, all communication had been channelled through the CPMP. There is provision for individual national authorities to refuse a market authorisation. However, when this happens the member state concerned must lodge its reasoned objections to granting an authorisation with the CPMP within 120 days of receipt of application. When objections are received, the CPMP is required to give an opinion on whether the product satisfies the criteria for authorisation set out in the EC directives. This opinion is communicated to the member states, who are required to reach a definitive decision within a further thirty days. However, CPMP opinion is not binding. The company concerned can also appeal direct to the CPMP and present relevant information.

This procedure is more popular than the old multi-state procedure and has been used more frequently. However, it seems that many pharmaceutical firms still prefer the traditional approach to the individual national authorities and are only using the multi-state procedure because of the huge backlog of approval applications being considered by the various national authorities. A major problem with any kind of centralised procedure for registration, such as the multi-state procedure, is that price fixing is still done at national level.

In 1988, the Commission reviewed the functioning of the multi-state procedure and stated:[7]

> It is unfortunate that, to date, every dossier has systematically been the subject of reasoned objections, in spite of the obligation on member states to take due consideration of the initial authorisation. The political willingness declared by certain member states to adopt the principle of mutual recognition, has not yet translated itself into actual administrative practice. If the multi-state procedure is to serve as a testing ground leading to a system of mutual recognition of authorisations, the experience so far is not convincing.

This is a reflection of the fact that any attempt at harmonisation is itself dependent on the way in which individual member states interpret Community legislation and the zeal and enthusiasm with which they reinforce its requirements.

Directive 87/22/EEC was passed in recognition of the problems caused by the level of disparity in the manner within which the pharmaceutical directives are implemented by the various national regulatory authorities. This disparity is recognised to be damaging to the highly innovative drug firms, particularly those in the high-technology areas and in biotechnology. This directive recognised that all the individual national bodies do not possess the required competence in each field, and provides a mechanism whereby the national bodies work in concert when considering an application for authorisation. In the case of products derived from biotechnological processes (recombinant DNA, hybridoma/monoclonal antibodies and cell culture), the competent authorities are obliged to consult with each other, and the CPMP, systematically before deciding to authorise, refuse or withdraw a product from the market. In the case of other categories of high-technology drugs, the consultation procedure takes place at the request of the firm concerned. At the end of the procedure, which must not exceed the time allowed for the examination of applications submitted under national procedures, the CPMP issues an opinion on whether the product satisfies the criteria laid down in the Community directives. This opinion is communicated to the member states, which are required to reach a definitive decision within a further thirty days. It is, as yet, too early to evaluate the degree of success which has been achieved with this directive, but early indications suggest[8] that the pooling of resources and knowledge is having a positive effect.

Following Directive 83/570/EEC, a working party of the CPMP was set up by the Commission to examine the possibility of preparing a standard format, acceptable to all member states, for the presentation of applications, together with a simplification of administrative and linguistic requirements. This has resulted in the *Guide to Applicants*, published in 1986. Since the adoption of Directive 87/22/EEC, this guide has been updated and details the requirements and procedures for obtaining a produce licence.

The Community registration system in the future

Both the Commission and the drug industry have been involved in on-going critical evaluation of the range of directives associated with pharmaceuticals. Such evaluation has helped to determine the appropriate nature of the registration system which will fulfil the basic requirement of ensuring that drugs meet the strict standards of control necessary to ensure safety, quality and efficacy. The system must also meet the need for an efficient means of granting new marketing authorisations.[9] The results of this evaluation suggest that a centralised approach, such as that offered for high-tech products (Directive 87/22/ EEC) should be available for all major new pharmaceutical products. A decentralised procedure, such as that available through the individual national regulatory bodies, should be available for products whose risk/ benefit ratio is already well understood and established. Such products would include over-the-counter medicines, or different formulations of products whose active ingredient has already been authorised. Where appropriate, it should be possible for major existing products to be the subject of an application to the central body should the licence holder wish to seek a single European licence. In the future, it is likely that the central body's opinions will be legally binding on the individual national regulatory bodies.

There is some strong feeling in the industry that the CPMP, as at present constituted, is inappropriate as the basis of such a central body. The composition of the CPMP is the root of the problem; it is not made up of superior independent scientists (as is the UK's Committee on the Safety of Medicines) but usually of nationally appointed civil servants who may be as influenced by their governments as by science. Indeed, the directive which set up the CPMP specifically states that committee members shall not be experts in the areas to be discussed. The feeling in the industry is that replacement of the CPMP by a truly independent committee of European experts would be not only fairer and more objective, but also in the long term interests of achieving good European standards. Such a body should also have a permanent secretariat and appropriate advisory committee structures to ensure that it could deal with the applications put to it quickly and efficiently, and provide the appropriate level of contact with companies and expertise in dealing with applications.[10]

Pharmacovigilance

Article 11 of Directive 75/319/EEC, which set up the CPMP, stipulated that the member states of the EC are obliged to report to the committee all appropriate information to ensure the quality, safety and efficacy of drugs. They must immediately notify the CPMP of any refusal or withdrawal of authorisation, and of any prohibition on the supply of drugs. For this purpose, the CPMP has established a procedure whereby information concerning the risks resulting from the use of pharmaceuticals, including the monitoring of adverse reactions, is exchanged. On the basis of this information, individual regulatory bodies can decide upon the appropriate action to take in their own territories prior to a final decision by the CPMP. The committee meets regularly to review such information and encourages the manufacturer to submit comments. In addition, the CPMP attempts to function as an interface between the European Parliament and the general public.

Guidelines

Since it was set up in 1977, the CPMP has attached a high priority to the preparation of guidelines on the quality, safety and efficacy of medicinal products. These guidelines serve a double objective. First, they are intended to provide a basis for practical harmonisation of the manner in which member states interpret and apply the detailed requirements for the demonstration of quality, safety and efficacy contained in the Community's directives. Second, they are intended to facilitate the preparation of applications for marketing authorisation which will be recognised as valid by all twelve member states.

In July 1987 the Council delegated to the CPMP the power to amend the annexe to Directive 75/318/EEC which contains the legal requirements for the conduct of the analytical and pharmaco-toxicological tests and clinical trials. Prior to this, any amendments to the above required the preparation of a directive, which is both time-consuming and incompatible with the need to ensure that the guidelines reflect the state of the art and are made available as soon as they are approved by the CPMP.[11]

Controls on the manufacture of pharmaceuticals

Directive 75/319/EEC established the principle that the manufacturers of drugs must be authorised, that they must be subject to inspection, and that manufacture must take place under the supervision of a qualified person who certifies that each batch conforms with its specifications. Batches certified in this way are exempt from further re-control within the Community. This directive also establishes that a single verification in an importing country of conformity with specifications, and the requirements laid down in the directives, for finished pharmaceutical products originating outwith the Community is sufficient for access to the Community market.

In 1988 a common position was adopted by the Council in favour of a Commission proposal (COM (87) 697) that the safeguards on the control of manufacturing operations should be reinforced through the introduction of a detailed Community code of good manufacturing practice. This is to be achieved by the CPMP working in close cooperation with the member states by a so-called 'Regulatory Committee' procedure.

Good laboratory practice

In addition to licensing manufacturers to produce drugs, there are also directives (86/609/EEC, 87/18/EEC, 88/320/EEC) which license investigators to study the effects of drugs in the laboratory, as required to comply with the directives concerned with gaining market approval. These specify the standard procedures which must be followed in performing and recording the results of experiments in which drugs are evaluated. They also provide details of the minimum requirements for the housing in which laboratory animals may be held and used. Furthermore, they also indicate a mechanism for inspection procedures through which it can be ascertained that the above directives are being complied with.

Technical standards and the European pharmacopoeia

Directives 83/189/EEC and 88/182/EEC were designed to harmonise the technical standards with which medicinal products must comply prior to gaining market approval. Furthermore, these directives require member states to notify the Commission, in advance, prior to the adoption of any new technical regulations or standards, explaining the reasons for such measures. This is to prevent the creation of new obstacles to trade. If appropriate, the Commission may propose that a harmonised solution to the problem be adopted for the whole Community.

Pharmacopoeias contain a detailed specification of the quality requirements for medicinal products and preparations. In 1964 the Council of Europe signed a convention to elaborate a European pharmacopoeia. Standardisation of the quality specifications has been a long-term objective of both the Community and the pharmacopoeia, and the binding effect of the European pharmacopoeia has been reinforced by Community directives. Only in the absence of a European pharmacopoeia monograph does the monograph of the national pharmacopoeia of the country of manufacture apply as the technical standard. All member states of the EC are parties to the convention and the Community has been negotiating with the Council of Europe in order to become a contracting party to the Convention on the European Pharmacopoeia.

Provision of information about medicinal products

Directives 65/65/EEC, 75/319/EEC and 83/570/EEC contain the basic requirements for labels and package inserts and summaries of product information. The Council has recently agreed on a proposal which would harmonise the information requirements and result in the provision of 'similar and better' information for both patients and doctors. These provisions apply to both prescription and over-the-counter medicines.

These directives also require that an insert should be included in the packaging of all medicinal products, unless all the relevant information can be provided on the labelling of the container.

Patent protection

The Commission has already recognised the deficiencies which exist in the protection of the intellectual property of pharmaceutical firms. They have introduced a limited form of protection with Directive 87/21/EEC for those products which follow the high-tech registration procedure. This applies particularly to medicinal products derived from biotechnology. The directive gave a ten-year protection to the information supplied by the innovatory firm in support of its application for approval of a new medicinal product regardless of the patent position of that product. This means that a second applicant cannot, without permission, refer to the information contained within the dossier of the initial applicant. This protection is limited, for, should the second applicant submit a complete dossier (with supporting data generated by themselves or from publicly published sources), they can proceed with their application for marketing authorisation. Such an application will be treated as a normal application.

The Commission has also recognised that patent period erosion is a major problem, in particular, for innovatory pharmaceutical companies and has tabled proposals to protect such companies. These proposals raise the possibility of a restoration of patent period for pharmaceuticals, on a product-by-product basis, with the period starting from the first approval in the Community, and possibly lasting twenty years. Such a move would be welcomed by the pharmaceutical industry.

Pricing and reimbursement

Directive 89/105/EEC was recently passed to address the anomaly of wide price variations for medicinal products, at both wholesale and retail level, across the Community. This directive is concerned with the pricing of medicinal products and the criteria for admittance to reimbursement schemes. While this directive does not specifically dictate a price for medicinal products it does lay down the general guidelines by which prices must be determined, and the factors which must be taken into account when determining whether a product should be admitted to a reimbursement scheme. In addition to price determination this directive also stipulates the considerations national governments must take into account when trying to control drug expenditure by price freezes (differentiated or otherwise) and/or profit margin controls, and the procedures available to companies to appeal against such actions.

The most important provisions with respect to pricing are that each product must be able to have its own price, calculated on the basis of its real cost, using a transparent method of calculation. Pharmaceutical firms must be able to take account of the various elements making up the cost of the products (research, raw materials, processing, advertising, transport, expenses and charges inherent in importing) in arriving at their price. When assessing the price requested by pharmaceutical companies the national authorities must take only such factors into consideration. In addition, marketing authorisation for a pharmaceutical product may not in any circumstances be refused, suspended or revoked, save on grounds relating to public health. This means that a member state cannot refuse, suspend or revoke a marketing authorisation simply because it considers the price of a pharmaceutical to be excessive. In addition, member states may not link the grant of a price rise, or derogations from price freezes, to conditions that can only be met by firms established within the territory of the state in question.

The directive also lays down objective criteria concerned with the admittance of a product to a positive list or exclusion from a negative list. It also specifically states the criteria which are unacceptable for the exclusion of a proprietary medicinal product from a positive list. Those criteria which are unacceptable for exclusion from a positive list are:

1 The existence on the market of other, less expensive, products having the same therapeutic effect.
2 The fact that the preparations in question are freely marketed without the need for any medical prescription.
3 Reasons of a pharmaco-therapeutic nature justified by the protection of public health.

This directive also lays down procedures by which companies can appeal against a decision to exclude their products from a reimbursement scheme.

The strength of this directive lies in its requirement that the various national authorities should be transparent in arriving at their pricing and reimbursement decisions. They must present in a clear and unambiguous manner the formulas they used in arriving at their decision. The continuous references to Articles 30–5 of the Treaty of Rome, concerned with competition policy, are what will make this directive effective.

CONSEQUENCES OF 1992 FOR THE PHARMACEUTICAL INDUSTRY

All the proposals identified as being essential to the creation of a single integrated European market in the 1985 White Paper *Completing the Internal Market* had been formally adopted as directives by January 1990. Without doubt the directives discussed above should eliminate, or at least greatly reduce the magnitude of, the barriers to such a single market. However, the effectiveness of these directives will be dependent on the manner and enthusiasm with which the various national governments interpret and enforce them. Past experience of the national governments' compliance with both the letter and the spirit of directives has not been encouraging. The determination of the Commission to enforce these directives, with the help of the European Court of Justice if necessary, will be of importance.

In all likelihood a single integrated European pharmaceutical market will not be created by, or on, 1 January 1993 but will evolve slowly by the selective enforcement of the directives discussed and various articles of the Treaty of Rome, particularly those relating to competition policy. This evolutionary process to, and the creation of, a single integrated European pharmaceutical market will result in marked changes in the structure of both the industry and the market and in the relative relationships of the various elements both within and between the industry and market.

Registration

There will be provision for both a centralised and a decentralised system for the registration of proprietary products. Which procedure is used will depend upon the nature of the proprietary medicinal product. Those derived from biotechnology and other highly innovative products will use the centralised system, whereas those products whose therapeutic efficacy and safety are already well established will use the decentralised system, with the facility of mutual recognition if appropriate.

Notwithstanding the criticisms of such a centralised regulatory body, the establishment of a central authority which can grant a single marketing authorisation for the whole of the EC should be to the advantage of the innovatory pharmaceutical companies. This will be particularly beneficial to those innovatory companies which do not have the resources, or the contacts with the various national authorities by way of local production facilities, because of their size. In contrast the smaller non-innovatory companies will suffer: those which serve local markets only and which benefit from the protection offered by the sourcing and pricing policies of the national authorities. At present such companies represent 20–30 per cent of the European pharmaceutical industry.

The maintenance of a fortified decentralised regulatory procedure for the vast majority of medicinal products has several benefits which include:

1 Inexpensive – no new body required.
2 Relatively little additional bureaucracy.
3 European companies with their current contacts and working relationships with individual national authorities would still be favoured over foreign companies.

4 No complete loss of sovereignty for national governments, while for highly innovative products the centralised procedure offers guarantees of impartiality and uniformity of approach.

By allowing flexibility, but at the same time guaranteeing that rigorous standards are followed, the proposed systems for registration should reduce the delay currently experienced in gaining marketing authorisation. According to a 1988 report, using 1984 as the base year, the incremental cost of the requirement for multiple registrations was minimal in comparison with the effects of time delays in obtaining marketing authorisation and the subsequent erosion of patent life. At 1984 prices this amounted to 160 million to 260 million ECU, or 0.5–0.8 per cent of total costs. This would have been sufficient to raise industry trading profits by 7 to 14 per cent. The proposal to extend patent life has important implications here.

From the preceding it would appear that the changes in the registration procedures will result in a more uniform and non-biased approach to the registration of proprietary medicinal products. This will be to the benefit of both the large and the small innovatory pharmaceutical companies.

Parallel imports

The simplification and harmonisation of product licence applications for marketing authorisation will make it easier for pharmaceutical companies to obtain pan-European authorisation. As the stated objective of the *Completing the Internal Market* programme was to ensure that any product legally manufactured and marketed within any member country could be freely sold throughout the Community, we would expect to see an increase in the level of parallel imports throughout the Community. In the past parallel imports of pharmaceuticals were not of any significance as Table 4.1 indicates.

However, the abolition of trade barriers within Europe, and the significant price differentials for proprietary medicinal products which currently exist, will encourage parallel imports. The standard deviation

Table 4.1 Parallel imports in some EC countries, as a percentage of sales, 1984

Country	% of sales
West Germany	1.0
Britain	1.0–1.5
Holland	3.0

Source: Economists Advisory Group (1988)

of ex-factory drug prices is ±27 per cent,[13] with prices in Portugal, France, Spain and Greece being roughly half those pertaining in West Germany, Denmark, Holland and Ireland. In the past, parallel imports across countries were limited, as patient information was country (language)-specific and copyright protected. There were also differing legal requirements for the packaging and classification of drugs and for admission to a positive list for reimbursement. These barriers have been largely eliminated by the directives outlined above. The European Court of Justice has also established the legality of parallel imports in pharmaceutical products even when the price differentials between countries are a result of governments, instead of manufacturers, price strategies. In addition the Court has ruled that contractual limitations on the export of pharmaceutical products from countries imposed by manufacturers are illegal under Article 30 of the Treaty of Rome.

Pricing and reimbursement

The price of proprietary medicinal products is expected to reach a common level throughout the Community. This price level will probably be slightly below the current Community average. It is doubtful whether this will happen by 1 January 1993 but it should evolve over a period of time. This will occur not just as a result of the price transparency directive and the resultant harmonisation of price-fixing formulas throughout the Community but, more important, (at least initially), owing to parallel imports. In the long term parallel imports will probably be insignificant, owing to a reduction in the magnitude of price differentials.

For products generally it would be reasonable to expect the level of demand to alter following a price change. Thus in countries in which the prices of proprietary medicinal products are currently relatively high, which incidentally have low consumption patterns, a decrease in price would be expected to cause an increase in demand. On the other hand, in the current low-price countries, which at present have high consumption patterns, an increase in price to the Community average would be expected to result in a decrease in consumption. However, the demand determinants for proprietary medicinal products cannot be considered to be normal.

The Economists Advisory Group[14] have determined the elasticity of demand for pharmaceutical products across the EC using the consumption patterns and price levels pertaining in 1984. They found that the demand for pharmaceuticals was practically inelastic ($e = 0.8$). They then determined the value of the European pharmaceutical market should prices become equalised at the European average and with demand elasticities of 0, 0.5 and 1.5. They concluded that the value of the market would change by 0, −471 million, and +1,464 million ECU respectively. This represents a percentage change of 0, −2 and 6.5 per cent respectively in the market value. Their opinion was that the reduction of 2 per cent was the most realistic of the three.

However, a more recent report[15] by Shearson Lehman Hutton suggests that should European pharmaceutical prices become equalised at those pertaining in Belgium, slightly below the European average, the value of the European market would decrease by 6 billion ECU (1988 prices). A reduction of this magnitude represents 20 per cent of the value of the European market.

While the percentage reduction in the overall value of the European market is thus significant, the changes in value of the individual markets may be of greater significance, particularly for those companies which are very dependent on a particular national market for a large proportion of revenues. Given the disproportionately large share which local firms possess of local markets (see Chapters 7 and 8), those which are dependent on the UK and German markets are likely to suffer most.

Related to the issue of pricing and market shrinkage are reimbursement and generic pharmaceutical products. With respect to reimbursement the directives concerned with the classification and conditions of supply of pharmaceuticals, i.e. prescription-only medicines or over-the-counter, and the criteria for admission to reimbursement schemes while facilitating the creation of the single market will contribute to the market shrinkage. The issue of generics is of major concern to the pharmaceutical industry, and the directive relating to the extension of patent life may provide future limited protection to innovative companies against market shrinkage.

In 1984 the relative percentage of drug sales for which generics accounted ranged from 20 per cent (Denmark) to 1 per cent (Italy)[16]. In general, the percentage share of the market held by generics was higher in high-cost drug countries than in low-cost countries. Any increase in price and harmonisation of criteria for admittance to reimbursement schemes will probably increase the level of consumption of generic products in those countries which are currently low-cost.

Industry structure

The fragmentation of the European market has resulted in a situation where the formulation facilities are dispersed throughout the Community. The R & D and active ingredient facilities are centralised and are generally in the home country of the pharmaceutical company. Thus, of the stages in the production of proprietary medicinal products, the only area where major economies of scale can be achieved is in the formulation stage.

According to EAG[17], 50 per cent of these formulation facilities are excess to requirements and this excess capacity accounted for 1–2 per cent of total industry costs in 1984. The success or otherwise of the directives, particularly the price transparency directive, relating to proprietary medicinal products will determine the nature of any restructuring of the industry. Three possible scenarios are the likely outcome of the price transparency directive, as follows:[18]

1 The directive is ineffective – prices continue to be linked to local activities and cost savings are limited to those possible through a unified registration procedure.
2 The directive is ineffective for the various political considerations which presently result in market fragmentation and lack of political will to ensure that a single market is created. However, companies withdraw manufacturing from marginal areas.
3 Directive is effective. Companies follow a policy of maximum possible concentration.

The net results of the above three scenarios on the pharmaceutical industry's costs will differ. If the price differentials between countries remain unchanged, rather than decreasing as previously suggested, then in the first and second instances the overall cost savings to the industry will be small. They will be in the region of 44 million to 116 million ECU (1984 prices) or 0.1 per cent to 0.3 per cent of total costs. In the third scenario there would be a major restructuring of the pharmaceutical industry's activities. This would result in cost savings in the region of 156 million to 273 million ECU (1984 prices). Thus the potential direct savings, from rationalisation of formulation facilities, as a result of unification of the European pharmaceutical market are relatively limited in terms of total industry costs (1 to 2 per cent).

As the average price of proprietary medicinal products across Europe is expected to fall, the effect on pharmaceutical companies will vary from country to country. Thus, the pharmaceutical industries of Italy, Spain and France may benefit, whereas those of Britain and Germany may suffer. In addition the companies most likely to suffer will be those which are highly dependent upon the sale of prescription medicines and include Glaxo of Britain and Bayer of West Germany.

A major strength of the British and, in particular, the German pharmaceutical companies is that they are vertically integrated, i.e.

they are divisions of large chemical corporations. Such companies include ICI of Britain and Hoechst of West Germany. In 1988 pharmaceuticals accounted only for 17 per cent of Hoechst sales. Thus these companies have the financial strength to survive and to acquire other smaller companies. At present the German giants are prevented from acquiring other smaller German pharmaceutical companies owing to the monopoly position they would enjoy within the German market. However, should competition policy switch from a purely national to a pan-European focus, German companies could find their scope for domestic acquisitions greatly enhanced. The West German market contains a number of major second-line groups, often family-owned, that could be extremely attractive to any predators. Examples include E. Merck, Boehringer-Ingelheim and Roehm. In addition the major British and German pharmaceutical companies are organised on truly multinational lines and are not dependent upon their home markets.

Thus it is probable that the larger companies, and in particular the larger of the British and German pharmaceutical companies, will become stronger while the small ones will suffer regardless of their home country. The small ones most likely to suffer are the non-innovative ones which are dependent upon their home market.

International competitiveness

The European pharmaceutical industry is highly competitive in international terms as judged by its profitability, innovative capacity and its ability to penetrate foreign markets as shown in Table 4.2. This table indicates that the European pharmaceutical industry had 10.5 per cent of the world pharmaceutical market which is outwith Europe in 1982. Of this 10.5 per cent, 8.8 per cent is shared in roughly equal proportions by the pharmaceutical industries of Britain and Germany.

However, sustainable competitive power in the pharmaceutical sector is dependent upon an ability to sustain R & D and the generation of new medicines. In 1987 there were sixty innovative European pharmaceutical companies. However, the European pharmaceutical industry which ten years ago accounted for 60 per cent of all new chemical entities in research accounts for 40 per cent of the world total now.[19] Whether this reduction is a reflection of a decreasing competitiveness or a more realistic commercial appraisal of R & D effort is open to question. The industry would argue that the fragmentation of the European pharmaceutical market and the high prices enabled the industry to become an internationally competitive force in the world pharmaceutical market. It argues that the expected decrease in the value

Table 4.2 Pharmaceutical market shares in the developed world outside Europe, 1982 (%)

To	Denmark	France	Germany	Italy	Holland	Britain	Total EC	US	Swiss	Other
US	0.2	0.7	3.9	0.2	0.1	5.1	10.2	80.0	9.2	0.6
Canada	0.5	2.8	3.3	0.5	–	7.1	14.2	52.1	10.0	23.7
Japan	0.2	0.6	4.8	0.2	0.3	1.9	7.8	12.2	2.8	77.2
Australia	0.5	1.1	6.4	0.6	0.3	16.4	25.2	30.9	7.6	36.3
New Zealand	1.7	4.0	8.0	–	2.6	26.6	41.2	31.9	9.6	17.3
South Africa	–	1.5	7.8	–	–	11.9	25.0	33.2	10.6	31.2
Total	0.3	0.8	4.5	0.3	0.2	4.3	10.5	50.4	6.8	32.3

Source: Economists Advisory Group (1988)

of the European pharmaceutical market, which in 1982 accounted for 89 per cent of the industry's revenues (Table 4.2), will seriously damage the industry ability to fund R & D and therefore its future viability. However the decrease in market value may be offset, to some extent, by the new possibilities of rationalisation of activities and increased economies of scale in addition to a more streamlined registration procedure.

Doubtless, there will be a major restructuring in the industry, with the weaker firms folding. However, the companies that are left will be more competitive. In addition the proposals with respect to the patent position of innovatory proprietary medicinal products will strengthen the competitive position of innovatory companies, regardless of size. It is unlikely that the creation of a single European market will favour European firms in the European market over their international competitors. This is so as many US and Swiss pharmaceutical multinationals have extensive production facilities in the EC. In addition the White Paper states that public resources should not be used to confer artificial advantage on some firms over others. Also Article 58 of the Treaty of Rome stipulates that EC companies of foreign parentage receive national treatment. It is unlikely that multinational pharmaceutical firms servicing the EC from facilities within the EC could be discriminated against in favour of domestic EC firms.

All pharmaceutical manufacturers are subject to three different forms of competition: the imitative, the initiative, and pure competition on goods. The single European market will not change this. The European pharmaceutical industry would, however, argue that the main beneficiaries of the single European Market will be the Japanese and American pharmaceutical companies, as these companies will be able to fund R & D through the higher prices which will probably prevail in their own domestic markets.

However, while this may be true, the European pharmaceutical industry is part of a global industry, and a total commitment to a European domestic market would be a great mistake. Although pharmaceuticals are a relatively high-technology industry, this should not lure the relatively successful European pharmaceutical firms into complacency. It would be impossible and highly dangerous to treat Europe in isolation from the rest of the world, and competition from the outside is increasing significantly. It is essential that innovation receives even more attention than before, even though the costs of R & D are escalating. Reliance on European markets will not recoup these costs. A global approach is the only possible answer and is the strategy which many major European pharmaceutical companies will adopt; witness the recent merger between Beecham and SmithKline, the expansion of both British and German pharmaceutical companies' activities in the US, and the spate of joint ventures with Japanese companies.

SUMMARY

The process of harmonisation in the pharmaceutical sector has varied greatly in speed, depending on what aspect is considered. By 1989 it was virtually complete as far as patents were concerned and had made good progress in the field of technical requirements for the registration of new products, best manufacturing practice and the conduct of clinical trials.

In the last two years the Commission has taken account of several of the pharmaceutical industry's fears and has made proposals for the further refinement of the regulatory procedure and for the extension of patent term. In addition it has addressed the major problem of divergent price levels for pharmaceutical products across the Community and national governments' incentives to local producers. It has also removed some of the last remaining barriers to free trade in pharmaceuticals within the Community, i.e. classification of drugs, packaging, labelling and information requirements.

It is doubtful whether a single integrated European pharmaceutical market will be created by 1 January 1993, the deadline established in the 1985 White Paper. This is so, not because the directives necessary for the establishment of such a market are not in force (which they are), but because of a lack of political willingness on the part of some of the member countries. It will probably be a further three to five years before a single European pharmaceutical market becomes a reality.

Perhaps the greatest danger in the creation of a single European market is the risk of the development of 'Fortress Europe'. In order to avoid the possibility of being refused access to the European market both the Swiss and the American pharmaceutical multinationals are increasing their presence within the EC. A manufacturing base is a prerequisite if there is any risk of 'Fortress Europe' developing, and a viable presence in any market can only stem from a strong local manufacturing base. However, the development of 'Fortress Europe' would also seriously injure the European pharmaceutical industry as it might be refused access to non-EC markets. The European Commission, recognising the negative effects for European industry in general of 'Fortress Europe', stated:

> The international market should not close in on itself. In conformity

with GATT, the Community should be open to third countries and must negotiate with these countries to ensure access to their markets for Community exports. It will seek to preserve the balance of advantage recorded, whilst respecting the identity of the internal market of the Community.

(EC summit, June 1988, Hanover)

On the assumption that the aims of 1992 are achieved, they should create a better climate in which a much needed industry restructuring can be carried out. At the very least there is likely to be a significant shake-out of the smaller, and even some of the larger, companies in the peripheral areas of the EC such as Spain, Portugal and Greece. In these areas, increased competition is likely to force many of the smaller companies out of business, while some of the larger ones could be acquisition targets.

This restructuring of the industry will leave only those companies which have a global outlook, strong product spread, solid R & D, technological strengths (particularly biotechnological) and leadership in the higher value-added areas surviving.

The main plus features of the single market are:

1 Standardised approvals for new pharmaceutical products.
2 Elimination of cross-border non-tariff barriers.
3 Single environmental standards.
4 Easier industry restructuring.
5 A single market with more power in international trade.

The negative features are:
1 Increased presence of non-EC companies in the EC.
2 Probable lower price standardisation and impact on R & D.

However, from an intra-European viewpoint the impact of the single market will be negligible overall and, on balance, marginally beneficial. It will create a more viable, more efficient and more internationally competitive European pharmaceutical industry, but smaller in terms of number. However, should the Japanese pharmaceutical industry, which is currently showing signs of expansionary activity outside Japan (e.g. Fujisawa), set up facilities in Europe, the nature and extent of the industry restructuring could be greatly magnified.

5 The competitive environment of the world pharmaceutical industry

In common with all other industries operating in free markets, the world pharmaceutical industry reacts to and is shaped by the external environment within which it operates. The strategies pursued by the various firms within the industry are likely to be shaped as a response to these external pressures and determinants. The purpose of this chapter is to analyse the external environment of the world pharmaceutical industry and to assess the importance of those parameters which are most likely to shape future strategy. The approach will follow the model set out in Figure 5.1. Here, the firm's external environment is subdivided into:

1 *The remote environment.* This consists of those economic, political, social and technological factors over which the individual firm has no control whatsoever, but which produce the opportunities and threats that are the basic building blocks of strategy. These opportunities and threats will, of course, affect every firm in the industry though the individual impact of each may be differential.
2 *The operating environment.* This consists of factors associated with suppliers, creditors, customers, competitors and the labour market upon which the individual firm may exert some indirect influence. The area covered by this analysis is, effectively, the industry itself and this will be termed the industry analysis. The purpose here is to evaluate these competitive forces which drive the industry and shape competitive responses.

Directly following the industry analysis, and closely linked with it, will be a consideration of the generic strategies which may be suitable for implementation within the world pharmaceutical industry. At this stage the strategy discussion will be limited to indicating those broad strategic directions which may be pursued by groups of similar firms within the industry, and to indicating which broad strategic directions

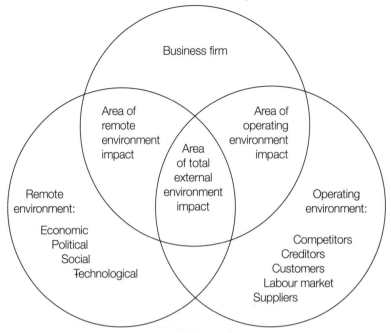

Figure 5.1 The external environment of the firm *Source*: J.A. Pearce II and R.B. Robinson Jr., *Formulation and Implementation of Competitive Strategy*, Irwin, Homewood, Ill., third edition (1988)

would be less helpful or even damaging. A discussion of firm-specific strategy comes later, and will be dealt with in Chapters 6–9.

THE REMOTE ENVIRONMENT OF THE WORLD PHARMACEUTICAL INDUSTRY

Economic factors

The market for pharmaceuticals is largely immune from the effects of normal economic cycles for two principal reasons:

1 It is difficult or impossible to put a price on good health, and if a drug has the potential to alleviate or cure an illness it will be demanded regardless of the state of the economy.
2 In most countries, the reimbursement system for ethical pharmaceuticals removes awareness of the high cost of drugs from the intermediary and end user, i.e. the doctor and the consumer.

Nevertheless, state-owned health agencies and health insurance companies are imposing increasingly tight controls on drug spending. This will have the effect of exerting downward pressure on prices and of motivating a change to cheaper generic products. In general terms, the relative economic prosperity of a country will have a degree of impact on overall price levels. As well as the obvious example of developing countries, major price differentials can exist between the various developed markets such as that between the less prosperous Mediterranean countries and the northern European countries such as West Germany and the UK.

A closely associated factor is the question of changes in the payment systems used in different countries. These are in response to the rising overall cost of drugs and include the changes made to the PPRS by the UK government, Italy's restricted formulary for government payment, changes to the insurance payment system in Germany, and direct buying by Medicare and hospital groups in the US.

International financial pressures and mechanisms also have a direct effect on the industry through the operation of exchange rates (including, specifically, the Exchange Rate Mechanism within the EC), differential inflation rates between countries, and regional factors like the economic impacts of the single European market (discussed in detail in Chapter 4).

Political factors

National governments have a greater influence on the world pharmaceutical industry than any other individual group or force. They are in the unique position of being the major customer, and also the regulator and pricing authority of the industry. This influence is felt in a number of areas:

1 Through the control of the licensing authorities a national government can influence the effective length of a drug's patent life and hence the period of monopoly a company has over selling a particular drug. Owing to increases in the length of time it takes for drug testing and clinical trials before a drug comes on the market, the industry is now lobbying vigorously for an extension of the patent period. Currently this is seventeen years in the US and around twenty years in most EC countries.

2 Through setting prescription guidelines; in keeping with cost-cutting requirements, doctors are being urged to prescribe generic drugs rather than branded products where possible.

3 Through control of drug pricing levels. For example, as noted above, the PPRS allows companies to set prices while keeping within profitability guidelines. These have been regarded as too high in the past, and have been reduced.
4 Regarding the single European market, political influence is crucial in two key areas. The EC is moving towards a pan-European drug licensing system which should reduce the expense and bureaucracy involved in licensing in different countries. A system of mutual recognition has proved to be cumbersome and met with little success. With regard to pricing, it is likely that differentials will encourage parallel importing for some years as a gradually unified pricing structure becomes established across the Community (see Chapter 4). The second area is the practice of allowing companies with substantial local investment to charge higher prices for their drugs in that country. This is likely to change as reference will instead be made to the investment in the EC as a whole. The result could be a reduction in duplication of manufacturing facilities across the Community.

Social factors

The size and composition of the population, as well as its standard of living, have a direct impact on the size and growth of the market for pharmaceuticals in any particular country. The overall size of the population affects the aggregate level of consumption, and population composition affects both the aggregate and the pattern of consumption (for example, products to treat diseases of childhood or afflictions of old age). With regard to standard of living, expectations of the quality of medical care tend to increase in developed countries as *per capita* income rises. In developing countries, the growth in GDP is likely to be a major determinant of growth in consumption.

The principal demographic trend over the next twenty years is for an increase in the number of older people and a decrease in the number of young people in populations. As well as requiring a shift in emphasis towards more geriatric-related drugs, etc., this will place a strain on welfare systems as a smaller working population must support the health service supplied to the non-working older population.

Concern for the environment, particularly waste chemical pollution, and consideration of animal welfare will have a considerable impact on research testing and manufacturing techniques.

Changing lifestyles will lead to greater demand for over-the-counter drugs instead of a surgery visit to be issued with a prescription; the trend towards 'care in the community' will lead to an increase in out-patient treatment; and quality of life considerations in prescribing will affect the propensity to treat illnesses with drugs, thus influencing the overall pattern of treatment demanded.

Technological factors

Biotechnology is now a well developed force for change in the world pharmaceutical industry but, while it has been high on promise, so far it has been lower on delivery. While some firms have been able to make successful products, sales have been disappointing. Among other reasons, this has been because injection is the principal (in some cases, the only feasible) method of delivery. Producing a more traditional delivery form is thus a major hurdle, and some firms have been allocating large sums to this area. While some in the industry believe that biotechnology represents a major route for future development, others believe that a clear picture will emerge only towards the end of the century. However, developments in biotechnology are expected to increase over that period, producing more efficient techniques of manufacture for new protein-based drugs, despite achieving current sales of less than 1 per cent of world drug consumption.

Information technology is advancing almost on a day-to-day basis, and pharmaceutical firms will be able to use it to improve efficiency in sales and in R & D. The latter is particularly important, as it is becoming recognised that small research groups tend to be more effective than large ones. However, for the large multinational company, the ability to link small research centres with a totally interactive data base may be the key to more effective management of R & D. The development of expert systems which help doctors reach a diagnosis will provide pharmaceutical firms with an excellent sales aid if specific branded drugs are recommended by particular expert systems.

Increased need for better, more efficient delivery systems which enhance therapeutic benefits and perhaps extend product life cycles will be a stimulus for increased research in this area. Drug delivery systems will become more 'user friendly', perhaps with less involvement from medical practitioners.

Finally, following the 1984 Bhopal disaster, the wider chemical in-dustry has had to re-examine disaster plans, safety rules and community relations programmes. This may have to include redesigning plants and installing automated process control systems to provide early warning of danger.

THE OPERATING ENVIRONMENT OF THE WORLD PHARMACEUTICAL INDUSTRY

Competition

The world pharmaceutical industry is highly fragmented, with the large majority of the top thirty firms having a market share of less than 2 per cent. Based on 1988 sales revenue, the world's largest drugs firm (Merck) has less than 4 per cent of the market. The structure of the industry has changed significantly, with a number of companies merging in order to obtain economies of scale in R & D and marketing, the best known examples being the mergers of SmithKline with Beecham, and Bristol-Myers with Squibb. Those companies with ambitions to compete on a global scale have recognised that the necessary critical mass has increased; however, companies that are prepared to remain as niche players may be able to compete in their current form. Whether this consolidation will continue is difficult to say, but some chief executives who have previously been against mergers are now open-minded on the subject, perhaps indicating that there could be more to follow.

In the US, the passing of the 1984 Waxman–Hatch Act (allied with government cost-reduction programmes) has led to the rapid growth of generic drug firms. This sector of the industry has tended to be populated by small independent companies. However, several large research-based multinationals have also entered this sector and up to half the market may now be in the hands of Bristol-Myers/Squibb, Warner Lambert, Ciba-Geigy, American Cyanamid, and Hoechst. Thus, it appears likely that, as this sector develops, it will be divided between small independents and large research-based firms which have the resources to develop profitable generics businesses. In this case, generics will be a major threat, but primarily to those companies which are reliant on (and unable to replace) drugs which are nearing the end of their patent periods.

Customers

As noted earlier, this industry is unusual in that 'customers' can be defined on three levels. There is the patient who consumes the drug, the doctor who prescribes the drug, and the agency which pays for the drug. In most countries, this last party is the government, although in the US the major buyers tend to be insurance companies and other commercial firms. Doctors tend to be loyal to products which they know will work, but in some countries they are under pressure from those who pay to prescribe generics or cheaper alternatives where these exist.

Governments are constantly trying to reduce drug bills, as are other buyers. They are reacting in a number of ways to rising pharmaceutical costs:

1 In the US, some federal government and employer health plans are attempting to force down drug prices on branded products by threatening to take them off lists of pharmaceuticals approved for reimbursement.
2 In Europe, there is evidence that the increase in parallel importing is being used to undermine the relatively high prices of drugs in some countries.
3 Many hospitals and other large users are demanding competing bids from manufacturers of similar patented products.
4 Other operators are joining together in groups to buy pharmaceuticals in an effort to match the bargaining position of the major drug players.

Thus, drug buyers are becoming increasingly price-sensitive, and this trend is likely to continue, leading to further bargaining-down of drug prices.

Suppliers/creditors

Raw materials represent a small proportion of the costs of making drugs, and suppliers are easily changed, as their inputs are largely commodities. Most large drug firms boast a strong capital position and are highly liquid; this ensures that credit will be readily available.

Labour supply

Most of the drug multinationals have good reputations as employers who provide good training and development programmes as well as a range of support benefits. Thus the ability of these firms to attract and retain quality employees is a fairly common factor.

INDUSTRY ANALYSIS

According to Porter,[1] focusing on future strategy leads the chief executive to formulate a series of questions:

1 'What is driving competition in my industry or in the industry I am thinking of joining?'

2 'What actions are competitors likely to take, and what is the best way to respond?'
3 'How will my industry evolve?'
4 'How can my firm be best positioned to compete in the long run?'

Porter's[2] approach to the structural analysis of an industry aims at assessing each of the competitive forces which act within the industry, and whose collective strength will determine the attractiveness and profit potential of the industry. These five competitive forces are: the barriers to entry and exit, the bargaining power of suppliers, the bargaining power of buyers, the power of substitutes, and the intensity of rivalry. They are illustrated in Figure 5.2, and are examined in detail below.

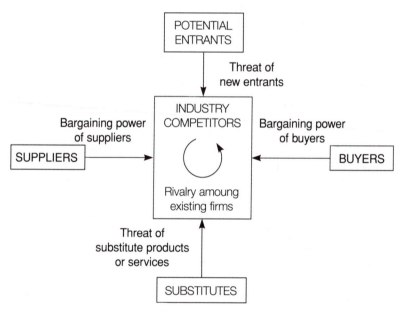

Figure 5.2 The forces driving industry competition *Source*: Porter (1980)

Barriers to entry and exit

New entrants to an industry bring new capacity, resources and competition. The threat of these new entrants depends upon how easy it is for them to enter, the barriers to entry that are present, and the reaction to potential entrants by the existing competitors. If the barriers to entry are high and reaction to entry is likely to be fierce, then the threat of entry is low. Porter identifies seven major barriers to entry:

1 *Economies of Scale.* This refers to the decrease in unit production cost with the increase in absolute volume per period. These economies of scale can be present in nearly every function of a business. Large firms are also able to share economies of scale between functions, e.g. one unit mass-producing parts for another unit, thereby making it even harder for the new entrant to compete. Firms enjoying such economies of scale possess distinct cost advantages.

2 *Product differentiation.* This occurs where established firms have brands to which their customers have developed a degree of loyalty. This loyalty can be the result of product performance, additional service, advertising or, as in the case of the pharmaceutical industry, simply by being first into the market with an efficaceous product.

3 *Capital requirements.* This refers to the amount of capital needed to start up in a competitive position. If linked with economies of scale, these present formidable barriers, especially if the risk is high.

4 *Switching costs.* If the costs of a buyer switching to the entrant's product are high, then the buyer must be presented with some increase in the ratio of relative value to price before a switch will occur.

5 *Access to distribution channels.* If the.product has difficulty in reaching buyers, then no sale will occur no matter how superior the product is. If the new entrant does not have its own distribution channels, then existing ones must be persuaded to handle the new product. This may mean using incentives, such as lower prices to the distributor. These incentives erode the profits of the new entrant and increase the height of the entry barrier.

6 *Cost disadvantages independent of scale.* Existing firms may have cost benefits not associated with economies of scale, for example proprietary technology, government subsidies, reliable access to raw materials; or they may be positioned further along the experience curve. Experience, with its accompanying skills, lowers cost not only in production but in sales, marketing, distribution, etc. Cost advantages which derive from the experience curve effect are often greater in labour-intensive industries, and will depend on a firm keeping its skilled workforce. However, advantages of this nature can be nullified by product or process innovations leading to a new experience curve.

7 *Government policy.* Government can control entry into an industry, limiting or even excluding entry by legislative measures like licensing or limiting access to raw materials. Government policy plays a major

determining factor within the pharmaceutical industry. Licences, patents, limited raw materials (for narcotic drugs) are all major tools currently used throughout the world. The industry is one of the most heavily regulated, and government policy presents a very high entry barrier.

Other properties of entry barriers are that:

1 They change as conditions change; for example, the Second World War brought several pharmaceutical firms together both in the US and in the UK to pool their expertise.
2 They change according to the changes in strength of the rivalry from the existing competitors.
3 A firm's strategy can change the mobility of entry barriers or their height, for example by backward integration into production of raw materials, thereby giving a new entrant a higher barrier to overcome.
4 A firm's internal skills or resources may be such that they fit the requirements of the industry and lower the entry barrier to the industry. For example, a cosmetics manufacturer would be better positioned for entry into the pharmaceutical industry than one producing gas turbines.

Potential entrants can face formidable entry barriers to an industry, and this is true for substantial sectors of the pharmaceutical industry. However, barriers can clearly be overcome, since new competitors do enter, often bringing with them new entry barriers. In other industries for example, window cleaning – the entry barriers are low and entry is cheap and simple.

Many of the factors which give rise to entry barriers also apply in reverse to shape the barriers to exit from an industry. These can also be high or low, and must be considered by a firm when contemplating the role of potential entrant. Porter sees the relationships between barriers and profitability as set out in Figure 5.3.

Entry and exit barriers in the world pharmaceutical industry In this industry, the entry barriers facing potential entrants are closely related to the nature of the highly specialised product. Owing to the very high degree of sophistication, differentiation, technical expertise, purity, reliability, safety, and R & D required – together with the long innovation time, government regulation and quality requirements – acceptable products are in themselves difficult to produce, without even any guarantee of commercial success.

They require skilled personnel, access to raw materials of acceptable

Exit barriers

		Low	High
Entry barriers	Low	Low, stable returns	Low, risky returns
	High	High, stable returns	High, risky returns

Figure 5.3 Barriers and profitability *Source*: Porter (1986)

quality, suitable technology, suitable premises controlled and acceptable to the authorities, the freedom to produce the product from restricting patents, or the innovative skill and resources to produce a new substance. The firm has to decide on its generic strategy and begin to compete with its rivals. For many years now pharmaceutical manufacturing has shown greater profitability as an industry than other forms of manufacturing. It is the high profitability of the industry which draws new entrants into it.

The industry is exceedingly research-intensive. The innovators within it are very few and very large; besides being strong in R & D resources, they show highly developed economies of scale. They are fiercely aggressive, especially towards potential new entrants. The list of the top fifty firms has stayed relatively constant over a number of years; the only significant change was in 1987, when Pharmacia – a Swedish firm – entered at forty-seventh position following its acquisition of Leo. This illustrates that a considerable increase in size and economic potential is necessary before making an impact on this industry.

Access to distribution channels is usually not the greatest of entry barriers in the developed countries, but is a substantial barrier in, for example, China, with its underdeveloped communication infrastructure and 3,750,000 square miles of land. The Chinese are now encouraging foreign investment in the Chinese pharmaceutical industry, through joint ventures, exhibitions, and trade delegations.[3] The industry employs about one million people, has 2,000 industrial enterprises and forty research institutes, according to *China Daily*.[4] With the PRC's population of 1,008 million, the market size is attractive, tempting new entrants from the West to take advantage of the now more receptive political climate.

Product differentiation is very prominent and presents a substantial entry barrier. The cost and the degree of research involved in producing a drug result in the innovative firms keeping within the therapeutic areas in which they are expert. There is not one company, not even among the very largest, that covers more than, at most, a few of the therapeutic segments, verifying that the industry shows a very high degree of product differentiation. The smaller companies are equally differentiated, the only difference being that they are producing 'me too' products instead of being industry leaders.

Exit barriers were lower in the ethical pharmaceutical industry at the beginning of the 1980s as assets were flexible for other uses and outside suppliers could satisfy the demand of remaining customers. Ciba-Geigy, for example, exited from production of sterile injectables when FDA requirements about packaging became too costly to satisfy and instead contracted to purchase them without difficulty. However, this should be regarded as an exit from one segment of the industry, not from the industry as a whole, from which the exit barriers are considerably higher, and are continuing to rise as the cost of innovation rises. Exits from the industry generally occur only with the much smaller firms.

Backward integration to production of the active ingredients and often beyond to the excipients is usual with the larger firms, but ultimately depends upon their resources and strategies. This can present problems of access to raw materials for new entrants.

Niche markets exist, such as insulin, mostly covered by such manufacturers as Eli Lilly (US) and Novo and Nordisk Gentofte from Denmark, with only a few other minor producers. Novo alone in 1987 had 34 per cent[5] of the world market. Organon, the Dutch firm, had for several years a leading position in the field of hormones, and endocrinology. Another successful firm operating within a niche market is Guerber of France, which specialises in X-ray contrast media, and with sales of $25 million is a giant within its own sector, since $25 million represents about half the world market for this kind of product.

Proprietary technology such as the biogenetic engineering developed by the Danish insulin producers, enabling the economic large-scale production of the superior product human insulin, presents very high barriers to new entrants on two counts. One, because of the superior production techniques, requiring proprietary knowledge, patented and inaccessible to the new entrant, and, two, because switching costs in changing from porcine or bovine insulin to the superior human insulin are so beneficial to the buyer that this represents another entry barrier for a new entrant. Where such linkages occur between entry barriers entry is even more difficult.

The last important mobility barrier is patent protection. The degree of protection conferred depends on whether the patent granted is for new compounds, a chemical process or medical use. It is significant that the major advances in drug innovation have taken place in countries such as US, the UK, the Federal Republic of Germany, and more recently Japan, where patent law is strongest, protecting and funding their active research and development bases. The comparative ease with which most drugs can be copied is cited as the reason for the importance of effective patents.

The barriers to entering and leaving the industry totally are so high as to be almost insurmountable. Barriers between the many sectors formed by the singularity of the products are also very high, making change from one sector to another a long and costly process, with fierce rivalry being shown by existing competitors. Governments play a dominant role in setting many of the barriers and adjusting their height, regulating the passage from one sector to another. Product differentiation, R & D resources, economies of scale with financial backing and patents present the most important barriers to entry.

Thus, when considering the potential entry of an innovative firm into the world pharmaceutical industry 'big league', the balance of forces can be characterised as in Table 5.1. From the formidable list on the left side of this table it will be seen that Porter's model predicts that the pharmaceutical industry is a very difficult one to enter, and this is borne out by recent history. Indeed, when the future trends of the parameters in Table 5.1 are considered, it might be said that the industry is becoming an impossible one to enter.

Table 5.1 Barriers to entry and exit

Very Strongly in favour of current members	*Very strongly in favour of new entrants*
Economies of scale	
Capital requirements	
R & D expertise	
Access to distribution	
Government policy	
Expected retaliation	
Access to raw materials	
Patent protection	
In favour of current members	*In favour of new entrants*
Proprietary product differences	New proprietary technology
Proprietary learning curve	Absolute cost advantage
Brand identity	

The bargaining power of suppliers

The power of an industry's suppliers lies in their ability to raise prices or reduce the quality of purchased goods or services. This affects the total profitability of the industry. Suppliers may be providing goods, services or labour. There are similarities between buyers and suppliers in what makes them powerful. For example. suppliers are powerful if:

1 They are few in number and more concentrated than the industry; a fragmented industry will stand in a weaker position.
2 There is no competition from substitute products; for example, in the textile industry, several different artificial yarns exist and a supplier of acrylic yarn would have to compete with a supplier of nylon, thus reducing its power, even when the supplier is large relative to the buyer.
3 The industry is not an important customer of the supplier group; this occurs particularly with suppliers selling to a range of industries, when the 'lesser' industries will be ranked in declining order of importance to the supplier.
4 The suppliers' product is important to the industry; when the buyers' industry is dependent on the suppliers' product, this gives the supplier leverage, especially with perishable goods.
5 If the supplier has built up switching costs, making it difficult, if not impossible, for the industry to change suppliers or to integrate backwards.
6 The supplier group poses a realistic threat of forward integration; when the industry is threatened with potential entry by suppliers, its negotiating position is weakened.
7 The supply is labour, and the labour supplied is highly organised and scarce.

The suppliers' bargaining power is also influenced by:

1 Industry strategy such as backward integration, bulk buying, or standardisation of industry products.
2 The degree of product information held by the industry, which will enhance or reduce the suppliers' bargaining power.
3 Governments; through regulation, environmental control, monopoly control, or even by the government itself becoming a supplier.

The suppliers' bargaining power varies from one industry to another and its total impact is the algebraic sum of the effects of all the above factors. Some of the parameters are susceptible to control or influence by the supplier group, such as differentiated products and switching costs; others, such as industry generic strategies, are difficult for them to influence.

The bargaining power of suppliers in the world pharmaceutical industry   The pharmaceutical industry is served by many different categories of suppliers which provide goods such as raw chemicals, bulk pharmaceuticals, biological products, packaging, laboratory equipment, production machinery and computers. Services that it buys include quality control, R & D, clinical testing and industrial information. The suppliers are many and varied both in size and in their products.

Pharmaceutical industry suppliers can be classified in three ways, each of which shows a different aspect of supplier bargaining power. First, they can be classified according to the firms they serve. The pharmaceutical industry is fragmented, with about 100 very large multinationals and over 2,000 small domestic and/or exporting firms. These can be further classified into medium and small, those producing branded products and generics. Each category will have different attitudes and negotiating strengths *vis-à-vis* their suppliers, based upon their buying clout and their dependence on suppliers' inputs. The large multinationals usually produce their own very complex active ingredients and easy-to-synthesise products in-house; the first to maintain strict security, the second to ensure an efficient and cheap supply. Such firms have equipment produced to their specifications, have little need of external laboratory services, and have in-house quality control covering their needs. They practise tapered integration; for example, special equipment produces on-line packaging (such as blister packaging and soft plastic infusion bags) as an integrated part of the production process.

Most suppliers are happy to supply their needs, considering it prestigious to be associated with the industry leaders. These pharmaceutical multinationals expect and demand quality and service from their suppliers, and are usually in a position to achieve this at a reasonable industry price.

The supplier needs of the very much smaller domestic firms are often greater, since they are lacking in the economies of scale, financial resources and in adequate skilled labour to integrate both backwards and forwards. Suppliers find a larger number of segments to serve with these buyers, although each individual segment is usually smaller than for the multinationals. There is generally more balance between the supplier and the buyer.

Second, suppliers can be classified according to the product they supply. This is especially important for raw chemicals, bulk pharmaceuticals and raw materials of biological origin, since the concentration of suppliers is usually higher than that of buyers (depending on the product), in which case those with the largest buying capacity or better buying relationship with their suppliers stand stronger than the others.

Medicinal herbs come extensively from the East European countries, placing the buyers in a vulnerable position, having very few, if any, additional sources. Even for the very large multinationals, a few products are difficult to obtain and the prices rise accordingly. Good examples are genuine rose oil, peppermint oil, and ginseng root. This type of raw material is subject to successful weather conditions providing a good harvest, and also on the economic situation in these countries. Many of the plants used grow wild in the countryside and are plucked by the population as an extra source of income. Should there be dramatic changes in lifestyle and the necessity of extra income, the supply situation could alter drastically.

Third, suppliers can be classified according to the regulations and the national drug policy/economic situation of the buyer's country. The regulating legislation of the buyer's country is important, as it is the country's economic situation and the national drug policy which directly steer the legislative demands made upon the industry and therefore indirectly upon its suppliers of raw materials.

The greater the wealth of the country and the more developed the country's national drug policy, the greater the regulation governing the pharmaceutical industry. This affects the country's pharmaceutical manufacturers, national and multinational subsidiaries, and those exporting to the country.

The regulatory legislation in the developed countries, and in those agreeing to good manufacturing practice, extends ultimately to the industry suppliers of chemicals and biological products. These products which ultimately become ingredients of drugs are subject to the same quality standards as those applied to the final product and each supplier is vetted and controlled by the buyer before being accepted as a supplier.

Between the two extremes of the developed nations and of countries such as Cameroon, having no wealth, no drug policy, very little pharmaceutical production to speak of and under 30 per cent essential drug coverage of the population, there is a whole range of differences of regulation to which the industry and its suppliers are subjected.

When these industry-specific points are taken into consideration, it is only a question of degree that separates the few very large firms from the hundreds of very small ones with respect to suppliers to the pharmaceutical industry. The various parameters are assessed in Table 5.2. Clearly, the actions of government stand out as an important factor, but this probably has a fairly equal effect on industry and suppliers. Otherwise, Table 5.2 characterises the bargaining of suppliers *vis-à-vis* the industry as an evenly balanced situation.

Table 5.2 Bargaining power of suppliers

In favour of suppliers	*In favour of the industry*
Switching costs	Differentiation of products
Presence of substitutes	Importance of volume
Supplier concentration	Threat of backward integration
Government	Government

The bargaining power of buyers

The buyer has specific needs for the industry's product (good or service), for which he is prepared to pay a price. Different buyers have different needs or variations of needs for the industry's range of products. The added value in the product is realised when it is sold, and the relative bargaining power of the industry and its buyer groups determines where the profitability flows; that is, in a competitive situation, it is the buyers' bargaining power that determines how much of the added value is retained by the producing industry and how much is captured by the buyers.

There are two broad groups of factors which determine the bargaining power of the buyers, bargaining leverage and price sensitivity. Bargaining leverage factors include:

1 *Buyer concentration versus industry concentration.* Are there very few buyers for which many industry firms are competing, or vice versa? The first situation will enhance the bargaining power of buyers, the second the industry's.

2 *Buyer volume.* If a given buyer or group of buyers purchases a large volume of industry output, then industry profitability is highly dependent on retaining their custom. This is especially so if the industry is characterised by heavy fixed costs.

3 *Buyer switching costs.* If these are high, buyers tend to be tied to a particular industry firm for supplies. If switching costs are low, buyer bargaining power tends to be higher.

4 *The ability of buyers to integrate backwards.* Buyers will be in a position to negotiate price and other concessions if they pose a

realistic threat of backward integration into the industry's area of operation.

5 *The existence of substitute products.* A substitute is only of interest if it lowers buyer cost or improves buyer performance relative to the industry's profit.

6 *Buyer information.* Any negotiator in possession of facts will always be in a stronger position than an ignorant one. The more facts possessed, the stronger the negotiator's position.

The second group of factors relating to the bargaining power of the buyer relate to price sensitivity, and include:

1 *Product differences compared to the different prices on offer.* This refers to the buyer's perception of what offering gives the optimum value for money. Thus, if the industry's offerings are undifferentiated, there is likely to be substantial buyer pressure for reduced prices.

2 *Proportion of buyers' total costs or purchases.* Buyers are usually less price-sensitive, and therefore are less motivated to use any bargaining power which does exist, if their purchases from the industry represent only a small fraction of their total purchases.

3 *Product quality.* Again, buyers are usually less price-sensitive when the quality of the industry's product has a great overall impact on the quality of the buyers' products.

These factors vary from buyers in one industry to another in the strength each exerts. Buyers may be large, small, single, grouped, consumers, commercial, industrial or institutional. This all influences their position and hence their bargaining power. Buyers within the pharmaceutical industry are in a special position, which is considered below.

The bargaining power of buyers in the world pharmaceutical industry The demand for medicines is derived, dependent on the incidence of disease or need to prevent certain types of illness, and the very use of the product often reduces the potential demand. The essential information needed to diagnose the disease and to determine the required product is possessed by an intermediary, a specialist in health care. The choice of product is made, for the most part, not by the buyer but by this middleman.

These medical personnel practise singly or in small groups; their emphasis is upon professional autonomy, and the right to chose what is considered best for the patient. In addition there is worldwide acknowledgement that 'Doctor knows best'. This makes them strong as a group, and the force they exert is considerable. For prescription drugs, therefore, the buyers would appear to be two-tiered, the choosers and the consumers.

The buyer 'group' as it is rapidly becoming is further extended by the influence of the question 'Who pays the cost of treatment?' Since governments form a very large and important group of buyers, it comes as no surprise that the pharmaceutical industry is subject to an unusual degree of regulation, which manifests itself in several ways. At least for prescription drugs, the greater percentage of buyers is composed of a three-tiered buyer group, the choosers, the consumers, and those who foot the bill.

Concentration was noted above as a leverage factor, and in Chapter 2 the high concentration of world buyers into a small number of developed-country markets was examined. The degree of concentration among buyers is demonstrated by hospitals and their buying routines. Hospitals are becoming increasingly cost-conscious, with yearly budgetary cuts a commonality. This has forced many hospitals to form buying groups to gain quantity discounts in drug purchases. Some even belong to several buying groups. In addition to which, hospitals are interested in buying the cheaper generic versions wherever possible. This places them in a very strong price negotiating position.

Backward integration ('do-it-yourself') is insignificant both in volume and in value, and its impact on the bargaining power of buyers may be dismissed. This places buyers in a vulnerable position *vis-à-vis* manufacturers. Switching costs are present in the industry and in certain segments can play an important role. An area where they are particularly forceful from the buyer's viewpoint is in the institutional sector. Switching from one type of infusion set, carried by one manufacturer, to another is often so expensive that it acts as a very real entry barrier for other competitors.

Switching cost also manifests itself in the role of information. A doctor becomes used to prescribing a certain drug, produced by one manufacturer, for a certain illness or range of illnesses. The doctor feels confident and acquainted with the dosage and the expected results. It entails considerable persuasion on the part of a new firm's sales representative, a real test of personal selling powers, before the average doctor will change to another product, assuming of course that the original product is satisfying the needs of the prescriber.

It is in the need for information that buyers from the pharmaceutical industry exert much of their bargaining power (albeit indirectly). However, they cannot exert this bargaining power in isolation; they need the support of a strong infrastructure in the form of political stability and government legislation. In this respect the wealthy developed countries are in a much stronger position than the newly industrialised and developing countries.

Sometimes the buyers' bargaining power is undermined from within in an insidious way. In the US, most states require or allow a pharmacist to substitute a cheaper, therapeutically equivalent product for a more expensive drug, unless the medical practitioner specifies otherwise. In Sweden, the industry association has held meetings with representatives of the medical profession to discuss how best to deal with doctors who demand financial and other concessions from companies before granting appointments. Both of these examples would seem to imply that the indirect buyers in the three-tier structure are aware of their power and are acting upon it.

Thus, Porter's approach to the bargaining power of buyers is an adequate description for the pharmaceutical industry and its three-tier buyer model. The fact that large buyers (hospitals, governments, doctors, consumers) are very concentrated in densely populated industrial countries gives them a measure of bargaining power over the industry and its firms. This is shown in several ways:

1 Governments footing the national insurance bills attempt to contain the overall cost by legislating on prices, etc.
2 Hospitals join together to form buying consortia to give themselves buyer volume in addition to concentration; this represents an attempt to maximise negotiating advantages with the industry, and has had some measure of success.
3 Another example is preferred drug lists in hospitals; many large firms struggle to get their products accepted on such lists.

These examples demonstrate the impact of price sensitivity, as postulated by Porter.[6]

The densely populated industrialised countries exert pressure through their political systems; in general, an electorate would not vote for a government that allowed prices to rise indiscriminately, or one that allowed demand to continually exceed supply. This is nicely demonstrated by the fact that these industrialised countries have the most legislation governing medicines, and are the most stringent in enforcing it.

The ability to integrate backwards is only a very weak force on the buyers' part; and because it is so weak the firms use it in their favour and always price new products very high for therapeutically new segments. This is not only because they have enormous R & D costs to cover, but also because they know that the buyers are dependent on their products.

Porter's[7] switching costs and information requirements apply in both directions in this industry. Some switching costs work in favour of the buyer (such as information); this gives the buyer strength due to his specialist knowledge (as illustrated by the Swedish doctors). Others give the firms strength, such as the cost of changing infusion sets in a hospital.

Thus, these examples illustrate clearly the determinants of buyer power through bargaining leverage and price sensitivity. In conclusion the balance may be represented as in Table 5.3. At the present time, the balance is quite heavily in favour of the industry, though there is likely to be some movement towards buyers in the future.

Figure 5.7 Bargaining power of buyers

In favour of buyers	In favour of the industry
Concentration	Brand
Volume	Product differences
Decision maker's incentives	Concentration
Substitute products	Volume
Information	Lack of backward integration

The threat of substitute products

A substitute product is one that can perform the same function as the industry's product. The existence of such a substitute determines a ceiling on industry prices (and profits), and can play a prominent role in determining industry demand. Substitution is also related to a firm's competitive scope within an industry as it narrows or widens the range of segments the firm may prospect.

It is not always easy to identify substitutes; for example, in certain instances of hypertension worsened by obesity and lack of general fitness, a substitute product could be a weight watchers' club or a health farm. All the impacts of a product on a buyer are relevant in defining substitutes and their relative performance. In the case of the weight watchers the reduction in weight, the better appearance of the buyer, giving more confidence, and the general improvement in fitness, would have to be considered as contributory factors in substitute product performance. This is also an example of a substitute product performing additional functions to those of an industry's product. The differing patterns of use of a substitute and an industry product often make a comparison impossible, since it is no longer of like with like.

One drastic option which can be considered a substitute is not to buy any product at all. A good example of this is cigarettes, where the impact of peer pressure and the anti-smoking campaigns leads people to give up smoking.

Used, recycled or reconditioned products are yet another source of substitutes. Reconditioned car tyres and used spare parts in cars, TVs, motor cycles, etc., speak for themselves.

A final potential for substitution is backward integration, or for the buyers to perform the function themselves. DIY is a constant substitute problem for master decorators.

Multiple substitutions interact in shaping the overall substitution rate in an industry; for example, sorbitol, aspartame and saccharin are all substitutes for sugar, but aspartame and sorbitol are also substitutes for the original saccharin. The total effect here is that the total size of the market segment has increased.

The number of substitutes will vary widely from industry to industry. Each potential product differs in how it replaces the industry product, and in the degree of threat it represents. There are two factors which affect the threat of substitution:

1 *The relative value/price of a substitute* compared to the industry's product. This is the value perceived by the buyer compared to the price paid. Porter[8] refers to this as RVP. For consumed products with no switching costs, the relevant RVP is only a function of present conditions; future circumstances are not important, as the buyer can easily change between the substitute and the industry product. For durable products, it is the expected RVP which measures the attractiveness of a substitute over time. The value of a substitute can be measured by the lowering of buyer cost, which includes variables like use rate and the cost of using the substitute over its entire life. Value can also be measured by an improvement of buyer performance relative to the industry's product. This includes the number of functions which can be performed with the substitute, and the uncertainty of the substitute being improved in future product generations. For example, a household might have delayed switching to a microwave oven until the second generation of these products was able to roast meat.

2 *Switching costs.* It is understandable that the higher the switching costs the more difficult the substitution. A household will reflect before changing to a gas cooker if the house is not connected to the gas mains. A businessman will calculate the cost of a season ticket to the city against the cost of petrol and parking expenses as the financial cost. Convenience, total travelling time, comfort and the stress/danger of daily driving in the rush hour are other factors to be

considered before the final choice is made. Buyers with different circumstances and in different industries will not all have the same propensity to substitute. Factors affecting the inclination to switch include financial resources, the buyer's individual risk profile, technological awareness and previous experience of substitutions.

The threat of substitution often changes over time. According to Porter,[9] these changes occur in the following areas: relative price, relative value, buyer's perception of value, switching costs, propensity to substitute. These changes in substitution over time occur both in the substitute and in the threatened industry, with the substitute industry on the offensive and the threatened industry on the defensive.

The path of substitution is shaped by how the factors affecting it evolve over time. Some substitutes gain quick acceptance, others never really penetrate. Generally, however, the path of successful substitution is S-shaped when substitution as a percentage of total demand is plotted against time (see Figure 5.4).

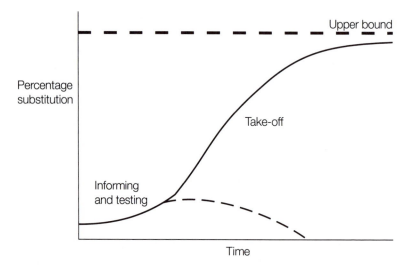

Figure 5.4 A typical S-shaped substitution path *Source*: Porter (1986)

The substitute product, at first little known, open to scepticism from buyers, is used only by a few risk takers who are willing to take the chance, or by those who perceive its potential to be worth a try. As the substitute gains ground and the experience of the first buyers is proved positive the substitute begins to penetrate the market (or, if unsuccessful, peters away).

There are a number of reasons for a rapid rate of penetration by successful substitutes, including:

1 Early success dispels the fear of risk and failure.
2 Successful switching may force new buyers to switch to maintain their cost position or differentiation.
3 Switching costs may decrease.
4 New buyers bring increased awareness and raise credibility.
5 Increased penetration often reduces costs through economies of scale and learning.
6 Introduction of new varieties of substitute product opens up new segments.
7 Increasing penetration prompts more aggressive pricing and marketing as competitors enter the substitute industry.

Buyers' use of the product may also change in such a way as to increase its demand. The RVP improvement offered is most important in determining the length of the testing time – the bigger the inducement, the shorter the testing period is. The time taken for the substitute industry to make necessary improvements and adjustments also affects the testing time.

The force of substitutes is complex, with many factors integrating to give the combined threat many facets. Substitutes may be prominent or difficult to recognise, with buyers playing a central part in their ability to penetrate a market as price sensitivity becomes enhanced.

The threat of substitutes in the world pharmaceutical industry
Substitute products for those of the pharmaceutical industry have been historically weak, but now seem to be growing in force and may develop considerable potency in the future. If substitutes are to be limited to alternative medicine, acupuncture, etc., then the threat within the developed countries is growing but not yet serious. Alternative medicines include such items as anthroposophic medicines and homoeopathic medicines. Their use does often entail a certain lifestyle and assuredly a certain philosophy. An increasing number of people in the Western world are turning to this type of remedy as awareness of environmental conditions, and the 'green movement', grows. Other new users are seen, especially among terminal illness cases, where conventional medicine has not been able to help.

Tradition, too, plays a part. Some countries have shown greater partiality to herbal preparations than others, as for example West Germany, with its special distribution channels for herbal products. In many countries lack of access through a well developed distribution channel prevents these substitutes from exerting any significant force.

For hundreds of years acupuncture has been used in China, where it represents a greater force than in the Western world. Chiropractors, osteopaths, and health farms could be considered by the pharmaceutical industry as a substitute 'rash' in some regions, where they exert a very minor impact, revealing themselves more as a diagnostic indication than as a substitute.

If the term 'substitute' is taken to include generics, then the picture is quite different. Since there are no crippling research and development costs the generics market at considerably less than the branded products. This gives them an immediate advantage, especially with institutional buying. The risk of failure is also minimised, since relevant testing has been carried out by the innovators.

Switching costs are often in favour of the buyer, and may include the following factors:

1 Generic names give the prescriber an indication of the drug's pharmacology.
2 The exclusive use of a single name for a drug reduces possibilities of confusion.
3 Generic names are almost universally used in undergraduate and postgraduate education, and in most medical and scientific journals.
4 Pharmacists could reduce their stocks with general generic prescribing.
5 Drug costs would be reduced.

However, there are also a number of negative (for the buyer group) switching costs, and the factors include:

1 Brand names are often simpler and easier to use.
2 The quality of generics has been claimed to be inferior, although, apart from a few well documented problems, most of the evidence appears anecdotal.
3 Differing appearance may be problematic for some patients.
4 Excipients may differ, and at present there is no requirement that manufacturers publish excipient variations.
5 The source of a generic often cannot be identified once it has been dispensed. With the implementation of product liability legislation, a need will arise for keeping appropriate records.
6 The effects on research, which could be very harmful to patients if cash flow from branded products is reduced by switching to generics.

Without the inclusion of generics, the threat of substitutes is very weak (though growing). As noted above, tradition is the main variable when alternatives to pharmaceuticals are considered for use. The main factors against alternatives are lack of buyer information to exert the necessary buyer force, and lack of adequate distribution channels to reach the market.

With the inclusion of generics as a valid substitute, the picture changes immediately, in line with Porter's[10] dictum:

Substitute products that deserve the most attention are those that:

- are subject to trends improving their price–performance trade-off with the industry's product; or
- are produced by industries earning high profits . . . where they can rapidly come into play if some development increases competition in their industry, and causes price reduction or performance improvement.

The pharmaceutical industry fits on both counts. The first, generics with no innovative costs, have a head start price-wise. Although some maintain that their performance is beneath that of the branded products, nevertheless there is no real feeling of the usual buyer risk associated with substitutes. Secondly the pharmaceutical industry is known to support high profits, and the removal of patent protection provides Porter's development to increase competition.

Switching cost as a determinant force is strong, as the buyer is faced with significantly reduced financial outlay, although some information or other installation costs may be incurred. The RPV is accepted as positive by the large buyer section of governments and hospitals. Since generics are based upon accepted and tested drugs, the element of risk usually associated with substitutes is minimal.

It is the special tiered structure of the buyer segment which now comes into play. Governments, even hospitals, are multi-layered and in the case of generics the layers are not always in constant agreement. This is shown by the difficulty of getting some generic products registered in countries which are also trying to make the cheapest prescribing (which is often generic) mandatory. In hospitals there is the preferred drug list, which the doctors and pharmacists choose for many reasons, cost being only one; and there is the hospital administrator's budget, which may look at a different perspective. Similarly, as noted, there is some resentment from the retail outlets, complaining about reduced profits. Porter's substitute model, therefore, does not apply so well to an industry having a multi-layer buyer segment, each with different priorities and strengths, if the layers are all regarded as the one buyer.

Lastly, there is buyer propensity to substitute. Governments are the first in line by choosing their national drug policy. Not all buying governments choose a generic policy, owing to the multi-layers acting against each other: the Ministry of Health against the Treasury. Given that the first tier shows a propensity to substitute, the second tier (the doctors) may not, as has often been seen to be the case. Here a multitude of reasons can exert an effect, such as laziness in learning a more complicated generic name, true confidence in a special brand, a connection with a pharmaceutical house (perhaps in research, or as a consultant), or just a case of 'old habits die hard'.

In summary, then the, threat of substitutes (excluding generics) is very weak. Even the threat of generics is much modified and weakened by the three-tier structure of buyers. In developed countries the situation may be represented as in Table 5.4.

Table 5.4 The threat of substitute products

In favour of substitutes	In favour of the industry
Switching costs	Low buyer propensity to substitute
RVP	

Intensity of rivalry

Rivalry within an industry can be active or passive, cut-throat, fierce, strong, moderate, slight or polite, existing as a driving force between the industry's firms as they compete for the best positions in the industry's market place.

A competitive move from one firm will result in a response from its nearest rivals. The quickness and strength of the response and method used, or the form which the response takes, are a measure of the intensity of the rivalry present within the industry. According to Porter,[11] the factors influencing rivalry are:

1 *Numerous or equally balanced competitors.* When there are numerous firms in an industry, an active competitor may try to move unnoticed, attempting strategies that would be disregarded in a smaller field. With equally balanced competitors, whether few or numerous, there is a more even distribution of market share, and hence a heightened sense of the need for protection of market share by the various competitors; this can lead to much in-fighting and retaliation. However, where the pecking order of relative strength is more obvious, industry leaders can discipline competition to some extent by using tactics like price leadership.

2 *Slow industry growth.* When firms cannot rely on the progress of industry growth alone for expansion, attention is channelled to expanding market share. This leads to increased volatility and rivalry, and to lower profits.

3 *High fixed storage costs.* The higher the fixed costs, the more the firm will try to improve capacity, but with excess capacity leading to price cutting. Fixed costs in relation to the value added to the product are more important for the firm than fixed costs in relation to the total costs. With products where storage is difficult, 'dumping prices' occur and reduce the industry's profitability.

4 *Lack of differentiation or switching costs.* These factors have been described earlier.

5 *Capacity augmented in large increments.* When augmentation can be only in large increments, the sudden large increases disrupt the industry's balance between supply and demand, resulting in over-capacity and dumping prices.

6 *Diverse competitors.* Where competitors are very diverse in origins, structure, culture, objectives and values they can and will interpret market signals differently. This makes it hard to establish industry rules for competing, and firms continually run head-on into each other, increasing rivalry and decreasing profits. This is especially so when the industry consists of a mix of foreign and domestic firms.

7 *High strategic stakes.* Rivalry is intensified if some firms have a particularly high strategic stake in the industry for reasons of status, technology, market position, etc. It can be a major factor for an inward-investing firm trying to establish itself in what it regards as a key market, e.g. the US, the EC, or Japan.

8 *High exit barriers.* These may consist of one or a number of: specialised assets which can be used only in one particular industry or location; high fixed costs of exit; strategic interrelationships between the business unit in the industry being analysed and the other business units within the same company; emotional barriers, usually based on management values and aspirations; government and social restrictions, particularly job loss effects. These factors can conspire to keep a firm operating within an industry despite making unsatisfactory profits.

If any of these factors affecting the intensity of competition changes, then there will be a corresponding change in rivalry. For example, technological changes can change the level of fixed costs; new cultures introduced by acquisition activity can change the industry culture; and changes in industry growth can have a particularly marked effect. A young industry usually has a high growth rate which slows down as the industry matures; this increases rivalry and leads to a shake-out, leaving only the strongest competitors to reap high returns.

Note that entry and exit barriers, and their combined effect, can also have a very significant effect on industry rivalry. These factors were discussed above and no further comment is needed here, but attention is again drawn to Figure 5.3.

Intensity of rivalry in the world pharmaceutical industry   It was noted in Chapter 1 that the pharmaceutical industry's sales are concentrated in developed countries. Reference to Table 5.5 indicates that this concentration is growing in two of the three major markets (North America and Japan), though Western Europe is still a very major market indeed. In these regions, drug consumption is based on expensive products which are used almost exclusively in the developed world. Also, it will be recalled that the concentration of research-based pharmaceutical firms is very high, with the top 100 firms accounting for about 80 per cent of world drug sales. These firms are based almost entirely in the three major markets noted above. This high concentration, together with the semi-oligopolistic nature of therapeutic sub-markets, tends to reduce rivalry in the industry.

Table 5.5 World consumption of pharmaceuticals by region, ex-Manufacturer Prices

Region	1976	1985	1976	1985	Average growth rate
	(US$ billion)	*(US$ billion)*	%	%	%
N. America	8.761	28.141	20.4	29.9	13.8
W. Europe	13.111	22.000	30.5	23.4	5.9
E. Europe	6.197	9.600	14.4	10.2	5.0
Japan	4.020	14.038	9.3	14.9	14.9
Oceania	0.480	0.700	1.1	0.7	4.3
Latin America	3.689	5.600	8.6	6.0	4.7
Africa	1.268	2.700	2.9	2.9	8.8
Asia *	2.920	6.600	6.8	7.0	9.5
China	2.600	4.700	6.0	5.0	6.8
Total	43.046	94.079	100.0	100.0	9.1

Source: WHO, *The World Drug Situation* (1988)
* Excluding China and Japan

Table 5.5 also indicates the compound growth rate of pharmaceuticals consumption in the period 1976–85. Taking inflation into account, the overall growth rate of 9.1 per cent is not notably high, but attention is drawn to the well above average figures for North America and Japan. This would suggest a lowering of rivalry in these two markets, with perhaps a quickening of the tempo in Western Europe.

Switching costs tend to be substantial, as discussed in a previous section. Product differentiation is also very high, owing to the singularity of therapeutic sectors and the specificity of modern drugs. This is especially so if the active ingredient is such that different formulations and drug administrations are pharmaceutically difficult to achieve or expensive to produce. Often the differences are in the bio-availability of the active substance, a factor which is not visibly obvious, thus creating a need for specialised and expensive personal selling to the appropriate tier of the buyer segment (the doctor). This may explain why the first on the market with a new formulation almost always retains the lion's share of the market. Overall, then, these factors tend to reduce rivalry.

The competitors in the pharmaceutical industry are certainly diverse. The presence of comparatively few but strong multinational subsidiaries in many countries of the world, both developed and developing, can bring new cultures and often misunderstandings to the domestic industries, and often increases the competitive emotions in the local firms.

The physical and economic ease with which bulk pharmaceuticals can be transported has been developed by the major firms to a competitive advantage. It is usual for drugs to be made up into dosage forms in the many worldwide subsidiaries. This gives the added profit of transporting in bulk, the close proximity to the market place and customer, and a better understanding and a closer working relationship with the national legislative authorities, and allows local product variations to be easily incorporated into the manufacturing process. Often, if a local workforce is employed, this results in savings in labour costs.

The very long innovation time and the very small chances of a new chemical entity being successful result in high stakes and intense competition for proprietary products. The attitude of the industry to patents, the abundance of economies of scale in production, and the very high entry barriers all support this. The rush to be the first with a drug, which in this industry is synonymous with a leadership position, is the ultimate factor in rivalry. In the 'me too' generic industry, with smaller firms, the stakes are considerably lower. With smaller, more flexible investments these firms, not financially bound in R & D, are able to change more quickly to meet market demands, their constraints being financial resources or product knowledge.

The very high financial commitments make exit barriers higher than most firms wish to tackle unless forced, thus keeping the competition within the industry longer than is the case where exit barriers are lower.

Summarising the effects of rivalry is rather more difficult than for the other four competitive forces. The major players in the industry, and the industry associations, continuously trumpet the fierce competition in pharmaceuticals; this analysis throws some doubt on rivalry as the source of any such competition. Industry growth is high enough to avoid the worst aspects of rivalry, and much the same could be said for the concentration and balance of firms. Informational complexity militates against extreme rivalry, as does the absence of costly large increments of capacity. Price control by governments prevents dumping, and ethical controls prevent companies encouraging consumers to use up over-capacity by taking unnecessary medicines. The only factors which may increase rivalry in this industry would seem to be the high strategic stakes of involvement and high exit barriers (for major firms). Thus the balance may be visualised as in Table 5.6.

Table 5.6 The intensity of rivalry

Factors increasing rivalry	Factors decreasing rivalry
High strategic stakes	Industry growth
High exit barriers	Industry concentration
	Balance of firms
	Brand identity
	Product differentiation
	Fixed storage costs
	Informational complexity
	Switching costs

The attractiveness of the world pharmaceutical industry

According to Porter[12], the ability of firms in the pharmaceutical industry to earn above-average rates of return is determined by the collective strength of the five competitive forces analysed above. It must also be borne in mind that the strength of any individual force is likely to vary over time, as will the overall attractiveness of the industry as measured by the sum of the five forces. The current and future positions of the world pharmaceutical industry are set out in Table 5.7. This indicates clearly that the industry is, indeed, a highly attractive one and is likely to remain so despite some increase in the bargaining power of buyers and the threat of substitutes. Thus the current high profitability of the industry is likely to persist.

Table 5.7 The attractiveness of the world pharmaceutical industry

Competitive force	Effect on current attractiveness	Effect on future attractiveness
Barriers to entry	•••	•••
Bargaining power of suppliers	••	••
Bargaining power of buyers	••	•
Threat of substitutes	••	•
Intensity of rivalry	••	••

This view is confirmed by revisiting Figure 5.3. Entry barriers to the industry are very high and are rising. Exit barriers are generally fairly low, though the sunk cost of on-going R & D would represent a major exit barrier for a research-intensive drugs multinational. Potential returns in the multinational sector of the industry could, therefore be characterised as high, with a moderate degree of associated risk.

As well as establishing the profit potential of the industry, the foregoing analysis will be an important stage in examining past and future strategies of the drugs firms covered in Chapters 6–8. Having diagnosed the competitive forces, firms must try to establish a defensible position against them. Porter indicates three possibilities:

1 Positioning the firm so that its capabilities provide the best defence against the existing array of competitive forces.
2 Influencing the balance of forces through strategic moves, thereby improving the firm's relative position.
3 Anticipating shifts in the factors underlying the forces and responding to them, thereby exploiting change by choosing a strategy appropriate to the new competitive balance before rivals recognise it.

GENERIC COMPETITIVE STRATEGIES

How are the competitors in an industry going to tackle the competitive situation? What guiding strategies are open to them? Porter[13] has developed the concept of generic strategies for coping with the five competitive forces and attempting to perform ahead of industry norms. These three generic strategies, shown in Figure 5.5, are:

1 Overall cost leadership.
2 Differentiation.
3 Focus.

These strategies can be used singly or in combination to create the defensible position discussed at the end of the previous section.

Overall cost leadership

Leadership through low cost in producing, marketing and selling the goods gives a firm a competitive edge over others in the industry, by enabling it to retain a larger share of the value added to the goods. Such a strategy requires full attention to every stage of the business process, with the emphasis on the cost incorporated at each stage. This type of strategy will base itself on economies of scale, the full use of appropriate technology, product standardisation, with low-cost design and a minimum of service, and the fullest possible use of the experience curve.

Once achieved and the position sustained, cost leadership can give the competitive firm protection in the form of:

1 Above-average returns.
2 Defence against buyers trying to minimise prices.
3 More leeway to cope with increased input prices.
4 Defence against competitors who must use profits in competing.

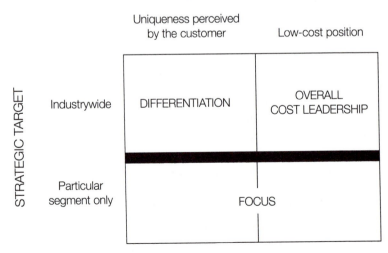

Figure 5.5 Three generic strategies. *Source*: Porter (1980)

Cost leadership often influences the company's culture, with such traits as attention to detail, discipline and frugality; the latter can manifest itself, for example, in spending rates on marketing and research activities, wages paid, training of personnel, specification of raw materials.

Cost leadership is achieved through daily attention to details and the constant implementation of improvements to rationalise. Often this attention is not given to areas where considerable economies can be made, such as:

1 Linkages between integrated functions.
2 Attention to all aspects of the business, including such areas as services, marketing, and the company's infrastructure.

Differentiation

Differentiation, or the extent in which one product differs from a competitor's, thereby creating a competitive gap, is the second major generic strategy which, if attained and sustained, will provide the firm with a competitive advantage.

A company following this strategy will usually veer away from standardisation, unless this can be incorporated into the business without adverse effect on the differentiation strategy. The company seeks out and exposes to the full the advantages incorporated in the difference between its product and those of competitors. Differences can present themselves as service, design, distribution channels, functionality, environmental protection and in a host of other guises. The differentiated firm does not ignore cost, but is willing to invest money in order to produce differentiation, even when the end result is more expensive than that of the competitors. Provided the product is perceived by the buyer to give value for its price, it will be bought.

As with the cost leader strategy, so will a strategy of differentiation colour the firm's culture to a certain extent. Such a firm would be willing to invest in research and would encourage individuality, not only in product design and function, but in distribution methods, marketing, after-sales service, etc. The firm is always on the look-out for methods of promoting the unique advantages of the product for which the buyer is willing to pay the higher price.

Once this position has been attained and held, the successfully differentiated firm achieves a competitive advantage over the others in the industry. This shows itself in the following manner:

1 Uniqueness of product.

2 Brand loyalty.
3 Higher margins, since buyers are prepared to pay a higher price for a specifically valued product.
4 The higher margins provide a buffer against increased input costs.
5 Customer loyalty protects against substitutes.

Since not all buyers will be willing or able to pay the higher price of the product, differentiation implies a smaller market share than cost leadership, but the greater degree of added value retained by the firm ensures profitability.

In the event of a firm being able to provide a differentiated product at a cost leader price, overwhelming success is guaranteed; but these two strategies are almost contradictory in principle and are therefore difficult to marry. However, firms rarely follow one generic strategy cleanly, but usually follow one generally and incorporate those facets from the others that do not harm the main strategy but which can actually enhance the competitive position of their product.

In both these two types of generic strategy the practising firms have targeted their products at a wide segment of the market, basing themselves on volume, either through price or through customer needs.

Focus

With focus as the generic strategy the firm targets itself in on a specific segment with special needs to which it caters exclusively, and not the market generally. By targeting in on a special problem, the focused firm becomes expert or specialist, thereby being able to produce the product more effectively than a competitor, and becoming a focus cost leader; or, by producing a better specialised product, being focus-differentiated.

Special characteristics are associated with focus – specialisation and a small share of the total market – although the individual firm can actually have a very large share of the small specialist segment, which is only a small part of the industry (a niche market). As suggested above, different skills are required for implementing the different strategies, both from the managers and from the workforce; this will result in different corporate cultures within the firms.

Stuck in the middle

A firm successfully competing in its industry is likely to be following a specific generic strategy, even if one modified in certain minor aspects. A firm that is neither cost-aware, nor has a product separating it from that of the competitors, has no competitive advantage with which to fight and is said to be 'stuck in the middle'. This is a position in which unsuccessful firms, losing their competitive edge, find themselves – a sure target for reduced profitability and lost market penetration.

Criticism of the generic strategies

Strategies change over time according to the product life cycle; for example, new products often begin as differentiated products, then go over to being produced by a cost leader as the product life cycle progresses. It is not always easy to judge the stage a product is at in its life cycle. This is due to the producer's incomplete knowledge of the buyer and the way the product is used by the buyer.

Other factors affecting generic strategy are those occurring in the external environment and these can be difficult to forecast or control. In some industries, owing to the nature of the product, there is no room for differentiation – just price manipulation. This is true in the pharmaceutical industry, to a certain extent, with some products. When a new product is successfully launched against a hitherto incurable disease costing enormous sums in both human suffering and social expense, the market cannot afford to haggle over the price. Such is the case of the new Wellcome product Retrovir, used against AIDS. It is alone, as yet, in a socially critical segment of the market and as such the price is very high. Even the strong regulatory control in the pharmaceutical industry has had to accept it. In its defence must be mentioned the innovation costs that have to be recouped.

The choice of which generic strategy to follow will depend on the strengths and weaknesses of the firm, and where the retaliation from the competitors will be least.

SUMMARY

In the evaluation of the remote environment of the world pharmaceutical industry it was seen that economic factors were broadly favourable, though changes in re-imbursement systems could pose significant threats in the future as all types of health agencies impose tighter controls on drug spending. There are potentially serious threats among political factors as government regulation of the industry increases, but this is likely to be mitigated – as it has been in the past – by the well developed relationships between governments and the pharmaceutical industry, both at the level of the individual firm and through the agency of national industry associations. Social factors are also generally positive, though changing lifestyles may cause a move to the less profitable over-the-counter drugs. There is a major threat lurking below the surface: in most developed countries there are a wide range of special interest and pressure groups (e.g. animal rights) whose views are antipathetic to the commercial interests of the drugs industry. They are largely without influence at the present time, but this is an area that the industry must watch carefully. Technology factors are also favourable, particularly since the pharmaceutical industry has developed a deep involvement with the emergent bio-technology via acquisition, joint ventures, strategic alliances, and organic development.

Many aspects of the industry's operating environment suggest opportunity rather than threat: competition is well regulated; good relations exist with customers, suppliers and creditors; and labour relations are generally good. Similarly, the five competitive forces in the industry analysis are quite positive for drug firms. Entry barriers are high and are likely to remain so; exit barriers are, with one exception, low. So we should expect high returns with a moderate degree of risk, and this is indeed typical of the pharmaceutical industry. While it may be subject to pressure on a number of points, it remains in a favourable position relative to the other competitive forces; suppliers are weak, buyers are not yet powerful and there are few meaningful substitutes. Therefore, the present pressures are not strong, but prob-lems could obviously be posed if they develop further. This could be counterbalanced by the confident expectation of future demand growth, ensuring that industry profits remain healthy, albeit not as high as has been the case in the past. The world pharmaceutical industry therefore remains an attractive one.

Regarding the generic strategies that are open to the industry, it must be borne in mind that the major pharmaceutical firms are characterised as follows:

1 Large, high-technology, multinational organisations.
2 Compete in world markets across the main therapeutic categories.
3 Intensive R & D strategies to ensure future product development and high profit margins.
4 Highly efficient, to ensure high profit returns in the short period of patent protection.
5 Strong brand image.

Considering the three generic strategies of overall cost leadership, differentiation and focus, it is not likely that all pharmaceutical firms will fall neatly into the one category. Rather, there will be a spread of philosophies, with many companies adopting more than one strategy. Certain generic-based companies could be classified in the general arena of cost leadership, while firms with market-leading drugs are able to command premium prices and so adopt a differentiation approach.

6 The United States pharmaceutical market

The pharmaceutical industry in the US is an important growth industry and represents a significant asset to the nation by virtue of its contribution to health care, its provision of alternative employment opportunities, and its strong and growing positive balance of payments. However, more than most other industries, pharmaceuticals attract considerable public examination and, indeed, controversy. In the US, ethical drugs are advertised only to the medical profession and are available for consumption by the public only if supplied by a pharmacist authorised by a doctor's prescription.

Evidence from a number of previous studies on the US pharmaceutical industry suggests that, of all the influences which act upon its structure, the most important is the increasing significance of advantages of scale in marketing, R&D, and production. Clearly, this favours the larger firms and provides substantial obstacles to would-be entrants. These advantages of scale apply not only to actual reduction of unit costs but also, in a broader sense, they allow companies to reduce the high risks associated with R & D and marketing in the advanced technology sector of the industry.

THE MARKET

In its annual report for 1990, Glaxo estimated the US market in 1989 at £23,000 million, an increase of 15 per cent over 1988. This represented the highest growth rate of any country in the developed world, thus emphasising the place of the US as a strategically important market. In terms of share of the world market, the US increased from 28 per cent to 29 per cent over the same period. In terms of retail pharmacy sales, Merck is by far the largest firm in the US (see Table 6.1), and has increased its revenues by 42 per cent since 1983. The next firm, SmithKline, has actually lost 3 per cent of its revenues since 1983;

when inflation is taken into account, this represents a serious loss of volume indeed – one factor which may have led to the 1989 merger with Beecham. Of the firms which were represented in the top ten in both 1983 and 1988, pride of place must go to Lilly, which has increased its sales by a massive 85 per cent. Three of the firms which have entered the top ten since 1983 – Glaxo, Marion, and Syntex – have been powered into position by individual high-selling drugs; Zantac in the case of Glaxo, Naprosyn for Syntex, and Cardizem for Marion. The four firms which have fallen out of the top ten since 1983 are Roche, Ayerst, Parke-Davis and Squibb.

Table 6.1 The top ten US companies in terms of retail pharmacy sales in 1988

Company	1988 sales ($ million)	1983 sales ($ million)	% change
Merck	1,400	983	+42
SmithKline	683	705	– 3
Upjohn	681	472	+44
Pfizer	658	622	+ 6
Glaxo	655	N/A	
Lilly	611	330	+85
Wyeth	567	427	+33
Marion	534	N/A	
Syntex	531	N/A	
Rugby	486	N/A	

Source: *Scrip Yearbook* 1990 and 1985

According to Pharmaceutical Data Services, the top ten drugs dispensed in the US in 1988 were:

1 Amoxil (amoxicillin, Beecham).
2 Lanoxin (digoxin, Wellcome).
3 Xanax (alprazolam, Upjohn).
4 Zantac (ranitidine, Glaxo).
5 Premarin (conjugated oestrogens, Wyeth-Ayerst).
6 Dyazide (triamterene + HCTZ, SK & F).
7 Tagamet (cimetidine, SmithKline).
8 Tenormin (atenolol, ICI).
9 Naprosyn (naproxen, Syntex).
10 Cardizem (diltiazem, Marion).

Two interesting points emerge from this: six of these drugs are manufactured by British-owned firms, and the largest US firm (Merck) does not figure in the list.

A major growth area in the US market is in drugs for the elderly, or for diseases that primarily affect the elderly. The Pharmaceutical Manufacturers Association estimated that there were 259 pharmaceutical products in the course of clinical trials in 1989 pertaining to such diseases. The forecast R & D bill in the US for research into these areas was $3,600 million, just under half the total industry estimated R & D spend for 1989. Of this total, about 50 per cent ($1,700 million) was directed at the chief cause of death among the elderly – cardiovascular diseases. Another curse of the ageing population – Alzheimer's disease – is also the subject of intensive research activity. In 1988, eleven companies had sixteen products under development for this indication. Whether this focusing of effort on the elderly section of the population is an effect of moral and ethical judgements by pharmaceutical firms, or whether it is merely due to the recognition of the rapidly rising spending power of senior citizens, remains to be seen.

New products

As noted earlier, increasing competitiveness is driving up R & D expenditure in an increasingly intense hunt for new chemical entities. However, for the industry as a whole, the bad news is that the number of new chemical entities introduced into their first markets in 1989 fell to thirty-five from a worldwide total of fifty-three in 1988.[1] The record of new chemical entity introduction over the last five years is shown in Table 6.2. This represents an average of fifty-one per year, so the 1989 performance represents a significant reduction on both the previous year's total and the overall average. In explanation, the suggestion has been made[2] that an increase in the proportion of total R & D resources devoted to biotechnology and genetically engineered products is the basic reason for the slow-down, as this type of new chemical entity moves more slowly through the different development stages than traditionally developed drugs. Of these thirty-five new entity chemicals, four were introduced in the US (though only one by a US-owned

Table 6.2 New chemical entities put on the US market, 1985–89

Year	No.
1985	57
1986	47
1987	61
1988	53
1989	35

firm) as opposed to twelve in Japan (eleven by Japanese firms). Five US-owned firms introduced a total of six new chemical entities in 1989; pride of place went to Merrell Dow with two new chemical entities (Perfan and Sabril).

It may be that the record for new chemical entities of US firms is about to move on an upward path again[3] with the following introductions being imminent:

1 Neubogen, an anti-cancer drug from Amgen.
2 Videx, an anti-AIDS drug from Bristol-Myers/Squibb.
3 Cognex, a CNS drug from Warner Lambert, a potential Alzheimer's therapy.
4 Ketorolac, a non-narcotic intramuscular from Syntex.
5 Clarithomycin, a broad-spectrum antibiotic from Abbott (Klaricid, licensed from Taisho).
6 Milrinone, a cardiostimulant from Sterling Drug.

Information needs

Of course, the increasing R & D expenditures and the concomitant rise in levels of competitiveness has had a direct effect on the size of US field sales forces in recent years. With the need to achieve fast and deep penetration with new product introductions, and the corresponding need for more frequent face-to-face communication with prescribing doctors, Pfizer[4] has noted the following major increases in sales forces for the years 1982–88:

Glaxo	+955	ICI	+395
Squibb	+423	Marion	+370
Roche	+406	Lilly	+329
Bayer	+404	SmithKline	+320
Merck	+395	Beecham	+279

Note that nearly 60 per cent of the total increase in this sample is accounted for by foreign subsidiaries operating in the US.

A final point may be observed here that flows from the general rise in competitiveness, and perhaps more specifically from the need for US generics firms to try to keep some kind of competitive edge as major branded products go out of patent. It may be that the effect of this, and the ever-increasing government-sponsored pressure on expenditure on drugs, has led to a degree of confusion among the public. Table 6.3 shows the results of a survey to determine what sources of information on prescription drugs are used in the US. Two factors are immediately obvious from this analysis: first, there has been a very large increase in dependence on health professionals, though public media are also playing a significant part; second, while each respondent in 1986 used (on average) 1.24 sources of information, by 1989 this had risen to 2.44. It is likely that this virtual doubling of the information requirement reflects the growing anxiety referred to above.

Table 6.3 Sources of information on prescription drugs in the US, 1986–89 (%)

Source	1986	1987	1989
Doctors	49	62	81
Pharmacists	32	29	53
Magazines	22	14	32
Television	8	5	29
Newspapers	7	7	25
Physician's Desk Reference	16	11	22
Other drug texts	10	6	2

Source: Scott-Levin Associates, quoted in *Scrip* 1476/7, p. 24

Industry analysis

A general industry analysis was carried out in Chapter 5; the purpose of this section is to note any differences in the strength of the five competitive forces as they act within the US market as compared to the global industry, and to evaluate the effect of any such differences. In the case of three of the competitive forces, no differences are discernible. These are: pressure from substitute products, bargaining power of buyers, and bargaining power of suppliers.

Because the US is both the largest and the best developed individual country market within the world pharmaceutical industry, it is virtually inevitable that barriers to entry will be higher than the norm. Patent protection is perhaps at its strongest in the US, where a very high value is placed on the protection of intellectual property rights. Economics of scale also act as important and high barriers to entry. The need for increasing R & D investments has already been referred to above; the full R & D bill for an new chemical entity in the US may now be in the region of $125 million to $150 million and thus represents a huge barrier to new entrants, even without considering the need to find and employ the high-level skills required. Much the same argument relates to economies of scale in quality assurance. Product differentiation leads directly to significant economies of scale in marketing activities, and this was touched on in the previous section in relation to field sales forces. Since the need for product differentiation is at its highest in such a well developed market, this also leads to a differential effect on entry barriers compared to the world market.

The well developed nature of the US market also has a significant effect on rivalry between the individual pharmaceutical firms. Successful product differentiation means that price competition is virtually absent in the branded segment of the market, though the use of generics could clearly have a significant effect here. Similarly, promotional techniques are aimed primarily at providing essential information to doctors rather than producing increased rivalry. Again, in such a well developed economy, such information parameters are likely to have a differential (reducing) effect on rivalry compared to the global industry.

In summary, with three of the competitive forces being similar to world levels, entry barriers being higher and rivalry lower, it is likely that the US industry will be more attractive than the global industry in general, and will therefore be more profitable for participants.

Opportunities and threats

These are the environmental factors which act on every firm in the industry; they are driven by economic, social, legal, political and technological forces. However, the strategic impact of these forces on any one company is likely to be somewhat different from that on any other, owing to the specific nature of the firm's internal make-up.

The opportunities facing the American pharmaceutical industry over the next few years are summarised below.

1 Within established markets demand for pharmaceutical products will continue to grow, with some therapeutic areas expanding at the rate of 25 per cent plus per annum.
2 The ageing population in most OECD countries is creating demand in a number of therapeutic areas which are underdeveloped.
3 Extended patent life, if and when implemented by the EC, will create significant revenue-earning opportunities by delaying the onslaught of generic competition.
4 The opening of new markets in Eastern Europe and the Pacific Rim will provide opportunities for significant long-term growth.
5 Advances in biotechnology could prove to be the source of many new drugs.
6 The over-the-counter market is expanding and is expected to grow significantly in the future, but it is regarded as being underdeveloped, particularly outwith the US.

7 When the proposed 1992 changes in the EC actually take place, this should allow rationalisation of manufacturing operations, resulting in substantial cost savings. Likewise one EC-wide licensing authority would also result in significant savings.

Short to medium-term threats which will pose strategic problems for the US industry are given below.

1 The desire of major drug buyers to reduce expenditure on drugs is resulting in downward pressure on prices.
2 Connected with the above, the rise of generic drug companies will be a continuing problem.
3 Increased governmental regulation will result in greater difficulty in having drugs approved, particularly 'me too' pharmaceuticals.
4 The effects of 1992 legislation in the EC will result, eventually, in the loss of preferential price structures.
5 Industry consolidation is creating more large players of roughly equal size, leading to increased competition.
6 Changing attitudes could have a number of effects in terms of the type of treatment people seek, any of which could affect ethical drug consumption.
7 Attitudes (e.g. backlash against animal testing) allied to demographic factors may result in fewer science graduates being produced by universities.
8 Biotechnology is also a threat in that a breakthrough could also lower one of the key barriers to entry into the industry.

In general, despite the problems facing the industry, the outlook for the future is favourable, with opportunities more than countering threats. To assess this and other pointers drawn above, the remainder of this chapter consists of a detailed analysis of three major US pharmaceutical firms: Merck, Abbott and Pfizer.

MERCK & CO. INC.

Company history and development

The firm originated from the German company known as E. Merck, founded by Heinrich Merck, which was involved in the pioneering and production of cocaine and morphine at the beginning of the nineteenth century. At the turn of the century Merck's grandson George established the US branch, Merck & Co., which expanded quickly. After 1918, business contacts with E. Merck in Germany were quickly terminated. Merck & Co. became a wholly American company and George Merck, followed by his son, was to build the pharmaceutical business into the basis of today's firm. In 1953 Merck merged with Sharp & Dohme, a British pharmaceutical company, to become Merck Sharp & Dohme – the amalgamation of two long-established and distinguished firms. Today Merck is the world's largest pharmaceutical firm and has its headquarters at Rahway, New Jersey.

Merck has followed a strategy based on innovation, with a continuous stream of new products more than compensating for sales losses incurred as mature products go off patent. Merck's own R & D efforts have been enhanced by trading existing products for new ideas. This innovation strategy has been supported by a range of licensing agreements and joint ventures. One of the most recent, and in many ways a milestone for Merck, was the setting up of a joint venture with Johnson & Johnson in the over-the-counter market. Having acquired the over-the-counter business of ICI (Americas), the joint venture company now ranks as fourteenth largest in the expanding American over-the-counter market.

Mission statement

Merck & Co. is a worldwide research-intensive health products company that discovers, develops, produces and markets human and animal health products, together with speciality chemicals.

It aims to supply products of the highest quality to its customers through the use of the most modern techniques in research, by using the most efficient manufacturing techniques and by providing balanced information about the safety and effectiveness of those products.

Merck aims to be a premier growth company whose performance in sales and income growth and return on invested capital will rank among the best in the United States, allowing the company to achieve its goal of enhancing shareholder wealth.

In order to achieve this success Merck must recruit and retain personnel of the highest calibre. The firm therefore seeks to recruit from those institutions with the best reputations in the fields most appropriate to its business, ensuring a continual stream of fresh talent into the company. To ensure that its personnel can operate effectively in an increasingly competitive environment Merck, through extensive training programmes, encourages personal development in a range of areas and at all levels. Merck is an equal opportunities employer interested in all talented employees irrespective of sex, colour, creed or disability.

As a major US company, Merck appreciates its public duty and therefore seeks to operate for the benefit of the communities in which it operates. Through promotion of scientific facilities within schools and universities Merck hopes to ensure that suitably qualified scientists can be produced to assist in the continued improvement of human and animal health. Through continually seeking to improve production and safety standards Merck aims to protect the environment from the effects of pollution and ensure safe working conditions for employees.

Merck, as a company, has always been driven by the challenge of unconquered diseases. Responding to that challenge affords Merck the single best way of meeting its obligations to patients, employees and other stakeholders, the interests of whom must be balanced against the goal of enhancing shareholder wealth.

Objectives

To maintain the very satisfactory progress of the last ten years, and to continue the momentum towards achievement of its mission, Merck will be looking to achieve a wide range of long term objectives. Among these are likely to be the following:

1 *Profitability*: to maintain a return of 20 per cent on total assets.
2 *Productivity*: in R & D, to reduce average development time by 10 per cent over the next five years; in production, to maintain productivity improvements while achieving a 90 per cent reduction in emission of chemicals over the next five years.
3 *Competitive position*: to remain the world's largest ethical drugs company; in animal health-care, to move from fourth largest to largest in the world rankings.
4 *Employee development*: to increase the number of personnel attending training courses each year by 10 per cent.
5 *Employee relations*: to seek continual improvement in safety programmes for employees.
6 *Technological leadership*: to utilise the best available technology at all times in order to enhance performance.
7 *Public responsibility*: to seek to improve the image of the company and the industry by philanthropic donations to charitable and educational causes.
8 *Shareholders*: to continue to enhance stockholder value at a rate that underlines the position of Merck stock as a key element of individual and institutional portfolios.

Business segments

Merck's business is divided into two segments – human and animal health products, and speciality chemicals and environmental products. The health products segment includes therapeutic and preventive agents, generally sold by prescription, for the treatment of human disorders as well as other products for human consumption. Among these are antihypertensive and cardiovascular products, of which Aldomet is the largest; anti-inflammatory products, of which Indocin and Clinoril are the major lines; antibiotics, of which Mefoxin is the largest; and ophthalmologicals, of which Timoptic is the best seller. Animal medicines include products used for the control and alleviation of disease in stock and poultry, as well as other products for animal consumption. The latter include the therapeutic classes of vaccines and other biologicals and psychotherapeutics. Prescription drug products are promoted by approximately 6,400 professional service employees throughout the world. Sales of prescription drug products are made primarily to drug wholesalers and retailers, physicians, veterinarians, hospitals, clinics and other institutions. Customers for other health products include distributors, wholesalers, retailers, feed manufacturers, veterinary suppliers and laboratories.

Speciality chemical and environmental products include granular activated carbon and water-saving equipment such as cooling towers, evaporative condensers, and closed-circuit fluid coolers for industrial, commercial and other large cooling, air-conditioning, and refrigeration applications. The company also sells speciality chemical products for a wide variety of applications such as use in water treatment, in the manufacture of paints and paper, in oilfields, in food additives, and in cleaning products. In addition, it manufactures and sells centrifugal pumps for a variety of uses. Sales of products and services are made in channels of trade including distributors, wholesalers, manufacturers, contractors, municipalities, utilities and other industrial users. Environmental water-saving products are sold primarily through independent manufacturers' representatives.

The total number of employees has increased by some 11 per cent since 1985, as follows:

1985	30,900
1986	30,700
1987	31,100
1988	32,000
1989	34,400

Employment with the company is highly prized; in 1989 the Merck Sharp & Dohme sales force was increased by 800, and applications for these new professional representative opportunities totalled some 60,000. Training at all levels is being increased regularly, with a particular target of strengthening the programmes for key executive development and succession in all international subsidiaries. Merck's status as an equal opportunities employer is emphasised by the fact that out of 3,032 new US employees in 1989, 53 per cent were female and 19 per cent were from minority communities.

Financial analysis

Geographical spread

An analysis of the geographical spread of the firm's activities over the last ten years is shown in Table 6.4. This shows that Merck's sales have been concentrated in developed markets, and that this concentration is growing over time. In 1980, 50 per cent of sales were made in the US, and 39 per cent in other OECD countries, with the remaining 10 per cent being accounted for by all other regions of the world. By 1989, this

Table 6.4 Merck geographical spread

Measure	1980	1985	1986	1987	1988	1989
Customer sales ($ million)						
Domestic	1,380.4	1,958.9	2,104.9	2,500.2	2,996.1	3,487.0
OECD	1,079.1	1,357.1	1,811.1	2,329.1	2,772.1	2,901.3
Other	274.5	231.5	212.9	232.0	171.3	162.2
Pretax profit ($ million)						
Domestic	374.2	645.0	656.4	851.9	1,089.5	1,557.6
OECD	256.3	197.2	387.5	579.6	759.0	722.4
Other	22.0	16.7	−5.0	−8.3	−2.1	−12.8
Identifiable assets ($ million)						
Domestic	1,530.3	2,120.2	2,263.6	2,404.2	2,614.9	3,150.6
OECD	929.0	1,539.3	1,612.0	1,933.0	1,735.0	2,028.1
Other	248.0	251.8	245.9	194.5	142.5	118.0
Return on sales (%)						
Domestic	27.1	32.9	31.2	34.1	36.4	44.7
OECD	23.8	14.5	21.4	24.9	27.4	24.9
Other	8.0	7.2	−2.3	−3.6	−1.2	−7.9
Return on assets (%)						
Domestic	24.5	30.4	29.0	35.4	41.7	49.4
OECD	27.6	12.8	24.0	30.0	43.7	35.6
Other	8.9	6.6	−2.0	−4.3	−1.5	−10.8

Source: Merck annual reports

last figure had fallen to only 2 per cent, which represents a virtual retreat from the developing world on the part of Merck. However, it should be noted that Merck has recently been given much public credit for its action in giving away ivermectin to 250,000 people in Central Africa afflicted by river blindness, an often disastrous tropical disease caused by parasite attack. Even in current dollar terms, sales to this segment had dropped by almost half. Over the same period, domestic sales have advanced to 53 per cent of the total and OECD sales to 44 per cent. Thus, the firm's domestic orientation has increased somewhat during the 1980s (see Figure 6.1).

This trend is reflected in the figures for identifiable assets in the three geographical segments, but is much more pronounced in the case of pre-tax profits. Here, the domestic proportion has increased from 57 per cent of the total in 1980 to nearly 70 per cent in 1989, while the OECD

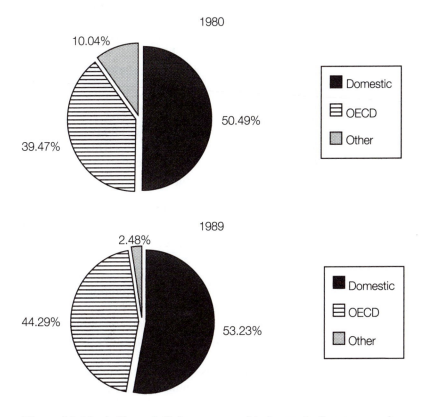

Figure 6.1 Merck Sharp & Dohme: geographical spread of customer sales, 1980 and 1989 (%) *Source*: Merck annual reports

proportion has dropped from 39 per cent to 32 per cent, and 'other' has gone from 3 per cent to a negative figure in 1989.

The data in Table 6.4 have also been reworked to give calculations of 'return on sales' (pre-tax profits to sales), 'return on assets' (pre-tax profits to identifiable assets) and 'asset turnover' (sales to identifiable assets). While great care should be exercised in interpreting these figures (especially with assets), they do give a broad measure of the efficiency of operations in the various geographical sectors. Thus, it can be seen that profitability on domestic sales has moved ahead strongly over the decade, with stability in the OECD countries and a move into the red in 'other'. The domestic return on assets has moved ahead even more strongly, with a good increase in OECD countries. Asset turnover has moved ahead in all sectors, with perhaps the best improvement in 'other'.

Overall, this analysis suggests a strategy of moving away from markets in less developed countries, positive moves to increase profitability in the favoured geographical sectors, acceptance of the US as the most important single market, and a determination to manage assets as efficiently as possible even where profitability is disappointing.

Results by segment of activity

For reporting purposes, Merck divides its turnover into two segments: human and animal health, and speciality chemicals. This analysis is shown in Table 6.5. This breakdown is not particularly helpful, as the health products make up a very large proportion of Merck's business. However, the table does show that the concentration on health products has increased from 84 per cent of all sales in 1980 to 92 per cent in 1989, while the proportion of pre-tax profits accounted for by the health segment moved from 93 per cent to 97 per cent. The return on sales is much better in health products (1989: 35.6 per cent) than on speciality chemicals (1989: 12.0 per cent), though both have shown satisfactory increases over the decade. Health products have moved ahead very strongly in return on assets, from 30 per cent in 1980 to 50 per cent in 1989, a very high figure indeed. Asset turnover has shown a good increase in health products, but has fallen significantly in speciality chemicals.

Fortunately, Merck also provides in its annual report a further breakdown of sales in the human and animal health sector, and this is shown in Table 6.6. Here, the full ten-year analysis is not possible because, from time to time, a newly identified product group is separated out of the 'other human health' category and shown as a

Table 6.5 Merck segment analysis

Measure	1980	1985	1986	1987	1988	1989
Customer sales ($ million)						
Human/animal health	2,286.5	3,097.1	3,770.0	4,630.2	5,473.4	6,058.1
Speciality chemical/ environmental	447.5	450.4	358.9	431.1	466.1	492.4
Pretax profit ($ million)						
Human/animal health	607.2	794.2	995.5	1,314.7	1,806.2	2,155.8
Speciality chemical/ environmental	43.5	58.4	50.0	57.7	61.5	59.3
Identifiable assets ($ million)						
Human/animal health	2,055.8	3,168.6	3,253.6	3,558.6	3,618.3	4,249.6
Speciality chemical/ environmental	383.8	369.2	430.6	429.4	426.0	470.0
Return on sales (%)						
Human/animal health	26.6	25.6	26.4	28.4	33.0	35.6
Speciality chemical/ environmental	9.7	13.0	13.9	13.4	13.2	12.0
Return on assets (%)						
Human/animal health	29.5	25.1	30.6	36.9	49.9	50.7
Speciality chemical/ environmental	11.3	15.8	11.6	13.4	14.4	12.6

Source: Merck annual reports

separate item; thus, antibiotics and ophthalmologicals in 1982, vaccines/biologicals in 1985, and anti-ulcerants in 1987.

However, some interesting points are immediately obvious. Over the decade, the make-up of the firm's sales in this sector has changed substantially. Antihypertensives and cardiovasculars have increased from 29 per cent of total sales to 40 per cent, thus becoming a sector of great strategic importance to Merck. At the same time, another sub-sector has declined markedly in overall importance: anti-inflammatories and analgesics, from 22 per cent to 10 per cent. Ophthalmologicals have also been losing ground, and vaccines/biologicals have been stable in terms of proportion of sales. Other bright sub-sectors have been antibiotics, animal health, and anti-ulcerants; all these (particularly the last) have had above-average sales growth compared to the sector as a whole (see Figure 6.2).

As in the previous section, this analysis suggests clear strategic intent on the part of Merck in concentrating on the human/animal health sector for increases in profitability and return on assets. Within this sector, the antihypertensives and cardiovasculars sector is clearly seen as being of key strategic importance; antibiotics, and animal health are also important growth sectors; anti-ulcerants seem to be one of

Table 6.6 Merck sub-segment analysis – human/animal health

Sales ($ million)	1980	1985	1986	1987	1988	1989
Antihypertensives and cardiovasculars	621.0	744.0	964.6	1,339.3	1,869.9	2,401.1
Antibiotics		452.3	576.8	692.2	800.2	791.1
Anti-inflammatories and analgesics	577.0	656.1	738.6	793.0	754.0	636.1
Anti-ulcerants				163.4	284.8	388.0
Ophthalmologicals		263.2	290.3	319.4	346.9	364.0
Vaccines/biologicals		135.9	165.6	201.7	217.9	271.1
Other human health	768.0	573.0	705.2	618.4	596.6	554.1
Animal health/agricultural	193.0	272.6	328.9	502.8	603.1	652.6

Sales (%)	1980	1985	1986	1987	1988	1989
Antihypertensives and cardiovasculars	29	24	26	29	34	40
Antibiotics		15	15	15	15	13
Anti-inflammatories and analgesics	27	21	20	17	14	10
Anti-ulcerants				4	5	6
Ophthalmologicals		8	8	7	6	6
Vaccines/biologicals		4	4	4	4	4
Other human health	36	19	19	13	11	9
Animal health/agricultural	9	9	9	11	11	11

Source: Merck Annual Reports

tomorrow's breadwinners; ophthalmologicals and vaccines/biologicals are in the 'cash cow' category.

Financial performance

Merck is not only the biggest pharmaceutical company in the world, it is also one of the best managed and controlled. This ability to develop the firm rapidly within fairly tight guidelines was suggested by the various analyses in the previous two sections, and it is amply confirmed by even a cursory glance at the company's ten-year financial record (see Table 6.7). Over the period, dollar sales have grown at a compound rate of 10 per cent per annum. Compared to this, marketing and administration expenses have grown at 11 per cent and R & D expenditure at 14 per cent. Thus, the compound growth of net profits after tax of 15 per cent is due almost entirely to the fact that materials and production costs have grown at the exceptionally low rate of 4 per cent per annum. This really does represent a triumph of management control and, linked to the fact that the number of employees has grown

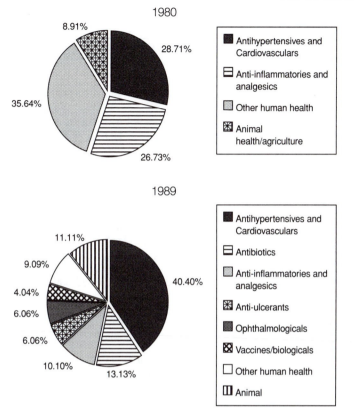

Figure 6.2 Merck Sharp & Dohme: sub-segment analysis, 1980 and 1989 (%)
Source: Merck annual reports

at only 1 per cent per annum, represents continuing major productivity gains for Merck. This has allowed net profits after tax to grow at 15 per cent per annum and dividends declared at 16 per cent per annum. This is illustrated in Figure 6.3.

A similar level of tight control has been maintained on working capital (growth rate: 7 per cent per annum) and growth in capital expenditure has been maintained at an average of 6 per cent per annum while long-term debt has actually fallen by 6% per annum over the decade, causing a reduction in the gearing ratio from 11.5 per cent to 3.3 per cent. Owing to Merck's multi-billion-dollar stock repurchase scheme, the growth of shareholders' equity has been limited to 7 per cent per annum and thus the return on shareholders' equity has increased from 23 per cent per annum in 1980 to 42 per cent per annum in 1989.

Table 6.7 Merck financial performance ($ million)

Measure	1980	1985	1986	1987	1988	1989
Sales	2,734.0	3,547.5	4,128.9	5,061.3	5,939.5	6,550.5
Materials and production costs	1,078.4	1,272.4	1,338.0	1,444.3	1,526.1	1,550.3
Marketing/administrative expenses	762.7	1,009.0	1,269.9	1,682.1	1,877.8	2,013.4
R & D	233.9	426.3	479.8	565.7	668.8	750.5
Net profit after tax	415.4	539.9	675.7	906.4	1,206.8	1,495.4
Dividends declared	178.1	235.1	278.5	365.2	546.3	681.5
Capital expenditures	256.5	237.6	210.6	253.7	372.7	433.0
Working capital	847.1	1,106.6	1,094.3	798.3	1,480.3	1,502.5
Fixed assets	1,185.2	1,882.8	1,906.2	1,948.0	2,070.7	2,292.5
Total assets	2,907.7	4,902.2	5,105.2	5,680.0	6,127.5	6,756.7
Long-term debt	211.4	170.8	167.5	167.4	142.8	117.8
Shareholders' equity	1,841.6	2,607.7	2,541.2	2,116.7	2,855.8	3,520.6
Number of employees	31,600	30,900	30,700	31,100	32,000	34,400
As % of sales						
Materials and production costs	39.4	35.9	32.4	28.5	25.7	23.7
Marketing/administrative expenses	27.9	28.4	30.8	33.2	31.6	30.7
R & D expenses	8.6	12.0	11.6	11.2	11.3	11.5
Net profit after tax	15.2	15.2	16.4	17.9	20.3	22.8
Dividends declared	6.5	6.6	6.7	7.2	9.2	10.4
As % of net profit after tax						
R & D expenditures	56.3	79.0	71.0	62.4	55.4	50.2
Dividends declared	42.9	43.5	41.2	40.3	45.3	45.6
Capital expenditures	61.7	44.0	31.2	28.0	30.9	29.0
Per employee						
Sales	86,519	114,806	134,492	162,743	185,609	19,042
Net profit after tax	13,146	17,472	22,010	29,145	37,713	43,471
Dividends declared	5,636	7,608	9,072	11,743	17,072	19,811
Capital expenditure	8,117	7,689	6,860	8,158	11,647	12,587
Working capital	26,807	35,812	35,645	25,669	46,259	43,677
Fixed capital	37,506	60,932	62,091	62,637	64,709	66,642
Total assets	92,016	158,647	166,293	182,637	191,484	196,416
Gearing ratio (%)	11.5	6.5	6.6	7.9	5.0	3.3
Return on shareholders' equity (%)	23	21	27	43	42	42

Source: Merck annual reports

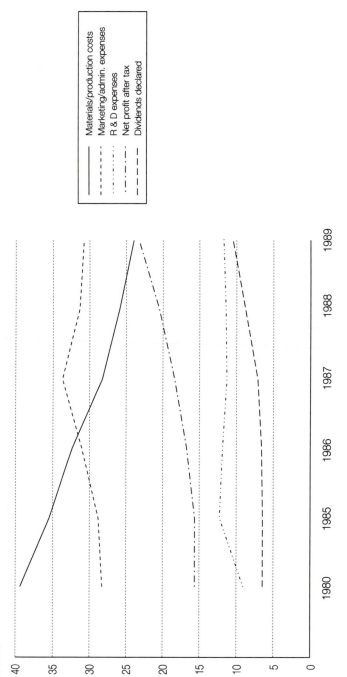

Per cent

Legend
—— Materials/production costs
- - - - Marketing/admin. expenses
········· R & D expenses
—·—·— Net profit after tax
– – – Dividends declared

Figure 6.3 Merck Sharp & Dohme: financial performance (as a percentage of sales), 1980 and 1988–9 *Source*: Merck annual reports

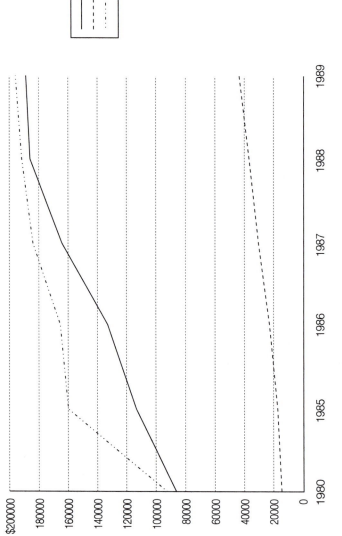

Figure 6.4 Merck Sharp & Dohme: productivity ($ per employee) *Source:* Merck annual reports

A breakdown of the firm's productivity record is also given in Table 6.7. While sales per employee have increased at a compound rate of 9 per cent over the decade, net profit after tax has increased at 14 per cent, a very satisfactory differential. The various asset productivity rates shown again demonstrate the tight management control within Merck, and the low rates of growth here suggest that the asset turnover rates are all satisfactory. The movement of some of these productivity variables is shown in Figure 6.4.

Perhaps the best way to summarise the results of Merck's exceptional management control of its functions and operations is to quote from Chairman Roy P. Vagelos's annual statement to stockholders for 1989, which, if anything, understates the position:[5]

> Broader worldwide acceptance of new products was the key to our fourth consecutive year of rapid growth. Earnings per share were $3.78, up 24% over 1988; net income was $1.5 billion, up 24%; and sales were $6.6 billion, up 10%.
>
> Our goal of *enhancing shareholder value* was well served by continued growth in earnings, which permitted two dividend increases in 1989 for a total payout of $1.64 per share, up 28%.
>
> In addition, we have sought to benefit stockholders by purchases of Merck stock for the Company treasury. Over the five years 1985–89, we purchased 47.6 million shares – 11% of the shares outstanding – and we are currently in the second year of a multi-year, billion-dollar purchase program. Over the last five years, increases in the market price of Merck stock – plus dividends – have provided stockholders with a total return on investment of 427%.

Thus, the company's pedigree and financial record are such that there is no reasonable diversification unavailable to it. However, the perceived strategy over the last ten years suggests that tight focus and 'sticking to the knitting' are in vogue at Merck. The firm is capable of raising a very large amount of capital by the sale of its treasury holding of its own stock, together with increasing its exceptionally low gearing rates and for issuing new stock. So Merck has the ability, and the track record, to support a bid for any pharmaceutical company that it wishes to go for, with very little regard for its size.

Activities

Products

Of the world's fifty top-selling drugs, Merck is responsible for six and there are eighteen Merck products in 10 separate therapeutic areas each of which sells more than $100 million annually. The firm's main therapeutic area is cardiovascular drugs which account for 37 per cent of sales revenue, although this is dominated by two main drugs, Vasotec and Mevocor. In addition, three other cardiovascular drugs have reached or exceeded the magic $100 million annual sales figure. The eighteen blockbusters are:

1 Vasotec is Merck's first billion-dollar seller; it is an angiotensin-converting enzyme (ACE) inhibitor for reducing high blood pressure and relieving congestive heart failure. It is claimed to be the only drug in its class that is proved to reduce mortality in cases of severe heart failure. Vasotec is the leading branded product in the US antihypertensive market in terms of both prescription numbers and purchases.

2 Mevacor is Merck's main cholesterol-lowering agent and is thought to be the world market leader in its field. It works in the liver to reduce the production of cholesterol by the patient. It was introduced in 1987 and was selling well in over thirty countries within two years. It broke the $1 billion annual sales barrier in 1991.

3 Moduretic is a high blood pressure drug whose patent in the US was recently successfully challenged by generic manufacturers. Because of this, and owing to its life cycle stage, it is likely that sales will dip under the $100 million mark in 1991–92.

4 Aldomet was Merck's best-selling drug as recently as 1986, surpassed in 1987 by Vasotec. It is also a high blood pressure medicine, and is also likely to slip under the $100 million sales barrier in 1991.

5 Zocor is a new drug, another cholesterol-lowering agent, and was successfully introduced into the UK, France, Italy, the Netherlands, Switzerland, and New Zealand in 1989, breaking through the $100 million sales level in its first year. As it is a second-generation compound, it is unlikely to be given fast-track treatment by the FDA, and so its date of introduction into the US market is uncertain.

6 Timoptic is a well established anti-glaucoma agent. Despite pressure from generics it is maintaining its market share against competition with an annual sales level of around $275 million.

7 Flexeril is a muscle relaxant which is also on a gradual decline in sales, perhaps principally because its patent has also recently been successfully challenged by generic manufacturers in the US.

8 Sinemet is a treatment for Parkinson's disease; it has never been a high-profile drug, but its performance typifies Merck's ability to maximise the income from past R & D inputs. Until recently it was

probably selling at the rate of some $200 million per year, though a sharper rate of decline is likely in the future.

9 Ivermectin, an anti-parasitic compound for livestock, was originally introduced in 1981 as Ivomec; it is a single injection formulation for cattle in several major countries outside the US. In 1989 this product had its largest year-on-year volume since 1984.

10 Primaxin is a broad spectrum antibiotic, and is the third most widely prescribed injectable antibiotic in the US, though in 1989 a larger proportion of its approximately $350 million total sales were made in Japan than in the US.

11 Mefoxin is also a broad spectrum antibiotic and while it was more in demand in the US than Primaxin in 1989, its total sales were drifting down towards the $200 million mark, while Primaxin was increasing its market penetration.

12 Noroxin is Merck's antibacterial agent for treating urinary tract infections. It is holding its market position and sales have broadly stabilised, probably around the $150 million level.

13 Pepcid is an H_2–receptor antagonist for treating duodenal ulcers. The FDA has also approved it for the treatment of gastric ulcers. It was launched in the US and several European markets in 1986, and has shown excellent growth. Its sales are likely to top $400 million in 1990, with no slackening yet in sight.

14 Clinoril is a non-steroidal anti-inflammatory drug for the treatment of arthritis. It was introduced in 1976 and, for a time, was a very successful drug for Merck. It is now in decline, with sales probably dropping down through the $200 million mark.

15 Indocin is an even older arthritis treatment than Clinoril; it is also declining faster and will probably drop through the $100 million level in 1991–92.

16 Dolobid is an analgesic designed for relief of pain and inflammation. It was originally launched in Europe, then introduced into the US in 1982. It is now experiencing competition from generics in that market, but is holding its annual sales above $100 million.

17 MMR II vaccine is a combination vaccine for measles, mumps and rubella. Sales increases are dependent on the incidence of outbreaks of these afflictions.

18 Hepatitis B vaccines include the first genetically engineered vaccine for the prevention of hepatitis B – Recombivax HB. This family of vaccines has only recently passed the $100 million sales level.

Thus, Merck has a very broad range of high-selling drugs. Some are old and in decline; some are in increasingly competitive sub-sectors, particularly where generics are involved, but are defending their market share vigorously; but the prime growth strategy is to aggressively develop the newer major drugs which have so much potential – Mevacor, Vasotec, Zocor, Pepcid, Primaxin and Prinivil (Merck's second ACE inhibitor for reducing high blood pressure).

Competitors

Merck's principal competitors are shown in Table 6.8. Of Merck's competitors only Glaxo is wholly an ethical drugs company deriving 99 per cent of its revenues from prescription drugs The other companies are also heavily involved in other areas: over-the-counter, agro-chemicals, chemicals, electronics, etc., and – for some – ethical pharmaceuticals account for a smaller element of their business, e.g. Bayer and Hoechst.

Table 6.8 Principal competitors of Merck

Company	Domicile	Ethical drug sales as % of total sales
Bristol-Myers/Squibb	US	48
Bayer	Germany	11
Ciba-Geigy	Switzerland	27
Glaxo	UK	99
Hoechst	Germany	14
Hoffman La Roche	Switzerland	41
SmithKline Beecham	US/UK	45

1 *Bristol-Myers/Squibb.* The merger of Bristol-Myers and Squibb created the second largest ethical drugs company worldwide after Merck. It has a major presence in cardiovascular drugs but its ACE inhibitor, Capoten (its lead product), has come under pressure, losing sales to Merck's Vasotec. Pravochol, a new anticholesterol drug, should soon begin to compete with Mevacor and Zocor, two of Merck's rising stars in this area.

With other areas coming under pressure, it is likely that BMS will react defensively through aggressive/innovative marketing. It has a strong balance sheet, will benefit greatly from the complementary resources which the two partners have brought to the new company; it has a strong R & D pipeline, albeit not always in the key areas in which Merck competes. BMS can be expected to be a significant competitor; indeed, Merck recently increased its sales force to match that of the post-merger BMS.

2 *Bayer.* Bayer's pharmaceutical business is in a healthy state at present, having a reasonably well balanced portfolio of drugs. However, it is suffering in its domestic market, as German health reforms encourage the use of generic drugs rather than off-patent brands. Bayer does, however, have a strong marketing network across the major European markets and is currently addressing its weakness in the US by recruiting an increased number of sales personnel. Bayer's antibiotic drug, Ciprobay, was launched successfully in the US in 1989 and is considered to have high potential. This is backed by the strength of Bayer's research effort, which although small in comparative terms is highly innovative. Bayer does, however, seem to have encountered problems with the FDA in having drugs approved, although this may be a reflection of its relative weakness in the US. With its commitment to the US market, Bayer can be expected to become a major competitor in Merck's home market, particularly in view of its reputation for innovation.

3 *Ciba-Geigy.* Currently No. 4 in terms of ethical drug sales, which account for some 27 per cent of group revenues. The performance of its ethical pharmaceutical business picked up during 1989/90, owing to sales of Voltaren in the US. Ciba-Geigy is thought to have a number of potentially successful cardiovascular products currently under development but many of its new drugs have offered little advantage over competitors', and there seems to be some validity in the view that the company's development pipeline is relatively weak. Its product line is also mature and open to attack by generics. Ciba-Geigy can be expected to continue to market its successful Voltaren and to protect its position in mature products. In this respect it seems more likely that it will be fighting off the generics rather than competing with Merck through innovation.

4 *Glaxo.* Glaxo is currently No. 3, with 1989 sales of $4.4 billion, of which its leading drug, Zantac, accounted for $2 billion. Glaxo's marketing has been excellent and with Zantac accounting for the dominant share of the company's profits, any entry into the anti-ulcerant market (by Merck's Losec) can expect severe retaliation. While this particular market is still growing it is likely to become more competitive over the next few years. Glaxo's management has been strengthened recently and, with the benefit of a rich research pipeline and a cash mountain, the company looks set to make significant progress in the next few years. While many of the products are in areas in which Merck does not compete there are a few developments which will need to be watched closely.

5 *Hoechst.* Hoechst's pharmaceuticals business is not in good shape.

The product line is very mature, with over 60 per cent of sales vulnerable to generic competition, leaving the company very much open to the effects of the West German health reforms. Despite boasting the world's second largest research department the company's pipeline contains no inspiring discoveries, with the majority of new products being 'me too' drugs which will be late entrants into their respective markets. Hoeschst's marketing efforts are biased toward Europe, with the North American operation much weaker. Clearly Hoechst is going through a difficult period at present and is not considered to be a threat to Merck at this time.

6 *Hoffman-La Roche.* Currently No. 13 in the rankings with a major contribution coming from its antibiotic Rocephin. Much of its portfolio of drugs is mature and Roche's very effective sales force will attempt to regain lost ground with the help of a new anti-arthritic drug which, although not innovative, should gain ground in view of the firm's marketing skills.

Roche made a number of acquisitions in various fields during 1989–90 and recently took a controlling interest in fast-growing Genentech, plugging itself into a good pipeline of new biotechnology-based products. Roche is bullish about the possible developments and, if Genentech maintains its rate of growth over the next few years, Roche could become an even more significant player.

7 *SmithKline Beecham.* Again, the product of a merger which propelled the new company to No. 5 in the world in terms of ethical drug sales. Both companies suffered from a lack of fresh ideas in the past and, while the research pipeline now looks more promising, a number of key pharmaceuticals will move off-patent by 1995; it is doubtful whether any of the new products will offset this. We can therefore expect the merged marketing force to fight hard to maintain market share, particularly of its principal pharmaceutical product, Tagamet. SKB is highly geared and may have to undertake a programme of disposals in order to reduce borrowing; top management faces a long and difficult task in integrating the two components of the organisation. There is also a question mark over whether the company has strength in depth at a senior managerial level. At this time, SKB does not appear to pose any real competitive threat to Merck.

Future developments

In an industry where the fortunes of a company can change dramatically on the discovery of a successful new drug, it is dangerous to make sweeping generalisations about the state of competitors. However, it appears likely that the main threat will come from Bristol-Myers/ Squibb, which presently competes in Merck's prime therapeutic areas, with Bristol-Myers in the past having a reputation as an aggressive competitor. Glaxo, Bayer and Roche could prove to be the source of a number of highly innovative drugs which could challenge Merck as a market leader. Another very important factor is that many European competitors, suffering from price reductions and political pressures at home (more so than in the US), are looking to strengthen their operations in the US – the world's largest market, and source of 50 per cent of Merck's revenues.

We have already concluded in Chapter 5 that rivalry in the industry is increasing; this has been borne out by consideration of Merck's competitors. Merck can therefore expect a more aggressive response from its competitors than has perhaps been the case in the past.

Research and development

It will be recalled from Table 6.7 that Merck's investments in R & D have been increasing rapidly in recent years. Thus, while R & D expenditure has fluctuated gently around 11.5 per cent of sales, it has fallen rapidly and consistently as a proportion of net profit after tax.

The firm's stated R & D goal[6] is to have the strongest research programme in the industry in every major disease area. To do this, and to provide a steady flow of new products, Merck continues to recruit high-quality scientists and provide them with advanced equipment and superior working conditions. The lion's share of the expected $855 million expenditure on R & D in 1990 (an increase of 14 per cent) will go on:

1 Cardiovascular medications: this will include the most extensive clinical trials ever conducted (and the first to include women) to study the role of Mevacor in reducing mortality. Also, Merck has established a collaborative programme with Du Pont to develop and market a new class of therapeutics for the control of high blood

Table 6.9 Merck R & D, 1985–89

Measure	1985	1986	1987	1988	1989
R & D expenditure ($ million)	426.3	479.8	565.7	668.8	750.5
Increase on previous year%	8.4	12.5	17.9	18.2	12.2
As % of sales	12.0	11.6	11.2	11.3	11.5
As % of net profit after tax	79.0	71.0	62.4	55.4	50.2

pressure, and the first product of this cooperation was in early clinical trials in 1990.

2 Gastrointestinal medications: Merck's ethical H_2-receptor antagonist for treatment of duodenal, peptic and gastric ulcers (Pepcid) was in clinical trials for over-the-counter use in certain gastrointestinal problems.

3 Infectious diseases: new indications are being evaluated for Noroxin and Primaxin. Mectizan (the human formulation of ivermectin) is being evaluated for use against elephantiasis. In collaboration with Repligen, Merck is conducting AIDS vaccine research.

4 Benign prostatic hypertrophy (enlarged prostate): Merck's drug in this area, Proscar, is currently being tested for reducing the size of an enlarged prostate and improving urine flow. In 1990, Proscar was in large-scale clinical trials.

5 Ophthalmics: MK-507 (a topical treatment for glaucoma) has success-fully passed through early clinical trials, and was planned to be in large-scale clinical trials by 1991.

6 Animal health products: alternative formulations of ivermectin con-tinue to be developed for control of external and internal parasites in a variety of animals. The active ingredient of Vasotec (enalapril) is being examined for treating congestive heart failure in dogs.

The bulk of Merck's R & D effort is concentrated at a 210 acre site in Rahway, New Jersey – adjacent to the firm's head office. However, there are also research establishments in Quebec (this has become Canada's largest industrial centre for the discovery of new drugs), France, Japan and the UK.

Merck is basically a very highly centralised company, both in terms of research and in terms of everything else, so that all major decisions concerning the strategy of the company emanate from Rahway.[7] Research is closely controlled and, given free choice, all research would be done at Rahway because of the ease of communication and because it is often necessary to duplicate the resources when research is subdivided into different places. Why, then, does Merck do research in other countries? Primarily, the firm has a perception that, if it is to do business in the UK (for example) and be as successful as Merck is, the government will look for a *quid pro quo*. Manufacturing facilities are one option, which Merck has pursued; the firm can also build a research facility.

When it is granted that the firm has to do some overseas research, the next question is where. Clearly, the most important aspect is the location of skilled staff. When Merck went to the UK to build a major neuroscience building near Cambridge, this was done for two reasons. One, the firm was able to hire a foremost scientist in the CNS field to head the operation. Second, Merck was aware that there were many scientists in the UK already in the CNS area. That became a very successful laboratory and the business continued to do well in the UK. Similarly, Merck built a toxicology laboratory in the middle of France, and that was probably a mistake because the firm could not hire toxicologists in France. They have to be imported from the US, from England, the Netherlands and Germany. So that was not a cost-effective way of operating, but clearly the firm was under pressure to do something in France, and in retrospect Merck probably picked the wrong thing to do and the wrong area in France to do it.

The case of Japan is different: Japan forces the firm to do work locally; it is a very nationalistic country, and the firm is obliged to play by Japanese rules or not play at all. So a firm that wants to have a major presence in Japan has to do the R & D work locally.

The question of 'critical mass', in terms of the minimum efficient size of a pharmaceutical R & D unit, is recognised by Merck as an important one. In defining critical mass, the firm looks at two aspects. First, if the firm is going to establish a grass-roots operation (like Merck's R & D unit in the UK), it must decide to support the facility completely. So there has to be basic research as well as all the aspects needed to support this activity. Second, the question of numbers has to be addressed. The firm must have a critical mass of chemists and biologists to do the basic research. From this base, Merck established that it needed approximately 200 scientists for the UK laboratory (total staffing about 300). Without numbers of this kind for a fully fledged R & D operation, the firm has no question that success is unlikely. So it accepts that if it wishes to do research in the full sense – basic research with substantial development capability – then this is a major undertaking.

Merck accepts that there is a view in the industry that an upper limit to research numbers in one unit may also exist, but the firm has yet to see it. It is a highly centralised organisation, and probably in more therapeutic fields than any other drug company in the world. Yet it is managed with a small group of people. The firm's view is that, if it can manage the current international spread of R & D operations with all the difficulties that distance brings, it would be no worse if all research was located at Rahway. So total size is not really seen to be a problem, though, as the research effort gets bigger over the years, it may become necessary to prioritise research projects more rigorously. Thus, physical constraints may eventually limit the size of R & D at Rahway to, say, fifty projects.

The role of the management group at Merck research is to define strategic targets about where science is leading the firm, what current and future medical needs may be, and where the firm's pharmaceutical research should go. A supplementary question concerns whether a particular emerging science is sufficiently ready to be exploited in order that an objective can be determined and achieved. For each programme of research, consideration is given to the resources needed, and how the programme will compete for resources with other programmes. This is Merck's basic approach to research management, and it has taken the firm from six therapeutic classes to thirteen in a relatively short period of time.

Management responsibility for R & D is devolved by therapeutic area, and this prevents the large central laboratory from becoming unwieldy. If top R & D management was forced to be involved in every decision, then the stage of physical impossibility would soon be reached. The key is for management to focus on the higher-priority items. As the research division gets bigger, top R & D management is involved less in lower-priority activity than a few years ago. It is feasible that, say, cardiovascular research could become so big as to be unwieldy within the corporate R & D structure. If this were to happen, the firm's response could be to spin off a specialist cardiovascular research company.

Control of finance and decisions on projects are strictly centralised functions. A budget is assigned to each facility for the year, then projects are assigned to keep it up to capacity. A central R & D database has been computerised and this will cover the whole research organisation; it is intended to be totally interactive, and should have the additional advantage of locating and utilising the by-products of mainstream research.

Strengths and weaknesses

At this stage, Merck's strategic strengths and weaknesses can be drawn out of the analysis. It is these strengths and weaknesses which, combined with the environmental factors outlined in Chapter 5 and in the section on the US pharmaceutical market at the beginning of this chapter, allow the construction of a number of future strategy options for Merck.

Strengths

1 Merck has a young product line and is less open to generic competition than any other pharmaceutical company.

2 Merck is the acknowledged leader within the industry in terms of management of R & D.
3 Merck is the world's No. 1 ethical drugs company and the only one with a major presence in the three principal markets.

Weaknesses

1 With 41 per cent of its sales in one therapeutic area, cardiovasculars, Merck could be vulnerable to any new revolutionary drug in the area.
2 By concentrating its research on enzyme blocking (the chief executive is a world-class enzyme chemist) Merck may miss advances in other areas.
3 Merck's earnings remain sensitive to movements in the US dollar exchange rate in view of its large overseas operations.

Strategy options and choice

With its substantial internal strengths, noted in the previous section, and bearing in mind the numerous environmental opportunities open to the firm, noted earlier, Merck should clearly pursue an aggressive strategy. This general strategic direction yields a number of specific strategy options which can be evaluated as follows.

1 *Concentric diversification.* This would be a poor option at the present time, as it would lead to Merck becoming more like its main competitors, and therefore less differentiated in terms of skills and operational characteristics. So concentric diversification would represent a backward step rather than a positive one.
2 *Product and market development.* These are certainly areas in which Merck should be active to help prolong the life of existing drugs by obtaining new use patents and by increasing global coverage. However, this is something which should be done as a matter of course and not regarded as a strategy for a company like Merck. Indeed, if it were the only strategy, the company would not be addressing the threats in its environment.
3 *Innovations.* Merck is already in the most advantageous position in the industry, as confirmed by the strategic mapping exercise. It is clear, however, that to maintain this position it must stay ahead of the pack in terms of the introduction of new and innovative drugs. It is evident, therefore, that a strategy based on innovation would be the most appropriate choice. This strategy not only builds on Merck's strengths, giving it the best chance to exploit the most lucrative

opportunities, but will also provide the best chance of insulating the company from the effects of generic competition and, to a lesser extent, pressure to reduce prices.

4 *Joint Ventures.* With Merck's resources, it could be argued, the joint ventures are not needed, but this would be a very short-sighted view and I believe they have an important role to play in the future development of the company. The use of joint ventures could perform a number of functions:

(a) As a means of obtaining additional new product ideas.
(b) As a defensive measure to stop good ideas going to competitors.
(c) As a means of generating extra revenue by converting older drugs for the over-the-counter market.

5 *Horizontal Integration.* Rather than use joint ventures, Merck could follow a strategy of horizontal integration and use its huge cash resources to buy small companies rich in research ideas. However, any hostile bid is likely to be counterproductive and while, Merck should be willing to consider any approach, it is likely that joint research ventures or licensing will be more fruitful. Clearly there is little point in buying a company which is open to generic competition, which rules out most large companies.

Conclusion

In choosing a strategy, clearly the role of past strategy is important. Merck has prospered in the past, using just such an innovation strategy as that which it has augmented recently with joint ventures. Clearly therefore such a strategy would be acceptable to the present management and would not need to overcome hurdles in terms of institutionalising the strategy.

Thus, it is likely that Merck's strategy will develop on two levels. The core strategy must be innovation, as new products which provide effective treatment for currently difficult diseases will ensure the future success of the company. Supporting this core strategy is likely to be a series of joint ventures of various types, aimed primarily at supporting and supplementing Merck's own research programmes.

ABBOTT LABORATORIES

Company history and development

Abbott Laboratories is based at Abbott Park, North Chicago, Illinois. The company dates back to 1888, when Dr Wallace C. Abbott started producing dosimetric granules in the kitchen of his apartment, behind his 'People's Drug Store' in Ravenswood, Illinois. Reportedly, his sales in the first year of operation amounted to some $2,000. The business went through all the normal development of a small firm starting as a family operation, expanding to take in 'outsiders', moving into advertising and catalogue selling of health products, and using the name Abbott Alkaloid Company. An early diversifier, the company was soon publishing and printing the journal *Alkaloid Clinic*, and in 1902 it also acquired an office stationery manufacturer.

By 1915 the company had adopted its present name and had moved into international business, selling over 700 Abbott products to 1,000 physicians in Europe and 500 in Latin America. In 1920, the company moved to a new site in North Chicago, and Dr Abbott died in the following year. The year 1929 saw the testing of company stock on the Chicago Stock Exchange and in the following year Abbott developed one of its most successful drugs, the barbiturate Nembutal, followed in 1936 by Pentothal, a best selling intravenous anaesthetic.

However, it was Abbott's activities during the Second World War that really set the course for the huge pharmaceutical multinational it was to become. One of its priorities was the production of dried blood plasma for the armed forces and, by the end of the war, Abbott had processed almost a million pints of whole blood. It also developed the Sterilope envelope which permitted easy dusting of Sulfanilamide powder over wounds in battlefield conditions. Probably the main impetus to growth came from Abbott's involvement in the government-sponsored push to mass-manufacture penicillin; in the post-war years this became a critically important field for Abbott, culminating in the marketing of Erythrocin in 1952. Nearly forty years later, this continues to be one of the safest and most effective antibiotics in use to combat the effects of Gram-positive bacteria.

The post-war years also saw a great increase in the internationalisation of the company, so that it now has important subsidiaries in over forty countries; it has wholly owned manufacturing facilities in seven countries outside the US, and majority-owned foreign manufacturing facilities in nineteen others. From 1980 onwards, by acquisition and organic growth, Abbott vigorously developed its line of speciality hospital equipment and diagnostics. A final notable feature of recent years has been the firm's highly developed ties with the Japanese pharmaceutical market and Japanese pharmaceutical firms.

Mission statement

Abbott Laboratories is in the business of developing, marketing and selling pharmaceutical, nutritional and hospital and laboratory products of superior quality to satisfy customers in key markets worldwide.

Our consistent strategy of growth from within emphasises our commitment to and dependence on continuing to focus our research and development efforts on health care while lowering its costs. We will through our strategy continue to achieve excellent return for our shareholders.

As a corporate citizen, Abbott Laboratories has a worldwide social responsibility which extends beyond its product line and balance sheet. Abbott Laboratories is committed to using its resources to make the world a better place to live.

This mission statement could be further illuminated by a quotation from the company's 1989 annual report:[8]

Abbott Laboratories has gained a reputation for its consistent performance and its discipline to manage for the long term. One of the important characteristics of our company is our emphasis on growth from within. We've been willing to invest significantly in research and development and, at the same time, achieve excellent return on equity for our shareholders. We believe this approach will continue to represent a blueprint for success in the future. One of Abbott's unique competitive strengths in the health care industry is its corporate-wide base of technology. Critical to our future success is continuing to focus our research and development efforts on technology that increases the quality of health care while lowering its costs. Technology must and will play a major role among the solutions as the world struggles with efforts to control the cost of health care. Abbott will take a leadership role in ensuring a future of improved quality health care within a cost-constrained environment.

Objectives

In order to achieve the (rightly) high ambitions set out in the statements in the previous section, important objectives in a number of areas will have to be met. It is likely that these will include the following.

1 *Profitability.* The pharmaceutical industry faces a decade with less prospect for supernormal profit than in the past. Abbott Laboratories should, through its focus strategy, be able to keep profitability up towards its exceptional high level for the 1980s. Profitability objective should be a growth rate of 13 per cent.

2 *Productivity.* Abbott has followed a strategy of strict cost control and focus on improved productivity. Selling, general and administrative expenses have been decreasing from 20.9 per cent in 1987 to 20.5 per cent in 1989. With a strategy of concentration, the productivity target should be 19 per cent within five years.

3 *Competitive position.* Abbott Laboratories has a very good competitive position in the US, its main market, to achieve further concentration. Successful connection with the biotechnology 'knowledge network' and ideas for products from joint venture partners will improve this position by development into further therapeutic areas.

4 *Employee development.* Successful innovation resulting in new products is the key to success in the pharmaceutical industry. Abbott provides a productive climate through employment of high-quality scientists and graduates. These will have the opportunity to work for periods in the research laboratories of Abbott's partners to exchange knowledge and stimulate innovation and personal relationships.

5 *Technological leadership.* It is essential for Abbott Laboratories to achieve technological leadership in some areas in order to generate new drugs to the market place.

6 *Public responsibility.* Abbott will continue its commitment to society through donations, support of disadvantaged businesses, and internship and employment opportunities for minority college students. Abbott will further use 0.5 per cent of R & D expenditure on the development of more environmentally friendly processes for manufacturing raw materials and drugs.

Business Segments

Abbott divides its business into two main segments: pharmaceutical and nutritional products, and hospital and laboratory products. Pharmaceuticals and nutritionals, with sales of $2.8 billion, represented 52 per cent of total company sales in 1989; this was a 7 per cent increase over 1988, compared to 11 per cent over 1987 and 13 per cent over 1986. Over this period, sales growth was better in international markets than at home. Of the total sales of this division, about 33 per cent represents pharmaceuticals and 57 per cent is nutritionals. The segment[9] includes a broad line of adult and paediatric drugs, nutritionals, vitamins and haemanites. These products are mainly sold on the prescription, advice or recommendation of doctors or other health care professionals. Also included in this segment are personal care products, agricultural and chemical products, and bulk pharmaceuticals. Taken together these represent about 10 per cent of total segment sales. Competition comes from other broad line and specialised health care manufacturers, and technological innovation is a significant competitive weapon in this market. In recent years, competitive pressures have also been increased by the substitution of generic products for prescribed brands. Personal care products are sold directly through marketing channels to the public and promoted by consumer advertising. Agriculture and chemical products are sold direct to distributors and industrial users. In both sub-sectors, price and technological innovation are significant competitive factors.

Hospital and laboratory products accounted for $2.6 billion of sales in 1989, 48 per cent of Abbott's total. Sales growth in this segment has been very good, the compound rate over the last five years being 13 per cent. In contrast to the position with pharmaceuticals and nutritionals, domestic growth has been better than international growth. Products in this segment included diagnostic systems for blood banks, hospital and clinical laboratories and other care and testing sites; intravenous and irrigating fluids and related administration equipment; venipuncture products; anaesthetics; critical care products; and other medical speciality products for hospitals, clinical laboratories and alternative care sites. This whole range of products is generally distributed through wholesalers and direct to hospitals, laboratories, and doctors' premises. This industry segment is highly competitive, both in the US and overseas. The principal competitive factors are price, technological innovation, product performance, and productivity-linked cost effectiveness.

The total number of employees has increased by 17.8 per cent since 1985, as follows:

1985	34,742
1986	35,754
1987	37,828
1988	38,751
1989	40,929

The company recognises that its long-term success relies on a talented, diverse, well educated and well motivated workforce. It is highly committed to the training and career advancement of young people from minority groups; it does this by prodiving internships, full-time job placements for graduates, financial and other contributions. Many of these students eventually join Abbott as permanent employees.

Financial analysis

Geographical spread

The analysis of the geographical spread of Abbott's sales over the last ten years is shown in Table 6.10. This shows very little movement over the period, except for the reduction in the proportion of sales accounted for by Latin America (LA) from 8 per cent in 1980 to only 3 per cent in 1989. However, within the period, it should be noted that domestic

Table 6.10 Abbott geographical spread

Measure	1980	1985	1986	1987	1988	1989
Customer sales ($ million)						
Domestic	1,437	2,625	2,880	3,288	3,746	4,167
Latin America	169	155	153	173	180	208
Europe, Mideast, Africa	346	480	638	824	957	1,028
Pacific, Far East, Canada	186	315	384	456	540	602
Pretax profit ($ million)						
Domestic	253	600	709	777	889	1019
Latin America	26	27	19	23	24	47
Europe, Mideast, Africa	61	85	131	170	183	188
Pacific, Far East, Canada	18	39	51	58	57	72
Identifiable assets ($ million)						
Domestic	916	1,811	2,070	2,320	2,610	2,998
Latin America	125	132	116	122	119	114
Europe, Mideast, Africa	258	381	453	595	638	737
Pacific, Far East, Canada	124	221	257	290	350	404
Return on sales (%)						
Domestic	17.6	22.9	24.6	23.6	23.7	24.5
Latin America	15.4	17.4	12.4	13.3	13.3	22.6
Europe, Mideast, Africa	17.6	17.7	20.5	20.6	19.1	18.3
Pacific, Far East, Canada	9.7	12.4	13.3	12.7	10.6	12.0
Return on assets (%)						
Domestic	27.6	33.1	34.3	33.5	34.1	34.0
Latin America	20.8	20.5	16.4	18.9	20.2	41.2
Europe, Mideast, Africa	23.6	22.3	28.9	28.6	28.7	25.5
Pacific, Far East, Canada	14.5	17.6	19.8	20.0	16.3	17.8

Source: Abbott annual reports

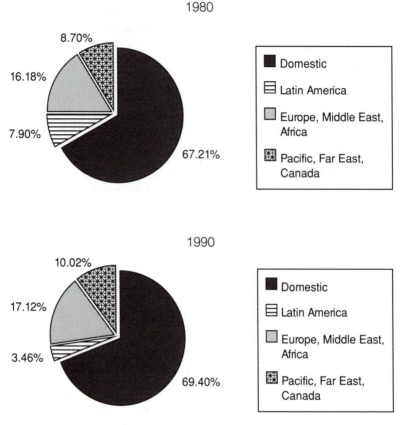

Figure 6.5 Abbott: geographical spread of customer sales, 1980 and 1989 (%)
Source: Abbott annual reports

sales rose as a proportion in the mid-1980s, only to fall back by 1989 while sales in Europe, the Middle East and Africa (EMA) showed the opposite trend (see Fig. 6.5). In dollar terms, sales in the US grew by about 200 per cent over the 1980s; by a slightly higher proportion in the Pacific, Far East and Canada (PFEC), by 200 per cent in Europe, the Middle East and Africa; and by only 23 per cent in Latin America.

When we turn our attention to pre-tax profits, the picture shows some interesting differences from that for sales, principally in that everywhere profits have risen much faster than sales. The growth of identifiable assets has shown a pattern very similar to that of sales.

Thus, the return on sales has increased everywhere, dramatically at home and in LA, satisfactorily in PFEC, but only marginally in EMA.

In like manner, there has been an astonishing increase (nearly double) of return on assets in LA, a good increase (up by a quarter) domestically and in PFEC, and only marginally in EMA. Note that the figures for LA are distorted by a major turn-round in profitability in this sector; the reasons for this are not known, nor can it be said to be a permanent turn-round or a short-term fluctuation; Abbott makes no appropriate comment in its annual report.

Overall, these figures show a strategy of concentration on the US market for increasingly healthy pre-tax profits and, to a lesser extent, for sales. It is ironic that Abbott, one of the international trailblazers among the American pharmaceutical multinationals, should be de-internationalising at a time when the whole industry is moving in the direction of increasing globalisation.

Results by segment of activity

Like Merck, Abbott reports its sales by only two segments, which is not very illuminating. However, this breakdown does throw some light on strategy, as it roughly corresponds to traditional markets (pharmaceutical, nutritional products: PN) and new markets (hospital, laboratory products: HL). The latter has been developed as a key strategic option in the last twenty years. In the 1975 Review of Operations,[10] the company observed:

> Decisions made in the past few years to place a high priority on the hospital segment of Abbott's business have proven sound; the hospital group continues to lead the way in Abbott's growth. This product group includes divisions responsible for domestic and international marketing of hospital, diagnostic, blood therapeutic products, and medical electronic equipment. The products of this group now account for 38 per cent of Abbott's sales. The group's worldwide sales for 1975 were $358 million, up 40 per cent from 1974.

This differential sales growth has clearly continued into the 1980s. Table 6.11 shows HL accounted for 42 per cent of company sales in 1980 and 48 per cent in 1989, for 34 per cent of pre-tax profits in 1980 and 38 per cent in 1989, for 49 per cent of assets in 1980 and 58 per cent in 1989. The underlying strength of the PN segment becomes apparent when attention is switched to other analyses in Table 6.12. Thus the return on sales of PN has increased from 20 per cent to 28.6 per cent over the decade; for HL, the corresponding figures are 14 per cent to 18.7 per cent. The return on assets of PL has moved from 32.6 per cent to a massive 45.1 per cent; for HL, the movement has been from 17.4

Table 6.11 Abbott segment analysis

Measure	1980	1985	1986	1987	1988	1989
Customer sales ($ million)						
Pharmaceutical, nutritional	1,180	1,839	2,057	2,333	2,599	2,785
Hospital, laboratory	858	1,521	1,751	2,055	2,338	2,595
Pretax profit ($ million)						
Pharmaceutical, nutritional	236	533	651	699	773	797
Hospital, laboratory	120	221	259	320	363	484
Identifiable assets ($ million)						
Pharmaceutical, nutritional	724	1,206	1,288	1,435	1,628	1,768
Hospital, laboratory	688	1,330	1,599	1,867	2,053	2,402
Return on sales (%)						
Pharmaceutical, nutritional	20.0	29.0	31.6	30.0	29.7	28.6
Hospital, laboratory	14.0	14.5	14.8	15.6	15.5	18.7
Return on assets (%)						
Pharmaceutical, nutritional	32.6	44.2	50.5	48.7	47.5	45.1
Hospital, laboratory	17.4	16.6	16.2	17.1	17.7	20.1

Source: Abbott annual reports

per cent to 20.1 per cent. In asset turnover, too, PL shows its strength and in recent years has generally been about 50 per cent higher than HL (1.6 to 1.1).

Fortunately, Abbott also gives another breakdown of sales, which helps us to see more clearly what has been happening within the PN segment. Table 6.12 shows that only the nutritional products can match the compound growth rate (13 per cent per annum) shown by the HL segment over the 1980s. The pharmaceuticals sub-sector has grown at just over half this rate (6.1 per cent). Figure 6.6 shows this change graphically, with pharmaceuticals dropping from 42 per cent to 32 per cent of all PN over the 1980s and nutritionals increasing from 44 per cent to 58 per cent.

Table 6.12 Abbott sales by segment of activity ($ million)

Segment	1980	1981	1982	1983	1984	1985	1986	1987	1988	1989
Pharmaceuticals	495	552	555	585	601	606	676	756	838	902
Nutritionals	518	630	745	838	933	1,059	1,171	1,343	1,486	1,598
Other PN	167	175	166	176	172	174	210	234	275	285

Source: Abbott annual reports

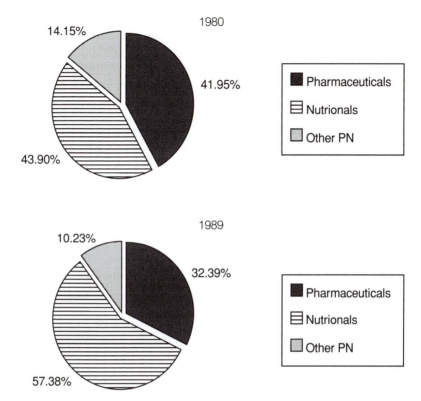

Figure 6.6 Abbott: segment analysis, 1980 and 1989 (%) *Source*: Abbott annual reports

As for the geographical spread above, the segment and subsequent analysis give some indication of the strategy that has been at work. Abbott is becoming less of a pharmaceuticals firm as time goes on, though it is still a significant player in the drugs industry. By 1989, only one Abbott sales dollar in six was coming from pharmaceuticals. There has been a long-term powerful move into hospital and laboratory products; while this may be a less profitable segment, it does provide a very useful diversification for Abbott as it is less susceptible to government pressure on health spending. The star performer, however, over the decade has to be nutritional products; sales have been growing as fast as those in HL, and it is likely that profits growth in this sub-sector has been powering Abbott forward.

So, taking the results of the geographical and segment analysis together, an interesting perspective emerges. Abbott seems to be moving slowly but definitely towards greater dependence on the US market for growth in nutritional products, and in hospital and laboratory products. This raises interesting questions for future strategy.

Financial performance

In some ways there is less evidence of tight management and control than there is in Merck; this may not, however, be a wholly fair comparison, as Merck is a highly concentrated business and almost entirely within one industry whereas Abbott is more decentralised and is spread over more sectors. The record of sales growth is good, with a compound growth figure of 11.4 per cent per annum over the 1980s (see Table 6.13). By comparison, marketing and administrative expenses have increased by 10.2 per cent per annum, and R & D investments have grown at the rate of 20 per cent per annum. To offset this, materials and production costs have grown at a compound rate of only 9.4 per cent; because this category of costs is much higher than for Merck (averaging 52 per cent of sales over the decade for Abbott as opposed to 32 per cent for Merck), the dollar saving from a small percentage of reduction in costs relative to sales more than outweighs the higher costs of R & D. Thus, net profit after taxation has grown at the compound rate of 16.7 per cent over the decade, a figure which is actually higher than Merck's. This manufacturing productivity increase has fed right through to dividends declared, which increased at an average rate of 17.2 per cent during the 1980s. This is illustrated in Figure 6.7.

Increases in capital expenditures and working capital are both quite high, at around 13 per cent per annum, but the firm has still managed to decrease long-term debt over the decade by 3 per cent per annum. Thus, the gearing ratio in 1989 had fallen to 5 per cent from 19 per cent in 1980, a performance which at least matches Merck's. Stockholders' equity has grown at 11.5 per cent per annum over the decade. Up to 1986, Abbott's shareholders were receiving a return significantly higher than Merck's, but since 1987 the latter have been receiving bumper returns of ten percentage points more; however, at 32 per cent in 1989, Abbott shareholders still had an excellent 0.32 per cent return on shareholders' equity.

Table 6.13 Abbott financial performance

($ million)	1980	1985	1986	1987	1988	1989
Sales	2,038.2	3,360.3	3,807.6	4,387.9	4,937.0	5,379.8
Materials and production costs	1,143.4	1,694.9	1,868.4	2,101.9	2,353.2	2,556.7
Marketing/administrative expenses	458.2	687.7	775.7	919.0	1,027.2	1,100.2
R & D expenses	97.6	240.6	284.9	361.3	454.6	501.8
Net profit after tax	214.4	465.3	540.5	632.6	752.0	859.8
Dividends declared	74.1	167.4	192.2	226.7	269.8	309.7
Capital expenditures	162.5	292.9	383.4	432.7	521.2	501.5
Working capital	239.7	891.9	585.4	668.7	913.3	719.2
Fixed assets	603.8	1,368.5	1,543.3	1,741.6	1,952.6	2,090.2
Total assets	2,062.8	3,468.4	3,865.6	4,385.7	4,825.1	4,851.6
Long term debt	191.3	443.0	297.4	271.0	349.3	146.7
Shareholders' equity	1,027.2	1,870.7	1,778.9	2,093.5	2,464.6	2,726.4
Number of employees	31,042	34,742	35,754	37,828	38,751	40,929
As % of sales						
Materials and production costs	56	50	49	48	48	48
Marketing/administrative expenses	22	20	20	21	21	20
R & D expenses	5	7	7	8	9	9
Net profit after tax	11	14	14	14	15	16
As % of net profit after tax						
R & D expenditures	46	52	53	57	60	58
Dividends declared	35	36	36	36	36	36
Capital expenditures	76	63	71	68	69	58
Per employee						
Sales	65,659	96,722	106,494	115,996	127,403	131,442
Net profit after tax	6,907	13,393	15,117	16,723	19,406	21,007
Dividends declared	2,387	4,818	5,376	5,993	6,962	7,567
Capital expenditure	5,235	8,431	10,723	11,439	13,450	12,253
Working capital	7,722	25,672	16,373	17,677	23,568	17,572
Fixed capital	19,451	39,390	43,164	46,040	50,388	51,069
Total assets	66,452	99,833	108,117	115,938	124,515	118,537
Gearing ratio (%)	19	24	17	13	14	5
Return on shareholders' equity (%)	21	25	30	30	31	32

Source: Abbott annual reports

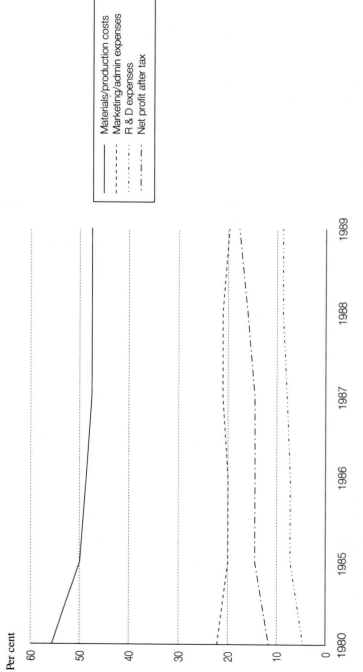

Per cent

Materials/production costs
Marketing/admin expenses
R & D expenses
Net profit after tax

Figure 6.7 Abbott: financial performance (as a percentage of sales), 1980 and 1985–89 *Source*: Abbott annual reports

Abbott's productivity record is also given in Table 6.13 and, again, this compares well with Merck's. The growth in net profit after tax per employee has been particularly satisfactory at 13.2 per cent per annum. Lower growth in some asset turnover ratios suggests, perhaps, good management control. The growth in fixed capital per employee, averaging 11.3 per cent annual growth over the decade, may be an indicator of a long-term strategy to substitute high technology in manufacturing for people, and this may be directly linked to the relative drop in manufacturing costs noted above.

Again a quote[11] from the Chairman of the Board (Mr Robert A. Schoellhorn) perhaps best illustrates the firm's strategic priority.

Abbott began the decade with a return on shareholder investment of 22.2 per cent for 1980. We increased that per cent each year throughout the 1980s, ending 1989 at 33.1 per cent. Our average return on shareholder investment for the 10-year period was 27.6 per cent, and our compound growth rate of earnings per share was 17.9 per cent, ranking Abbott among the top US companies for the decade of the 1980s for strength and consistency of performance.

To provide an appropriate context for these two performance measures, we point out two additional facts. First, that Abbott's performance for shareholders was accompanied by strong and steady increases in spending for research and development – critical to the long-term success of our technology-based company. Our research and development spending level in 1979 was 5.0 per cent of total sales. We ended the decade with R & D expenditures of 9.3 per cent of total sales.

Second, Abbott's performance was achieved amid a decade of extraordinary marketplace changes.

So we can see that Abbott is undoubtedly in a strong financial position as a health care company. Whether this strength will be used to develop its position in the pharmaceutical industry is a question that can only be answered after analysis of Abbott's product range, its competitors, and the recent past and likely future outputs of its R & D effort.

Activities

Products and competition

The firm's pharmaceutical sales are highly concentrated in two lines, the erythromycin range (antibiotics) and Tranxene (a mild tranquilliser for anxiety). These two lines account for over half of all Abbott's drug sales. The company has exploited existing products through a series of line extensions, and it has tackled the problem of product maturity by establishing a joint venture with the Japanese pharmaceutical company Takeda in 1977. This has resulted in Takeda-Abbott Pharmaceuticals (TAP), which is equally owned by the two companies. This venture was expected to yield several new products for the US and Canadian markets. However, TAP's only major addition to the product line, so far, has been Lupron (a new therapy for prostatic cancer).

During 1988, Abbott has negotiated a number of agreements with Japanese makers of antibiotics;

1 Tanabe Seiyaku Co. – to develop and market Temafloxacin, a new quinoline antibiotic.
2 Toyama Chemical Co. – cross-licence agreement for the sale of another new quinoline antibiotic Tosufloxacin.
3 Taisho Pharmaceutical Co. – Abbott will apply to the Japanese Ministry of Health for sales approval of clarithromycin, a new macrolide antibiotic discovered by the Japanese company.

These agreements are unlikely to have a major impact on the company's future in international pharmaceutical markets.

Abbott's own view[12] of its pharmaceutical business is that it 'focuses on maximising the profitability of its existing strong products while the revitalised pharmaceutical research and development efforts have set the stage for worldwide launches of two major products'. The existing products are divided over three areas: anti-infective and metabolic (chiefly antibiotics), neuro-science (CNS), and cardiovascular (including blood products).

The antibiotic segment represents approximately 45 per cent of pharmaceutical sales. The erythromycin antibiotic range is by far Abbott's worldwide best seller. It is estimated that sales of this product alone account for over 8 per cent of corporate turnover. These products have been off-patent for some time, but the company has continued to increase sales of the range, maintaining its No.1 position in the worldwide erythromycin market. This has been achieved by defensive strategies such as line extension into niche markets (Eryped, a fast-acting paediatric form, and Eryderm for common acne). Abbott have also been involved in price cutting to meet competition as well as indication extension through continued research. Hence, the company has kept this range running by effective marketing management.

In 1986 the product range was further diversified with the introduction of polymer-coated erythromycin (PCE). This product is likely to strengthen Abbott's position in this market, offsetting the decline in sales of erythromycin ethyl succinate (ESS). According to the company, PCE sales have made it the most successful new erythromycin product ever marketed.

The importance of PCE is that it reaffirms Abbott as an innovator in the erythromycin market and gives it a highly promotable new entry with no generic counterpart. PCE is a proprietary technology for the company and it has applications to other Abbott products.

In 1989, the firm filed new drug applications in the US for two important anti-infectives: clarithromycin (a new broad-spectrum macrolide antibiotic) which will be marketed under the trade name Klacid in Europe, and Temafloxacin (a highly active quinalone) which will be marketed in Japan by the firm's subsidiary, Dainabot.

It is estimated that the CNS segment represents approximately 20 per cent of pharmaceutical sales. Tranxene (a tranquilliser licensed from Sanofi) is the company's main product in the mental health market. Tranquillisers remain a major market sector in the US and Abbott has achieved continued growth, around 15 per cent per year up to 1986. However, growth slowed considerably in 1987 owing to the loss of patent protection.

To offset the negative impact of generic competition, Abbott has introduced triangular-shaped Tranxene T tablets, in place of the original capsules. This has differentiated the product and increased its sales while slowing the overall sales reduction in the Tranxene range. The anxiolytic market is becoming crowded with brands such as Upjohn's Xanax and Bristol-Myers' Buspar. In addition generic substitutes are also eating into Tranxene's market share.

Abbott also markets two main anti-epileptic products, Depakene (another Sanofi licensed product) and Depakote. The former's sales have levelled off, but it is still an important anticonvulsant in the US and Canada. The latter, Depakote, has been developed with an enteric coating to prevent gastric irritation. Abbott holds the worldwide marketing rights for this presentation. In 1987 sales of Depakote in the US increased by 50 per cent compared with 1986. These products should provide a solid base for earnings in the future, especially Depakote, which continued to be the fastest-growing anticonvulsant in the US in 1989.

The CNS and blood products segment is estimated to represent 20 per cent of the company's pharmaceutical sales. In this sector Abbott markets K-Tab and K-Lor (potassium replacement therapy), and haemitic products (drugs to increase haemoglobin and red blood cells) as well as Enduron and Enduronyl; these are Abbott's diuretics and their market is generally declining, owing to more modern therapies.

Abbokinase is a drug given intravenously to dissolve blood clots and to clear catheters. It has become one of Abbott's fastest-growing drugs. It is used for the treatment of pulmonary embolism as well as for intracoronary administration in heart attacks. The firm is still awaiting FDA approval for the use of Abbokinase in the treatment of blood clots in peripheral veins and arteries, and for intravenous administration in treating heart attacks. Competition from Genentech's Activase and Beecham's Eminase may adversely affect this product's future earnings. Abbokinase may also have a price disadvantage because of the high cost of extracting urokinase (the basic necessary compound) from its source (human urine). Nevertheless, commercial indications for this product are good.

Hytrin (an antihypertensive vasodilator) was introduced to the US market in 1987 and is co-marketed by Wellcome. There is strong competition in the antihypertensive market, therefore Hytrin may find it difficult to gain a major market share.

Through licensing agreements Abbott has access to other important cardiovascular products, Loftyl and Cordilox. Abbott markets the former worldwide, with the exception of the US and France. Loftyl's growth was strong in 1987 and it is likely that these products will lead to increased earnings in the future.

Future developments

The major problem facing Abbott is the lack of discovery and development of significant new products from the company's own research to revitalise its pharmaceutical business.

However, there are some products that have the potential to become stars over the next ten years. Difloxacin is a quinolone antibiotic developed in-house, and is due to be launched in the early 1990s. By the mid-1990s there is expected to be competition from quinolone antibiotics. Carteolol is a beta-blocker licensed in from the Japanese company Otsuka and was launched in 1991.

Cefomonil and Somnatrol are TAP products which have resulted from Takeda's research. These products were expected to be launched in 1990.

With relatively poor R & D productivity in the past, and few important products in development, Abbott's domestic pharmaceutical business is likely to depend on the TAP joint venture and licensing for additional substantial product lines. This may indicate a question mark over the degree of future commitment that the firm will make towards its drugs business.

Research and development

Table 6.10 indicated the rapid rise in Abbott's recent annual investments in research and development and, clearly, there is a strategy at work here which is being implemented in a very determined fashion (see Table 6.14). Thus, R & D expenditure has been increasing rapidly as a proportion of sales, even at the expense of also increasing as a proportion of net profit after tax. Of the 1989 figure of $501.8 million it is likely that approximately $110 million was devoted to pharmaceuticals research; this represents a figure not too far away from the industry's 13.5 per cent norm.

Table 6.14 Abbott R & D

Measure	1985	1986	1987	1988	1989
R & D expenditure ($ million)	240.6	284.9	361.3	454.6	501.8
Increase over previous year (%)	10.0	18.4	26.8	25.8	10.4
As % of sales	7.2	7.5	8.2	9.2	9.3
As % of net profit after tax	51.7	52.7	57.1	60.5	58.4

At present R & D is increasingly being 'bought in' from the Takeda joint venture and licensed-in compounds. A large proportion of R & D funds is spent developing licensed-in products as well as developing new formulations of existing products. Hence, Abbott devotes a relatively small amount of sales revenues to research into new chemical entities or fundamental research.

In January 1987 the company introduced a 'venture group' concept for research. The teams take responsibility for the entire project; each team has one person in charge who manages the budget and reports to the vice-president of R & D. At present there are five venture groups active in research; the company believes that these have significantly increased the potential for developing new drugs.

International R & D operations

In the course of the last ten years, Abbott has made the transition from a highly centralised research operation to a somewhat decentralised research operation in a rather unusual way. What has been decentralised is the corporate research as an entity. This has been done in functional areas; that is, pharmaceutical research, diagnostic research, hospital products research and so on. In that way, research groups have been compartmentalised.

With regard to hospital research and nutritional research, these are very small groups which have no satellite operations at all. Hospital products R & D is centralised in North Chicago and nutritional products R & D is centralised in Columbus, Ohio.

With regard to the diagnostic business, there is a principal research unit at North Chicago which has grown rapidly over the last ten years. Abbott is now probably the largest company in diagnostics in the world, but there is also a diagnostic R & D capability in Germany and another one in Japan.

What remains of the pharmaceutical division at Abbott Park is the old corporate research entity. There are a large number of functions and services which are operated from North Chicago which are not duplicated elsewhere. Servicing work is done for other research divisions and this includes toxicology, pathology and metabolism Thus duplication is avoided of activities which are not intrinsic to the research programme. On top of that is the standard pharmaceutical R & D operation.

The unit which exists in the UK is principally an analytical and formulation unit.[13] It does not do basic research. It formulates compounds; it does analytical work with compounds through its clinical arm; and, with its regulatory arm, it does the appropriate work to register new drugs in the UK. This unit is used as a springboard to the market. For example, the phase 1 regulatory testing procedures are much more complex in the United States than in the UK. In the UK, it is much more on the investigators' shoulders to make decisions for testing in normal subjects than it is in the US. So occasionally, when phase 1 testing is required quickly, Abbott knows that it can move material quickly into the UK formulation facility, and that they can, in turn, go into immediate phase 1 testing, using existing commercial groups at Guy's Hospital or other areas. So the utilisation of this facility is the only way that North Chicago gets involved in UK activities. Thus, the UK R & D includes part of the pre-clinical stage and a wide range of clinical work.

Abbott in North Chicago does very little in-house clinical work. It has a large number of clinical workers, but their job is to put the work out to professional clinicians throughout the United States and indeed throughout the world for the clinical work to be carried out in that way. All of the new molecular research within Abbott is done at North Chicago. In the past, ten years ago and over, Abbott had a number of regional product programmes going through R & D but over the last ten years these have been significantly reduced. The situation in the developed world is that the disease entities are common to all countries. In the Third World, however, there is a totally different disease structure, and the economic opportunity is significantly reduced. So the major endeavours at North Chicago relate to the First World and to the principal economic opportunities. These include cardiovascular disease, renal disease, anti-infectives and antibacterials, and anti-ageing treatments. Thus the approach is now very strongly towards standardised global markets.

The cost of developing a new drug in the US today is between $130 million and $150 million. This is the main reason for a change in market approach. Thus it is generally uneconomical to develop drugs which are not for global markets although, in some instances, drugs will be developed in European markets or markets outside Europe where appropriate opportunities exist.

The decentralisation which took place was functional decentralisation, so there have been benefits of increased functionality in the various research groups. The pharmaceutical business is structured on a regional basis. There is a UK operation working within an international pharmaceutical operation. The international drug development centre at Queenborough in the UK is part of the international division and is not directly related to the North Chicago facility, although they work quite closely together and exchange information freely. Thus North Chicago does not control the UK research group although it uses its facilities frequently. The UK research arm works wholly in support of Abbott International, which comprises all of Abbott except the US.

Critical mass

The company does not find critical mass easy to define precisely. At North Chicago, there are 300 molecular research scientists and 500 employees divided between administration and development work. The number of molecular research scientists has doubled since 1980. While this is well above the critical mass level, there are still certain research areas within North Chicago where the claim could justifiably be made that more scientists are needed to reach an efficient scale of research in particular projects.

The stage at which inefficiencies begin to be noticed is not so much tied to an absolute number as to a desire to retain functional purity. Developing a drug requires handing the project on from one group to another. Over several stages of development, the problem of functional purity appears when problems arise at the interface between groups and the groups avoid taking responsibility for the problem. This causes some projects to move through the process at a less than optimal speed.

In the autumn of 1986, Abbott carried out a review of the development side of the North Chicago drugs R & D unit because there was a feeling that the operation had grown somewhat inefficient due to increasing size. The result of this review was the establishment of the venture groups described above. It is probably too soon to say that this reorganisation of R & D effort is an unqualified success, but the early indications are promising.

Strengths and weaknesses

The firm's strengths and weaknesses can now be drawn out of the foregoing analysis, as an intermediate step in developing Abbott's future strategic options.

Strengths

1 The company is in a strong financial position, certainly strong enough to buy back a proportion of its shares as a defence against being acquired.
2 The joint venture with Takeda yields a source of new drugs and gives a substantial boost to Abbott's foothold in Japan.
3 Productivity has been rising sharply in recent years.
4 Innovation, particularly in antibiotics, has been gradually increasing over the last ten years. PCE (see above) has certainly reaffirmed Abbott as an innovator, and the venture group concept may help to confirm this. In another field, the co-marketing of Hytrin with Wellcome represents an important innovation.
5 Abbott has developed considerable skill in searching out and finalising suitable marketing and licensing agreements, and in making successful acquisitions.

Weaknesses

1 Abbott's own R & D has a relatively poor long-term record in producing major products, resulting in mature product lines and dependence on agreements with other pharmaceutical firms. This results in patchy sales in international markets.
2 The company's drugs operation is small in relation to the major players in this market.
3 Abbott has no strongly developed biotechnology expertise or connection.
4 The firm's global presence is not strong, and the trend in recent years has been for further concentration in the US market to take place.

Strategy options and choice

Abbott's strategic strengths (compared to other firms in the industry) are not so powerful as Merck's, and so the firm has correspondingly less room for financial manoeuvre. However, it is possible to identify four principal strategic options which are open to Abbott's pharmaceutical business.

1 *Concentration.* Invest heavily in research and development to rejuvenate its product portfolio. The foundation for such a strategy must be a belief that pharmaceuticals will provide attractive business opportunities in the future. Abbott's recent experience in diagnostics and the lack of impact of the Takeda joint venture does not encourage this view.

  This strategy would require a considerable increase in R & D funding. The company's existing commitment seems to be weighted in favour of the diagnostic division, with the opening of two facilities in 1987 in the US and Germany.

  The increasing pressure within the pharmaceuticals industry through government regulations and increased concentration is likely to mean that Abbott's future profit margins will be squeezed and its business opportunities limited.

2 *Acquisition of a complementary pharmaceutical company.* The aim of this strategy would be to buy-in new products and R & D expertise. This is a viable option as Abbott has a strong balance sheet, but the competition for such an acquisition (if one exists) is likely to be fierce and the asking price high. However, Abbott's recent strategic moves have been concentrated in other business areas, the exceptions being the joint venture with Takeda and the co-marketing agreement with Wellcome.

3 *Sell the Pharmaceutical Products Division (PPD).* The division's limited product portfolio and lack of success in R & D suggest that future survival will be difficult.

  This option would allow Abbott to concentrate its energy and resources on those areas of the business with the highest potential for growth and profits.

  PPD might be attractive to a major pharmaceutical company wishing to strengthen its marketing and distribution.

4 *Milk the pharmaceutical business over the next ten years.* This option is consistent with Abbott's existing position. Operations can be maintained by:

(a) Exploiting the limited product portfolio.

(b) Joint ventures such as with Takeda.
(c) Licensing agreement requiring limited investment.
(d) Joint marketing and distribution arrangements with the other business areas.

This final option is the one that is best recommended to Abbott. Milking the pharmaceutical business over the next ten years and investing the cash flows in other business areas is the strategy that best fits the firm's strategic strengths to the commercial opportunities available in its operating environment. Specifically, this recommendation is consistent with the following observations:

1 The pharmaceutical industry is becoming increasingly competitive, with limited business opportunities.
2 Investment in R & D is a high-risk strategy and patent protection is under attack in the more developed markets.
3 Abbott is only a small player in the ethical pharmaceuticals business. Size is becoming an increasingly important feature in this industry.
4 Lastly and most importantly, Abbott seems to have more attractive investment opportunities in the other business areas.

Conclusion

On first reading, it may seem unnecessarily negative to suggest that Abbott should treat its pharmaceutical division as a cash cow, and turn its business development strategies in other directions. However, this could also be regarded as proactively implementing what has been happening reactively over the last twenty years. It gives Abbott the chance of maximising the return on past pharmaceutical investments, and developing the firm's health care interests in a segment where its skills and abilities are better suited to the longer-term competitive environment.

PFIZER INC

Company history and development

Like so many American multinationals, Pfizer Inc has its origins in a partnership that was established between two young emigrants from Europe – Charles Pfizer and Charles Erhart. Founded in Brooklyn, New York in 1849 it has now celebrated 150 years of continuous operation and is by any standards an 'established' company that has formed a view of its place in the world.

Beginning life as a fine chemicals company supplying bulk chemicals to processors and packagers for incorporation into their branded products, the beginnings of Pfizer's diversification into health care and pharmaceuticals can be dated quite precisely. The critical turning point was the military demands of the Second World War when Pfizer's expertise in large-scale chemical fermentation technology was enlisted into the US war effort and led to a breakthrough in the bulk production of the penicillin that accompanied the Allied troops on to the beaches of Normandy.

By the end of the war the company accounted for some 85 per cent of US penicillin production and it was this experience, 100 years after its foundation, that led it into its second century. The change of direction that followed the war was based upon three critical decisions which began to transform the company and have shaped its pattern of growth ever since:

1 To move away from being a simple supplier of bulk chemicals towards marketing the products of its science and technology under its own label.
2 To build upon its war experience overseas – establishing a manufacturing and marketing organisation on a worldwide basis.
3 To apply its new-found expertise in antibiotics to animal care, to increasing food productivity for what it perceived as a hungry world.

Following the results of a worldwide soil screening programme which, in 1949, led it to discover the first of the new broad-spectrum antibiotics, Terramycin, it began to apply the critical decisions it had made, establishing a separate Antibiotics Division to market the new drug under the Pfizer name. This decision marks its entry into pharmaceutical marketing and it was a move that was quickly consolidated by the formation of a number of foreign trade subsidiaries – now known as Pfizer International.

By the end of the 1950s Pfizer had developed a broad range of antibiotics and had begun to market a number of other ethical drugs in the areas of diabetes and mental health and had established manufacturing plants in both the UK and France.

The 1960s were a period of diversification, with the acquisition of interests in consumer products and materials science, a move which led in the 1970s to a concentration upon the themes that now form the core of its mission. Pfizer began to commit itself to large-scale investment in research and development in its main business areas of pharmaceuticals, agriculture, speciality chemicals and minerals, spending more than $750 million on R & D and a further $1 billion on capital investment in production and marketing facilities.

As a result of this proliferation, in 1972 the various R & D activities spread throughout the group were brought together with the establishment of the Central Research Division, which provided a sense of direction and cross-fertilisation between research laboratories and programmes in the US, England, France and new facilities established in Japan.

The results of this emphasis upon research were to be seen in the discovery and clinical development of a number of significant pharmaceuticals, including Minipress, the cardiovascular antihypertensive and the drug which sustained the company's growth throughout the early 1980s, the anti-arthritic Feldene. Numerous other drugs were added to the product range via licensing, including Cefobid (a third-generation injectable antibiotic), Spectrobid (a broad-spectrum penicillin) and, most important of all, Procardia (a new cardiovascular).

By the end of the 1970s the international ambitions set out in the critical decisions taken at the end of the war had largely been fulfilled. The company now operates in 140 countries, has established a manufacturing presence in sixty-five of them and has located major research facilities in each of the world's major drug markets – the US, UK, Germany and Japan. One of Pfizer's strengths has been its ability to focus upon longer-term issues in the areas of product and market development.

In terms of its products, its research activities have led to the introduction of major, if now somewhat dated, drugs such as Feldene and the company has in place an aggressive licensing strategy to ensure that it has a balanced portfolio of new drugs throughout the 1990s.

It has also established a framework for work towards the elusive promise of biotechnology with the formation of a molecular genetics group that has already registered its first breakthrough, the discovery of the molecular structure of the natural gene for human renin, a kidney enzyme involved in the regulation of blood pressure. This direct involvement has been extended with an equity investment in the bio company Oncogene Science and research agreements with five others – Genetics Institute, Xoma, Genzyme, British Biotechnology and California Biotechnology.

Mission statement

An international research-based company, operating in all of the major markets of the world, Pfizer is founded upon limited and related diversification. Its task being that of developing, manufacturing and marketing advanced products in the areas of pharmaceuticals, medical

equipment and supplies, agricultural medicines, high-technology part-
icle coatings, oxides and refractories, in speciality chemicals and in
consumer health and beauty products.

While focused upon human health care, the company strives to apply
the advances of science in meaningful ways which extend and improve
life, encompassing increases in the efficiency of food production and
improvements in the quality of products for home and industry.
Dedicated to long-term growth in income of 10–15 per cent per annum,
it is driven by a belief in the value and necessity of continued
investment in research and development and seeks to be in the forefront
of therapeutic innovation.

Objectives

To satisfy the demands of this mission statement to continue the
satisfactory growth of the last ten years, and to consolidate its place in
the pharmaceutical industry into the next century, Pfizer is likely to
have developed a series of objectives, including:

1 Maintain high levels of R & D spending to ensure leadership in a
  substantial number of therapeutic lines.
2 Increase market share of existing products by introducing new
  dosage forms and new indications.
3 Develop heavy involvement in the evaluation of promising lines of
  biotechnology which will add to an already wide portfolio of
  research investments.
4 Maintain a diversified product portfolio with risk-spreading characteristics in a cyclical worldwide business.
5 Develop additional strategic alliances, like that with Bayer AG for
  the marketing of Procardia XL or the research collaboration with the
  Oxford-based British Biotechnology Ltd, to increase the ability to
  meet the increasing competitive requirements of a globalising
  industry.
6 Improve operational performance in all divisions to achieve an
  annual growth in net income of 10–15 per cent.

Business Segments

Pfizer Inc, with a large number of wholly owned subsidiary companies
worldwide and a number of companies where it holds minority
interests, is divisionally structured into five business segments. Each
segment is organised into a number of subdivisions reflecting target
markets by products.

Health Care

This business segment accounted for 64 per cent of Pfizer's net sales in 1989 and contributed 80.7 per cent of the 1989 operating profit of $1,024 million. While net sales increased compared to the previous year's figures by 5.1 per cent, operating profit decreased by 8.4 per cent. It is probably too early to call this a trend but it shows that prices have come under some pressure due to competition from generics and government regulations (demanding additional testing and documentation for new drugs clearance procedures, price regulations). These show their impact on operational profit.

Pfizer's over-reliance and dependence on pharmaceuticals, which contribute 75 per cent sales to the whole Health Care division, could become a major threat for the company in the future, especially if it does not succeed in developing and launching new competitive products as replacements for its current strong brands, with patents expiring within the next few years. Pharmaceuticals are concentrated around the main therapeutic lines of: antibiotics, cardiovasculars, anti-inflammatories, central nervous system agents and anti-diabetes agents.

Hospital products, with a growth in sales of 17 per cent, have shown the fastest growth rate of all Pfizer businesses since the division was founded in 1972. Hospital products include seven operating units, all of which showed good to strong results in 1988 and are expected to develop their businesses further with similar growth margins.

Health care products are largely promoted through the medical profession and sold direct to medical institutions, or distributed to wholesale and retail drug outlets, hospitals and clinics.

Agriculture

This business segment is largely concerned with animal health products and can be viewed as the counterpart to pharmaceuticals in the health care division. Therefore, there is a possible benefit from research and product development within pharmaceuticals.

Net sales of the Agriculture division increased by 16.3 per cent, while operating profit increased by a record 15.3 per cent. Products within this division are sold to the main key livestock markets; pigs, cattle and poultry.

Government regulations, as experienced in the mid-1980s by US cattle exporters, and increasing consumer sensitivity to livestock treated with antibiotics could have an adverse long-term effect on the business.

Specialty Chemicals

The Specialty Chemicals division increased sales by 4.5 per cent and operating profit by 18.4 per cent. This division constitutes an important supplier of base chemical intermediates for Pfizer's pharmaceutical and agriculture divisions, while simultaneously selling proprietary speciality products to the food, beverage and pharmaceutical industries.

Beta-thymidine, used in the manufacture of the only approved AIDS treatment drug, Retrovir (produced by Burroughs Wellcome), contributed significantly to the good performance of this division.

The division's strength in fermentation technology should give a competitive advantage in commercialising more biotechnological products.

Consumer Products

Consumer Products increased sales by 5.2 per cent while operating profit decreased by nearly 50 per cent (attributable to high start-up costs for four new product launches, two in each business unit). These two business units are Coty cosmetics and fragrances and Leeming/Pacquin over-the-counter health care products. While Coty products performed well in an industry-wide decline, over-the-counter health care products came under heavy pressure through increased competition.

Materials Science

Like the Specialty Chemicals division, the Materials Science division performance benefited from greater operating efficiency and the concentration on development of high-technology proprietary products. Sales increased by 5.1 per cent and operating profit by 3 per cent. This Pfizer division produces magnetic particles used for the production of magnetic tapes (for video and cassette) and is a major producer of precipitated calcium carbonate (PCC), used in paper production worldwide. Building PCC satellite production plants on-site at paper mills has become a major success and will be pursued in the future.

Other divisions and head offices

Apart from the five purely market and sales-oriented divisions there exist the following other divisions, many of them central head offices, all of them providing services for the above-named business segments:

1 Public Affairs and Government Relations.
2 Operations.
3 Personnel.
4 Licensing and Development.
5 Corporate Strategic Planning.
6 Pfizer International Bank.
7 International Subsidiaries (all overseas activities are managed through this division).

Pfizer does not have a central corporate marketing sales division. Marketing and sales activities are organised through business segments.

Employees

By 1987 Pfizer had 40,700 employees worldwide, distributed by region:

United States	17,200
Europe	9,600
Asia	6,900
Canada/Latin America	4,300
Africa/Middle East	2,700

It is company tradition to recruit local managers for operations outside the US. There are just fifty expatriate employees in overseas subsidiary companies.

Financial analysis

Geographical spread

A record of Pfizer's activities in various parts of the world is shown in Table 6.15. This shows clearly that domestic sales are becoming very important to the firm, rising from 43 per cent of global sales in 1980 to 55 per cent in 1989. During the decade, sales in Asia have remained fairly steady at around 14–15 per cent of the total, but other areas of the world are becoming progressively less important to Pfizer (see Figure 6.8). Table 6.15 also shows that, in terms of pre-tax profit, the dependence on the US market is growing even faster. During the decade, the proportion of profits coming from this source increased from 37 per cent to 60 per cent, while the proportions in all other market areas fell. The proportion of company assets identifiable to each market has shown much more stability over the 1980s. The analysis of return on sales and return on assets in Table 6.15 quantifies these differential changes in proportion, and gives some valuable clues about the broad strategy that has been followed by Pfizer. In the domestic market, there has been a rise over the decade in both return on sales (from 13.8 per cent to 18.2 per cent) and return on assets (from 14.8 per cent to 23.2 per cent). The corresponding figures for Europe and for Africa/Middle East have shown encouraging upward trends until 1988, but have been disappointing for Asia and Canada/Latin America. While

Table 6.15 Pfizer geographical spread

Measure	1980	1985	1986	1987	1988	1989
Customer sales ($ million)						
Domestic	1,308	2,343	2,483	2,651	2,884	3,097
Europe	806	654	856	1,052	1,176	1,190
Asia	429	473	584	704	808	876
Canada/Latin America	339	396	389	399	406	386
Africa/Middle East	148	160	163	114	111	123
Pretax profit ($ million)						
Domestic	180	613	684	635	685	564
Europe	158	185	218	247	282	239
Asia	80	35	45	85	73	83
Canada/Latin America	48	62	61	50	47	51
Africa/Middle East	19	16	18	18	17	10
Identifiable assets ($ million)						
Domestic	1,222	1,521	1,673	1,885	2,132	2,432
Europe	823	895	940	1,252	1,316	1,453
Asia	417	504	624	739	774	745
Canada/Latin America	263	255	266	302	296	285
Africa/Middle East	127	110	87	86	84	83
Return on sales (%)						
Domestic	13.8	26.2	27.5	23.9	23.8	18.2
Europe	19.6	28.2	25.4	23.4	24.0	20.1
Asia	18.7	7.4	7.7	12.0	9.1	9.5
Canada/Latin America	14.0	15.7	15.7	12.5	11.5	13.2
Africa/Middle East	13.1	10.2	10.8	15.7	15.5	8.1
Return on assets (%)						
Domestic	14.8	40.3	40.9	33.7	32.1	23.2
Europe	19.2	20.6	23.1	19.7	21.4	16.4
Asia	19.2	6.9	7.2	11.5	9.5	11.1
Canada/Latin America	18.1	24.4	23.0	16.5	15.8	17.9
Africa/Middle East	15.2	14.7	20.3	20.7	20.6	12.0

Source: Pfizer annual reports

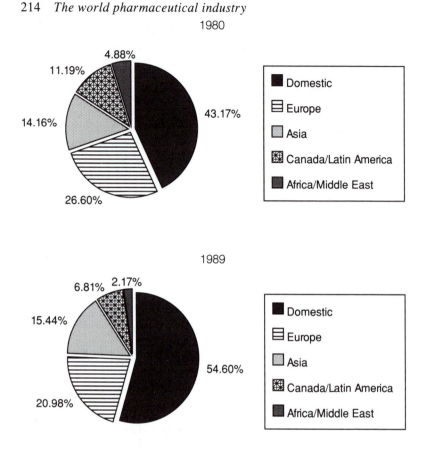

Figure 6.8 Pfizer: geographical spread of customer sales, 1980 and 1989 (%)
Source: Pfizer annual reports

this strengthens the view that concentration on the domestic market has probably been Pfizer's principal strategy, it is clear that the firm has devoted great effort to securing good returns from Europe and Africa/ Middle East. In terms of the Boxton Box model, these markets could be termed 'cash cows'.

Results by segment of activity

The basic analysis is given in Table 6.16. Again, this gives some clear indications of the way Pfizer has developed strategy in the 1980s. The proportion of sales accounted for by the Health Care segment has increased from 54 per cent to 64 per cent over the decade (see Figure 6.9), with the pre-tax profits proportion rising from 78 per cent to 81 per cent. Identifiable assets, too, have become more concentrated in this sector. For all three of these parameters, the other sectors have fallen back; the only exception is in the Consumer segment, where there have been modest advances. The result of this has been that return on sales in the Health Care segment has increased from 23.5 per cent to 26.1 per cent in 1988 before dropping back to 22.8 per cent in 1989, and the return on assets from 29 per cent to 35 per cent in 1988 (28.7 per cent in 1989). The performance of other segments has been disappointing, though for a time in the mid-1980s, returns in the Consumer segment were much more attractive.

Table 6.16 Pfizer segment analysis

Measure	1980	1985	1986	1987	1988	1989
Customer sales ($ million)						
Health care	1,644	2,516	2,878	3,118	3,453	3,629
Agriculture	464	473	492	519	540	628
Specialty chemicals	416	392	416	514	512	489
Consumer	252	343	365	396	484	509
Materials science	254	301	327	374	396	416
Pretax profit ($ million)						
Health care	386	790	851	832	902	826
Agriculture	45	48	35	54	59	68
Specialty chemicals	24	17	41	70	49	58
Consumer	25	54	65	63	76	39
Materials science	13	19	25	29	34	33
Identifiable assets ($ million)						
Health care	1,334	1,706	2,040	2,455	2,578	2,875
Agriculture	392	382	377	434	453	493
Specialty chemicals	451	400	439	483	489	401
Consumer	152	165	183	227	445	538
Materials science	258	320	341	383	391	368
Return on sales (%)						
Health care	23.5	31.4	29.6	26.7	26.1	22.8
Agriculture	9.7	10.2	7.1	10.4	10.9	10.8
Specialty chemicals	5.8	4.4	9.8	13.6	9.5	11.9
Consumer	9.8	15.8	17.8	16.0	15.7	7.7
Materials science	5.2	6.4	7.5	7.7	8.6	7.9
Return on assets (%)						
Health care	29.0	46.3	41.7	33.9	35.0	28.7
Agriculture	11.5	12.7	9.3	12.4	13.0	13.8
Specialty chemicals	5.3	4.3	9.2	14.4	10.0	14.5
Consumer	16.3	32.7	35.4	27.9	17.0	7.2
Materials science	5.1	6.0	7.2	7.5	8.7	9.0

Source: Pfizer annual reports

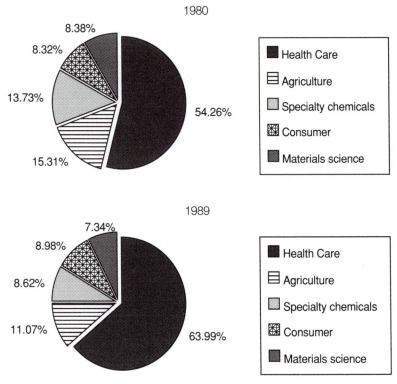

Figure 6.9 Pfizer: segment analysis, 1980 and 1989 (%) *Source*: Pfizer annual reports

Thus, Pfizer is becoming very concentrated in the Health Care segment, and Table 6.17 gives a further breakdown of sales in this segment. Again, this analysis illustrates some aspects of strategy with crystal clarity. As a proportion of all Health Care sales, the Hospital sub-sector has increased from 21.5 per cent to 35 per cent over the 1980s. Within the Pharmaceutical sub-segment, even greater changes have taken place (see Figure 6.10), with cardiovascular products advancing from 10 per cent of the whole to 27 per cent, and anti-inflammatories moving from 6 per cent to 24 per cent. In addition, it can be seen that the sales performance of the important anti-infectives group was turned round in 1986, and by 1989 was accounting for 31 per cent of the Pharmaceutical sub-segment. This turn-round was probably due to increased sales of derivatives of Cefobid.

Table 6.17 Pfizer health care segment analysis: sales ($ million)

Segment	1980	1981	1982	1983	1984	1985	1986	1987	1988	1989
Hospital	353	323	366	474	513	555	674	787	914	942
Pharmaceutical:	1,291	1,454	1,694	1,866	1,891	1,961	2,203	2,331	2,539	2,687
Anti-infectives	609	631	634	647	570	565	653	691	750	835
Cardiovascular	127	155	248	325	389	465	546	597	662	722
Anti-inflammatories	76	181	344	415	432	486	539	556	649	645
Antidiabetes	102	119	140	158	189	135	130	143	153	171
CNS	157	160	146	152	150	149	155	144	122	112
Others	220	208	182	169	161	161	180	200	203	202
Total	1,291	1,454	1,694	1,866	1,891	1,961	2,203	2,331	2,539	2,687

Source: Pfizer annual reports

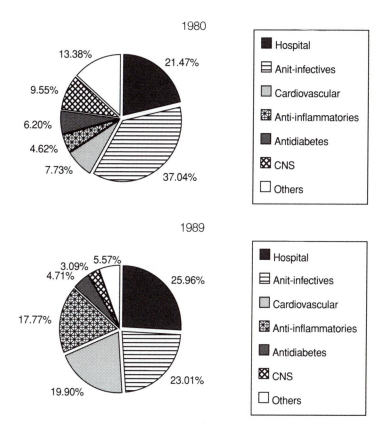

Figure 6.10 Pfizer: health care segment analysis, 1980 and 1985–89 (%) *Source*: Pfizer annual reports

Financial performance

Pfizer's ten-year record is set out in Table 6.18. It is immediately obvious that compound annual sales growth over the 1980s at 7.1 per cent has been significantly lower than that of Merck (10.2 per cent) and Abbott (11.4 per cent). However, as with the other two firms, the interplay of relative reduction of materials and production costs only partially offset by relative increases in marketing/administrative expenses and R & D (see Figure 6.11) has meant that net profits after tax have increased from 8 per cent of sales to 12 per cent over the decade. The poorer performance in 1989 has not, however, shown through in dividends declared, which rose substantially against a drop in profits. Indeed, over the period 1980–89, dividends declared grew at a higher compound rate (14.7 per cent per annum) than sales (7.1 per cent per annum), R & D (14.1 per cent per annum) or net profit after tax (11.5 per cent per annum).

Increases in working capital have been kept low, evidence of tight management control in this area. Long-term debt has been reduced by two-thirds over the 1980s, and the gearing ratio has fallen from 37 per cent to 4 per cent. This is a substantially better performance than that of either Merck or Abbott.

Shareholders' equity has grown at the rate of 12.4 per cent per annum over the decade, but the movement in return on shareholders' equity has been disappointing. From 16 per cent in 1980, it rose to a peak of 20 per cent during 1983–85, only to fall back to 15 per cent in 1989. Compared to the other two American pharmaceutical multinationals examined earlier, this is a very poor performance.

Pfizer's productivity record compares relatively well with the other two firms'; in particular, net profits after tax per employee have grown at 13.2 per cent over the 1980s, precisely the same rate as Abbott's. The spurt in capital expenditure per employee since 1985 may be an indicator of the realisation that major investments in high technology offer Pfizer a feasible path back to the industry leadership position it once occupied.

What is the explanation for the 1989 reversal of Pfizer's steadily improving financial performance over the 1980s? Often, a chairman's annual statement merely gives well rehearsed excuses for such a reversal but, in this case, Edmund T. Pratt Jr. notes:[14]

> Although a decline in earnings has been a rarity at Pfizer, it is largely explained in 1989 by what we believe is the most promising Pfizer story for some time ... Our strategy is to remain a leading innovator by building on Pfizer strengths. Those strengths include excellent R & D and marketing skills; adaptable, high quality manufacturing, and a highly qualified staff.

Table 6.18 Pfizer financial performance ($ million)

	1980	1985	1986	1987	1988	1989
Sales	3,054	4,025	4,476	4,920	5,385	5,672
Materials and production costs	1,464	1,546	1,720	1,897	2,020	2,062
Marketing/administrative expenses	942	1,313	1,465	1,681	1,881	2,110
R & D expenses	162	287	336	401	473	531
Net profit after tax	255	580	660	690	791	681
Dividends declared	106	241	270	297	330	364
Capital expenditure	164	196	196	258	344	457
Working capital	1,089	1,709	1,729	2,144	1,751	1,593
Fixed assets	830	1,269	1,352	1,506	1,655	1,784
Total assets	3,384	4,490	5,228	6,923	7,638	8,325
Long term debt	585	324	285	249	227	191
Shareholders' equity	1,580	2,927	3,415	3,882	4,301	4,536
Number of employees	41,600	39,200	40,000	40,700	40,900	42,100
As % of sales						
Materials & production costs	48	38	38	39	38	36
Marketing/administrative expenses	31	33	33	34	35	37
R & D expenses	5	7	7	8	9	9
Net profit after tax	8	14	15	14	15	12
As % of net profit after tax						
R & D expenditure	63	49	51	58	60	78
Dividends declared	41	42	41	43	42	53
Capital expenditures	64	34	30	37	43	67
Per employee						
Sales	73,421	102,666	111,900	120,880	131,672	134,730
Net profit after tax	6,127	14,788	16,500	16,958	19,347	16,178
Dividends declared	2,541	6,153	6,743	7,292	8,071	8,646
Capital expenditure	3,940	4,995	4,903	6,346	8,403	10,843
Working capital	26,185	43,589	43,220	52,681	42,800	37,843
Fixed capital	19,962	32,360	33,788	37,000	40,467	42,378
Total assets	81,356	114,538	130,688	170,088	186,738	197,743
Gearing ratio (%)	37	11	8	6	5	4
Return on shareholders' Equity	16	20	19	18	18	15

Source: Pfizer annual reports

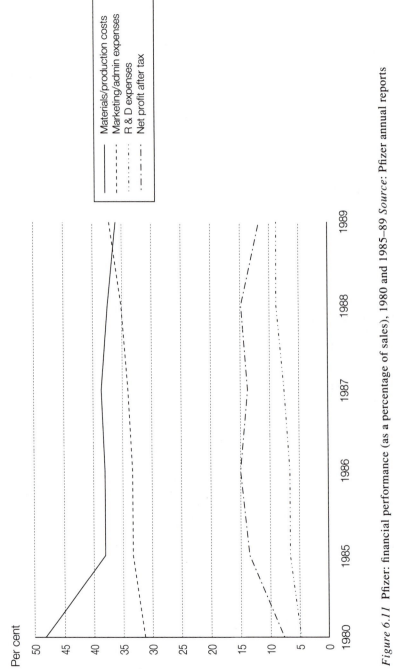

Per cent

Materials/production costs
Marketing/admin expenses
R & D expenses
Net profit after tax

Figure 6.11 Pfizer: financial performance (as a percentage of sales), 1980 and 1985–89 *Source*: Pfizer annual reports

Throughout the 1980s, our R & D expenditures have almost quadrupled, totalling more than $3 billion for the decade. And we spent more than 17 per cent of that sum in 1989. In addition, we continue to invest in new R & D facilities and manufacturing plants both in the US and overseas.

The result of these expenditures is that we now have a range of exciting new products in each of our businesses. Several have already been introduced in a number of countries, including the US. Their excellent acceptance to date is very promising for Pfizer as we continue to introduce them around the world.

Thus, the case is being made strongly that the 1989 financial performance represents a once-only downward movement because of large advance revenue expenditures made to launch and commercially develop a number of promising new products. The new products are certainly there, as will be seen in the next section. Time will tell if they return the expected performance, but the early signs are good.

Activities

Products and competition

In pharmaceuticals Pfizer has focused its research, development and marketing efforts upon drugs designed to combat chronic and debilitating diseases such as angina, arthritis, diabetes and serious fungal infections. Its current portfolio, summarised by therapeutic area, is set out in Table 6.19, together with an indication of the sales revenue the various classes generated in 1987–89, providing an indication of the relative importance to the company.

The following descriptions outline those that are of strategic importance in so far as they provide the current base of its revenues and those intended to take over that role in the future. The percentage figures quoted alongside each major product are James Capel's[15] estimates of market size and growth rates.

Feldene: anti-inflammatory; ($5 billion; + 10 per cent per annum)
Although a 'mature' product – first introduced in 1979 – Feldene, a once-a-day anti-inflammatory agent for the control of arthritis, continues to be the company's largest-selling drug, accounting for 23 per cent of its pharmaceutical turnover.

It is now facing increasing competition in a crowded market, from new product launches in the US by American Home and SmithKline

Table 6.19 Pfizer worldwide sales of therapeutic lines and most recently launched major products ($ million)

Product	1989	1988	1987	Annual Change 89/88	Annual Change 88/87
Worldwide pharmaceuticals	2,687	2,539	2,331	+6	+9
Anti-infectives	835	750	691	+11	+9
Cefobid	127	137	163	−7	−16
Sulperazon	108	84	60	+29	+40
Unasyn	140	82	22	+71	+273
Diflucan	44	2	–	*	–
Cardiovasculars	722	662	597	+9	+11
Procardia	420	364	305	+15	+19
Procardia XL	40	–	–	–	–
Minipress/Minizide	210	250	246	−16	+2
Minipress XL	4	–	–	–	–
Cardura	6	–	–	–	–
Anti-inflammatories	645	649	556	−1	+17
Feldene	612	616	524	−1	+18
Antidiabetes agents	171	153	143	+12	+ 7
Glucotrol	115	93	79	+24	+18
CNS agents	112	122	144	−8	−15
Other	202	203	200	–	+ 2

Source: Pfizer Annual Report 1989, p.19
* Growth more than 1,000%

Beecham and from generic substitution in its overseas markets. The company recognises its potential vulnerability and is attempting to maintain its position by the continued introduction of new dosage forms – tropical, injectable, suppository and dispersible tablets. This has had some success and although Pfizer is positioned in what is perhaps the largest single therapeutic market it is doubtful whether its position can ultimately be sustained in the face of significant competition from newer drugs.

Main competitors:

Voltaren	Ciba-Geigy	US launch 1988
Naprosyn	Syntex	
Indocid	Merck	
Clinoril	Merck	
Relifex	SmithKline Beecham	
Ultradil	American Home	

Procardia and Procardia XL: cardiovascular; ($3.5 billion; + 20 per cent) Procardia – a licensed drug – was the first oral calcium channel blocker introduced into the US. Originally indicated for angina, a new improved version, Procardia XL, has extended its application to hypertension and makes use of an advanced oral delivery system that delivers a near constant dosage throughout a twenty-four hour period.

In its first five months XL gained 13 per cent of all new US prescriptions for CCBs and has begun to be prescribed in place of other cardiovascular agents, e.g. diuretics, beta blockers, ACE inhibitors and nitroglycerin. It is estimated that 2.5 million Americans suffer from angina and over 60 million from hypertension, hence the importance of the XL extended indication. The base form of the drug is also produced by BASF and Searle as well as Pfizer, and the company's new calcium antagonist Cardura is an attempt to broaden its base in a therapeutic market that is seen to have significant growth opportunities.

Main competitors:

Cardizem	Tanabe, Marion	
Adalat	Bayer	out of patent
Perdipine	Yamanouchi	
Bayotensin	Bayer, Yamanouchi	

Potential new drug entrants

TA-3090	Tanabe
Plendil	Astra
Nisoldipline	Bayer

Diflucan: anti-infective First introduced into the UK and France in September 1988 and subsequently approved for the US market in January 1990, Diflucan is regarded as a significant antifungal agent and a potential 'blockbuster'. Indicated for infections of the urinary tract, peritonitis, pneumonia, and cryptococcal meningitis as well as fungal treatment for AIDS, cancer patients, transplant recipients, diabetics and those on long-term antibiotic regimes, it achieved 40 per cent market share within five months of its introduction onto the Japanese market. It is currently the leading oral antifungal in French hospitals and has been introduced into seven other European countries – Italy, Belgium, Denmark, Ireland, Sweden, Switzerland, and Iceland as well as Hong Kong. Pfizer intends to introduce the product into a further twenty-one countries during 1990. It is positioned against a single competitor, with few other development drugs likely to enter the market in the short to medium term. Diflucan is set to become the company's 'star' performer.

Main competitors:

Sporanox   Johnson & Johnson

Potential new drug entrants:

Sch-39304   Schering-Plough

Cardura: cardiovascular Launched in 1989, Cardura builds upon the Pfizer's experience with Minipress, the first of the selective alpha blockers – a class of agents discovered by Pfizer. It is intended as a once-a-day monotherapy providing an alternative to Pfizer's ageing Procardia. Launched in nine countries to date – Denmark, the UK, Ireland, Norway, Netherlands, West Germany, Hong kong, Austria and Korea – fifteen additional launches were planned for 1990, including the US. Japanese regulatory approval was gained in January 1990. Although a useful addition, industry opinion does not regard it as a breakthrough drug.

Main competitors:

Cardizem	Tanabe, Marion	
Adalat	Bayer	out of patent
Perdipine	Yamanouchi	
Procardia	Pfizer, BASF, Searle	
Bayotensin	Bayer	

Potential new drug entrants:

TA-3090	Tanabe
Plendil	Astra
Nisoldipline	Bayer

Sulbactam antibiotics: anti-infectives; ($3 billion; + 10 per cent per annum) This is a family of oral and injectable antibiotics based upon Pfizer's enzyme inhibitor sulbactam and includes – Unasyn (oral), Unasyn IM/IV and Sulperazon, which combines sulbactam with Pfizer's cephalosporin antibiotic Cefobid. This family is in competition with just about every major antibiotic.

Future developments

To a large extent, Pfizer's product line development supports the indications of the chairman's statement quoted above. A noticeable deficiency occurred in the anti-diabetes segment after the withdrawal of Sorbinil, but the new anti-diabetes Glucotrol surpassed sales of $100 million in 1989, thereby plugging the gap. Similarly, there is a relatively weak presence in the CNS segment, where Pfizer currently holds only about 1.5 per cent share of the market – well below all the other segments in which it is engaged. This weakness in CNS is expected to continue until the introduction of Sertraline in the early 1990s. In addition to Sertraline (an antidepressant), Pfizer's other important new drugs in the pipeline are cetirizine (antihistamine). azithromycin (microlide antibiotic). fluconazole (antifungal). Xomen E5 (monoclonal antibiotic).

Research and development

Pfizer has about sixty drug substances under research and development, of which about two-thirds are from its own laboratories and the remainder are under licence from other companies. Also, the firm has more than a dozen drug candidates passing through advanced clinical testing and development towards new product launches.

In recent years, Pfizer has increased R & D investments very quickly indeed; in fact, as a percentage of sales, the figures are almost the same as those noted earlier for Abbott Laboratories, and there is likely to be a similar strategy at work, being implemented in the same determined fashion (see Table 6.20). Specifically, in the health care business, Pfizer's R & D investments as a proportion of sales amounted to 8.8 per cent (1985), 9.4 per cent (1986), 10.4 per cent (1987), 11.3 per cent (1988) and 12.2 per cent (1989). Thus in the pharmaceuticals business above it is likely that R & D expenditures approach (possibly surpass) the industry norm of 13.5 per cent.

Table 6.20 Pfizer R & D

Measure	1985	1986	1987	1988	1989
R & D expenditure ($ million)	287	336	401	473	531
Increase on previous year (%)	12.5	17.1	19.3	18.0	12.3
As % of sales	7.1	7.5	8.2	8.8	9.4
As % of net profit after tax	49.5	50.8	58.1	59.7	78.0

The internationalisation of pharmaceutical research and development

Most of Pfizer's R & D capability is within a single organisation but that organisation is international in character. Almost 40 per cent of its human resources are overseas, so Pfizer research is essentially a decentralised operation. The main centre is at Groton, Connecticut, which carries out the full range of activities. An R & D unit was established at Sandwich, England, in 1958 and its mission is to develop products for worldwide use with a specific product development function for the European market. In the early 1960s, a second overseas R & D unit was established at Amboise, France. It does a great deal of drug safety evaluation for Sandwich. Finally, in 1972, a third offshore unit was opened, at Nagoya in Japan. Perhaps its principal contribution to Pfizer's global research output has been in the area of screening soil samples for fermentation-derived biologically active compounds.

The UK laboratory is an excellent example of Pfizer's approach towards decentralisation. It is perfectly capable of doing everything in the entire process that can be done in the US and so, to a degree, Pfizer has the advantages of decentralisation in a fairly centralised set-up. The best term to describe the Pfizer approach is 'participative centralisation' in the sense that the overseas laboratory in the UK recommends what its programme should be; and although the central administration has the ultimate say, in practical terms it rarely insists on changes in what has been recommended because over the years the basic research strategies have come to be well understood, and very little intervention is required in programme planning.

There are some advantages to centralisation. First, nowadays, with the enormous sophistication of science as well as of the technology that is used in research, with the phenomenal level of research competition that is now faced on a worldwide basis, it is very necessary to reach critical mass at any research centre, so it would be dangerous to have such a particulate organisation that it was made up of little pieces. It is very doubtful if any one operation would have the momentum and strength to cope. So if the firm is going to be research-intensive at the level of the largest firms in the industry, it is absolutely necessary to have at least some large laboratories which have critical mass in human resource terms.

The biggest challenge of all in decentralisation is communication. It is astonishing how difficult it is to remain fully and adequately in touch, especially on fast-breaking matters and development matters, even when the main laboratories are in English-speaking countries that are connected by every modern form of communication.

Control in research organisations becomes increasingly challenging on the basis of sheer size alone. It is certainly more difficult to exert management control over a laboratory on the other side of the ocean than it is when head office is right in the centre of it.

Critical mass

The way Pfizer has come to think about critical mass in recent years as the company has grown larger is to ask what level of productivity from research in the form of major new pharmaceutical products is required in order to achieve the growth objectives of the company, which are defined quite explicitly. This is coupled with a restrospective analysis of what amount of resources it takes to develop and discover a new product based on Pfizer's own experience. Pfizer's own data for the past decade or more tell the firm roughly what is necessary to do the job.

At Groton there are about 1,500 people. For a company of Pfizer's size, with the needs it has and with the level of competition it confronts, and with the regulatory requirements it faces, it would not be possible to be smaller than that in the largest facility; otherwise the firm would probably be suffering from lack of facilities, lack of equipment or lack of basic research power. So the firm's view is that it is necessary to have the main lab with one level of critical mass at the larger end. This allows it to have subsidiary labs with smaller critical masses.

On the small side, for Pfizer's situation, anything smaller than 500 people in total would have to be viewed as a satellite. A satellite is a laboratory that is not expected to be self-sufficient. It is one that has some role in collaboration with a larger centre. For example, the lab in France and the one in Japan would be regarded as satellite laboratories under this definition. However, these two are very different. The one in France is devoted entirely to safety evaluation work and it serves the British laboratory in that capacity. So that is a satellite laboratory which need not reach the critical mass of 500. It need only be staffed to do its specific job, which is narrowly defined. The Japanese laboratory, which is smaller still, is still only at the experimental stage where the firm is building up the manning. The firm will determine over the next four or five years just what the potential is for Pfizer to invest in innovative research in Japan with its own laboratory. So this is still in the experimental stage and it is also handled as a satellite to Groton, i.e. the work they do there is very closely tied in to one of the project teams in Groton.

The 500 minimum figure mentioned above is for total staff. This would imply something in the region of 300 research professionals.

Strengths and weaknesses

From this examination of Pfizer and its operating characteristics, it is now possible to derive the firm's strategic strengths and weaknesses, from which a range of future strategic options may be developed.

Strengths

1 *Global presence*: in the form of a large, effective sales and marketing organisation sited in all the world's major drug markets, including a recent 20 per cent increase in its US field staff. Although this is not unique Pfizer's is regarded as having an organisation that delivers an identifiable competitive advantage.

2 *Aggressive licensing organisation.* Although competent in research Pfizer has shown itself to be alert to the strategic opportunities presented by the licensing of appropriate compounds and possesses the resources necessary to undertake subsequent development.

3 *Good working relationships with regulatory bodies, particularly the FDA.* The advantages of this have been amply demonstrated by the whirlwind approval it secured in the US for Diflucan, its breakthrough antifungal agent.

4 *Appropriate research focus.* Given the actual and forecast increase in the proportion of elderly and very elderly people in the populations of most Western countries, it is likely that this will lead to a shift in the demand for various therapeutic classes of drugs, most obviously those directed towards the treatment of chronic and degenerative illness such as arthritis, dementia, senility, CNS disorders and immune deficiency. These are the areas upon which Pfizer has focused its research effort and in which it has built up considerable expertise.

Weaknesses

1 *Ageing portfolio.* Although the company claims to have more new drugs in its research pipeline than ever before, this should not obscure the fact that its most successful drug – the anti-arthritic Feldene – has been on the market for twelve years and is now facing stiff competition from Merck, AHP and SmithKline Beecham in the US. It is still reliant upon it for 23 per cent of its sales turnover and Procardia, its second-biggest revenue earner, is also feeling the pace and is having its life extended by advanced XL delivery systems.

2 *Patent expiration.* The company faces significant exposure to generic competition as a result of patents expiring during the next few years.

Strategy options and choice

Matching Pfizer's strengths and weaknesses with the environmental opportunities and threats (developed in Chapter 5) yields a number of future strategy options for the firm.

1 Further expansion (forward vertical integration) into the over-the-counter market. The over-the-counter market is expanding at a higher rate than ethical drugs, particularly in the US. A move in this direction would make use of the company's established and strong chemical/pharmaceutical processing skills and Pfizer could well outperform competition by benefiting from economies of scale. Pfizer through its Consumer Products division, already shows presence in the over-the-counter business sector. The company started along this road when purchasing Oral Research Laboratories in September 1988. However, its relative lack of expertise in the retail business would suggest an alliance as the best way of taking advantage of this opportunity.

Direct acquisition is a further possibility in order to gain a more substantial foothold in the over-the-counter business. As in the alliance option, this would take advantage of its manufacturing skills but would require strong management skills to manage a non-core activity in the retail business. The profitability of the US market has been steadily increasing whilst profits from other geographical areas are decreasing.

2 Make use of already established channels of distribution and manufacturing plants and use them as platforms for moving into new markets such as China and the Far East. Operations already exist in Japan and ties through licensing agreements are extant. A relatively politically stable area offers parallel opportunities for growth of business in other divisional segments.

3 Move into the USSR and other Eastern Bloc countries as they move towards more market-oriented economies. The Soviet Union or Hungary would be particularly interested in benefiting from the transfer of technology and expertise from a company as strongly established as Pfizer. At the same time there should be no restriction imposed by either the American government or European counterparts, as basic pharmaceutical technology is not proscribed. There is a need for a European partner to facilitate a move into this area, however, clarification on how to repatriate profits would be required (cf. Shell's and Enichem's moves into the USSR) prior to making any moves in this area. Developments in this geographical area should be monitored by Pfizer, while awaiting suitable opportunities.

4 Closer alliances in marketing, R & D and distribution with other pharmaceutical companies along the lines of current agreements between Bayer of Europe and Taito (a Pfizer subsidiary) in Japan. Agreements of this sort would result in mutual benefits from utilising

distribution and marketing channels already in place, thereby increasing profitability.

5 Development of the generic division to take further advantage of well established brands. Buying from other major pharmaceutical companies brands which have come out of patent should also be considered. Government intervention to lower the cost of state health care means that increasing emphasis is being placed on generics. Pfizer could benefit in this growth area by cashing in on the benefits offered from economies of scale in its manufacturing business, and by using its established brand names. Undoubtedly generics are the major growth area in the years ahead.

6 Acquisitions and/or mergers in the pharmaceutical industry to complement existing portfolio, cover the current drug cycle gap and take advantage of the strong overseas marketing division. A possible target would be Upjohn, which lacks worldwide marketing and distribution channels but whose portfolio could augment deficient areas of Pfizer's ethical business. Upjohn is particularly strong in CNS and antidiabetes, where Pfizer's portfolio is lacking.

7 Buy and/or sponsor university R & D, as many universities are lacking long-term funding for more ambitious R & D projects. This option becomes even more attractive as many universities are looking very actively for industry funding as part of privatisation trends and reductions in government funds. This option would as well have a positive impact on the recruitment of high-calibre R & D personnel.

8 Last, but not least, Pfizer could opt for a strategy of 'logical incrementalism'. However, such a strategy would only work if the strategic goals and objectives were clearly set and logical incrementalism became implementation of a strategy of small steps without major changes to current business practice.

A number of the above options could be combined, in pursuing Pfizer's growth over the next decade. The over-the-counter market can be expanded in the US by building on Pfizer's corporate image and expertise in ethical pharmaceuticals as a basis for moving into medicated over-the-counter products. This should be done in niche segments, such as oral products.

In order to further strengthen Pfizer's presence in the Pacific Rim, the company should continue to work towards expanding operations in that area. This would allow early entry into growing markets, based on an existing commitment to the Asian market.

Pfizer should also continue with the existing strategy of licensing substances, as well as of acquisitions of smaller, research-based companies with potentially important drugs. This should primarily focus on the areas where Pfizer's current portfolio is reduced owing to expiring patents and lack of research breakthroughs, as in CNS drugs. This strategy should also be further developed in order to gain entrance to new markets, e.g. cancer and AIDS. Mergers with larger companies offering a strategic fit, allowing access to new markets and new products, should also be further considered, allowing increased economies of scale.

Sponsoring and/or buying university-grown R & D seems to be a promising way for a cash-rich company such a Pfizer to gain access to high-quality research, mainly in areas of basic research.

The company should further build on its technological strengths in the field of computer-aided graphic biogenetic modelling and simulation. This technological high end area of computer applications could give the company a leading edge in this field.

Conclusion

From the analysis that has been carried out, the company appears to face the same type of decision that confronted SmithKline and Beecham as separate companies. Although it has substantial resources at its disposal, the concentration that is taking place within the industry is forming even bigger players. Given an ageing portfolio of drugs and imminent patent expirations, it is unlikely that the one real winner Pfizer appears to have in Diflucan will be able to generate sufficient internal resources to enable it to compete effectively in an increasingly competitive global market into the future.

Pfizer appears to face a choice between pursuing its future as a diversified company, in which case more attention needs to be given to the Chemicals, Materials Science and Consumer Products divisions; and releasing these resources to focus the firm's attention upon its health care business and growth within that sector by merger or acquisition.

The choice appears crudely simple. However, companies well into their second century are apt to have formed a view about their place in the world, to carry with them an historical legacy that pushes them towards the maintenance of a separate and identifiable existence. This is the case with Pfizer and by that inclination they would prefer market and product development strategies. In the last analysis it comes down to the perceptions and expectations of management and the arrival of a willing and complementary suitor.

7 The British pharmaceutical market

In a report[1] published in 1986, the Pharmaceutical Economic Development Council took particular care to underline the importance of the UK ethical drugs industry to the economy as a whole, emphasising that growth had been very satisfactory over a long period of time, that innovative companies continued to be profitable, and that the UK industry's high rate of internationalisation had led to a substantial surplus trade balance. Clearly, the existence and vigorous development of the nationally based pharmaceuticals business had led to substantial benefits in employment, investment and (perhaps most important of all) in the nation's technological capacity. For the EDC, this industry typifies the type of sector that the UK must sustain and develop in order to maintain international competitiveness; it also provides a suitable development template for other high-technology sunrise industries.

Thus, while the industry's output is less than 2 per cent of UK manufacturing industry as a whole, it is – in net terms – the second largest manufacturing contributor to the UK balance of trade.[2] Also, while UK consumption of pharmaceuticals is about 3 per cent of the world total, around 8 per cent of the total drugs R & D expenditure is in British laboratories. Despite this record of success, the Association of the British Pharmaceutical Industry (ABPI) believes that the industry is subject to wide-ranging political criticism, much of which is perceived by drug firms as being hostile and ill-informed.[3]

Certainly, the objective observer (if such exists!) would probably agree that the UK industry had something of a surprise in the 1980s, in that its relationship with the Conservative government was significantly less smooth than had been the case in the past. The reason is more likely to be the severe and growing pressure on public expenditure of all kinds than any real change in ideological perspective by either side.

THE MARKET

Glaxo[4] estimated the UK market for 1989 at some £2,500 million, an increase of 10 per cent on 1988. While this probably represented a real increase in volume, it was a lower growth rate than that recorded by some other European countries (e.g. France 11 per cent, Italy 12 per cent, Spain 15 per cent). UK consumption as a proportion of the global total has been steady around 3 per cent for the past few years.

Table 7.1 shows the output of the UK pharmaceutical industry by the main therapeutic classes for 1977 and 1987. Overall, the average annual rate of growth over the period was just under 10per cent per annum; the corresponding figure for the various therapeutic groups varies widely around this mean from a low of −3.31 per cent per annum for the blood class to 16.33 per cent per annum for the sensory organ therapeutic group. When inflation is taken into account, it can be seen that there has been significant real volume growth in five of the twelve therapeutic classes: sensory organs, muscular and skeletal, alimentary tract, genito-urinary, and respiratory. Similarly, there has been negative volume growth in dermatologicals, antiparasitics, and the blood groups. Analysing the figures in Table 7.1 by cash increases yields another perspective; the big winners are seen to be alimentary (increase of £291

Table 7.1 UK pharmaceutical output by the main therapeutic classes, at current manufacturers' prices

Therapeutic class	1977 (£ million)	1987 (£ million)	Average annual growth (%)	% of total 1977	% of total 1987
Central nervous system	155	287	6.35	16.83	12.33
Cardiovascular	150	374	9.57	16.29	16.07
Blood and blood forming organs	28	20	−3.31	3.04	0.86
Respiratory system	108	323	11.58	11.73	13.87
Alimentary tract system	122	413	12.97	13.25	17.74
Genito-urinary (incl sex hormones)	26	78	11.61	2.82	3.35
Hormones (excl sex hormones)	14	30	7.92	1.52	1.29
Muscular and skeletal system	70	282	14.95	7.60	12.11
Dermatologicals	56	98	5.76	6.08	4.21
Sensory organs	13	59	16.33	1.41	2.53
General anti-infectives	169	353	7.64	18.35	15.16
Antiparasitics	10	11	0.96	1.09	0.47
Totals	921	2,328	9.72		

Source: Census of Production and Department of Industry

million over the ten years), cardiovascular (£224 million), respiratory (£215 million), muscular and skeletal (£212 million), general anti-infectives (£184 million) and CNS (£132 million). Taken together, these six therapeutic classes account for £1,258 million increase, or about 90 per cent of the total increase in cash output.

Table 7.2 shows the growth in National Health Service sales of ethical drugs over the period 1977–87; the average annual rate of increase was 13.6 per cent. Note also that sales as a proportion of industry output and of GDP also rose significantly during this ten-year period.

According to the ABPI,[5] imported goods account for only about one-sixth of UK domestic medicine consumption, and this proportion has been fairly stable since 1984. Table 7.3 gives an indication of UK pharmaceutical trade performance. This shows that while the positive trade balance has grown by over £450 million between 1977 and 1987, as an average annual growth rate this comes out to only 8.2 per cent. In contrast, imports have been growing at 16.3 per cent per annum. Similarly, the comparative position of pharmaceutical exports per head still looks good in sterling terms beside the equivalent figure for all other manufactured exports; however, pharmaceutical exports per

Table 7.2 UK ethical pharmaceutical home market at current manufacturers' prices

Year	Total NHS sales (£ million)	Sales per head (£)	Sales as % of gross Output	Sales as % of gross GDP
1977	605	10.75	38.01	0.41
1987	2,162	38.05	44.50	0.52
Average increase (%)	13.6			

Source: ABPI

Table 7.3 UK pharmaceutical trade

Year	Exports FOB (£m)	Imports CIF (£m)	Trade balance (£m)	Pharmaceutical exports per employee (£)	All UK exports per employee (£)
1977	555	174	381	7,812	3,524
1987	1,621	786	835	18,543	11,807
Average Increase (%)	11.31	16.28	8.16	9.03	12.85

Source: HM Customs and Excise, and Department of Employment

employee grew by only 9 per cent per annum over the ten years, compared to 12.1 per cent per annum for all UK manufactured exports. Thus, while the UK position in the international pharmaceuticals trade remains strong, the industry is not quite the pre-eminent performer it was in the 1970s.

The regulatory regime

As noted above, there is a clear perception within the industry that it has been subjected to increasingly severe restrictions on its commercial operations, with government controls on prescribing and further squeezes on profitability, prices and promotion. The effect of this may have been to reduce the growth rate of the UK pharmaceuticals market and make the UK a less desirable locus of foreign direct investment for global players in the industry.

Ethical drug prices in the UK are controlled via the Pharmaceutical Price Regulation Scheme (PPRS) which was established in 1978; the objective of the scheme is to control the cost of drugs to the government while allowing for a satisfactory (but restricted) return on capital. To increase its control in this area, the government introduced a 'limited list' which was further divided into a 'white list' containing the drugs that doctors could prescribe under the NHS regime, and a 'black list' containing drugs where the prescription would not be reimbursed by the NHS. The criteria for inclusion on the white list are therapeutic need and cost. Some pharmaceutical firms have argued that the limited list is virtually a vehicle for the introduction of mandatory generic pre-scribing in the UK, but this is probably carrying the argument too far.

However, it should be noted that the limited list regulations may not have affected all companies in the same way. For instance, not all pharmaceutical firms are affected by the limited list, as they do not all have major product ranges in the therapeutic groups covered. Also, some of the affected firms have found better ways of overcoming the problem, e.g. Wellcome minimised the commercial difficulty caused by the removal of Actifed from the white list by developing the product in the over-the-counter sector and resorting to heavy public advertising.

Similarly, the pharmaceutical industry's profits on sales to the NHS (by far its largest customer) are effectively controlled by the PPRS. Under this scheme, each firm is allocated a target rate of return on capital by the regulatory authority. This target is arrived at after accounting for the circumstances of the individual firm and of the contribution it makes (or is likely to make) to the economy in terms of investment, foreign earnings, employment and research. In addition, the scheme allows for an additional discretionary 'grey area', the margin above a firm's profitability target within which it could be allowed to retain additional profit earned on NHS sales. It is argued that this part of the PPRS favours large British firms.

In 1984 the UK government reduced the allowable return on capital to 21 per cent, and further reduced it in 1985 to between 15 and 17 per cent. Naturally this resulted an in outcry from the industry, together with a measure of cancellation or postponement of capital investment projects. It is likely that the government has tacitly accepted that the profitability squeeze has been overdone, because there has been a degree of relaxation since 1986.

Other restrictions include profit regulation through prices. For example, if the 'Annual Financial Returns Forecast' (a requirement of the PPRS) for an upcoming year showed a deficit on the profitability target, the government would then grant a price increase. However, if the company exceeded its profit target, it would be required to repay the excess to the government or accept a year with no price increases.

The long-run effect of this gradual tightening of controls could be characterised as follows:

1 Although the overall effects of profitability restrictions have been significant, nevertheless UK profits represent only a small proportion of total profits for most British-owned companies and especially for British subsidiaries of major pharmaceutical multinationals.
2 Investments by overseas companies have been reduced, deferred or cancelled; into this category would come Lilly and A.H. Robins.
3 Companies have been forced to concentrate resources on their most profitable products.
4 Generally, regulations have become a source of comparative advantage to large firms, while small ones have been disadvantaged and forced to invest less in R & D.
5 There has been a slight shift (beginning of a trend?) in sales from the ethical to the over-the-counter market segment.
6 Annual growth in sales to the NHS has declined.

The most recent attempt at government regulation of the industry came in January 1989 with the publication of the White Paper *Working for Patients*. This will impact the pharmaceutical industry through its proposal that family doctors should be given 'indicative drug budgets' in an effort to restrict the upward spiral of expenditure on medicines. According to the ABPI[6] the implication will be to encourage doctors to prescribe the cheapest therapy for their patients and to avoid the more expensive innovative new products. This is perhaps an overly pessimistic conclusion and assumes that doctors will meekly fall in with government cost-cutting intentions without having proper regard for patient needs. However, the long-run effect may well be to reduce the industry's incentive to produce new and better therapies, and to discourage doctors from running screening programmes. Only time will tell.

New products

In the view of the ABPI,[7] confidence in the UK as a preferred location for pharmaceutical R & D has recovered, and record levels of investment are now taking place. The width and depth of this investment may be assessed by consideration of the following range of R & D activities:

1 Glaxo has successfully launched the first of the second generation of oral cephalosporin antibiotics in Japan and France, and its 5HT research is yielding promising results in control of emesis in cancer patients and in antimigraine treatment. Other areas of activity include a new bronchodilator, a calcium antagonist to treat hypertension and a steroid to treat seasonal and perennial allergic rhinitis.
2 Beecham has developed a new topical antibiotic treatment for nasal staphylococcal bacteria, and a thrombolytic drug which has been launched successfully in Europe. Its new bedfellow, SmithKline, launched a new vaccine to protect children against measles, mumps and rubella; it announced a new treatment for gastro-oesophageal reflux disease; and it was active in the hypertension therapeutic area.
3 ICI Pharmaceuticals has been very active with launches of an injectable anaesthetic preparation, a once-a-month formulation for treating prostate cancer, a new ACE inhibitor, and a new approach to the treatment of heart failure.
4 The Wellcome Foundation introduced a new drug for the treatment of allergic rhinitis and urticaria.
5 Fisons were also busy with a product launch in the respiratory therapeutic area, with the development of a new corticosteroid licensed from Squibb; other development work is concentrated in the fields of inflammation and immunology, cardiovasculars, and gastro-intestinals.
6 Wyeth introduced an antidiabetes compound which will help with complications in long-term diabetes.
7 Pfizer introduced the first of a new class of antifungals, and also launched a novel alpha-blocking agent to combat hypertension.

8 Syntex introduced a new antiviral, and continued with development work in non-steroidal anti-inflammatories, endometriosis, peptic ulcer disease, ischaemic heart disease and hypertension.

9 Janssen concentrated its clinical research programme in several areas, including anti-allergics, anaesthesia, cardiovascular treatments, gastro-enterology, mycology, virology and psychiatry.

10 Other active firms included Cilag (renal disease), Roche (anaesthetics) Lederle (angina and hypertension), Lilly (CNS), Farmitalia Carlo Erba (coronary heart disease), Amersham International (CNS), and Hoechst (acute myocardial infarction).

Industry analysis

The general industry analysis in Chapter 5 evaluated the five competitive forces which work on the pharmaceutical industry and its profitability. For three of these, there are no real differences – entry barriers, pressure from substitute products and the bargaining power of suppliers. The remaining two competitive forces are evaluated below.

In the UK, as in many other countries, the government is the major customer for the industry's output, and also regulates safety standards and profitability on sales to the NHS. In short, customer bargaining power is high and the industry has been subjected to increasing restrictions as the government attempts to contain its NHS costs. The strict safety guidelines may contribute to delay in the commercialisation of new products as well as to the escalation of fixed overheads, particularly in R & D. Also, the buyer has virtually full information on which to base its view of the equitable return on investment that should be allowed to the industry. However, in evaluating this force, it should be remembered that despite the recent squeeze on profitability, the UK pharmaceutical industry still remains one of the most profitable manufacturing sectors in Britain. The outcry about price constraints is probably more realistic when considered relative to both the risk and the investment involved in R & D activity.

As in other countries, rivalry among existing competitors is mainly in the form of product innovation. With the relative decline in the home market for ethical drugs, the tendency will be to position a new product so that it gets on to the NHS white list to be eligible for GP prescription.

To compensate, in a conscious or unconscious move to reduce rivalry in the ethical sector, companies have rationalised their organisations, concentrating on fewer areas of R & D – mainly in the areas of relatively high market value such as cardiovasculars, AIDS, and cancer treatments. The dominance of multinationals is likely to continue, with the growing importance of successful product innovation contributing to increased concentration in the industry.

Taking these two competitive forces together, we can see that while the increased bargaining power of the government tends to reduce the attractiveness of the industry in the UK, this may be counteracted by the longer-term effect of oligopolistic behaviour among rivals tending to increase attractiveness. The net effect of the five competitive forces, compared to the global position outlined in Chapter 5, is probably to make the UK a less attractive (and therefore less profitable) market than the international norm, with a tendency to converge in the longer term.

Opportunities and threats

As with the industry analysis, so the UK-specific analysis of environmental opportunities and threats tends to be similar to the global factors outlined in Chapter 5. There are, however, some differences which relate to the geographical location of the UK, to the historical perspective which links/separates Britain with/from the rest of the world, and the particular form of development followed by the UK pharmaceutical industry. Thus, the UK-specific opportunities facing the industry over the next few years include:

1 The highly internationalised nature of the UK pharmaceutical industry means that particular opportunities will increasingly open up as the world economy develops and trade is liberalised. The most notable of these opportunities are the opening up of the Japanese, Eastern European and Chinese markets, and the harmonisation of EC regulations following the completion of the single European market in 1992.
2 The proposal to increase patent protection to twenty years in Europe will be particularly beneficial to large international drug firms.
3 Regulatory and market changes will encourage significant growth in the over-the-counter and generic sectors; again, this could be particularly beneficial to flexible, fast-moving drug multinationals.

Similarly, the UK-specific threats facing the industry over the next few years include:

1 The advent of the single European market in 1992 will also pose a particular threat to UK-based firms because the price premiums obtained in the UK market will be difficult, even impossible, to

maintain. Also, the pressure on costs and the harmonisation of standards will lead to significant rationalisation of European operations, and low-cost countries will tend to benefit at the expense of higher-cost centres like the UK.

2 The growth in the UK over-the-counter and generic sectors indicated above will be a particular threat to those firms whose product line is weak and/or which have many out-of-patent products.

3 The advent of indicative drug budgets, outlined above, may prove in time to be the biggest single threat to the industry that will emerge during the 1990s.

However, despite the particular problems facing the UK industry, most observers and players still see a broadly favourable outlook. To evaluate the range of parameters described above, we now turn to a detailed analysis of three major UK-owned pharmaceutical multinationals: Glaxo, ICI Pharmaceuticals, and Wellcome.

GLAXO HOLDINGS PLC

Company history and development

The company which was to become the Glaxo Group, the UK's leading pharmaceutical organisation, had its origins in New Zealand more than a century ago. Glaxo first became known as a supplier of dried milk for infant feeding in the early 1900s and then moved into the medical products market in 1924. The company entered the antibiotics field in 1943 as one of the first manufacturers charged with the task of pioneering the mass production of penicillin. Extensive research in the antibiotics field culminated in the launch in 1964 of cephaloridine, a broad-spectrum injectable antibiotic effective against a wide range of infections.

In the late 1950s, Glaxo began an expansion programme which was to give an even broader base to its operations. Allen & Hanburys Ltd (Britain's oldest surviving pharmaceutical company) was acquired in 1958 and Edinburgh Pharmaceutical Industries Ltd in 1963. Other acquisitions included Evans Medical, the pharmaceutical wholesalers Vestric, and the infant foods and nutritional products company, Farley Health Products Ltd.

These and other companies, each with its own network of overseas subsidiaries and distributors, were brought under the Glaxo umbrella in the 1950s and 1960s to create the UK's and one of the world's largest pharmaceutical groups. The tradition they brought with them gave added impetus to the Glaxo Group's already fruitful R & D programme, which has resulted in a portfolio of more than 250 products in a wide variety of preparations. Among the key therapeutic areas in which the group has an interest are gastro-intestinal diseases, asthma, infectious diseases, skin disorders and cardiovascular problems.

During the 1960s and 1970s the Glaxo Group embarked on a worldwide expansion programme which was to lead up to it becoming the only British organisation among the world's top twenty pharmaceutical companies. Rapid growth was achieved throughout the world, but particularly in the leading pharmaceutical market-places.

The group acquired a subsidiary in the US in 1978 and this has grown rapidly to become one of the top ten companies in the US pharmaceutical industry. In Japan, the second largest pharmaceutical market after the US, Glaxo has been represented for over thirty years and is one of the leading non-Japanese companies. The group is also among the leaders in the major markets of Europe such as Italy and Germany. In many countries Glaxo also has joint venture and licensing arrangements with local pharmaceutical companies. During the period of substantial growth in the 1980s the group's mainstream business was gradually rationalised into prescription medicines, and a number of historic business interests were sold. These included wholesalers Vestric, Farley, Evans and the veterinary interests.

The modern Glaxo is ranked second by sales in the world industry league. It has subsidiary and associated companies in over fifty countries and is the leading pharmaceutical company in many of them, including the UK, Italy, the Netherlands, New Zealand, Ireland and Hong Kong. More than half the group's subsidiaries have their own manufacturing facilities and they, together with a network of agents and distributors, ensure that Glaxo's products are available in virtually every country in the world.

Mission statement

The firm's own view of its mission statement is encapsulated in a recent publication:[8]

> Glaxo is an integrated research-based group of companies whose corporate purpose is the discovery, development, manufacture and marketing of safe, effective medicines of the highest quality.
> The cornerstone of the Glaxo Group's growth has been its commitment to research and development with the objective of discovering and developing better and safe medicines of the highest quality and benefit.

There are over 31,000 employees worldwide, and products are sold in 150 countries through a network of seventy subsidiary and associated companies.

Since Glaxo has developed from being a small company in 1980 to one of the global pharmaceutical giants by the end of the decade, its underlying strategy has obviously been effective in pursuing the mission statement.

In the early 1980s Glaxo decided to concentrate on prescription medicines, and has since shed its Wholesaling Division, Surgical Products Division, Veterinary, Foods and Generic Divisions (1984–87).

It committed itself to generate growth from internal resources and decided to devote its resources and management effort to develop the mainstream business, which was not only of high quality but also with potential for high growth. The then new chairman, P. Girolami, developed a four-point plan:

1 To concentrate Glaxo's resources and efforts on medicines of the highest quality and benefit to society.
2 To expand Glaxo's activities and markets worldwide.
3 To expand and improve Glaxo's research, development and technological resources as the base for the successful pursuit of these goals.
4 To create a flexible international organisation capable of adapting itself to meet the changing and complex needs of a worldwide business.

Objectives

Unlike some other pharmaceutical multinationals, Glaxo is not very forthcoming about its business objectives. However, these would appear to be based on four sets of parameters which the firm sees as crucial to success:

1 Availability of capital to invest in R & D, production facilities (primary and secondary) and to build marketing and sales networks in the three main markets of Europe, the US and Japan. Ability to sustain this type of investment in the long term is also critical.
2 Innovation, generation of new products and also the extension of current product life cycles, in the main therapeutic markets.
3 Manufacturing efficiency – economies of scale and technological-innovations especially in primary production.

4 Ability to maximise the sales of new products by launching them on to the three major markets as quickly as possible, and having the appropriate size of sales teams to do the job efficiently. This is perhaps both the key area and potentially the most expensive outlay; great savings can be made here by economies of scale.

The relationship of this mix of abilities to the achievement of objectives is perhaps best illustrated by an excerpt from the chairman's annual statement to Glaxo shareholders:[9]

If we are to continue long-term growth, it is necessary to carry on enlarging the prospects for discovering new products, both by intensifying our efforts in existing therapeutic areas and by extending our research into others. To succeed we must be prepared not only to invest heavily in plant and equipment but also to harness the skills and talents of scientists of different cultures and different countries, organised in such a way as to give free rein to their inventiveness. With that aim we have chosen to expand overseas the number of establishments involved in research, each forming part of a major trading company and each with delegated freedom to invest, and not to create one huge establishment.

For the more immediate future, we continue to have a programme of unprecedented size for developing a large number of compounds which promise to become major products. As marketing authorisations come through, there is, in addition, the immense task of providing the medical community around the world with the information about these important new medicines to enable them best to serve their patients. All this has to be done without relaxing our efforts on our existing products, which still have a great potential for growth, while at the same time pursuing the challenge of untapped markets. Although there is not another market available to give us the decisive increase in sales that we gained in the United States in the past decade, other areas of the world remain undeveloped for Glaxo products. The changes that have taken place in Eastern Europe give us a welcome opportunity to develop markets which were previously outside our reach. In the Far East, a region of great economic vitality, the potential for our products in terms of population far exceeds the prospects in Eastern Europe. In these areas, and in Latin America, we have the prospect of laying the foundations for bigger and more prosperous businesses in the course of the decade.

Business segments

Until recently, Glaxo was a highly diversified company operating in many fields, but is now virtually entirely concentrated in ethical pharmaceuticals. Three of Glaxo's products feature on the list of the world's top twenty best-selling drugs. Zantac (an anti-ulcerant) heads the list; the others are Ventolin (an anti-asthmatic) and Zinnat (an oral antibiotic). The firm is involved in producing drugs in five main therapeutic categories: anti-ulcerants, respiratory, systemic antibiotics, cardiovascular, and dermatologicals; in the first two, Glaxo is the major player.

In 1990 Glaxo employed 31,300 people directly, though the total employment figure rises to over 40,000 when associated companies are included. Nearly one-third of these are located in the UK, and the remainder in some fifty other countries where the firm conducts operations. Great efforts are made to increase employee motivation and identification with company objectives by the use of suggestion schemes, newspapers, videos and an annually produced 'Report to Staff' in seven languages. Employment policies are rigorously equal opportunity, and the firm has an enlightened attitude towards jobs for the disabled. In terms of management development, Glaxo's human resource planning is done on a national basis, with central arrangements to identify and develop promising managers on an international basis.

Financial analysis

Geographical spread

Glaxo's sales are often described as being 'highly internationalised', but this is only strictly true if the comparison is made between, say, 1981, when only 44 per cent of sales were made outside Europe, and 1990, when the proportion had risen to 55 per cent. In effect, what has happened since 1981 is that a major market (North America) has been added to the firm's geographical spread, but the proportion of sales accounted for by all other market areas has decreased (with the exception of Europe). This can be seen from the data in Table 7.4. Over the period 1981–90, total sales increased at an average rate of 16.7 per cent per annum which is a truly staggering rate of increase. Effectively, it means that Glaxo's sales increased by a factor of four over the decade. The rate of increase varied widely from one region of the world to another, but the net effect is shown in Figure 7.1. The position is perhaps best understood by looking briefly at each market area.

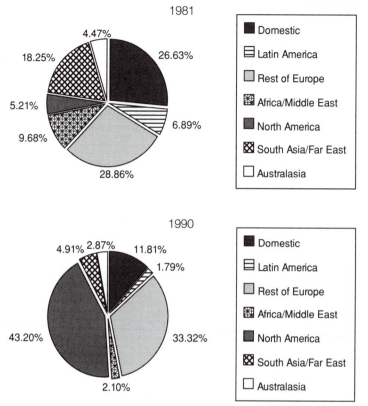

Figure 7.1 Glaxo: geographical spread of customer sales, 1981 and 1991 (%)
Source: Glaxo annual reports

United Kingdom. In 1990 total sales increased by 10 per cent to a record £337 million. The contribution made by Zantac to sales growth in the UK seems to be falling off: in 1988 Zantac sales increased by 31 per cent, in 1989 by 12 per cent; the 1990 figure is not reported, but is likely to have been less than half that for the previous year. During the 1980s as a whole, domestic sales increased at an average rate of 10 per cent per annum; while this is a very healthy rate of increase, never-theless UK sales as a proportion of the total fell from 27 per cent in 1981 to 12 per cent in 1990. Glaxo's total exports from the UK amounted to £683 million in 1990, representing nearly one-third of all drug exports, a performance which won the firm a 1990 Queen's Award for Export Achievement.

Table 7.4 Glaxo geographical spread

Measure	1981	1982	1983	1984	1985	1986	1987	1988	1989	1990
Sales (£ million, excluding UK wholesaling)										
Domestic	143	158	173	195	228	232	233	277	305	337
Europe (excluding UK)	155	203	274	319	383	503	597	660	776	951
North America	28	45	66	193	333	469	662	831	1,163	1,233
Latin America	37	36	30	33	30	35	34	31	38	51
Africa and Middle East	52	65	62	62	68	54	56	73	59	60
Southern Asia and Far East	98	110	120	74	106	94	111	128	156	140
Australasia	24	46	54	39	38	42	48	59	73	82
Sales (% increase on previous year)										
Domestic	34	10	9	13	17	2	0	19	10	10
Europe (excluding UK)	7	31	35	16	20	31	19	11	18	23
North America	27	61	47	192	73	41	41	26	40	6
Latin America	28	-3	-17	10	-9	17	-3	-9	23	34
Africa and Middle East	41	25	-5	0	10	-21	4	30	-19	2
Southern Asia and Far East	27	12	9	-38	43	-11	18	15	22	-10
Australasia	41	92	17	-28	-3	11	14	23	24	12
Sales (Indexed)										
Domestic	100	110	121	136	159	162	163	194	213	236
Europe (excluding UK)	100	131	177	206	247	325	385	426	501	614
North America	100	161	236	689	1,189	1,675	2,364	2,968	4,154	4,404
Latin America	100	97	81	89	81	95	92	84	103	138
Africa and Middle East	100	125	119	119	131	104	108	140	113	115
Southern Asia and Far East	100	112	122	76	108	96	113	131	159	143
Australasia	100	192	225	163	158	175	200	246	304	342

Sales (% of total by area)

Domestic	27	24	22	21	19	16	13	13	12	12
Europe (excluding UK)	29	31	35	35	32	35	34	32	30	33
North America	5	7	8	21	28	33	38	40	45	43
Latin America	7	5	4	4	3	2	2	2	1	2
Africa and Middle East	10	10	8	7	6	4	3	4	2	2
Southern Asia and Far East	18	17	15	8	9	7	6	6	6	5
Australasia	4	7	7	4	3	3	3	3	3	3

Source: Glaxo annual reports

Europe (excluding UK). The group's sales continued to grow in all other main European markets, increasing by 23 per cent in 1990 to a figure of £951 million. This represents 33 per cent of total group sales, an advance from 29 per cent in 1981. Sales increases over the previous year varied widely:

Eastern Europe	over 200%
Turkey	83%
France	28%
Greece	27%
Spain	26%
Portugal	18%
Italy	15%
Germany	12%

In addition, Glaxo managed to edge its market share forward in most countries. Especially encouraging was the fact that several products other than Zantac made significant advances, particularly in the major markets.

North America. In the US, the world's largest single market for pharmaceuticals, Glaxo's market share was approaching 6 per cent in 1990, and sales in this market accounted for 39 per cent of group turnover. The firm has now become a very major force within the US pharmaceutical industry. Zantac consolidated its position as the largest-selling drug in the US with a sales increase of 17 per cent, but increases of up to 45 per cent were recorded by the firm's respiratory products. In Canada, respiratory products also performed well, but Zantac lost market share to fiercely competitive generic ranitidine. Taking the North American market as a whole, sales increased by only 6 per cent in 1990, which must be some concern to the firm, as this market powered the group's major advance during the 1980s. From accounting for only 5 per cent of total sales in 1981, it rose to a massive 43 per cent in 1990 (down from 45 per cent in 1989). As an average annual rate of increase, this comes out as an enormous 52.3 per cent per annum.

Latin America. This is not an important market for Glaxo; over the 1980s it has fallen from 7 per cent to 2 per cent of group sales. However, the optimism about Latin America noted above in the chairman's 1990 statement perhaps reflects the fact that in 1989 and 1990 sales increases amounted to 23 per cent and 34 per cent respectively. Particularly good performance is being achieved in Mexico, but in other parts of the region Glaxo faces severe economic and political conditions, not the least of which is inadequate patent protection.

Africa and the Middle East. This is another market that has become progressively less important (in comparative terms) for Glaxo, falling from 10 per cent of Group turnover in 1981 to 2 per cent in 1990. Unlike Latin America, there are few signs of optimism or a recovery. Sales increased by only 2 per cent in 1990, having fallen by 19 per cent in 1989. However, within the region, South Africa was promising, with a sales increase of 22 per cent, as was Nigeria, which recorded 77 per cent. This, however, merely highlights how poor must have been the aggregate performance in other countries.

Southern Asia and Far East. This region contains Japan, the second largest single market in the world for pharmaceuticals; this country has been targeted by Glaxo for close attention in the future. The region, as a whole, accounted for 18 per cent group sales in 1981, and this had slumped to only 5 per cent in 1990. Over the decade, the average rate of sales increase was only 4 per cent per annum. Good individual sales increases in 1990 were recorded in Taiwan (143 per cent), the Philippines (42 per cent), Korea (29 per cent), Pakistan (18 per cent) and India (18 per cent. Glaxo's market share in Japan (less than 1.5 per cent) is its lowest of any major market and does not seem to be increasing owing (the firm claims) to constraining policies by the government aimed at limiting medical expenditure.

Australasia. This is a relatively stable market for Glaxo. While sales here have grown at the attractive rate of 14.6 per cent per annum over the 1980s, this has been below the average rate for the group, and Australasia now accounts for only 3 per cent of Group turnover (4 per ent in 1981). Again, there are some bright spots within the region, and satisfactory sales increases have maintained Glaxo's position as leading pharmaceutical company in both Australia and New Zealand.

Results by segment of activity

There is a marked though understandable tendency to regard Glaxo as a one-product company, but even a glance at Table 7.5 shows that this is not the case. Sales of Zantac commenced in 1982, and in this section that will be used as the base year for comparison. Thus, in the eight years up to 1990, respiratory products and systemic antibiotics between them added some £924 million of sales; this represents a compound growth rate of 21 per cent per annum, for the former and 23.1 per cent per annum for the latter. These are highly attractive growth figures by any measure. However, the growth of the anti-ulcerant segment is truly spectacular. Accounting for only 6 per cent of group sales in 1982, this had advanced to 49 per cent by 1990 – a compound growth rate of 57.5 per cent per annum.

Table 7.5 Glaxo segment analysis

Measure	1981	1982	1983	1984	1985	1986	1987	1988	1989	1990
Sales (million)										
Anti-ulcerants	0	37	97	248	432	606	829	989	1,291	1,401
Respiratory	115	148	179	217	255	287	362	457	585	682
Systemic antibiotics	80	91	94	95	112	181	226	299	396	481
Cardiovascular	10	12	22	19	33	36	46	48	46	44
Dermatologicals	61	67	66	70	74	77	86	96	101	105
Other pharmaceuticals	148	149	158	130	154	174	149	138	138	131
Animal health	33	40	48	48	37	26	30	25	5	3
Foods	68	95	93	65	64	42	13	7	8	7
Sales (% increase on previous year)										
Anti-ulcerants	N/A	N/A	162	156	74	40	37	19	31	9
Respiratory	37	29	21	21	18	13	26	26	28	17
Systemic antibiotics	25	14	3	1	18	62	25	32	32	21
Cardiovascular	100	20	83	-14	74	9	28	4	-4	-4
Dermatologicals	17	10	-1	6	6	4	12	12	5	4
Other pharmaceuticals	17	1	6	-18	18	13	-14	-7	0	-5
Animal health	14	21	20	0	-23	-30	15	-17	-80	-40
Foods	24	40	-2	-30	-2	-34	-69	-46	14	-13

Sales (Indexed)

Anti-ulcerants	0	100	262	670	1,168	1,638	2,241	2,673	3,489	3,786
Respiratory	78	100	121	147	172	194	245	309	395	461
Systemic antibiotics	88	100	103	104	123	199	248	329	435	529
Cardiovascular	83	100	183	158	275	300	383	400	383	367
Dermatologicals	91	100	99	104	110	115	128	143	151	157
Other pharmaceuticals	99	100	106	87	103	117	100	93	93	88
Animal health	83	100	120	120	93	65	75	63	13	8
Foods	72	100	98	68	67	44	14	7	8	7

Sales (% of total by segment)

Anti-ulcerants	0	6	13	28	37	42	48	48	50	49
Respiratory	22	23	24	24	22	20	21	22	23	24
Systemic antibiotics	16	14	12	11	10	13	13	15	15	17
Cardiovascular	2	2	3	2	3	3	3	2	2	2
Dermatologicals	12	10	9	8	6	5	5	5	4	4
Other pharmaceuticals	29	23	21	15	13	12	9	7	5	5
Animal health	6	6	6	5	3	2	2	1	0	0
Foods	13	15	12	7	6	3	1	0	0	0

Source: Glaxo annual reports

Over the 1980s cardiovasculars have shown a high growth rate (17.6 per cent per annum compound), though by 1990 this segment still had only £44 million of sales – accounting for 2 per cent of the total. Dermatologicals, on the other hand, had put on a healthy £38 million sales increase, but saw its proportion of group sales fall over the eight years from 10 per cent to 4 per cent.

In the other product groups, sales are now lower than in 1982. Indeed, Glaxo has made strategic decisions to move out of three of these segments. In foods, the Australian beverages division was sold in 1984, and Farley Health Products Ltd in 1986; in 'other pharmaceuticals', Evans Medical Ltd with its UK generics business was sold in 1986; and in animal health, various interests in different regions were sold in 1988 (see Figure 7.2).

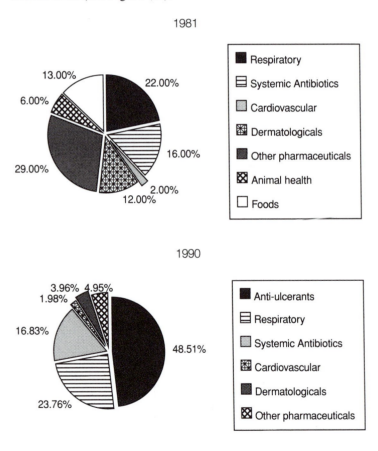

Figure 7.2 Glaxo: segment analysis, 1981 and 1990 (%) *Source*: Glaxo annual reports

One further major strategic decision was made during the period under review which is not reflected in the data of Table 7.5. In 1985 Glaxo disposed of its drugs wholesaling subsidiary, Vestric Ltd. At the time of disposal, sales were running at the rate of some £350 million, but continuing pressure on margins and the poor strategic fit of this business convinced the board to terminate the wholesaling activity.

Financial performance

Glaxo's ten-year record is shown in Table 7.6, and it is very impressive by any measure. As noted earlier, sales have grown at the compound rate of 16.7 per cent per annum over the 1980s, but this growth rate has been far outstripped by other parameters: R & D expenditures (29.1 per cent per annum), trading profit (30.5 per cent per annum), dividends declared (37.3 per cent per annum) and capital expenditures (30.9 per cent per annum). Figure 7.3 shows the movement of some of these parameters in graphical form with, for comparison, the addition of employee remuneration. Thus, R & D has climbed steadily from 6 per cent of sales in 1981 to 14 per cent in 1990; trading profit from 13 per cent to peak at 40 per cent in 1987 before dropping back to 35 per cent in 1990; net profit after tax starting at 9 per cent of sales in 1981, climbing to 28 per cent by 1986, then stabilising at that level; and employee remuneration drifting down to a low in 1987/89 before rising to 23 per cent in 1990.

Perhaps a further degree of illumination is cast on Glaxo's financial performance by Figure 7.4 which analyses four variables as a proportion of net profit after tax; the variables are R & D, dividends, capital expenditures and employee remuneration. All four variables, most especially the latter, fall steadily till the 1986/87 period; then all start to drift upwards again, capital expenditures most rapidly.

Several interpretations could be made of the data from Figures 7.3 and 7.4; perhaps the most likely is that, by 1987, most of the benefits of scale efficiencies had worked their way through the company, that pressures on historically high margins were beginning to show, but that the strategic decision to maintain and increase investments in technology and facilities had been taken and were being implemented.

The productivity ratios are all highly satisfactory. Over the decade, sales per employee have grown at 15.4 per cent compound while all the other ratios have grown much faster, e.g. net profit after tax per employee by 31.4 per cent compound and dividends declared by 35.7 per cent compound. The only exception is remuneration per employee,

Table 7.6: Glaxo financial analysis (£ million)

Measure	1981	1982	1983	1984	1985	1986	1987	1988	1989	1990
Sales	710	866	1,027	1,200	1,412	1,429	1,741	2,059	2,570	2,854
Trading profit before R & D	131	183	242	326	469	630	844	994	1,199	1,397
R & D	40	50	60	77	93	113	149	230	323	399
Trading profit	91	133	182	249	376	517	695	764	876	998
Net profit after tax	61	80	109	169	277	400	496	571	688	793
Dividends declared	19	24	33	48	74	104	141	185	260	329
Capital expenditures	55	65	70	98	126	201	193	275	373	619
Working capital	189	242	279	343	470	662	946	1,116	1,419	1,405
Fixed assets	219	256	281	347	413	536	650	829	1,124	1,569
Total assets	442	481	565	697	846	1,108	1,471	1,809	2,318	2,769
Long term debt	57	90	50	53	75	98	107	116	192	89
Shareholders' equity	382	428	542	675	827	1,090	1,450	1,784	2,291	2,732
Employee remuneration	177	199	224	254	296	316	358	425	537	645
Number of employees	28,218	28,106	27,768	25,053	25,634	24,728	24,954	26,423	28,710	31,327
As % of sales										
Trading profit before R & D	18	21	24	27	33	44	48	48	47	49
R & D	6	6	6	6	7	8	9	11	13	14
Trading profit	13	15	18	21	27	36	40	37	34	35
Net profit after tax	9	9	11	14	20	28	28	28	27	28
Employee remuneration	25	23	22	21	21	22	21	21	21	23

As % of net profit after tax									
R & D	50	47	40	30	28	34	46	55	63	66
Dividends declared	41	38	32	28	26	27	28	30	30	31
Capital expenditures	78	54	48	39	50	45	58	64	81	90
Employee remuneration	81	78	74	72	79	107	150	206	249	290
Per employee									
Sales	91,104	89,516	77,925	69,768	57,789	55,083	47,898	36,985	30,812	25,161
Net profit after tax	25,314	23,964	21,610	19,877	16,176	10,806	6,746	3,925	2,846	2,162
Dividends declared	10,502	9,056	7,001	5,650	4,206	2,887	1,916	1,188	854	673
Capital expenditure	19,759	12,992	10,408	7,734	8,128	4,915	3,912	2,521	2,313	1,949
Working capital	44,849	49,425	42,236	37,910	26,771	18,335	13,691	10,048	8,610	6,698
Fixed assets	50,085	39,150	31,374	26,048	21,676	16,111	13,851	10,120	9,108	7,761
Total assets	88,390	80,738	68,463	58,948	44,808	33,003	27,821	20,347	17,114	15,664
Employee remuneration	20,589	18,704	16,084	14,346	12,779	11,547	10,139	8,067	7,080	6,273
Gearing ratio (%)	3	8	7	7	9	9	8	9	21	15
Return on shareholders' equity (%)	29	30	32	34	37	33	25	20	19	16

Source: Glaxo annual reports

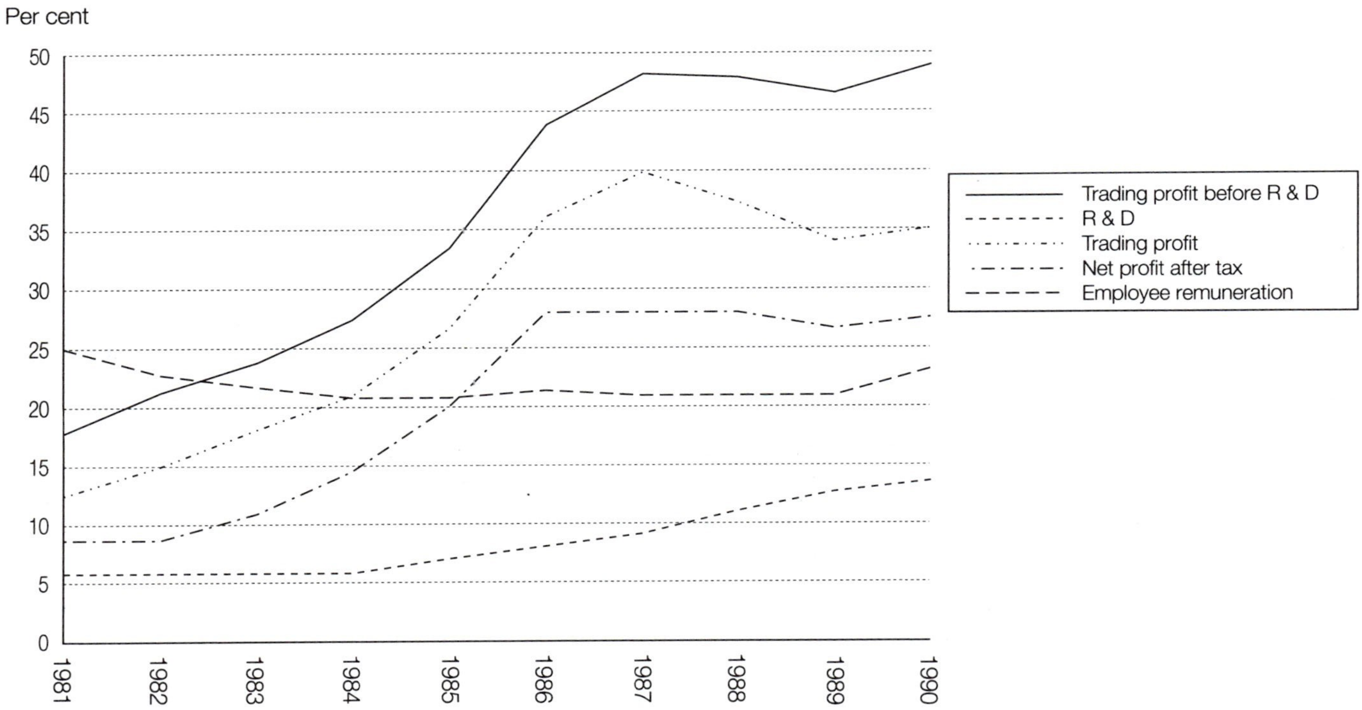
Per cent
50
45
40
35
30
25
20
15
10
5
0
1981
1982
1983
1984
1985
1986
1987
1988
1989
1990
Trading profit before R & D
R & D
Trading profit
Net profit after tax
Employee remuneration

Figure 7.3 Glaxo: financial performance (as a percentage of sales), 1981–90 *Source*: Glaxo annual reports

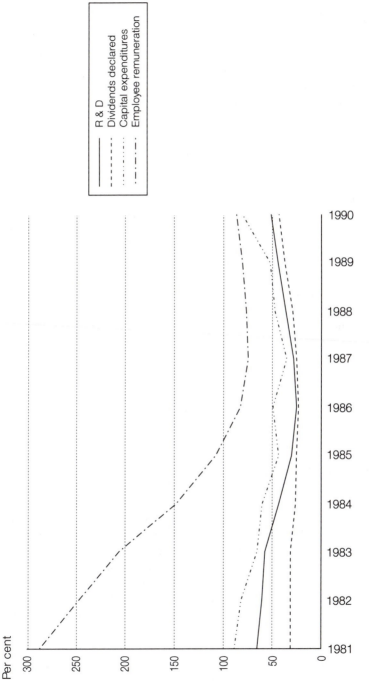

Per cent

| R & D |
| Dividends declared |
| Capital expenditures |
| Employee remuneration |

Figure 7.4 Glaxo: financial performance (as a percentage of net profit after tax), 1981–90 *Source*: Glaxo annual reports

which has grown at a lower rate than the sales ratio, indicating good management control.

The soundness of management control is also evidenced by the very low growth in long-term debt, which has meant that the gearing ratio has dropped from 15 per cent to 3 per cent over the 1980s. Broadly in line with the aggregate of these movements is the return on shareholders' equity, which stood at 16 per cent in 1981, peaked at 37 per cent in 1986, and had drifted back to 29 per cent by 1990. In response to this, the firm would probably observe that, over the same period, dividend per share has increased each year, from £0.014 in 1981 to £0.22, in 1990, representing an astonishing compound growth rate of just under 36 per cent per annum.

What strategic conclusion can be drawn from the geographical, segment and financial analyses? In this case, a brief summary probably gives a reasonably fair picture. Faced with the explosive growth of Zantac, the firm wisely decided to focus its activities virtually entirely on the ethical pharmaceuticals market as the decade progressed, and chose to emphasise Europe and the US in market development terms at the expense of Japan. Now that the huge growth rates in Zantac sales are beginning to level out, the firm can be seen to have made strategic investments in technology, facilities and locations in order to develop new products and new markets. Throughout, the company's shareholders have benefited hugely.

Activities

Products and competition

Glaxo competes principally in five therapeutic segments, and in each it faces competition from major pharmaceutical multinationals. However, the company does have a sound product and segment mix and, together with the R & D strategy which is analysed below, this provides a strong platform for building a wide-ranging sustainable competitive advantage. The products in the five principal therapeutic groups are now examined, together with details of competing products and firms.

Anti-ulcerants. Glaxo is currently the market leader in this segment with Zantac; the key success factors here include Glaxo's emphasis on quality, its aggressive marketing strategies, and the lack of product side effects. The keenest competitor is SmithKline Beecham with its Tagamet. However, new entrants including Roxatidine (Hoechst) and Omeprazole (Astra and Merck joint launch) may affect the market share position to some extent. In Japan, Zantac's major rival Gaster has suffered a setback which may adversely affect its market position.

Zantac continues to be the leading therapy for the treatment of peptic ulcers and related conditions, though it is now being used across a broader range of acid-related disorders.

Respiratory. Glaxo's Ventolin is the top-selling bronchodilator, and also the thirteenth best-selling drug in the world. Its nearest competitor is Terbutaline, manufactured by Astra. Competition in this market tends to be in methods of drug administration rather than in new products; e.g. Riker have introduced Aerolin Autohaler.

Ventolin is a combination of salbutamol and albuterol. Glaxo has developed other delivery systems for these substances including Diskhaler (dry powder inhalation) and Volmax (controlled release oral delivery).

Becotide and Becloforte, based on the steroid-based anti-asthmatic beclomethasone dipropionate, perform well where inhaled steroids are used for the relief of asthma. Beconase is an intranasal form for the treatment of allergic rhinitis.

Systemic antibiotics. Lilly is the leader in this market, but Glaxo is represented in the sector by Fortum (ceftazidime), a third-generation injectable cephalosporin. An earlier product, Zinacef, helps to maintain the firm overall sales in this sub-sector.

Zinnat (cefuroxime axetil) is an oral antibiotic which has been launched in all major markets, though under a variety of names. Ceporex is an earlier oral cephalosporin, which is still making a useful contribution to Glaxo's presence in this sub-sector.

Cardiovascular. This is a small but growing sector for Glaxo and it is dominated by large pharmaceutical multinationals that have specialised in this market, including ICI Pharmaceuticals and Merck. The firm's representative in this sector is Trandate (labetalol).

Dermatologicals. Glaxo has a long-established range of topical steroids which span a wide range of needs and applications in this market. While the segment is unlikely to be a main plank of the firm's future strategy, it is probably regarded – and used – as a cash cow.

Future developments

Glaxo's success has been largely due to an increased product range, especially in anti-ulcerants, respiratory and systemic antibiotics. Large investments have been made in R & D and in primary and secondary production facilities to develop a strong product portfolio both for the short and the long term. In addition, large investments have also been made in setting up a marketing structure in Europe and America, and the equivalent structure is planned to be in place in Japan by 1995.

The corporate structure has been reorganised; Glaxo is now nominally an integrated business, with geographically dispersed activities linked and unified by a common strategy. This highly developed system of central coordination is combined with clear and forceful leadership; delegation of operating responsibility to subsidiaries throughout the world has been fairly fully implemented.

Thus, Glaxo believes that it is in a powerful position to take full advantage of opportunities as they arise in the still expanding markets of Europe, Japan and North America in the 1990s and beyond. The question is, will it all work, and will Glaxo avoid the earlier fate of SmithKline? The answer, as with SmithKline, will depend almost entirely on the outputs from the huge investments in R & D made by the firm from the massive cash flows deriving from the success of Zantac. Glaxo has grown too big too quickly to stand still now. Its future comes down to two fairly stark alternatives: advance to become the world's largest drugs firm through successful new product development, or find protection in strategic alliance and/or merger.

Research and development

For most of the 1980s, Glaxo's R & D expenditures lagged well behind the industry norm of 13.5 per cent of sales. However, in 1989 and 1990 the figures were 12.6 per cent and 14 per cent respectively. These large investments are used to pay for the efforts of a veritable army of R & D staff, around 5,700 in 1990. Of these, 62 per cent were located in the UK, 14 per cent in the rest of Europe, 13 per cent in the US, 4 per cent in Japan, and 7 per cent in the rest of the world.

Management of R & D

There are three main centres for R & D, each responsible for different biological objectives in seven major therapeutic areas of research (Table 7.7). The local subsidiary controls the R & D activities in that country and the satellite facilities in nearby countries.

The overall policies relating to these centres are directed and controlled through Glaxo International Research Ltd (GIRL). The annual reviews in each therapeutic area are undertaken by the chief executive of GIRL. Thus the reviewing group consists of the Chief Executive (GIRL) Research, clinical and development directors of the relevant research company, plus the chairman and senior managers of each of the relevant Research Management Committees (one of which

The British market 261

Table 7.7 Glaxo main centres for research and development

Country	Company	Therapeutic areas
UK	Glaxo Group Research (GGR)	CNS GI Respiratory CV Infection
US	Glaxo Inc	Cancer and Immunology Metabolic
Italy*	Glaxo Italy	Infection CNS

Source: Author
* (Shared responsibilities with GGR)

oversees the day-to-day running of research in each therapeutic group).

Each therapeutic area has three to five projects. In total, Glaxo is exploring thirty different new approaches or diseases. All the projects are concerned with applied science. The company sees basic science as being the job of the academic community.

Although the firm is currently working in seven therapeutic areas, Table 7.8 shows that three of these account for the bulk of expenditure. Each of the seven therapeutic areas is controlled by a Research Management Committee (RMC) which defines what a new drug must be able to do, and what it must not do to be an improved drug for inadequately treated diseases. The RMC is responsible for discontinuing non-productive work at the earliest feasible moment.

There are two External Scientific Affairs Committees, one in the UK and one in the US. They have several roles:

1 To maintain contacts in therapeutic areas not within the core of Glaxo R & D.

Table 7.8 Glaxo R & D effort (measured by employment)

Therapeutic area	% of total R & D effort
Infectious diseases	22
Cancer and immunology	22
Cardiovascular	20
CNS disease	16
Gastro-intestinal disease	9
Respiratory disease	6
Metabolic disease	5

Source: Glaxo annual report 1989

2 To provide the seven therapeutic groups with technology and information.
3 To establish formal collaborations through new Chairs or joint ventures.
4 To acquire new technology.

The chairmen of the External Scientific Affairs Committees sit on the RMCs to ensure that their committees have a detailed knowledge of what external assistance is required by research.

The process of R & D

In the perception of Glaxo, the key factor for success in R & D is having testable ideas. Ideas must be practical from the biological, chemical and medical aspects. In order to end up with a new entity, the expected clinical improvement must be significant, and the medics must be able to show the advantage in patients. In addition the drug must be safe and must be able to be made on a production scale. The decision to follow a particular train of thought must always be backed up by a hypothesis which shows the logic of the thinking.

Glaxo's R & D is idea-based. As a result, the company views the real limiting step in drug development as being the generation of ideas. Not surprisingly, the quality of its people is seen as the company's most important strength. The quality determines the thinking, the motivation and the hard work. Acquiring the technology or the equipment to take ideas forward is not seen as a problem of costs or availability.

Glaxo is committed to using any technology that can help to develop ideas. The company may develop and patent its own technology, but usually relies on the industrial sector for new technology. Animal models can be well developed, such as those for anxiety testing or hypertension, or new ones may be developed for new therapeutic areas. Physical and organic chemistry will continue to be important. Glaxo's 175 research chemists in GGR synthesise about 3,500 compounds a year; in certain cases this work stems from identifying an active compound in fermentation broths. Physical chemistry is important for an understanding of molecular shape and behaviour. Clear understanding of drug-receptor theory is essential for the biologists and has implications for the screening programmes generated.

Glaxo's new therapeutic areas involve more complex systems than its research of a few years ago, and more detailed models and tools are required to analyse them. Tissue culture models are useful for analysing otherwise difficult processes, such as those in the CNS. Mammalian cell culture is used as an expression system for genetically engineered products, and is often associated with the other genetics-related techniques. The understanding of complex protein systems is increasingly important and molecular modelling is especially important for complex mediators such as peptides. For simpler neurotransmitters, a blackboard is adequate.

Research portfolio

There are currently (1990) eighteen compounds at the end of the research phase. Thirteen drugs are in full development or are reaching the end of exploratory development, up from seven in the previous year. Four new drugs will be launched in the next couple of years. Nine drugs are in the mature phase and two are declining. The latter are in areas of intense competition, to the extent that bulk antibiotics are a commodity product. The range of products is shown in Table 7.9.

Table 7.9 Glaxo stages of product development

Therapeutic area	Indication	Product	Stage
Infectious diseases	Antivirals	Various	D
	AIDS	?	D
	Antibiotics (cephalosporins)	Cefuroxime GR 69153	G D
Cancer and immunology	Cancer	Various	D
	Cancer emesis	Ondansetron	D end
Cardiovascular	Thrombosis	GR 32191	R/D
	Hypertension	Lacidipine	D
CNS disease	Cognitive disorders, schizophrenia, anxiety	Ondansetron	D
	Depression	GR 50360A	D
	Migraine	Sumatriptan	D
GI disease		Sufotidine	stopped
Respiratory disease	Asthma	Salbutamol CR Salmeterol	G D end
Metabolic disease	Topical steroids	Fluticasone	D end
	Cholesterol	?	D

Source: Author
Note: R research, D development, G growth, in last column

Strengths and weaknesses

From the above analyses of Glaxo's operations and activities a list of company strengths and weaknesses can now be drawn up. These parameters, and the environmental opportunities and threats described at the beginning of this chapter, will be the building blocks of the strategy options that are developed in the next section.

Strengths

1 Glaxo is financially sound and has enjoyed continued growth all the way through the 1980s. The firm has more than adequate funds to support growth by developing and aggressively marketing new compounds in the world's major markets.
2 Zantac is currently the world's best-selling drug and has powered Glaxo into No. 2 spot in the world rankings.
3 Glaxo has strong distribution and marketing networks in its existing major market areas (US and Europe). Where necessary, Glaxo has also shown a keen ability to develop co-marketing arrangements with other firms in markets where it is temporarily short of sales staff.
4 Glaxo is currently operating in a number of major therapeutic groups which have good growth prospects; the portfolio of products is excellent.
5 The firm's resources and operations are highly concentrated in the ethical pharmaceutical industry.

Weaknesses

1 The firm's almost total concentration on ethical pharmaceuticals may also be regarded as a weakness in some ways, as it also concentrates risk on one sector. However, it has to be said that this is quite clearly not the view that the company's management takes.
2 There is very heavy reliance on Zantac for sales, profits and cash flow. The need for a replacement mega-seller is obvious.
3 Historically, R & D expenditure has been low compared to industry norms. This has been rectified in 1989 and 1990. Doubtless, the firm would argue that its R & D investments must reflect its management judgement about how to deploy resources and that it cannot follow some crude rule of thumb. That said, it must yet be observed that, had Glaxo's R & D percentage of sales approached the industry norm of 13.5 per cent during the five-year period 1984–88, a total of £397 million of additional expenditure would have been made; this is equivalent to the sum spent in 1990.

4 Expiry date of patents on the firm's main revenue generators are now clearly in sight, and this problem may well be exacerbated by the increasing competitive pressures from generics manufacturers.

Strategy options and choice

In order that advantage be taken of Glaxo's unique combination of internal strengths and external opportunities, it is unlikely that anything other than an aggressive competitive strategy would maximise the firm's potential. There are four broad possibilities:

1 Market penetration strategies:
   (a) Further penetrate the market by the introduction of different systems of drug administration.
   (b) Developing further strategic alliances in regions where the firm is not strong e.g. joint marketing, as with the Hoffmann La Roche arrangement of the mid-1980s in the US market.

2 Market development strategies:
   (a) Increase market share in Japan.
   (b) Increase market share in China.
   (c) Increase operations in the Third World and developing countries.
   (d) Increase operations in the Pacific Basin.

3 Product development strategies:
   (a) Expansion into biotechnology.
   (b) Develop a range of drug that address real needs in the market place.

4 Diversification:
   (a) Diversification into the generic market.
   (b) Diversification into the over-the-counter market.
   (c) Diversification by acquisition of companies involved in related activities, e.g. surgical equipment.

Medium-term strategy recommendations

As any well run company would, Glaxo will consolidate its present operations by maintaining market share in the anti-ulcerant sector, and will increase its marketing activities in this sector to fend off the threat of new drug introductions. Beyond that, strategy in the next five years should include the following elements.

1 *Market Penetration*. Increase the penetration of Glaxo into the other

important market segments (respiratory, systemic antibiotics, cardio-vasculars) by developing strategic alliances where appropriate and by introducing different systems of drug administration for existing products.

2 *Market Development.* Increase its market share and presence in Japan, which is the second largest pharmaceutical market (after America) by buying over one of its current associate companies. Thereafter, manufacturing and research facilities should be set up to cater for Japanese market needs and demand.

3 *Product Development.* The need here is to increase the firm's R & D activity in cardiovasculars, respiratories, gastro-intestinals, antibiotics, anticancers and immunology. In addition, there should be a focus on real needs in the market place (e.g. diseases of the ageing population) where new drugs can fill important health care requirements.

Long-term strategy recommendations

For the period beyond 1995, Glaxo will need a powerful strategy to power shareholder value ahead in a way that will satisfy already high expectations. The above medium-term strategies will make a significant contribution toward this requirement, but a gap may still remain which a prudent management team will want to fill. With this in mind, the strategy recommendation made here is for the company to diversify into the over-the-counter market.

It is unlikely that this proposal would find much favour with the company (or with stock market analysts) at present, if for no other reason than an attachment to the greatly misconstrued 'sticking to the knitting' theme. However, there are several positive reasons that would recommend such a move:

1 This market offers Glaxo an opportunity to diversify into closely related product areas and reduce its dependence on ethical drugs.

2 The technologies involved in the production and marketing of over-the-counter drugs are relatively similar to those used for ethical pharmaceuticals.

3 The over-the-counter market is growing at a very fast rate, especially the American market, owing to the increased popularity of self-medication.

4 This market is not subjected to strict governmental control in terms of pricing and product restrictions.

5 Consumers are less price sensitive than the government, owing to

their concern regarding their own health; this fits nicely into Glaxo's high product quality perspective.

6 Over-the-counter drugs are more limited in the range of illness which can be treated. However, since many of the common diseases (particularly those of developing countries) could be treated by non-prescriptive medicines if adequate support were provided by local national governments, the potential is very great.

Conclusion

Summarising the Glaxo position is fairly simple. The firm must use its massive cash flows from Zantac to finance its development away from such heavy dependence on this product, principally by evolving a stream of new 'blockbuster' products. The management team must be very aware of the problems encountered by SmithKline (with Tagamet) at a similar stage of development. Another urgent need is to expand operations rapidly in the third of the triad of critical world markets (Japan). Finally, the risk involved in being so totally committed to ethical pharmaceuticals should be spread in the longer term, if not by the method suggested above, then by an alternative strategy which offers the same or better consequences.

ICI PHARMACEUTICALS LTD

Company history and development

ICI is one of the world's largest manufacturing and trading organ-isations. Described as a 'chemicals, plastics, and paints producer', it has manufacturing facilities in twenty countries and sells to 150 countries. *Business Magazine* ranks ICI as the No. 5 British company in terms of sales value. The present operations of ICI are organised in three divisions:

1 Consumer and speciality products.
2 Industrial products.
3 Agricultural products.

The pharmaceuticals operation is part of the Consumer and Speciality Division, in which it accounts for about 70 per cent of divisional profits. Its fortunes have been varied: while it made a key contribution to keeping the company afloat in the early 1980s, the mid-1980s showed no increase in its rate of growth. Today pharmaceuticals have surged ahead once more, contributing 27 per cent of profits on 10 per cent of total turnover in 1989, and are the anchor of the company's value-added product strategy.

In global terms ICI Pharmaceuticals is ranked as the No. 19 company in the industry, specialising in the cardiovascular market and competing with the top ten giants such as Hoechst, Bayer, and Ciba-Geigy. In this segment it has two major products, Tenormin and Inderal, whose superiority made ICI arguably 'the' cardiovascular company of the 1980s.

ICI underwent enormous changes under the chairmanship of John Harvey Jones (1982–87). They included the disposal of oil refining units, the determined move into the pharmaceuticals area, and changes in management style. These policies demonstrate the style of company that is being created. The firm is committed to assuring its long-term profitability as a global trading organisation and will pursue the following corporate targets to that end:

1 Maintaining distribution and production capacity worldwide.
2 Commitment to being a major competitor in markets able to offer high margins; at present the pharmaceuticals industry is the best example of this within ICI.
3 Redirection of the technological base to support new market opportunities.

ICI's involvement in pharmaceuticals dates back to the 1930s; like other European chemical firms, it used its expertise in the synthesis of dyestuffs as the entry point. By 1934 the Dyestuffs Group Research Department had produced both an antiseptic dye and an inhalation anaesthetic. Within a few years, a small research team of chemists and biologists was formed to synthesise medically active compounds, and the effort was rewarded in 1941 with the successful development of Sulphamethazine, regarded for many years thereafter as the sulphonamide for routine use.

Further successes in the 1940s included Paludrine (a synthetic antimalarial) and Hibitane (a very effective topical antibacterial). Later, the development of Mysoline (a highly effective anticonvulsant) allowed thousands of patients to lead more normal lives.

ICI's total commitment to long-term success within the pharmaceutical industry probably dates from the move into new laboratories at a 400 acre greenfield site near Macclesfield in Cheshire, followed by further pharmaceutical research facilities developed in Australia, France and the US. The main pharmaceutical production unit was also developed at Macclesfield, which now handles nearly 200 medical and dental products which are distributed to 150 countries.

ICI Pharmaceuticals has become a truly international concern with manufacturing and processing units in Australia, Bangladesh, Belgium, France, Germany, India, Indonesia, Italy, Japan, Mexico, New Zealand, Nigeria, South Africa, Spain, Taiwan and the US. Today, subsidiaries of ICI market its pharmaceutical products in almost every country in the world, and ICI can safely be regarded as one of the world's major drug firms.

Mission statement

The ICI group publishes a formal mission statement in its annual report, as follows:[10]

ICI's business addresses the essentials of life – health, food, clothing, shelter, transport – and helps to make them available to as many people as possible. By focusing on specific market needs, applying its technological skills, developing innovative products and selling them internationally, ICI continued in 1989 to meet world problems with world solutions.

The chemical industry is a major force for the improvement of the quality of life across the world. ICI aims to be the world's leading chemical company, serving customers internationally through the innovative and responsible application of chemistry and related sciences.

Through the achievement of our aim we will enhance the wealth and well-being of our shareholders, our employees, our customers and the communities which we serve and in which we operate.

We will do this by:

- seeking consistent, profitable growth;
- providing challenge and opportunity for our employees, releasing their skills and creativity;
- achieving a quality of standard and service internationally which our customers recognise as being consistently better than any of our competitors;
- operating safely and in harmony with the global environment.

Clearly, all of the above will apply as much to ICI Pharmaceuticals as it will to any other ICI business, but additional division-specific factors may be characterised as follows:

The pharmaceuticals business of the ICI Group ranks among the largest drug companies in the world. Its purpose is to invent, develop and market drugs and other medical products for human use. Products discovered by ICI account for a major part of the business. By focusing on high-technology research and development, ICI Pharmaceuticals seeks to introduce products which will make a worthwhile contribution to human health. It is presently concentrating on cardiovascular disorders; cancer; infection; pulmonary, metabolic and arthritic diseases; and disorders of the central nervous system.[11]

Objectives

ICI Pharmaceuticals operates within the Consumer and Speciality Products Division whose contribution to corporate growth is to move the company in the direction of higher profit margins and stable sectors of the chemical industry and away from the cyclical fortunes and lower profit margins associated with commodity-type enterprises. This is being achieved by maintaining and increasing ICI's presence in the high value-added areas of the chemical industry, of which pharmaceuticals is of overwhelming importance. Goals in this area must be:

1 To increase representation in the Japanese, US, and EC markets, which at present account for 75 per cent of world pharmaceuticals expenditure.
2 To maintain and pursue global coverage to minimise vulnerability to economic downturns and exploit upturns.
3 To cement the company's position in the profitable cardiovascular segment either by product life extension (e.g. Tenormin LA), new products (e.g. Corwin and Visacor), or by augmenting the line-up by obtaining the licence to sell related products (e.g. the licensing of Zestril from Merck & Co.).
4 To extend the product line-up to create a presence in other profitable sectors of the pharmaceutical industry, in order to reduce dependence on any one sector.

Business segments

In recent years, the orientation of ICI Pharmaceuticals has been changed significantly. The number of areas in which major research is undertaken has been reduced from seventeen to seven, concentrating on those where proven expertise exists, such as cardiovascular agents and cancer treatments. These are: cardiovascular, cancer, infection, pulmonary, metabolic, arthritic and central nervous system. Between them, cardiovascular and anticancer drugs account for about three-quarters of the firm's drugs sales (see Table 7.10).

Table 7.10 ICI pharmaceutical sales by therapeutic category, 1988

Therapeutic category	% of sales
Cardiovasculars	60
Anticancers	14
Antiseptics	10
Antacids	5
Other	11

Source: *Scrip Yearbook* 1990, p. 326

Around one-third of all R & D expenditure is focused on cardio-vascular areas, with a large proportion of the remainder on cancer (see Table 7.11). In line with this policy of concentration, sales forces are increasingly specialised by therapeutic area. Products of commercial potential developed in areas lacking strong marketing resources are increasingly licensed out: this has been done recently with Statil, a diabetic treatment which will be marketed by Merck. Conversely, licences for complementary products developed by other companies are sought where they are seen to fit the ICI marketing and customer profile: this has been done with the important ACE-inhibiting agent Zestril, developed by Merck.

Table 7.11 ICIP R & D expenditure by therapeutic area, 1988

Therapeutic area	% of R & D spend
Cardiovasculars	30
Anticancers	18
CNS	12
Respiratory diseases	12
Anti-infectives	11
Metabolic dysfunction	11
Anti-arthritis	2
Other	2

Source: *Scrip Yearbook* 1990, p. 326

A strong involvement in biotechnology has been retained, with good links into academic centres. Resources in both R & D and marketing have been augmented substantially overall, with increases of 30 per cent and 50 per cent respectively in manpower being implemented over the period 1985–90.

It is not clear how many people are employed by ICI Pharmaceuticals, but the 1989 figure was likely to have been around 16,000. Of these, the sales force would account for around 2,600 and the R & D staff for around 3,300. In common with other divisions, the employees of the drugs business benefit from a long-standing and liberal corporate human resources philosophy. People are said to be the group's most valuable resource; many companies make this claim, but ICI also recognises that its competitive edge depends on the talents of its people. The firm's aim is to give its employees in all parts of the world the chance to develop full potential through the training and opportunities it offers. The equal opportunities philosophy is being developed continuously, and high priority is given to training and development within this ethos. In its worldwide subsidiaries ICI allows and encourages personnel policy to be developed nationally; however, in line with most superior multi-national companies, the firm also encourages exchange of best human resources practice across business and national boundaries.

Financial analysis

Because ICI Pharmaceuticals is a division of a much larger corporate entity, there is less detailed information about its operations than is the case for, say, Glaxo or Wellcome. However, it is still possible to develop a reasonably clear picture of what is going on within the business.

Geographical spread

Table 7.12 shows the share of some important world markets held by ICI Pharmaceuticals. The nature of its products governs, to a large extent, the market penetration in developed countries, particularly in the case of cardiovasculars and anticancer drugs. The firm has a strong position in the UK, fairly strong in Europe (but not Italy) and North America, and a relatively weak position in Japan. Within this pattern, there have been several particularly bright spots. Tenormin (beta-blocker) and Tenoretic (combination beta-blocker and diuretic) have been performing well in the US, with Zestril a star performer in 1989; sales of Tenormin and Inderal (beta-blocker) have been developing strongly in Japan, with Nolvadex (breast cancer treatment) showing well in 1989; and Tenormin was successfully launched on to the potentially huge Indian market in 1989.

Results by segment of activity

Cardiovasculars. Tenormin is the leading product in its class, and is now selling well also as part of the combination drug Tenif; the older

Table 7.12 ICI pharmaceuticals' share of world markets, 1987

Country	% of Market
Australia	4.7
UK	4.2
Sweden	3.9
Belgium	3.6
Netherlands	2.8
Switzerland	2.1
US	2.0
Canada	1.2
France	1.1
West Germany	0.9
Spain	0.9
Japan	0.8
Mexico	0.6
Italy	0.6
Argentina	0.5

Source: *Scrip Yearbook* 1990, p. 326

beta-blocker Inderal continues to sell profitably; and the new star in this sector, Zestril – an ACE-inhibitor licensed from Merck – is carving out a growing market share in the treatment of both hypertension and congestive heart failure. The cardiovascular sector has been historically a very good one for ICI Pharmaceuticals, and prospects are encouraging.

Anticancers. This is becoming a very important sector for the firm, possibly 'tomorrow's breadwinner'. Nolvadex is now the world's leading anti-cancer drug by value of sales and Zoladex, a treatment for prostatic cancer which uses implant technology requiring administration only once a month, has become the fastest-growing product in its category. Zoladex was due to be launched in the US in 1991, and should confirm ICI Pharmaceuticals as a major player in the anticancer market.

Other. ICI's drugs division is also showing good performance in a number of other sectors, notably in anaesthetics, anti-infectives, diabetes treatment, and antiseptics. Additionally, in 1990, ICI gained a small though potentially valuable foothold in the antidepressant category as a by-product of divesting its over-the-counter range in the US.

Financial performance

Table 7.13 shows the development of ICI's pharmaceutical business over the last five years. Remembering that, as recently as 1982, pharmaceuticals made up 18 per cent of group sales but 38 per cent of group trading profits, it can be seen how much the group has changed in a short time. The pharmaceuticals business is still the jewel in the crown, but other businesses within the group have closed the gap. This favourable assessment, however, rests largely on the performance of ICI Pharmaceuticals (ICIP) in 1989. For the four years before that, trading profits had been static on sales that were rising at nearly 8 per cent per annum; thus, ICIP trading profit fell from 32 per cent of sales to 27 per cent over these four years. The position was largely recovered in 1989, with sales rising by 14 per cent, trading profits by 24 per cent, and profitability was restored to 30 per cent.

Table 7.13 ICI financial performance (£ million)

Measure	1985	1986	1987	1988	1989
Pharmaceuticals					
Sales	936	1,047	1,105	1,172	1,334
Trading profit	304	311	322	321	399
R & D	120	137	150	170	190*
Trading profit %	32	30	29	27	30
R & D as % of sales	13	13	14	15	14
R & D as % of trading profit	39	44	47	53	48
Group					
Sales	3,533	3,912	3,750	4,092	4,856
Trading profit	978	1,049	1,297	1,470	1,467
R & D	341	391	461	565	639
Trading profit %	28	27	35	36	30
R & D as % of sales	10	10	12	14	13
R & D as % of trading profit	35	37	36	38	44
Pharmaceuticals as % of group					
Sales	26	27	29	29	27
Trading profit	31	30	25	22	27
R & D	35	35	33	30	30

Source: ICI annual reports
* Author's estimate

The improving performance of the group as a whole relative to ICIP can be seen graphically in Figures 7.5 and 7.6 Because of the global nature of ICI's business, trading profits tend to be volatile; however, the overall outcome of the past five years' trading has been that group profitability has generally risen to that of ICIP, though there have been variations above and below. Similarly, and giving a strong indication of the underlying strategic shift, the group R & D expenditure as a percentage of sales has risen to the point where it is broadly in line with

Per cent

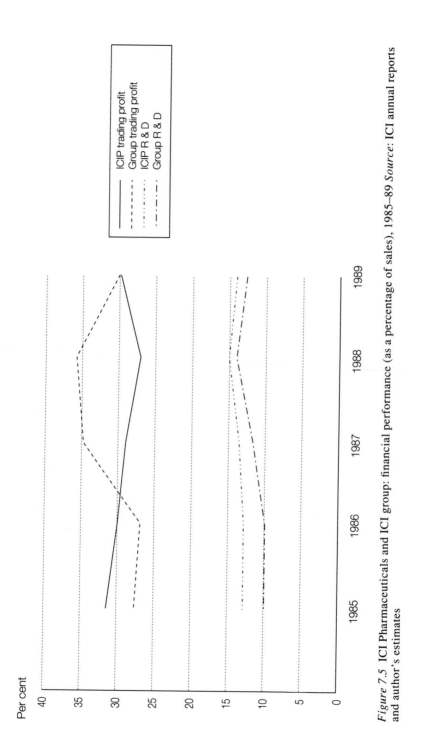

ICIP trading profit
Group trading profit
ICIP R & D
Group R & D

1985   1986   1987   1988   1989

Figure 7.5 ICI Pharmaceuticals and ICI group: financial performance (as a percentage of sales), 1985–89 *Source*: ICI annual reports and author's estimates

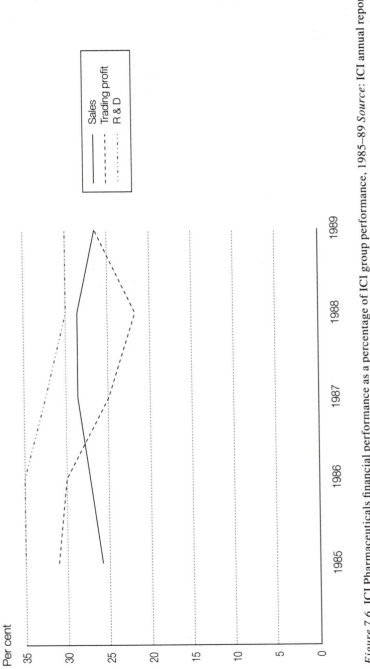

Figure 7.6 ICI Pharmaceuticals financial performance as a percentage of ICI group performance, 1985–89 *Source*: ICI annual reports and author's estimates

the traditionally research-intensive ICIP. This is despite the fact that ICIP expenditure on R & D has risen at a compound 12 per cent per annum during 1985–89, with R & D as a proportion of sales rising above the industry norm of 13.5 per cent. Thus, from being a highly profitable unit of a dull group, ICIP could now be regarded as a profitable part of a profitable whole.

Activities

ICIP's product portfolio of pharmaceuticals ranges from the blockbuster drug Tenormin to several newer, niche products.

Cardiovascular. ICIP has considerable credibility and customer franchise in this area, having developed the beta-blocker family of drugs. It has strong specialised sales forces in Europe and the US, dealing with a relatively small group of buyers. Tenormin is an industry leader, turning over some £570 million in 1989. However, it is now at the end of its patent life, with no obvious successor and a number of generic companies gearing up for production. Inderal is a much smaller market and revenues are shared with American Home Products. Corwin is very promising in clinical tests. However, it is an acute failure treatment (i.e. customers are not 'locked in'), coupled with which it has attracted some adverse press concerning (unproven) safety fears. Withdrawal was contemplated and rejected, but sales may be affected.

Zestril has great potential, and provides an entry to the fast-growing ACE-inhibitor segment, complementary to beta-blockers. Principal competitors in this area are Merck, Bristol-Myers/Squibb, and Astra/Ciba-Geigy.

Anticancer. Nolvadex is patent-expired with the exception of the US, where a long extension has been awarded, owing to significantly expanded therapeutic benefit discoveries in the treatment of breast cancer. This involves substantially increased dosages being administered. Prospects are good. Zoladex is likely to be a leader in the prostatic cancer niche. This product will grow, but not massively. There are a number of companies in this field and much research work is under way, but the breast and prostatic segments are not yet highly competitive. Revenue prospects in the medium term are good, but less so in the longer term without substantial extension to the present range of products.

Anaesthetics. Halothane is well established in the fairly static inhaled anaesthetic sector. Diprivan, an intravenously applied product, is also occupying a niche, where growth is likely to be unexciting. Both of these products have numerous competitors; competition is likely to increase further as numerous entrants are expected in the intravenous sector.

Research and development

International operations

To a large extent, ICIP products aim to serve a standardised global market, and this is certainly the case with products which are now going through the research and development process. The benefits of centralising R & D are seen to be the easier achievement of a critical mass in a multi-disciplinary structure. Basic research is becoming more dependent on heavy analytical equipment and it is more effective to centralise this type of facility. Centralisation also leads to constructive interaction between project teams. It lends itself to better library information services and other back-up services. However, on the disadvantage side, hot projects are more difficult to move along quickly.

A number of problems have been experienced following the decentralisation of R & D which are mainly historical. There is no problem in principle with a well thought out strategic disposition. The problem then becomes one of having a big enough base to attract good people. This is one of the benefits of having a large mass at Macclesfield. The ICI group has a very strong interaction with the centres of excellence, and this is self-perpetuating in that ICI as a group wishes to attract high-quality people. Ultimately, pharmaceutical R & D is an ideas business and ideas emerge from people. So fundamental to success is the ability to attract high-calibre people.

Internationalisation of R & D

Moving into a new market attracts its own problems. Japan is at one end of the spectrum and America at the other end. Americans are generally enquiring, are risk-takers and are more likely to join a start-up project. So for a greenfield start, America is a better base than Japan.

ICI's method of entry into the US has precipitated many of the existing problems in coordinating pharmaceutical R & D. The US was seen as a highly important market, being one-third of the total world market. A presence there was important, particularly for sales, but also for the sheer importance of a visible presence and the necessity of underpinning marketing and development with the research activities. This is particularly so if the firm can tap a new centre of intellectual excellence, and there is no doubt that the US is pre-eminent in the bio-sciences.

For a long time, the US has been a powerful intellectual community with many centres of excellence, so ICI's strategy in the 1970s depended heavily on moving into the US. This was done by acquiring the Atlas Chemical Company in 1972, a broad-based concern with a product range not unlike ICI's own. Part of the logic of acquiring Atlas was the fact that it included a small but very successful pharmaceutical operation. The sales of this drug operation were almost entirely built around one product and in addition there was supposed to be some kind of research capability. The original plan was to use that as a base to build a facility the size of Macclesfield. This was drastically scaled down later when it emerged that the research capability was much less strong than had been supposed. This difference between expectations and reality has been the source of many of the problems in running R & D in the US. It turned out that ICI had actually bought a firm with a low-output research group. The people had come from other businesses and they had no idea what real research in the pharmaceutical industry was. They had the wrong skills, and most of the 1970s was spent in getting rid of the old and replacing it with the new.

Development was the first activity, because new products were being pushed through. This started somewhat slowly but was very effective in the end. The company has one of the leading products in the States and the US pharmaceutical operation is going very well. The research presence has also grown somewhat, but it is unlikely ever to reach the original projected size. People with expertise have been brought in from other companies, and staff from the British unit have been sent across the Atlantic to help. By the mid-1980s there was a very professional research team in the States, about 600 in total, of whom 200 are researchers.

Knowledge protection is not a major practical problem. If the company is sufficiently explicit in identifying what is secret and makes that clear to people, then decentralisation has no effect on knowledge protection. Provided the people see the company's secrets as integral to their own future interests, then they will preserve confidentiality. However, with over 3,000 miles between the two research facilities there has occasionally been some confusion about the precise status of a piece of information.

Critical mass

There are several dimensions to ICI's approach to the concept of critical mass. Firstly, to operate in the pharmaceutical industry, certain basic skills must be present. In addition to this expertise dimension there is the difficulty of making judgements in inherently complex areas. Some of the judgements which have to be made include: how much does the company need to do itself, how much can be tapped from the outside, how much can be done collaboratively? This leads the firm to an understanding of what numbers of scientists of different types are necessary to make an impact in any particular field.

In the case of a start-up, the company's view is that the minimum work load would be three disease areas. These must not be all of the same level of difficulty. For example, it would be unwise to mix antivirals, cancer and immunology. The risks should be spread to some degree. To do multi-disciplinary research in three areas would require well over 100 people, which would mean an expenditure in excess of £10 million a year. The same approach would apply to a development lab, with roughly the same numbers involved.

Of the R & D spend, 30 per cent is in research and 70 per cent is in development. The more successful a company is in invention, the more the bias in expenditure will move toward development. The implication of this is that an R & D lab is going to be of a minimal size of between 300 and 400 people. This would be under a participative centralisation model. ICI works on the Bayliss model, which suggests that for every eight chemicals moving from research into development, four will be lost in pre-clinical development, another two in clinical development and finally only one would be introduced onto the market. Therefore much more care is put into the selection stages in terms of identifying potential shortcomings in toxicology and pharmacology profiles, etc.

Management of R & D

As noted above, there are now three main research centres – the UK, the US, and France. In 1988 there were approximately 2,200 R & D employees in the UK facility, 650 in the US, and 450 in France.

In the UK, the single large research centre was split into Research 1 and Research 2, each with a Director of Research. The majority of ICIP research work is concentrated in this dual facility, which is situated at the company's Macclesfield site.

The pharmaceuticals business of ICI is run by the International Pharmaceutical Council (IPC), which is advised by the Therapeutic Area Strategy Committee (TASC); in turn, TASC is presented with strategic options by the Therapeutic Area Teams (TATs). Neither TASC nor TAT is executive; there is one TAT for each therapeutic area, but only one TASC.

Each TAT comprises up to eight middle managers from the clinical, research, development and commercial functions of ICIP. It may take advice from outside consultants. The team has the following tasks:

1 To analyse competition.
2 To keep up to date in academic areas not related to core research.
3 To assess licensing opportunities.
4 To assess research projects and development projects.

The IPC chooses the strategy by considering the flow and impact of products, resources, risk, time scale of development and the product's potential. The strategy is then implemented by the New Product Development Committee (NPDC) and the Research Policy Committee (RPC). The NPDC meets monthly and comprises the technical, medical and marketing directors, the US vice-president of R & D and the general manager of development. The committee has an executive role in four areas:

1 Objectives of development.
2 Time.
3 Cost.
4 Competitive position.

The process of R & D

The Research Policy Committee is to research what the NPDC is to development: an executive that implements and manages the strategy chosen by the IPC. It meets twice a year. The intention of this review is to balance effort between therapeutic areas and between biology, biotechnology and chemistry.

ICIP believes that the art of effective research is to find the right balance between sustaining creativity and delivering focused effort. This balance is important at all levels from the individual scientist up. The management of research is very much about managing failure – 95 per cent of research leads nowhere in commercial terms.

Ideas can come from anywhere and pass through TATs. Licensing opportunities or new approaches are treated equally. TATs and the NPDC and RPC try to avoid the not-invented-here mentality. The importance that ICIP attaches to maintaining creativity is illustrated by the way in which resources are allocated. The RPC keeps 10 per cent free to explore ideas that come forward during the next review period. This can be a hard decision to make when all the TATs are clamouring for resources.

The aim of ICIP is to improve therapy. A drug must have a better (more marketable) profile than existing treatments, but 'me toos' are not to be sneered at. There is an emphasis on a balanced portfolio. Breakthrough products are regarded as those with a significant therapeutic advantage.

Ideas from within TATs are the main source of new products. Basic research is not uniformly scanned except in the seven therapeutic areas and it seems unlikely that an opportunity in other areas would be noticed early. However, a considerable proportion of the applied research within the company is what ICIP calls systems research. This is research on physiological systems such as neurotransmitters (5HT), other messenger systems (thromboxanes) or enzyme systems (aldose reductase). If a compound can affect these systems in a selective manner, it may be the starting point for a useful drug in several therapeutic areas. For example, the discovery of a thromboxane inhibitor has implications for asthma and heart disease.

People are seen as the most important part of R & D, since it is they who have the ideas and solve the problems. The least tolerable weakness in R & D would be a lack of creative people. ICIP puts emphasis on motivating research staff through involvement in TATs and by allowing 10 per cent of R & D spend to be unallocated. Until a few years ago, there was little management of R & D and creative individuals were left to their own devices. The result was a large number of projects and missed opportunities as more focused competitors got there first. The need to have large teams working in a given field has led to a reduction in the number of therapeutic areas from eighteen to seven. ICIP acknowledges that it is diffcult to balance the pressures to contain costs, reduce development time and still cover enough areas to give a balanced portfolio. The systems approach described above is one way of providing coverage in research.

ICIP has five products in late research and fourteen in the development stage; they are listed in Table 7.14 and annotated for the different stages in the R & D life cycle.

Strengths and weaknesses

Strengths

1 R & D spend is above the industry average at 14 per cent of turnover, and the size of the R & D staff (3,300) ranks ICIP at about seventh in the industry on this variable, well above its ranking in terms of sales volume. The possibility of new products is therefore theoretically high. In addition, the ICI group's record of innovation is good and is being thoroughly exploited through a major public awareness campaign based on the 'world class' theme.

2 ICIP is relatively secure in a number of product sectors, with good growth potential in the medium term.

Table 7.14 ICIP stages of product development

Therapeutic area	Indication	Product	Stage
Cancer	Prostate	Zoladex	early G
		Castadex	early D
	Benign prostate hypertrophy	Zoladex	R
		Castadex	R
	Breast	Nolvadex	G/M
	Solid tumours	Ricin-tagged Ig	R/D
	Chemotherapy	?	R/D
Cardiovascular		?	early D
		Diuretic	early D
	Heart disease	Corwin	end D
	Angina	Visacor	end D
Central nervous system	Psychosis	ICI 204636	early D
	Anxiety/migraine /depression	Two $5HT_2$ ligands	D
	Anaesthesia	Diprivan	early G
Pulmonary	Emphysema	Elastase-inhibitor	D
	Asthma	Leucotriene inhibitor	D
		Thromboxane antagonist	D
Metabolic	Diabetes neuropathy	Statil	end D*
	Clinical obesity	B_3 agonist	early D
Infection	antibiotics (cephalosporins)	Cefotan	G
		carbapenem	early D
Arthritis		ICI 207968	R

Source: Author
* Withdrawn due to lack of efficacy
R research,   D development,   G growth, in last column

3 The firm has powerful marketing resources in its two largest therapeutic sectors (cardiovascular and cancer), with well established
customer relationships and sales forces in the US and Europe. The
US market has been a particular strength for ICIP since 1985.

4 Potentially valuable relationships have been developed with Merck
(US) and Yamanouchi (Japan) with respect to cross-licensing.

5 Perhaps the key element in the recent success of ICIP has been the
change in management culture, perspective, and impetus given to the
division by the leadership of John Harvey Jones, ably followed
through by his successor Denys Henderson – who was directly
responsible for ICIP for a number of years before his appointment as
Group Chairman. The company management is now focused upon
areas of high growth and profitability, and upon developing new
competences to take advantage of emerging markets.

Weaknesses

1 Recent R & D successes have been in relatively small niche markets,
as a result of which no obvious successor to Tenormin is forthcoming
when the patent expires in 1991. ICIP is excessively dependent upon
this drug, as no other potential blockbusters appear to be in the
development pipeline.

2 The company has no significant presence in counterbalancing areas
such as generic production and over-the-counter sales. This is
contrary to the trend within comparable companies towards spreading
risk across different sectors. It has abandoned a promising US over-
the-counter presence which could have offset market setbacks elsewhere.

No strong presence has been established in the massive Japanese
market; indeed as a proportion of sales this area has declined since
1985.

Strategy options and choice

ICIP's strategic problem can be stated simply: it must take the best
possible advantage of its present leading position in two therapeutic
areas before that position is undermined. The decision about how to
accomplish this is largely one of whether to do so primarily by focusing
on external factors or by harnessing external resources. In the former
case the prescribed strategies would be a choice or combination
of concentration, market development, product development and

innovation. In the latter case the possibilities are horizontal integration, concentric diversification and joint ventures.

To a large extent this decision must be based on the degree to which internal actions are capable of meeting the challenges faced. ICIP has already taken a number of necessary steps to rationalise its R & D marketing structures. However, the growth of the minimum economic scale of these activities means that continuation of these approaches alone will not suffice. In particular, the evidence that even a well established, highly regarded R & D operation cannot guarantee major new products must be acted upon more decisively. ICIP must also accept that outside researchers are likely to be the source of many new product innovations. To an extent, ICIP has 'externalised' through limited licence agreements and the link-ups with Merck and Yamanouchi; however, this alone will not obviate the critical threats.

In general, then, the company must look externally for ways to cope with changing conditions. In the immediate term the position of major products must be protected as far as possible, though some loss in market position is unavoidable. At the same time, the longer-term supply of competitive products must also be assured, especially if in-house research cannot guarantee this.

So, if we accept that ICIP is possibly in a weaker position longer-term, the more appropriate strategy options may be horizontal integration or divestiture. The prospect of divestiture is highly problematic to a diversified company such as the ICI group, as its recent strategy has focused on high added-value sectors such as pharmaceuticals, and its earnings position would be very badly affected. The option of concentration has been followed as far as possible, and the option of horizontal integration is proposed as an externally orientated route to greater security. It appears to offer considerable benefits to ICIP in combination with present strategy: concentrated research and marketing in two principal and several smaller areas could continue with 'product gaps' plugged through acquisition. However, the likelihood of finding a suitable 'full-range' candidate at a realistic price is not high. The product areas of interest are all high-growth and this route, applied widely, will be very costly.

A better series of options would be to gain the benefits of new products, and of complementary marketing resources, through tighter, permanent joint-venture agreements with similarly sized research-based companies in the US and Japan. This would allow highly concentrated marketing efforts in each geographical market, whilst cutting down on duplication of R & D programmes. It would also be more likely to appeal to potential partners, as to some extent the environmental threats are shared. The obvious candidates would be Merck and Yamanouchi; loose arrangements with both are already in place, and ICIP shares broad therapeutic areas with both without 'head-on' competition.

There would be several potential benefits from such an arrangement. Truly global marketing capability would be gained at relatively little cost; the arrangement would yield sustainable representation in the Japanese market for both cardiovascular and cancer segments; and a massive sales force could be utilised in the US for co-operative marketing to the dispersed cardiovascular market. At the same time, the ability to match new products to sales specialities would be strengthened for future new product swaps and at an earlier stage of development. Given this resource, the effects of generic competition on Tenormin are most likely to be minimised.

At the same time, relationships with – or the acquisition of – small indpendent pharmaceutical research groups should be examined. A major programme of funding or collaborative research is likely to increase the odds in favour of breakthroughs in basic research, allowing the allocation of more internal resources to product development activities. The possibility of moving the research effort for smaller programmes (metabolic, pulmonary) into such companies should be followed up if possible, and these research groups encouraged to pursue promising courses with greater autonomy. This would exploit the 'unpredictability' of primary research success and widen as far as possible the research base.

In summary, then, ICI should follow a policy of continued concentration with regard to internal R & D, whilst broadening the overall research base through external arrangements. At the same time, joint ventures should be extended from their present limited use into the prime weapon of competitive strength.

Some loss of income is unavoidable over the next few years because of patent expiries, primarily that of Tenormin. With the above measures in place, however, ICI should weather this period and continue to be a major force in the world ethical pharmaceuticals industry.

Conclusion

In a fairly short space of time ICIP has moved from being the outstandingly profitable division of a fairly unexciting multinational chemical giant to being one of a number of high-tech, research-based, expanding divisions. Among other things, this must have drastically reduced the bargaining power of ICIP *vis-à-vis* the corporate entity. A few years ago, a good case could have been made for floating ICIP off as a separate company; no doubt this occurred to more than a few executives of the pharmaceuticals business at the time, and it may even have been discussed internally. Now, such an outcome is most unlikely; ICIP is firmly bound to its parent and the relationship has become one of mutual support.

This has had, necessarily, a major effect on ICIP's strategic outlook. As part of ICI, the question of overall commercial risk is best considered at corporate level. Thus ICI will regard its spread of businesses in drugs, paints, petrochemicals, fibres, advanced materials, etc., as being wide enough to spread its risk. Thus, from this perspective, it makes perfectly good sense for ICIP to be required to concentrate on ethical drugs and eschew all other markets. This may explain ICIP's retreat from the over-the-counter sector in the US. If the firm was an independent entity, there would be a strong argument – as there was with Glaxo – for considering significant diversification into this related sector to spread its risk.

Clearly, this is not an option at the present time; the key question is whether membership of the ICI family will be sufficient to protect ICIP from the increasingly fierce competition and shake-out which will be a feature of the world pharmaceutical industry for the remainder of the twentieth century.

WELLCOME PLC

Company history and development

Wellcome is one of the world's most highly respected research-based pharmaceutical companies and almost all of its broad product range is the result of internal innovation.

The business was established in London in 1880 by two young American pharmacists, Silas Burroughs and Henry Wellcome, both of whom later assumed British nationality. After the death of Burroughs in 1895 Wellcome expanded the business internationally and the Wellcome Foundation Ltd was established in 1924. When Sir Henry Wellcome (as he then was) died in 1936 all the shares of the foundation were vested in the trustees (the Wellcome Trust), who were directed to 'apply the income received from the Company towards the advancement of medical and veterinary research and the maintenance of research museums and libraries'.

No further expansion of Wellcome's geographical operations occurred in the next thirty years, and this led to a stagnation of the business and a decline in sales in real terms after 1924. However, since 1950 an increase in activities has been evident, and several acquisitions took place, with subsidiaries being set up in various countries. Since 1965, however, expansion has been mainly organic with the exception of the major acquisition of Calmic in 1967.

In January 1986 25 per cent of the equity in the Wellcome Foundation Ltd was floated, this being the consequence of a decision by the trustees to diversify the Trust investments. The shares at the flotation were issued for the company Wellcome PLC, of which the Wellcome Foundation Ltd is a wholly owned subsidiary.

The research programmes funded by the Wellcome Trust are administered completely separately from those undertaken by the Wellcome Foundation Ltd and are directed towards separate aims. The trustees do not play a role in the management of the company apart from exercising their rights as shareholders.

The most recent development of note has been the announcement that it had been agreed that Coopers, the animal health business jointly owned with ICI, was to be sold. Animal health had been a problem for ICI and Wellcome for several years and this led to a pooling of their interests in 1985. Long-term prospects are poor, demand is sluggish, and it is considered that a large share of the market is necessary for this type of business to make money.

Whilst a profit of £9.9 million had been made on turnover of £170.5 million in 1988 Coopers had been absorbing a disproportionately large amount of management time in relation to earnings. The sale raised over £65 million for Wellcome; it also freed management resources and ended the involvement in a business area with an unexciting future.

Following the introduction of the AIDS drug Retrovir, Wellcome took over from Glaxo as the British pharmaceutical company with the highest profile. Whilst in 1987 the company was in twenty-fourth position in the world pharmaceutical league it was predicted that this ranking would be substantially improved by 1992.

Wellcome's strong background in virus research has suited it perfectly for two of the major medical developments of the 1980s – herpes and AIDS. Zovirax, the herpes treatment, is currently the company's top performer. However, Retrovir is predicted to become one of the world's top ten ethical drugs by sales during the early 1990s unless a more effective treatment is discovered.

The company has also been involved in the development of tPA, which dissolves blood clots and is a direct product of genetic engineering. Indeed this drug could become the first major ethical product to emanate from the new technology.

Wellcome is also a force in over-the-counter health care and has a major share of the market for cough and cold treatments in the UK and US.

Mission statement

The firm's own view of its mission is published in the annual report and accounts:[12]

> Wellcome is an international group devoted to the research, development and marketing of products for the promotion of human health. Its origins go back more than a hundred years. Today, it operates in all the world's major pharmaceutical markets and has manufacturing operations in eighteen countries. Worldwide the group employs some 19,000 people, 18 per cent of whom are engaged in research and development.

This represents a clear statement of purpose, but to flesh it out a bit and add some colour and perspective to this formal statement, it may be useful to turn to excerpts from the new chairman's statement to the shareholders in 1990:[13]

> We have a broad base of products, with particular strengths in several therapeutic areas and a leading position in antivirals. Our research base is strong, with teams of excellent scientists on both sides of the Atlantic investigating new treatments in a number of exciting areas. The links which our scientists have with academics and other external groups are strong and productive. We also have excellent development capabilities with a record of compiling good quality clinical data to support the use of our products.
>
> Geographically, we operate worldwide, with well-established and successful subsidiaries in many major countries. During the year just ended, we have made some organisational changes which we believe will improve the efficiency of our worldwide operations. We have continued to provide the international infrastructure, resources and management that some of our subsidiary businesses require for fruitful development, but we continue to scrutinise all areas of our business, in the search for improved efficiency and performance.
>
> The process must and will continue. Our Group will prosper best if it builds on its past strengths, while at the same time adapting to contemporary needs. Paramount among those needs is a development of a clear focus for the Group, a single-mindedness to concentrate on those areas of business where we are or can become strong.

Objectives

It is not very clear what the objectives of the company are; perhaps this is something the new management team will turn its attention toward. However, inspection of the chairman's and directors' reports for the past few years suggest that the following are likely to be included among Wellcome's objectives:

1 To expand and develop markets outside the UK, particularly in Europe and Asia.
2 To maintain strong R & D activities, thus ensuring the future prosperity of the company.
3 To provide and maintain an attractive return on investment for the shareholders, and particularly for the Wellcome Trust.
4 To develop a customer-focused orientation, especially in the US.
5 To ensure quick penetration into the market of new products, thereby maximising revenues and the length of the patent-protected life.
6 To develop a strong branding operation with out-of-patent drugs (or other forms of product differentiation) to maximise the profit flows outwith the patent life, thereby protecting revenues in markets with a strong presence of generic products.

Business organisation

Therapeutic sectors

Just under a quarter of total group sales are made outside the ethical pharmaceutical market; this includes sales in a range of over-the-counter medicines, to relieve coughs and colds, and a range of non-pharmaceutical products, including diagnostics, hygiene products and environmental health products. The remainder of group sales, amounting to 77 per cent of the total, is spread across seven principal therapeutic groups; these are antivirals, systemic antibacterials, topical anti-infectives, cardiovasculars, antigout treatments, muscle relaxants and immunosuppressants. A final sub-sector is termed 'other pharmaceuticals' and includes a lung surfactant, an antihistamine, a decongestant, vaccines, analgesics, tropical medicines and a number of anticancer products. Taken together, this is a very wide range of products for a firm whose sales are less than £1.5 billion.

Structure

Because of the wide geographical spread of Wellcome's operations it has adopted a regional structure to exercise general management control. There are four operational regions:

1 UK, Ireland, Australia, New Zealand, South Africa.
2 Western Europe (excluding the UK and Ireland), East Africa, India, Iran, Japan, Nigeria, Pakistan.
3 North, Central and South America.
4 Rest of the world. This area is the responisbility of Wellcome International Trading, which is involved principally with the export of products from the UK to countries where Wellcome does not have an operating plant or subsidiary, e.g. in Africa, South East Asia, the Middle East, Eastern Europe.

In the UK the regional management structure covers both marketing and selling while other aspects of the business are controlled by a functional structure. Elsewhere the regional management structure is used to control marketing and selling and, in addition in those countries where a local subsidiary operates, all other aspects of the subsidiary's business.

Marketing

The company attaches great importance to the marketing and promotion of its products and in recent years has devoted an increasing proportion of its resources to this function. As it is important to recover costs and also generate a return on capital within the period of patent protection, Wellcome has adopted an international perspective in its marketing approach. That is, once a product has been fully developed and approved by the necessary authorities it is launched as soon as is practicable in all appropriate world markets.

If the product is one that can be obtained on prescription only, its launch will be accompanied by conferences and exhibitions to inform the medical profession of its uses and advantages over competitors' products. Once a product is on the market Wellcome's medical sales representatives play an important role in informing the medical profession of the attributes and uses of the product. The development of a product is continued following launch and this factor along with vigorous marketing and the company's reputation for quality help to sustain product sales and brand loyalty following patent expiry.

Over-the-counter products are now being promoted direct to the consumer via television advertising and point-of-sale displays, and the firm claims that this activity has stabilised its market share in a mature and highly competitive sector. The US is a particularly important market for Wellcome's over-the-counter products.

Ethical drugs are distributed through drug wholesalers for sale to chemist shops, hospitals and nursing homes. Over-the-counter products are distributed to retail outlets either direct or through wholesalers which are not necessarily drug specialists. Sales are also made to governments, in some cases by tender.

The group has recently undertaken a substantial review of the health care environment, assessing the continuing containment of costs, the growth of drug purchasing operations, the impact of gradual ageing of the population and the structural change in the industry overall. The group, and in particular the North American division, is responding to the changing environment through a substantial reorganisation of its marketing operation. It is establishing five strategy business units responsible for over-the-counter sales, physician sales, diagnostics, hospital sales and national accounts. Each unit will be a self-sufficient profit centre, the idea being to shift the focus of activity to the customer. The establishment of the strategic business unit system is expected to make the operation substantially more effective, whilst reducing marketing expenditure. The marketing effort will become customer-driven and well placed to cope with the changes occurring in the health care market.

Drug companies' sales used to increase simply because the consumption of drugs in a particular market increased; however, now the companies are trying to grab market share from each other. One example is the fight for the $1 billion – $2 billion market in anti-heart attack medicines. Genentech, Beecham, Wellcome and Hoechst are all building up teams to promote their products, advertising heavily in medical journals or even on cable television, and offering free samples to hospitals.

Human resources

Wellcome attaches great importance to the maintenance of good staff relations, to communication by means of regular briefings, staff meetings and in-house magazines and to the training and developing of its personnel. Indeed at Burroughs Wellcome managers must be treated fundamentally the same as other employees where gaining support, as already mentioned, requires informing, involving and interacting.

A major factor in the group's growth has been the commitment of its employees and indeed on the public flotation in 1986 they pruchased 17.9 million shares at a cost of £21 million, 84 per cent of the shares available to them. Employees' share schemes are being introduced where practicable and most of the group's major operations have arrangements to provide employees or their dependants with benefits upon termination of service. The Wellcome Foundation Ltd has long-standing consultative links with employees' representative bodies at both site and national levels, to ensure that the views of employees are taken into consideration.

Wellcome has not long since come through something of a management crisis. In 1987–88 the firm lost a number of high-quality senior people and was facing succession problems on the retirement of the chairman, Alfred Shepperd, in mid-1990. A solution was sought by bringing in Sir Alistair Frame as deputy chairman, becoming chairman on the retirement of Sir Alfred (as he became). John Robb, previously chief executive of Beecham, was appointed chief executive. John Precious joined as finance director from Tioxide. Altogether, in 1989–90 three executive directors retired and three were appointed, reducing the average age of the board by more than four years to fifty-three. In this respect, at least, Wellcome seems well geared up for the future.

Financial analysis

Geographical spread

After two distinct phases of international expansion Wellcome has become a major force in the global pharmaceutical industry (see Table 7.15). It now has over forty operating subsidiaries throughout the world, and its products are sold in over 120 different markets. The firm has developed a particularly strong presence in North America since 1983 to the extent that it now derives 45 per cent of its sales and 61 per cent of trading profits from this market. (Note, from Table 7.15, that sales and trading profit are measured on different bases and are not, therefore, strictly comparable.) The key to Wellcome's development in the US was its entry into the over-the-counter cough and cold preparations market with Actifed in 1983. Sales of this product grew quickly and powered the growth of the US subsidiary through 1984 and 1985. Since then, growth has been spearheaded by the antiviral Zovirax and the cardiovascular Lanoxin, products which registered cash sales growth of around 30 per cent per annum (in local currency) during 1986–90, resulting in a major increase of the market share of Burroughs

Table 7.15 Wellcome geographical spread

Measure	1981	1982	1983	1984	1985	1986	1987	1988	1989	1990
Sales (£ million, by location of customer)										
UK	79.8	84.4	92.6	99.5	113.9	110.8	117.8	131.4	144.0	147.0
Rest of Europe	76.5	87.7	98.8	117.3	145.9	176.8	215.0	257.1	287.6	355.8
North America	137.6	179.0	139.7	319.4	446.9	428.0	475.4	519.1	594.3	659.1
Rest of World	206.4	241.0	243.3	270.2	296.9	289.8	324.2	342.9	382.5	307.0
Sales (% increase on previous year)										
UK	21	6	9	7	14	−3	6	12	10	2
Rest of Europe	−6	15	13	19	24	21	22	20	12	24
North America	22	30	−22	129	40	−4	11	9	14	11
Rest of World	12	17	1	11	10	−2	12	6	12	−20
Sales (Indexed)										
UK	100	106	116	125	143	139	148	165	180	184
Rest of Europe	100	115	129	153	191	231	281	336	376	465
North America	100	130	102	232	325	311	345	377	432	479
Rest of World	100	117	118	131	144	140	157	166	185	149
Sales (% of total by area)										
UK	16	14	16	12	11	11	10	11	10	10
Rest of Europe	15	15	17	15	15	18	19	21	20	24
North America	28	30	24	40	45	43	42	42	42	45
Rest of World	41	41	42	34	30	29	29	27	27	21

Trading profit (£ million, by location of company)										
UK	50.1	60.0	52.7	49.5	53.0	65.3	77.5	109.5	131.5	164.7
Rest of Europe	2.2	1.5	4.4	5.2	5.7	10.1	13.7	17.7	16.5	22.4
North America	41.9	46.8	74.8	114.9	167.4	163.7	193.4	225.3	266.0	291.0
Rest of World	19.6	23.5	22.9	27.0	32.4	30.8	35.1	44.1	0.4	0.0
Trading profit (% increase on previous year)										
UK		20	−12	−6	7	23	19	41	20	25
Rest of Europe		−32	193	18	10	77	36	29	−7	36
North America		12	60	54	46	−2	18	16	18	9
Rest of World		20	−3	18	20	−5	14	26	−99	−100
Trading profit (indexed)										
UK	100	120	105	99	106	130	155	219	262	329
Rest of Europe	100	68	200	236	259	459	623	805	750	1018
North America	100	112	179	274	400	391	462	538	635	695
Rest of World	100	120	117	138	165	157	179	225	2	0
Trading profit (% of total by area)										
UK	44	46	34	25	21	24	24	28	32	34
Rest of Europe	2	1	3	3	2	4	4	4	4	5
North America	37	36	48	58	65	61	60	57	64	61
Rest of World	17	18	15	14	13	11	11	11	0	0

Source: Wellcome annual reports

Wellcome in US hospitals, where it is now one of the top ten players. This growth rate of business in the US was further underlined by the launch of a second major antiviral (Retrovir), which had broken through the $100 million sales barrier in 1989. Following, possibly because of, intense public pressure regarding the price of Retrovir, a reduction of a further 20 per cent was made in September 1989 (another 20 per cent reduction had been made in December 1987); notwithstanding, the cash sales of this product still rose by some 30 per cent in 1990.

After the US, the UK remains Wellcome's second largest market and its principal export base. In 1990, sales to UK customers accounted for 10 per cent of the group total, and exports totalled £336 million – a rise of over 24 per cent on the 1989 performance. The home market is, however, proving a difficult one, with both parallel imports and generic prescribing having a significant effect. Europe, in contrast, holds far greater potential and features prominently in Wellcome expansionary plans. Indeed, as a consequence of the firm's strategy to improve its performance in Europe, year-on-year sales increases have been very much higher than those in the US since 1985.

In the Japanese market, significant development dates from 1976, when a joint-venture agreement was made with Sumitomo to form Nippon Wellcome. In 1985 Zovirax was introduced to this market and sales entered a rapid growth phase; as a result, Wellcome can now be considered as a serious competitor in this market. By 1990 the firm's sales in Japan had topped £80 million, and this is now Wellcome's third largest country market after the US and the UK.

Figure 7.7 is a graphical representation of the composition of the group's worldwide sales. During the 1980s North America became much more important (increasing from 28 per cent of sales in 1981 to 45 per cent in 1990), as did continental Europe (15 per cent to 24 per cent). The UK became relatively less important, but the real loser was the 'rest of the world' segment, which fell from 41 per cent of total sales in 1981 to only 21 per cent at the end of the decade. Since this sector includes the growing Japanese market, it can be seen that the under-performing areas were Central and South America, Africa and the Middle East, and Australasia. While the sale of the Coopers animal health business had a significant negative effect on these markets, it must also be recognised that these regions are becoming comparatively less important to Wellcome because of its developing range of products and possibly because of explicit strategy.

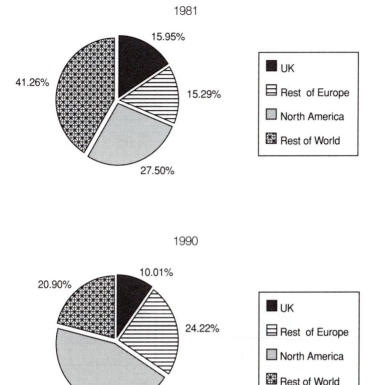

Figure 7.7 Wellcome: geographical spread of customer sales, 1981 and 1990
(%) *Source*: Wellcome annual reports

This picture is further amplified by Figure 7.8. Again, it must be emphasised that the data for Figure 7.7 are sales by location of customer, while for Figure 7.8 trading profit is computed by location of operating company. Nevertheless, the overwhelming importance of the US market in profit terms is driven home by this analysis, as is the fact that the 'rest of the world' no longer generates any significant trading profit (none at all in 1990!). Another feature of this chart is the relatively low proportion of trading profit being derived from operations in continental Europe, though the position has improved somewhat since 1981.

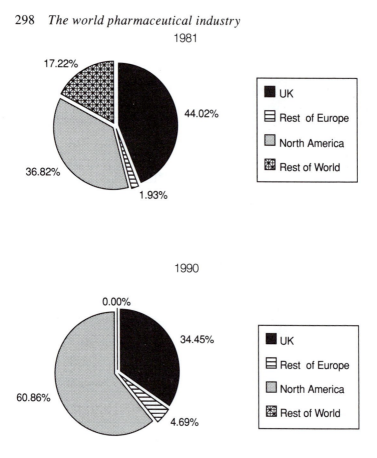

Figure 7.8 Wellcome: geographical spread of company trading profits, 1981 and 1990 (%) *Source*: Wellcome annual reports

Results by segment of activity

These are shown in detail in Table 7.16. Over the years 1984–90 group sales grew at a compound rate of 13 per cent per annum. By comparison, this growth rate was exceeded by antivirals (65 per cent), diagnostics (17 per cent), 'other' pharmaceuticals (15 per cent), and equalled by cardiovasculars. The big loser over this period was systemic antibacterials, which lost an average of 8 per cent of sales per year. Thus, the pattern of sales has changed completely over these seven years, with antivirals growing from 4 per cent of sales to 37 per cent; over this period, no other sector increased as a proportion of group sales. This is shown graphically in Figure 7.9. Indeed, if the antiviral group had never existed, Wellcome's claim to be an ethical pharma-

Table 7.16 Wellcome segment analysis

Segment	1984	1985	1986	1987	1988	1989	1990
Sales (million)							
Antivirals	27	62	105	176	306	427	545
Cough and cold preparations	103	142	135	127	126	148	151
Cardiovasculars	40	60	66	75	79	79	82
Antigout preparations	79	80	73	79	79	83	81
Topical anti-infectives	73	83	81	83	71	77	79
Muscle relaxants	20	37	38	42	47	58	73
Systemic antibacterials	106	99	89	82	67	64	64
Diagnostics	15	17	22	29	29	32	38
Other pharmaceuticals	86	104	103	142	151	164	197
Other non-pharmaceuticals	133	141	131	123	125	122	159
Sales (% increase on previous year)							
Antivirals		130	69	68	74	40	28
Cough and cold preparations		38	−5	−6	−1	17	2
Cardiovasculars		50	10	14	5	0	4
Antigout preparations		1	−9	8	0	5	−2
Topical anti-infectives		14	−2	2	−14	8	3
Muscle relaxants		85	3	11	12	23	26
Systemic antibacterials		−7	−10	−8	−18	−4	0
Diagnostics		13	29	32	0	10	19
Other pharmaceuticals		21	−1	38	6	9	20
Other non-pharmaceuticals		6	−7	−6	2	−2	30
Sales (% of total by segment)							
Antivirals	4	8	12	18	28	34	37
Cough and cold preparations	15	17	16	13	12	12	10
Cardiovasculars	6	7	8	8	7	6	6
Antigout preparations	12	10	9	8	7	7	6
Topical anti-infectives	11	10	10	9	7	6	5
Muscle relaxants	3	4	5	4	4	5	5
Systemic antibacterials	16	12	11	9	6	5	4
Diagnostics	2	2	3	3	3	3	3
Other pharmaceuticals	13	13	12	15	14	13	13
Other non-pharmaceuticals	20	17	16	13	12	10	11

Source: Wellcome annual reports

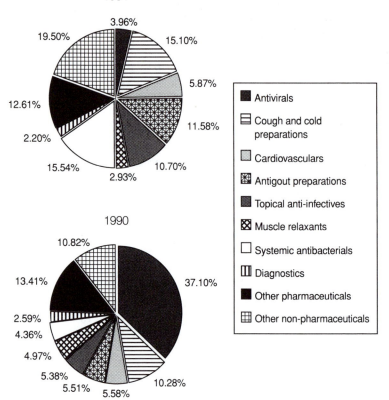

Figure 7.9 Wellcome: segment analysis, 1984 and 1990 (%) *Source*: Wellcome annual reports

ceuticals company would have been much diluted by 1990, with only just over 40 per cent of the remaining sales being in this category.

Within the key antivirals therapeutic category, the pattern of growth of the two major products has been as in Table 7.17. The natural decline in the year-on-year growth figure is clearly shown in the case of Zovirax. The increase in cash terms has actually been greater as each year has passed but, because of the limiting factor of market penetration, the proportion of increase will naturally fall off over time. What must be much more worrying for the company management, however, is the greatly accelerated rate of decay in the growth figure which is so clearly evident in the case of Retrovir. Obviously, the public disquiet about the price (totally refuted by Wellcome) and the two successive price

Table 7.17 Wellcome sales of Zovirax and Retrovir, 1984–90

Product	1984	1985	1986	1987	1988	1989	1990
Zovirax							
Sales (£ million)	27	62	105	160	216	293	375
Proportion of group total (%)	4	7	12	16	20	23	25
Year-on-year growth (%)		130	69	52	35	36	28
Retrovir							
Sales (£ million)				16	90	134	170
Proportion of group total (%)				2	8	11	12
Year-on-year growth (%)					463	49	27

decreases (each of 20 per cent) have had a bad effect on growth rates. Only three years after launch, the rate for Retrovir (at 27 per cent) had fallen below that for Zovirax, which was launched as long ago as 1981.

Financial performance

Wellcome's mission statement reflects a focus on R & D more than on profitability. In its 1985 prospectus to prospective shareholders, the marketing objectives state that the company has a high focus on increasing sales in order to recover R & D costs and provide an adequate return on investment. The use of the word 'adequate' is the interesting point here. It could be considered that the management team is, to some extent, shielded from the normal commercial pressures because its majority shareholder (74.5 per cent shareholding) is the Wellcome Trust, which is committed to philanthropic causes. In addition, the firm is safe from acquisition because of this controlling interest held by the Trust. It may be said that some of the consequences of this are apparent in the analyses in Table 7.18 (and also in Tables 7.15, 7.16).

However, there are also many positive aspects of the financial performance, and some of these are shown in Figure 7.10. Over the period of rapid development of the antiviral products, Wellcome's performance compares reasonably well with that of Glaxo over a similar phase of development (shown in Figure 7.3). In particular, trading profit and net profit after tax have performed very well after a static period up to 1986.

Figure 7.11 compares some important parameters as a proportion of net profit after tax and, again, these compare fairly well with Glaxo (see Figure 7.4), except that progress has not been quite so smooth.

Table 7.18 Wellcome financial analysis

Measure	1981	1982	1983	1984	1985	1986	1987	1988	1989	1990
Sales (million)	500.3	592.5	674.4	806.4	1,003.6	1,005.4	1,132.4	1,250.5	1,408.4	1,468.9
Trading profit before R & D	102.2	121.4	142.6	185.6	243.7	257.8	311.5	384.9	464.8	536.3
R & D	52.0	66.3	80.9	96.6	122.0	132.5	142.4	163.7	189.3	221.2
Trading profit	50.2	55.1	61.7	89.0	121.7	125.3	169.1	221.2	282.8	315.1
Net profit after tax	33.0	36.9	38.1	48.0	64.8	61.3	97.7	131.8	172.3	197.3
Dividends declared	10.5	13.0	14.0	17.0	23.8	17.4	23.7	30.4	42.8	55.2
Capital expenditures	40.9	41.4	38.5	57.7	73.7	88.3	108.2	132.5	146.9	178.0
Working capital	68.0	73.7	86.7	94.6	81.8	121.6	112.1	130.3	229.0	186.2
Fixed assets	234.1	253.1	281.4	326.0	356.8	392.0	446.9	522.3	592.2	681.6
Total assets	302.1	326.8	368.1	420.6	438.6	513.6	559.0	652.6	821.2	867.8
Long term debt	99.9	123.4	145.7	172.2	169.2	169.7	194.6	190.3	173.0	124.0
Shareholders' equity	302.1	326.8	368.1	420.6	438.6	513.6	559.0	652.6	821.2	867.8
Employee remuneration	152.9	182.2	207.3	234.3	275.3	283.1	309.1	337.4	375.9	403.1
Number of employees	18,501	18,706	18,645	18,608	18,342	18,764	19,338	20,236	21,213	18,853
As % of sales										
Trading profit before R & D	20	20	21	23	24	26	28	31	33	37
R & D	10	11	12	12	12	13	13	13	13	15
Trading profit	10	9	9	11	12	12	15	18	20	21
Net profit after tax	7	6	6	6	6	6	9	11	12	13
Employee remuneration	31	31	31	29	27	28	27	27	27	27

As % of net profit after tax										
R & D	158	180	212	201	188	216	146	124	110	112
Dividends declared	32	35	37	35	37	28	24	23	25	28
Capital expenditures	124	112	101	120	114	144	111	101	85	90
Employee remuneration	463	494	544	488	425	462	316	256	218	204
Per employee										
Sales	27,042	31,674	36,171	43,336	54,716	53,581	58,558	61,796	66,393	77,913
Net profit after tax	1,784	1,973	2,043	2,580	3,533	3,267	5,052	6,513	8,122	10,465
Dividends declared	568	695	751	914	1,298	927	1,226	1,502	2,018	2,928
Capital expenditure	2,211	2,213	2,065	3,101	4,018	4,706	5,595	6,548	6,925	9,441
Working capital	3,675	3,940	4,650	5,084	4,460	6,480	5,797	6,439	10,795	9,876
Fixed assets	12,653	13,530	15,093	17,519	19,453	20,891	23,110	25,810	27,917	36,153
Total assets	16,329	17,470	19,743	22,603	23,912	27,372	28,907	32,249	38,712	46,030
Employee remuneration	8,264	9,740	11,118	12,591	15,009	15,087	15,984	16,673	17,720	21,381
Gearing ratio (%)	33	38	40	41	39	33	35	29	21	14
Return on shareholders' equity (%)	11	11	10	11	15	12	17	20	21	23

Source: Wellcome annual reports

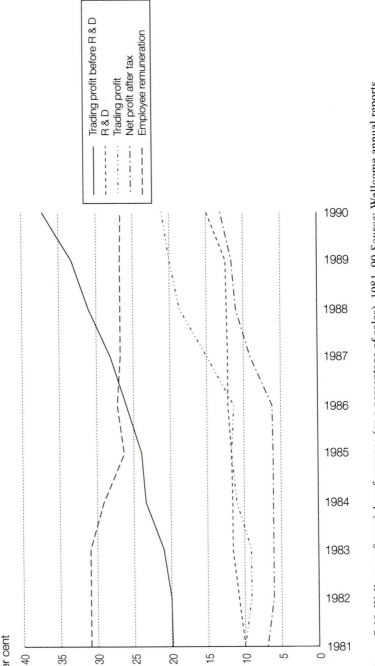

Figure 7.10 Wellcome: financial performance (as a percentage of sales), 1981–90 *Source:* Wellcome annual reports

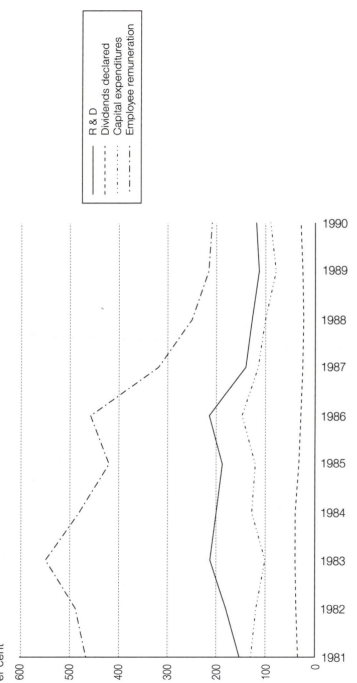

Figure 7.11 Wellcome: financial performance (as a percentage of net profit after tax), 1981–90 *Source*: Wellcome annual reports

Perhaps another similarity that could be drawn with Glaxo is that it is only recently that R & D spend has achieved (and exceeded) the industry norm. For a company which is so dependent on one product group, and which is achieving such high cash flows from it, this is perhaps a worrying factor; all the more so becuase of the emphasis placed on R & D in the mission statement, mentioned above.
However, many of these favourable comparisons with Glaxo are in terms of the pattern of performance. When the employee productivity parameters are compared. Wellcome comes out worse – and very markedly worse – on every one with the single revealing exception of employee remuneration. Even the firm's gearing ratio, which has come down significantly since 1987 and especially on the sale of Coopers Animal Health, is still well above the norm for the industry and Glaxo's 3 per cent.
Thus, on the aggregate level, Wellcome's overall financial performance seems to be acceptable. However, when it is disaggregated in almost any way, some doubts begin to arise. This will be examined again later, in the strategy analysis section, and the dicussion will be continued about the linkage between the firm's shareholder pattern and its strategy and performance.

Activities

Products and prospects

Wellcome's product portfolio covers a broad spectrum of therapeutic markets but has been dominated by mature products, many of which are subject to generic competition. Increasingly since 1988, the group's product base has become more focused on the newer antiviral products, Zovirax and Retrovir. Wellcome's pioneering work with both Zovirax and Retrovir has resulted in the company becoming the acknowledged leader in the antiviral field. Developing Retrovir was an exceptional achievement and one that illustrates the quality of the group's scientists.
Nine years after its launch, Zovirax remains the drug of choice for a variety of herpes infections. It is now registered in seventy countries and has become Wellcome's largest-selling product. There is undoubtedly further scope to expand Zovirax sales; some of the more important factors are:

1 The number of genital herpes sufferers continues to increase.
2 There is scope for further approvals for the high-dose treatment of shingles in a number of important geographical markets.

3 Confirmation of the synergistic benefits of combined Acyclovir/ Interferon use for hepatitis B.

4 Approval of combined Retrovir/Zovirax therapy in AIDS.

As the only drug yet to have been licensed for the treatment of AIDS, Retrovir has the potential to enhance the fortunes of the group significantly. It is for this reason that Retrovir and AIDS require deeper analysis to understand fully the potential impact on Wellcome's medium-term future.

Currently Retrovir is indicated only for cases of full-blown AIDS and for severe ARC (AIDS Related Complex). However, despite its availability since the spring of 1987, not all patients are using the product. Many doctors have reacted negatively to wide publicity on the potential side effects of the drug. These have to be set against the devastating nature of the disease. The result of negative publicity has been that Retrovir use per patient is running at levels lower than that which would be indicated by the recommended dosage regimen. Nevertheless, as a result of growing physician favour of the product, the number of patients taking Retrovir is growing significantly, with consequent effect on sales revenue.

The number of drugs in development aimed at treating AIDS is proliferating at a phenomenal rate. However, to date, the progress of these alternative therapies has been disappointing. The greatest promise in the short term is in drugs which enhance the body's own defence mechanism. One such product to reach prominence recently with a detailed write-up in the *Lancet* is Ditiocarb (also called Imuthiol) from Institut Mérieux. Others include Isoprinosine from Newport Pharmaceutical and pentapeptides such as Johnson & Johnson's Thymopentin and Serono's TPI. Interferons, including those from Wellcome and Hoffman La Roche, operate in a similar manner and are also being investigated, as are Interleukin 2, and GMCSF from Glaxo and Sandoz.

In commercial terms, however, it is generally agreed that the development of these new products will not be a threat to Retrovir for a number of years. First, the human trials of these drugs are principally in combination with Retrovir, and therefore evidence and data as to their efficacy will mainly be available in their use alongside that treatment. Second, these products work in an entirely different way from Retrovir, which is active against the virus itself. This is another reason why it is predicted that these products will be used alongside Retrovir rather than against it.

Turning now to Wellcome's drugs outside the antiviral sector, it should be noted that most of these products are mature and, whilst some continue to register solid growth, this is being largely offset by weakness in other areas. The key products include the cough/cold treatments Sudafed and Actifed, Septrin (a systemic antibiotic), Zyloprim/Zyloric (an antigout agent) and Lanoxin (a treatment for heart failure). Amongst the remaining categories the most notable are Tracrium (a muscle relaxant) and the group's diagnostic products.

The largest single single market for cough/cold treatments lies within the US and the market is dominated by products which have been switched from prescription to over-the-counter only. Compared with the mid-1980s, this market is not showing tremendous growth, is becoming intensely competitive, and market share has largely become a function of promotional expenditure. Wellcome products in this market include Sudafed and Actifed.

Wellcome's antibacterials are well past the peak of the product life cycle. Septrin, the major product in this therapeutic category, is struggling to maintain volume growth. Although achieving prominence in Third World countries, where it is valued as a relatively cheap and effective broad-spectrum antibiotic; elsewhere its market and price are under pressure.

Although the antigout products are off-patent, problems in reproducing the properties of Zyloric have largely deterred generic manufacturers from making inroads into this market. There are now signs, however, of some headway being made in the US, but with few proprietary products on the horizon Zyloprim (the US trade name) should continue to be a good revenue generator for the group.

The cardiovascular Lanoxin is another off-patent drug that is registering strong performance against generic competition, particularly in the US, where it is now the second most prescribed product behind SmithKline's Dyazide. However, although undoubtedly effective in relieving some of the symptoms of heart failure, because its effect on mortality is inadequately known, its efficacy and safety have recently come into question. Potential competition is also on the increase. As a consequence, Wellcome has mounted a new promotional campaign in the US. There is, however, little doubt that Lanoxin volumes will suffer over forthcoming years even though a lingering reluctance to switch entirely to new therapies may persist.

Amongst the remainder of the non-antiviral portfolio are a number of niche products that are still registering very respectable growth. These include Tracrium and Leucovorin, the best-selling amongst Wellcome's anticancer range.

Diagnostic products are another area registering good progress, largely due to Wellcome's dominant position in the HIV test market, particularly in the UK. With the introduction of its second-generation kit, Wellcome will be well placed to match the competition in this field.

Competitors

The main competitors in the various major segments that Wellcome is operating in are listed in Table 7.19.

Table 7.19 Wellcome's competition

Main market segment	% of Wellcome's health care turnover	Main competitors
Antivirals	37	Rhône-Poulenc, Johnson & Johnson, Glaxo, Hoechst
Cough/cold	10	Glaxo, Beecham, Fison
Topical anti-infectives	5	Beecham, Sankyo, Glaxo
Antibacterials	4	Takeda
Antigout	6	Glaxo, ICI
Cardiovascular	6	ICI, Fison
Muscle relaxants	5	Fison
Diagnostics	3	ICI, Glaxo
Other pharmaceuticals	13	Beecham, Glaxo, Fison
Non-pharmaceuticals	11	Glaxo, Hoechst

Research and development

The management of R & D

The main centres for R & D are Beckenham in Kent and Research Triangle Park in North Carolina. Both centres share research in all therapeutic areas. The numbers employed and cash deployed are shown in Table 7.20. The selection of therapeutic areas (Table 7.21) was made three years ago by top management and was intended to align strengths and opportunities. The five areas give a wide market coverage and include the largest world markets of CNS, cardiovascular and anti-infectives.

The proportion of spend in each therapeutic area has remained more or less constant since 1988, except that the antiviral area has grown slightly as the development of Retrovir enters the more expensive

Table 7.20 Wellcome R & D employment, 1989

Country	Number	%	Spend %
US	1,200	35	57
Europe, rest of the world	2,190	65	43
Total	3,390		

Source: Author

Table 7.21 Wellcome pharmacological R & D effort measured by spend, 1989

Therapeutic area	% of total R & D effort
Anti-infectives	36
Cardiovascular	17
Anti-inflammatory/allergic	15
CNS	11
Cancer	14
Other	7

Source: Author

stages. There is an element of reinforcement in the distribution of expenditure; if one area is particularly successful, the tendency is to put more money into it to maximise the expertise, the market experience and the market opportunity.

The Research Committee is the executive function that controls the discovery (research) stage. It comprises the director of research and the heads of each therapeutic area. The discovery process is divided into three. The early stage is concerned with the bright ideas of the chemists and biologists and is managed by the department head. Both the systems approach and targeting of a disease are used to drive the generation of ideas.

The middle stage is looked after by the Therapeutic Area Group and starts when a group of compounds look interesting. Resource allocation is planned and links between interested therapeutic areas are established. Clinical and commercial input is provided at this stage and the Research Committee starts to take an interest through monthly inputs from the therapeutic area review. The final stage of discovery – the programme stage – starts when selected compounds pass into toxicology, pharmacokinetics and chemical development. Chemical development is concerned with choosing the most appropriate synthetic pathway and with the feasibility of scale-up for production. There is considerable commercial and clinical input at this stage.

To be taken on by development (termed a 'project' by Wellcome), usually a single compound must be selected, a disease target identified and a patient profile prepared. After approval from the appropriate research division, the scientific, clinical and commercial case is developed with the Project Forum by the therapeutic area leader, the project manager and sometimes the individual whose idea has been followed through. The Project Forum provides a route for communication between department heads and between divisional heads and is non-executive. After approval from the RDM (Research, Development and Medicine) director, a project manager is appointed to oversee the development stages. Each manager covers more than one therapeutic area and is likely to have several projects on the go at once. The executive management review and the Project Forum review approved projects against objectives and consider development resource and commercial resource allocation, equipment problems and other delaying factors.

The process of R & D

From the point of view of the whole company, R & D is successful if it provides new products that generate new revenue streams. As far as the R & D function is concerned, a product launch marks a measure of success, even if it does not do well subsequently. It seems that R & D transfer ownership once the commercial people accept the product.

Wellcome is prepared to admit orphan drugs to R & D, even though the markets for them are relatively small. The informal limit for market entry is a size of £50 million per annum, half that accepted by ICI and Glaxo. The expenses are covered by collaborating with bodies such as the World Health Organisation. The cross-fertilisation between therapeutic areas, which is a benchmark of good communication, has paid dividends for Wellcome, as one of its anti-malarial compounds may have applications in other protozoan diseases and even in AIDS.

The therapeutic areas are a focus for discovery, but the systems approach adopted allows applications of the same discovery in different areas. The case for starting a discovery programme based on the systems approach must be made with some justification that a disease treatment can result. The discovery process, as Wellcome calls the research stage, is idea-driven.

The duration of the research stage varies by therapeutic area, taking up to twenty years in the case of antivirals. Wellcome is about average in the development time taken, but still says that it is always too long. Regulatory approval times are kept to a minimum if the product has a significant therapeutic advantage and this is part of the rationale of keeping to novel compounds. While the company agrees that concentrating research in a few areas is essential, the policy breaks down by being non-exclusive.

Biotechnology receives a lot of attention at Wellcome, partly because of the company's history and the continued involvement in vaccine manufacture for the UK. Biotechnology is divided into two parts, one dealing with immunoprophylaxis and the other with protein engineering. The latter is not vaccine-orientated but concentrates on therapeutic proteins, for example the second generation tPA, which are essential to a continued presence in the market.

There are currently seventeen products in development and these are laid out in Table 7.22.

Table 7.22 Wellcome stages of product development

Therapeutic area	Indication	Product	Stage
Anti-infectives	AIDS	Retrovir	end D
	Herpes	Zovirax	G
	Malaria	556C	early D
	Hepatitis B	Wellferon	D/G
	Hepatitis non		
	A non B	Wellferon	D
Cardiovascular	Myocardial Infarction	tPA	end D
		nPA	early D
CNS	Epilepsy	Lamotrigine	end D
	Depression	Wellbutrin	G
Anticancer	Solid tumours	Two compounds	early D
	Leukaemia	CAMPATH 1-H	early D
	Renal cell	Wellferon	end D
Anti-inflammatory/ anti-allergic	Anti-histamine	Duact/Semprex	end D
	Asthma	Two compounds	early D
Others	Respiratory Distress Syndrome		
	(neonates)	Exosurf	end D
	(adults)	Exosurf	early D
	Muscle relaxant	Doxacurium	end D
		Mivacurium	D
		Tracrium	G
	Sickle cell anaemia	589C	early D

Source: Wellcome annual report 1989; author
R research,   D development,   G growth, in last column.

Strengths and weaknesses

Analysis of Wellcome's internal operations yields the following lists of potential strengths and weaknesses, which will be carried forward to the strategy analysis in the next section.

Strengths

1 Wellcome is the world's leading antiviral company, with Zovirax and Retrovir as lead products.
2 Retrovir is patent-protected till 2005.
3 Use extension of existing products has been a significant development, e.g. Zovirax for shingles.
4 The firm's presence in Japan is improving (though slowly).
5 The R & D resource is excellent, with a high worldwide reputation; in particular, the US facility has played a key role in the development of both Zovirax and Retrovir.
6 The US marketing team is strong.
7 Strong and developing European presence.

Weaknesses

1 Over-dependence on Zovirax and Retrovir.
2 There is some evidence that the old, pre-flotation management approach is still operating in the company, though clearly this may change radically following the recent board changes.
3 The UK marketing team seems to show a comparative weakness, at least in relation to the US team, if not to the UK efforts of other drug majors.
4 Again compared to other pharmaceutical multinationals there seems to be lower coordination between the UK and the US.
5 Zovirax is out of patent in the mid-1990s, and is likely to face stiffening competition in 1993–5.

Strategy options

From the foregoing analysis, there would seem to be two principal strategic directions open to Wellcome PLC; they are:

1 To compete, as at present, as a medium-sized partially internationalised firm.
2 To compete as a truly international company.

The first of these involves no real change in present strategy. Wellcome has recently reorganised its US operations in order to give it a more specific customer focus. Another objective of the reorganisation is to make marketing effort more cost-effective. This reorganisation should enable Wellcome to consolidate and expand its existing market share in its major market.

Continuing with the existing strategy would also involve further gradual expansion of existing operations in Europe and other international markets, an on-going focus on marketing drugs developed by Wellcome itself, and – above all – retaining the current broad-focus research.

The alternative strategic direction of significantly more rapid internationalisation would also require an increased focus on profit. Japan is Wellcome's third largest market, but only accounted for 6 per cent of global turnover. This might suggest that Wellcome's market share in major countries other than the US and the UK is too small to be profitable in the long term.

A truly internationalised drugs firm is one which is firmly established as an insider in the three critical markets of the US, Europe and Japan. It does not mean, as is the case with Wellcome, trying to run operations in as many countries as possible without a clear emphasis on profitability. It is likely that the restructured board will want to keep the profitability of various international operations under close review, but it will also be necessary to take a more commercial view of loss makers and – at the same time – aggressively develop the potentially profitable markets of continental Europe and Japan.

Where Wellcome finds it necessary to close down operations in particular country markets, it should examine the potential of licensing distribution and/or manufacture of its major off-patent drugs. This kind of rationalisation will release cash flow and management time to concentrate on the development of key markets.

In line with this market development strategy, it will be vitally important to re-focus R & D in order that resources are concentrated on areas of significant commercial potential. At present, over 60 per cent of R & D expenditures are still made in areas outside the key antiviral therapeutic segment; these areas are not yet providing the required commercial results.

Other specific strategies required to develop this major internationalisation thrust might include:

1 Joint ventures such as that with Sumitomo of Japan to establish a big enough base and sufficient depth of local management expertise from which to expand a target market.

2 Acquisition of foreign firms in target markets to achieve the same purpose.

3 Licensing of production and/or distribution in target markets where either of the above two strategies cannot be implemented.

4 Expand R & D into other major therapeutic areas with potential for significant commercial success.

5 Expand into selected manufacture and sale of generic drugs in those target markets where this can help in generating scale economies.

6 In those target markets where it has an established brand presence, Wellcome should consider adding to its range of over-the-counter drugs by internal development, by licensing, or by acquisition.

Conclusion

Arriving at a conclusion for Wellcome PLC is considerably more difficult than for other major pharmaceutical firms because of the nature of the past, present and future development of the two-way relationship between the company and the Wellcome Trust. Before flotation, Wellcome had a century of proud history as an organisation which put human health – particularly in developing countries – above all other considerations. The profit that was earned, and it was substantial, was used by the Wellcome Trust for an admirable range of philanthropic purposes.

Of course, this did not all change because 25 per cent of the company was floated on the stock market. The old corporate culture lingers on and will for many years to come, no matter what measures top management may or may not take. However, Wellcome's (partial) entry into the competitive world of commercial pharmaceutical multi-nationals will have a continuing and growing impact. The top management of the firm is becoming – and will continue to develop as – increasingly commercial. This must inevitably induce stress into the relationship between PLC and Trust.

The view taken here is that if the Wellcome Trust wishes to have a continuing and growing stream of dividends from its majority shareholding in Wellcome PLC in the long term, it must recognise the inescapable economic and strategic imperative that the firm must internationalise in strength in the developed markets of the US, Europe and Japan – perhaps at the cost of a (relative) withdrawal from some historic markets. In an ideal world, the Trust might even see its way to encourage this vital strategic thrust, as the alternative for Wellcome PLC is inevitable stagnation.

8 The European pharmaceutical market

THE MARKET

Some of the parameters of the European pharmaceutical industry have already been covered in Chapter 4 in terms of the single European market; the purpose of this chapter is to widen the scope somewhat to cover the whole of continental western Europe.

The European pharmaceutical market is valued at 33 billion ECU and is the second largest market in the world, accounting for approximately 30 per cent by value of the total world market. The value of European pharmaceutical production is in the region of 43 billion ECU (1986) and the industry makes a positive contribution to the total European balance of payments.[1] Of the world's top fifteen pharmaceutical companies in 1989, in terms of pharmaceutical sales, six were of European origin. These include Hoechst and Bayer of West Germany, which were ranked third and fourth respectively; Ciba-Geigy (fifth), Sandoz (eighth) and Roche (fifteenth) of Switzerland; and Glaxo of Britain, which was in second position.[2]

The importance of the European pharmaceutical industry is not in its size, accounting as it does for less than 1 per cent of total European GDP,[3] but the fact that it is one of the few high-technology industrial sectors in which Europeans are successful in global terms. Furthermore it is one of the few high-technology sectors in which R & D investment is funded entirely by the industry itself. This investment in R & D amounted to 4 billion ECU in 1988.[4] Indeed, if commitment to innovation is judged purely on the percentage of sales spent on R & D, eight of the leading fourteen companies worldwide are of EC origin.[5]

The pharmaceutical market is also the most highly regulated market, given the non-typical characteristics of the supply and demand for medicinal products, and national government's natural concern about the health of their citizens. As a result, there are twelve national markets within the EC, each with its own approval and registration procedures and each with its own price structure. In other words a single integrated European pharmaceutical market does not yet exist, as pointed out in Chapter 4.

Demand characteristics

Traditionally, ethical drugs have represented about 80 per cent by value of the European pharmaceutical market, with the remaining 20 per cent being accounted for by over-the-counter medicines. The large majority of consumers are insured against the cost of prescription drugs and are thus not interested in prices. Their main concern is in the effectiveness of the drugs and for this they must rely on the prescribing doctor, who is interested principally in the effectiveness, therapeutic value and possible side effects associated with drugs. However, prescribing doctors are now taking an increasing interest in prices, as a result of pressure by governments throughout Europe to control health care expenditure. The objective of this pressure is to contain national drug costs by encouraging the prescription of generics, or cheaper equivalent products, and not to increase overall consumption of drugs.

Within the EC there are vast differences in the propensity to consume drugs. Generally southern Europeans consume more drugs *per capita* than northern Europeans. Allied with these different consumption propensities are wide price variations, with the high consumers having lower prices than the low consumers. This would suggest that there is an element of price elasticity in relation to the demand for pharmaceutical products. A report published in 1988[6] suggests that this elasticity is low – below unity in all probability – but not zero. However, of greater significance to the demand for pharmaceuticals is not some minor element of price elasticity but the differing medical traditions and sociological factors between northern and southern Europe.

In addition, unlike most other markets, the pharmaceutical market is comprised of several sub-markets based upon therapeutic category. The dominant share of pharmaceutical consumption is accounted for by chronic diseases such as asthma, rheuma, diabetes and anti-infectives of which there are several sub-markets. The existence and importance of these totally distinct sub-markets are reflected in the fact that not even the leading pharmaceutical companies possess more than 4 per cent of the total world pharmaceutical market.

Trade in pharmaceuticals

The supply of pharmaceuticals within Europe is highly international-ised; most countries have a trade surplus, the exceptions being the less developed economies such as Greece and Portugal. However, within national markets of the EC, as an example, a disproportionately large share of the local market is held by local manufacturers. According to EAG,[7] national markets were on average supplied as follows:

1 By locally based companies (subsidiary of a multinational or purely national company): 43 per cent.
2 By imports from other member states: 23 per cent.
3 By imports from third countries, especially the United States and Switzerland: 34 per cent.

More recent data compiled by Shearson Lehman Hutton[8] in 1989 supports the above. They found, in 1988, that 23 per cent, 34 per cent, 14 per cent and 25 per cent respectively of the local markets in West Germany, France, Italy and Britain were held by companies of the respective markets' nationality. In addition, of the top ten products in each of the above markets seven, five, three and seven respectively were products of companies of the respective markets' nationality. This is a reflection of the more favourable treatment that companies with a local presence have traditionally received from national authorities. This leads to substantial foreign production of drugs within the EC, particularly by American and Swiss companies.

Pricing and reimbursement

National governments are the major clients of the pharmaceutical industry and an indication of the cost of health care provision, in terms of drugs, can be had from Table 8.1. Although the table is constructed from 1984 data, health care provision is still a major burden on public finances. In 1988 the national governments paid between 44 per cent (Denmark) and 88 per cent (West Germany) of the total ethical drug bill. The EC average was 67 per cent.[9]

The national governments have differing policies with respect to the pricing of pharmaceuticals. In Italy the price allowed is very much based on a multiple of direct production costs, including raw materials and labour. In France the price is determined by an assessment of the R & D effort, the therapeutic advantage offered and the novelty of a new drug. In Britain the key determinant is the use of a profit control which limits the return on investment which the pharmaceutical company can

Table 8.1 Public and private health care expenditure as a percentage of GDP

Country	Total	Private	Public
France	9.1	2.6	6.5
Holland	8.6	1.8	6.8
West Germany	8.1	1.7	6.4
Ireland	8.0	1.1	6.4
Italy	7.2	1.1	6.1
Denmark	6.3	1.0	5.3
Belgium	6.2	0.5	5.7
UK	5.9	0.6	5.3
Spain	5.8	1.5	4.3

Source: OECD *Financing and Delivery Healthcare*, OECD, Paris (1987)

make on its sales to the National Health Service (NHS). Only in West Germany can the pharmaceutical industry set the price itself, and this may explain why historically drug prices have been highest in Germany.

In addition to controlling the prices of ethical drugs, all European countries employ additional control mechanisms in the form of positive and negative lists of drugs; being listed positive is essential for reimbursement from the state. The criteria used in rating a drug positive or negative vary between one country and another. Finally, the actual contribution made by the individual consumer to the retail cost of drugs also varies widely, with West Germany (approximately 12.5 per cent) at the lower end of the scale and Denmark (about 55 per cent) at the upper.

Facility location and supply of pharmaceuticals

Facilities for the formulation of pharmaceutical substances are strategically dispersed throughout Europe in order to maximise revenues and gain access to markets. Recall the fact, noted above, that pharmaceutical companies with a local presence possess a disproportionately large share of local markets. This is due, in part, to national agencies sourcing their drug requirements locally, even when it would be possible to import them at a lower price.

The manner in which pharmaceutical products are supplied and distributed within Europe also shows marked differences. There are differing legal requirements as to the packaging and pack size of pharmaceuticals and a large degree of non-uniformity as to the classification of drugs, e.g. whether they are ethical or over-the-counter. For example Nurofen (ibuprofen) is available over-the-counter in Britain and West Germany for general pain relief but is not available over-the-counter in Spain. This has implications for admittance to reimbursement schemes. In addition, there are differences in the retail outlets allowed in the various European countries; over-the-counter medicines can be purchased outside a pharmacy in Britain, West Germany and Holland but not in Spain, France, Belgium or Italy.

There is also a marked concentration in the pharmaceutical wholesale sector. In each country the pharmaceutical wholesalers are licensed by the respective national authority and in Germany, France, and Britain only three or four local groups handle 60 per cent of the non-hospital trade. The non-hospital sector generally accounts for about 80 per cent of the total ethical market. At the retail level there are also legal differences in that a pharmacist can only own one outlet in West Germany and not a chain of outlets as in Britain.

Industry analysis

A global industry analysis was carried out in Chapter 5; the purpose of this section is to highlight any significant differences in the European situation. Such differences do exist, largely due to the advanced stage of market development that has been reached, and also due to the multi-country nature of the market structure.

Barriers to entry into the industry are possibly higher than the global norm, owing to a number of factors:

1 High and growing economies of scale in the area of sales and marketing.
2 Twenty-year patents on new drugs, meaning that companies must either instigate an expensive R & D programme or be in a position to sell other companies' products.
3 Large 'up front' capital requirements for R & D and marketing of new products.
4 Increasing difficulty in gaining access to distribution channels in the major markets.
5 Loyalty of doctors to existing brands, although this is reducing due to governmental pressure.
6 Existence of learning and experience curves for each individual market within Europe.

In addition to these barriers to entry, potential new entrants are likely to be deterred by the potential retaliation from existing firms competing within the industry. They have much to protect and will use all their considerable resources to fight off any attempts to enter the market.

Episodes of intense rivalry are likely to become more frequent within the European market as the industry becomes more competitive, particularly in view of the series of major changes which will result from the single European market legislation. The major firms are now of such a size that considerable exit barriers from the industry have been built up, and are increasing. This combination of high entry barriers and growing exit barriers will shift the European industry from the position of making high stable returns to the point where the high returns carry an additional element of risk.

The bargaining power of buyers will also increase; in EC countries this will be a direct consequence of single-market legislation; in other countries it will be an indirect consequence as non-EC governments instigate 'copy-cat' legislation in those areas where EC countries appear to be achieving more control over rising drug costs.

In summary, then, while the European drug industry will continue to be an attractive one for the foreseeable future, it will be marginally less so as each year passes principally due to increasing rivalry and added buyer bargaining power.

Opportunities and threats

Europe-specific opportunities in the environment within which the drugs industry must work are as follows:

1 The opening up of Eastern Europe.
2 Mutual recognition of drugs, leading to swifter market entry and hence longer patent protection.
3 An increase in the elderly population, which is likely to lead to continued growth in the market.
4 Standardisation of delivery systems, leading to economies of scale in production.
5 Original pack dispensing with opportunities for consumer recognition of branded drugs.

Environmental threats could be characterised as:

1 Increasing bargaining power of buyers especially governments, who are trying to cut their costs by encouraging generic drugs.
2 Increasing rivalry within the industry.
3 An increase in parallel importing.
4 A falling number of school leavers to recruit.
5 Changing values within society, leading to reduced demand for drugs.

To assess the future of the European pharmaceutical industry, the remainder of this chapter consists of a detailed analysis of a major Swedish drug multinational (Astra), a Swiss giant (Ciba-Geigy), and an EC-based firm (Hoechst).

AB ASTRA

Company history and development

Astra is by far the largest manufacturer of pharmaceuticals in Sweden, indeed in the whole of the Nordic region. It was founded in 1913 as a drug company, and developed its own research programme in the 1930s. By the end of the 1930s it had produced its first original product. By 1948 Xylocaine had been introduced; this is a local anaesthetic and remains one of Astra's best-selling products to the present day.

A few years later, a major programme of internationalisation was initiated, which included plans for a worldwide network of subsidiaries, agents and licensees. Again, this programme has been maintained and developed right into the 1990s. Over the same period, the firm also pursued a diversification strategy to spread commercial risk beyond the pharmaceutical industry. This led to a number of totally unrelated projects, including investments in agricultural and plant protection companies, a firm which produced ski wax, and ventures were established to manufacture and market personal hygiene products and rust prevention treatments for the automobile industry. In 1977 Ulf Widengren was appointed company president and, as a result of his strategic review, all these non-pharmaceutical activities were divested between 1978 and 1980.

The firm's R & D programme has produced a number of significant original products, including the cardiovascular products Aptin and Seloken, the ampicillin Penglobe, and the anti-asthma agent Bricanyl. Astra now claims to be among the industry leaders in the fields of beta-blockers (the major category of drugs used for cardiovascular disease) and bronchodilators (for respiratory diseases). In recent years, it has developed great hopes of adding the anti-ulcer market to its list of world leaderships.

The company's headquarters are in Sweden at Södertälje, and most of its research and manufacturing operations are concentrated in the home country. However, it does have (or has planned) ten pharmaceutical manufacturing plants in other countries; it has twenty wholly owned foreign marketing subsidiaries, and it also markets its products in an additional 100 countries through a network of licensees and agents.

Mission statement

Like many other pharmaceutical multinationals, Astra does not publish an explicit mission statement. However, it can be fairly accurately inferred from using a variety of published sources to describe the philosophy of the firm.

The aim of Astra is to cure and prevent disease. This is achieved through the development and marketing of ethical pharmaceuticals. Astra focuses on areas of research where, by virtue of its expertise, it can develop highly innovative pharmaceuticals that can contribute to medical therapy. Effort shall be concentrated in each research area on products that satisfy urgent medical needs, as this is considered the best way to maximise the profits for our shareholders.

Both in research and in marketing and production, Astra's strength in relation to its international competitors shall be utilised and developed. In priority product areas, Astra's objective shall be to attain a position among the largest companies in its important geographical markets.

Marketing efforts will concentrate on transferring the knowledge that has accumulated during the period of product development. The objective shall be to enjoy the confidence of public authorities, the medical profession and other health care personnel.

Astra owes its success to its employees, all of whom are encouraged to become stockholders. Worker participation at board level ensures that the views of employees are taken into account in the decision-making process.

Objectives

Astra has always been a research-led company. The 1989 annual report, however, appears to reveal a shift of emphasis towards marketing. The underlying message seems to be that Astra intends to capitalise on good new products in order to become a major global player. The company seems to rule out a merger on the grounds that there are few economies of scale to be obtained in the field of R & D. It hints, however, at possible further alliances in the area of marketing.

Notwithstanding, it would still be reasonable to characterise Astra's objectives as:

1 *Advanced research.* Astra will focus on areas of research where, by virtue of its expertise, it can develop innovative pharmaceuticals that can contribute toward improving medical therapy.

2 *Medical needs.* Efforts will be concentrated in each research area on products that satisfy urgent medical needs.

3 *Relative strength.* Both in research and in marketing and production, Astra's strength in relation to its international competitors will be utilised and developed.

4 *Market share.* In priority product areas, Astra's objective will be to attain a position among the largest companies in its important geographical markets.

Business segments

Astra's substantial and continuous growth record has been entirely organic, with no acquisitions of any kind. The firm believes that a well developed marketing organisation is essential for success, and that the marketing of pharmaceuticals involves the transfer of all the knowledge that has accumulated over the long development period. It built up its marketing companies during the 1970s in northern and southern Europe, Canada and Australia. Astra's large US subsidiary was engaged primarily in the hospital and dental market, while the large out-patient market in the US was being developed chiefly through licensees.

These markets were significantly strengthened during the 1980s; during this period of expansion and consolidation, the firm followed two important guidelines:

1 Not to license products resulting from Astra's research to agents in large, important markets.

2 With the exception of Mexico and Argentina, the company's Latin American markets were assigned lower priority, with a new business focus on South East Asia. A joint venture was set up in China, where Astra has been one of the first pharmaceutical firms to appreciate the value of the Chinese market, and has also demonstrated keen awareness of the importance of timing in Chinese market entry.

Astra has five core therapeutic areas. Cardiovascular products were the largest area during the 1980s, though the growth rate is now starting to fall off somewhat, owing principally to the relative decline of beta-blocker products. Respiratory products currently represent the fastest-growing of the firm's historically important product groups, a trend which has been in place for most of the 1980s. Astra still has a major and growing presence in local anaesthetics, a product area that the firm entered over forty years ago with Xylocaine. Anti-infectives have been a solid performer for Astra over the last ten years, but annual growth here has now dropped well below that of the total pharmaceutical market.

The fifth group of products, treatments for gastro-intestinal diseases, is Astra's new 'star'. Launched in 1988, Losec has grown very rapidly indeed and threatens to outshine the performance of Tagamet (Smith-Kline) and Zantac (Glaxo).

Astra also has a line of medical care equipment which is hardly a dynamic performer and a catch-all 'other products' category which has recently shown good growth.

Astra is a very Swedish company. Although it operates in a global market, almost half its employees are located in Sweden. In the key area of research, 1,300 out of 1,650 people are based there. Only in marketing are the majority of employees outside Sweden. At board level, Astra has two worker representatives. One is from research and one is from production; both are based in Sweden. The board appears strong, with good non-executive representation. There is, however, a lack of an international dimension. It is curious that the executive vice-president (who is a large private stockholder) is in charge of finance and control, as well as being responsible for regional marketing for America. Given the increased importance of the US, it would make sense to have this as a separate appointment. The opportunity could be used to give the board the international dimension it presently lacks.

The company has instigated a stock option scheme for all its staff. This had a 87 per cent take-up in Sweden but only 35 per cent take-up elsewhere. All employees are involved in the profit-sharing scheme. The implication would seem to be that whilst employees at home are highly loyal to the company, elsewhere they may be less committed. Unless this can be overcome it would be sensible to continue concentration of the most important activities in Sweden.

Financial analysis

Geographical spread

Astra's international spread of sales is shown in Table 8.2, and indicates that the internationalisation programme has been maintained and extended right the way through the 1980s. Overall, the firm's sales growth for the decade averaged some 16 per cent per annum, a significantly higher figure than that recorded for the Nordic market (11 per cent per annum) over the same period. Performance in North America has been patchy, with good year-on-year gains being made early and late in the 1980s, with a period of falling sales between 1985 and 1987 – mainly as a result of aggressive price competition in local anaesthetics. Between 1982 and 1989, sales in non-Nordic Europe increased by a very satisfying 18 per cent per annum, mainly owing to

Table 8.2 Astra geographical spread

Measure	1982	1983	1984	1985	1986	1987	1988	1989
Sales (SEK million)								
Nordic Countries	981	990	1,015	1,157	1,260	1,452	1,694	1,974
Other European Countries	863	1,120	1,188	1,391	1,770	2,043	2,376	2,709
North America	378	547	698	764	754	671	793	1,005
Asia/Pacific	350	704	776	834	943	996	1,154	1,493
Other Markets	170	203	234	290	233	244	261	276
Sales (% increase on previous year)								
Nordic Countries		1	3	14	9	15	17	17
Other European Countries		30	6	17	27	15	16	14
North America		45	28	9	−1	−11	18	27
Asia/Pacific		101	10	7	13	6	16	29
Other Markets		19	15	24	−20	5	7	6
Sales (% of total by area)								
Nordic Countries	36	28	26	26	25	27	27	26
Other European Countries	31	31	30	31	36	38	38	36
North America	14	15	18	17	15	12	13	13
Asia/Pacific	13	20	20	19	19	18	18	20
Other Markets	6	6	6	7	5	5	4	4

Source: Astra annual reports and author's estimates

superior performance in major markets like France and the UK. Astra seems to have a clear view of the triad of crucial international markets – Europe, the US, and Japan; its development in Europe in the 1980s meant that this market overtook and greatly surpassed the Nordic market as the firm's chief source of sales.

However, in terms of compound growth of sales, pride of place must go to the Asia/Pacific market, which has been growing at a compound rate of 23 per cent since 1982. There have been major surges here in 1988 and 1989 and, if the present rate of growth continues, Asia/Pacific will overtake the Nordic countries as Astra's No. 2 market by 1992. Like all pharmaceutical firms, Astra was under severe pressure in Japan from 1985 onwards owing to government insistence on price controls and price cuts, but the Japanese business turned in a sparkling performance in 1989 following (and because of) the acquisition of Hoei Pharmaceutical Co. Ltd. This acquisition was made towards the end of 1988 primarily for the purpose of increasing market capacity in preparation for the future introduction of Astra's research products on to the Japanese market. The short-term benefits, however, have been in the local anaesthetic products.

Growth in 'other markets' has been disappointing at only 7 per cent compound per annum since 1982. Figure 8.1 shows the change in sales pattern between 1982 and 1989. 'Other markets' have fallen from 6 per cent of the total to 4 per cent, Nordic countries from 36 per cent to 26 per cent, while North America increased from 14 per cent to 18 per cent in 1984 then fell back to 13 per cent by 1989. Evidence of Astra's geographical strategy can, however, be seen in the advance of Europe from 31 per cent of total sales to 36 per cent, and of Asia/Pacific from 13 per cent to 20 per cent. In terms of the 'triad' of markets concept, this leaves the US as very much the weak link, and this point will be returned to later.

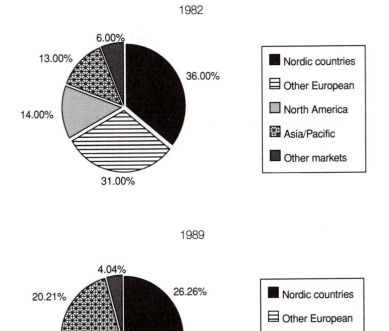

Figure 8.1 Astra: geographical spread of customer sales, 1982 and 1989 (per cent) *Source*: Astra annual reports

Results by segment of activity

Table 8.3 gives Astra's sales broken down by segment of activity and, again, a useful comparison can be drawn against the firm's overall 16 per cent per annum sales increase over the 1980s. Only two segments – respiratory products and gastro-intestinals – were above the average, with compound growth figures of 22 per cent per annum and 35 per cent per annum respectively. In the case of respiratory products, the growth has been fairly steady throughout the decade; they overtook 'other pharmaceuticals' in 1982 as Astra's third largest segment, and moved ahead of local anaesthetics into second place in 1987. They are now Astra's biggest product group.

However, the 'star' segment of the 1990s is likely to be the gastro-intestinals, where the growth of Losec has powered ahead in a phenomenal fashion in 1988 and 1989. Its early growth pattern is very similar to (and even more rapid than) SmithKline's gastro-intestinal

Table 8.3 Astra segment analysis

Measure	1980	1984	1985	1986	1987	1988	1989
Sales (SEK million)							
Cardiovasculars	596	1,249	1,343	1,467	1,580	1,735	2,008
Respiratory	246	719	888	1,044	1,254	1,539	1,828
Local anaesthetics	375	932	1,065	1,135	1,210	1,394	1,558
Gastro-intestinals	73	88	85	82	77	104	569
Anti-infectives	242	340	350	396	398	485	517
Other pharmaceuticals	380	469	581	691	709	819	768
Medical care equipment	76	114	124	145	178	202	209
Sales (% increase on previous year)							
Cardiovasculars	19	6	8	9	8	10	16
Respiratory	16	27	24	18	20	23	19
Local anaesthetics	15	19	14	7	7	15	12
Gastro-intestinals	16	−7	−3	−4	−6	35	447
Anti-infectives	20	4	3	13	1	22	7
Other pharmaceuticals	11	−9	24	19	3	16	−6
Medical care equipment	13	10	9	17	23	13	3
Sales (% of total by segment)							
Cardiovasculars	30	32	30	30	29	28	27
Respiratory	12	18	20	21	23	25	25
Local anaesthetic	19	24	24	23	22	22	21
Gastro-intestinals	4	2	2	2	1	2	8
Anti-infectives	12	9	8	8	7	8	7
Other pharmaceuticals	19	12	13	14	13	13	10
Medical care equipment	4	3	3	3	3	3	3

Source: Astra annual reports and author's estimates

Tagamet or Glaxo's Zantac. If Losec turns out to be a blockbuster like either of these, it will completely transform Astra's operations and its prospects.

Although the year-on-year sales increases of cardiovasculars dropped off in the mid-1980s, performance improved again towards the end of the decade as sales of beta-blockers stabilised and new product launches added some sparkle to the range. This is still a very important segment for Astra where it has established a good reputation based on an excellent range of products, and backed by an increasingly productive R & D programme.

The overall effect of these changes can be seen in Figure 8.2, which shows anti-infectives falling from 12 per cent of total sales in 1980 to 7

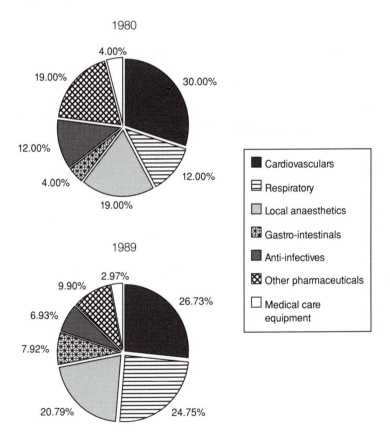

Figure 8.2 Astra: segment analysis, 1980 and 1989 (per cent) *Source*: Astra annual reports

Table 8.4 Astra financial performance (SEK million)

Measure	1980	1985	1986	1987	1988	1989
Sales	1,988	4,436	4,960	5,406	6,278	7,457
Cost of goods sold			1,459	1,507	1,670	1,964
R & D	243	647	742	823	956	1,032
Marketing and administration			1,849	1,971	2,319	2,752
Employees' share in profits					41	58
Depreciation	75	194	232	258	293	348
Operating earnings	180	967	1,068	1,243	1,355	1,668
Earnings before tax	107	705	914	1,273	1,366	1,798
Net earnings	72	407	483	625	682	962
Working capital	1,158	3,378	3,945	4,306	4,892	6,710
Fixed assets	834	1,991	2,374	2,757	3,386	3,387
Total assets	1,992	5,369	6,319	7,063	8,278	10,097
Long term debt	247	217	129	123	174	161
Employee remuneration	710	1,298	1,407	1,574	1,728	2,102
Number of employees	6,213	6,405	6,768	6,880	6,977	7,800
As % of sales						
R & D	12	15	15	15	15	14
Operating earnings	9	22	22	23	22	22
Net earnings	4	9	10	12	11	13
Employee remuneration	36	29	28	29	28	28
As % of net earnings						
R & D	339	159	153	132	140	107
Employee remuneration	992	319	291	252	254	218
Per employee (SEK)						
Sales	319,974	692,584	732,861	785,756	899,814	956,026
Operating earnings	28,939	150,913	157,787	180,727	194,210	213,846
Net earnings	11,524	63,575	71,424	90,785	97,692	123,346
Working capital	186,399	527,400	582,890	625,872	701,161	860,256
Fixed assets	134,267	310,851	350,768	400,727	485,309	434,231
Total assets	320,666	838,251	933,658	1,026,599	1,186,470	1,294,487
Employee remuneration	114,277	202,654	207,890	228,779	247,671	269,487
Pre-tax return on capital						
Employed (%)	14	24	22	22	22	23
Return on shareholders'						
equity (%)	16	30	25	22	22	24

Source: Astra annual reports and author's estimates

per cent in 1989, and 'other pharmaceuticals' dropping to 10 per cent from 19 per cent. Cardiovasculars, local anaesthetics and medical care equipment have been relatively stable over the decade while respiratory products (12 per cent to 25 per cent) and gastro-intestinals (1 per cent in 1987, 8 per cent in 1989) have forged ahead.

Financial performance

The financial information published by a Swedish firm in its annual report and accounts is calculated on a different basis, and developed for a marginally different purpose, from that given by a British or US firm. However, Table 8.4 gives a reasonable view of Astra's operations over the 1980s, though many of the variables may not be strictly comparable with those given in Chapters 6 and 7.

Perhaps the most interesting analysis that can be drawn from the figures is given in Table 8.5. Thus, as with Merck, improvements in manufacturing techniques (causing reductions in the cost of goods sold) are enabling high levels of R & D and marketing to be maintained. The significance of the drop in R & D as a proportion of sales is not yet apparent; it may be a one-off, or a function of project development within the fiscal years. Having regard to Astra's history and its prospects, it is unlikely to be a signal of long-term reduction in R & D investments.

Table 8.5 Astra financial performance analysed

As % of Sales	1986	1987	1988	1989
Cost of goods sold	29.4	27.9	26.6	26.3
R & D	15.0	15.2	15.2	13.8
Marketing and administration	37.3	36.5	36.9	36.9

Figure 8.3 is again reminiscent of the Merck performance, with employee remuneration as a proportion of sales falling steadily and significantly throughout the 1980s. The other notable feature of this graph is the excellent growth shown in operating earnings, surely the sign of an effective and integrated management team.

The long-term reduction in employee remuneration as a proportion of sales shows through very strongly in the productivity ratios in Table 8.4. Of particular interest here is the very rapid rise in operating earnings and net earnings per employee, again the sign of a well run firm. Financial management has also been prudent over the 1980s, with controlled increases in working and fixed capital, and a significant drop in the amount and proportion of long-term loans within the firm's capital structure. All this has had a predictably beneficial impact on the two measures of return on investment.

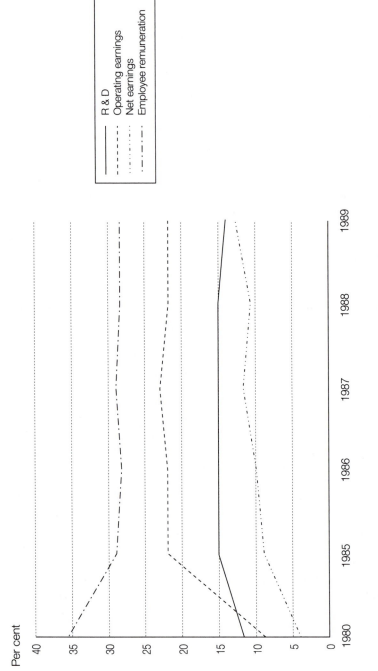

Per cent

	R & D
	Operating earnings
	Net earnings
	Employee remuneration

Figure 8.3 Astra: financial performance (as a percentage of sales), 1980 and 1985–9 *Source*: Astra annual reports

Activities

Products and competition

In the cardiovascular segment, there are four dominant groups of products: calcium antagonists, ACE inhibitors, beta-blockers, and diuretics. Astra's largest-selling product is a beta-blocker called Seloken which brought in SEK1,310 million of direct sales in 1989, and a further SEK1,585 million from licensed sales. (Ciba-Geigy sells the product under the name Lopresor.) In total, sales of Seloken accounted for 18 per cent of the global market for beta-blockers, a market which is forecast to grow by some 7 per cent per annum for the next few years.

Astra has also launched a second-generation calcium antagonist called Plendril. It is the first of this group of drugs to have a single daily dosage, and is considered to be a major advance over existing products. Sales of Plendril in 1989 were just SEK95 million in a world market worth over SEK22 billion. The overall market is thought to be growing rapidly and Plendril seems to be well placed to take advantage of this, having quickly achieved a market share of 10 per cent in those countries where it has been introduced. Astra has signed a cooperation agreement with Hoechst covering that firm's ACE inhibitor Ramace and Plendril. Ramace is not a novel product, but it does give Astra an entry into an important sub-segment of the antihypertensive market in a number of countries.

Finally, in the cardiovascular area, Astra has the anti-angina agent Imdur, which had sales of SEK105 million in 1989. The firm has signed a licensing agreement with Schering-Plough to cover marketing rights in the US, where it is scheduled to be introduced in the early 1990s.

The total world market for respiratory treatments was thought to be worth SEK47 billion in 1989; anti-asthma preparations accounted for about 45 per cent this figure, and the sub-segment was thought to be growing at approximately 20 per cent per annum. Astra has two main products in this therapeutic area, Bricanyl and Pulmicort. Both are available in conventional form or with the Turbohaler powder inhaler. Unlike some competitive products, this applicator uses the natural inhaling action of the patient, thus avoiding the need for CFCs. In 1989 sales of Bricanyl amounted to SEK567 million through direct marketing, with a further SEK950 million coming from licensee sales – mainly in the US. The largest direct markets for Bricanyl are Sweden and the UK. Pulmicort had sales of SEK510 million, up by 59 per cent on the 1988 level. This product has the fastest-growing sales in this therapeutic area. The largest markets for Pulmicort are West Germany and the UK. While it is far out-performing the market average, Bricanyl is lagging marginally behind. Other products are showing steady growth, but not building global market share. Concentration on Pulmicort whilst maintaining other products would seem to be the obvious move in this therapeutic area. Among these other products are Theo-Dur (1989 sales SEK278 million), Rhinocort (SEK121 million) and Mucomyst (SEK178 million).

Local anaesthetics make up a very mature market with total world sales of about SEK3 billion in 1989; the growth rate is low, likely to be under 5 per cent. Astra's Xylocaine, developed in the 1940s, is the world's best-selling product in this area. In 1989 Xylocaine maintained its market share, with sales of SEK1 billion. Two other products in this area, Marcain and Carbocaine, are also showing good growth, with 1989 sales of SEK205 million and SEK111 million respectively. Nesacaine, a much smaller product marketed only in the US, had 1989 sales of SEK35 million. R & D in this area is looking at new forms of application such as creams, CFC-free aerosols, and adhesive plasters. However, the main research focus is on discovering new methods and substances for blocking pain.

It is in the gastro-intestinal therapeutic area, with the new anti-ulcer agent Losec, that Astra hopes to experience its greatest growth in the medium term. The world market was about SEK80 billion in 1989; estimates of the growth rate vary, but are all towards the 20 per cent mark. The H_2-receptor antagonists have about 40 per cent of this, and include Zantac and Tagamet. Losec is a different type of pharmaceutical substance – acid-pump inhibitor – that seems to have proved more effective than H_2-receptor antagonists in the treatment of diseases such as peptic ulcers and reflux oesophagitis. Its clinical trials have attracted a great deal of international attention and a satisfactory degree of acceptance. Losec has shown astonishing growth in its first full year, and this is expected to continue. In the US, where the product is marketed by Merck, it has achieved sales of some SEK80 million after just two months on the market.

Anti-infective products represent a small and declining therapeutic area for Astra, with most of the sales concentrated in the Nordic countries. Penglobe is the biggest single Astra product in this sub-segment, with 1989 sales of SEK233 million (down 6 per cent on the previous year), though a further SEK249 million of sales were made through licensees. Other representatives in this area are Kavepenin, and the new drugs Lexinor and Foscavir.

The CNS area has been unimportant for Astra historically, but it hopes to achieve significant sales in a fast-growing sub-sector with Roxiam, a treatment for schizophrenia. Many applications for registration have been lodged, and it is hoped to launch the product in 1990. Another schizophrenia product, Raclopride, is currently being evaluated in clinical trials.

Astra's efforts in the medical care equipment sector are centred on LoFric (a drainage catheter with a special surface that binds water) and Iopamiro (an intravascular x-ray contrast medium which is well tolerated by patients. Sales of the first are growing rapidly, and the best markets have been the UK, West Germany and the Netherlands.

Future developments

In its core pharmaceutical product areas, Astra is actively pursuing the development of new and existing products with the medium-term aim of establishing strong positions in global markets. However, the key factor for Astra is not the success or failure of this progressive strategy but whether Losec becomes a blockbuster like Zantac and Tagamet before it. Both of these drugs completely transformed the medium-term performance of the respective companies. SmithKline grew very quickly but perhaps found the problems of following such a success too much, and eventually merged with Beecham. Glaxo seems to have learned some of the lessons; it has increased R & D expenditures, improved the control of R & D projects, and moved strongly to improve production and marketing. If Astra can learn from these role models, Losec could power it to being one of the global pharmaceutical industry giants by the end of the 1990s.

Research and development

Astra is a research-intensive company. Its four 'product companies' in Sweden are research-based, each concentrating on one or two therapeutic areas. The firm spends a high proportion of sales on R & D; for most of the 1980s, expenditures exceeded the industry norm of 13.5 per cent of sales. However, in 1989 the proportion dropped to 13.8 per cent from 15.2 per cent in the previous year. This may represent a policy decision, or it may merely mean that 1989 sales rose considerably faster than the management team expected. Perhaps a bit of each is involved; management might not have expected sales to rise by (as it turned out) 19 per cent, but must surely have expected a better outcome than the 8 per cent which was added to R & D investments.

The four product companies are:

1 Astra Pain Control:
Therapeutic area – pain relief.
Number of employees – ninety-three.
New products – none.
2 Astra Research Centre:
Therapeutic area – diseases of the central nervous system and infectious diseases.
Number of employees – 357.
New products – Roxiam.
3 Draco:
Therapeutic area – respiratory diseases.
Number of employees – 382.
New products – Bambuterol.
4 Hässle:
Therapeutic area – cardiovascular and gastro-intestinal diseases.
Number of employees – 562.
New products – Plendril, Losec.

Astra Pain Control is undertaking long-term research into pain relief and supporting the existing successful products in this area. This is reflected in the relatively small number of employees and the lack of new products.

Astra Research Centre is carrying out long-term research into diseases of the nervous system as well as supporting the existing anti-infective agents. The new product, Roxiam, was launched in 1991. The only development in infectious diseases is the acquisition of marketing rights over a 'me too' oral cephalosporin for the Nordic region.

Draco is supporting Astra's major agents for respiratory diseases as well as developing new products in this area. They have been successful with Pulmicort and with their Turbohaler and hope for similar success with Bambuterol.

Hässle is the largest of the product companies and is divided between cardiovascular diseases and gastro-intestinal diseases. It has developed Astra's two most exciting new products – Plendril and Losec, one in each area. Its resources will now be split between these two different types of drugs.

Strengths and weaknesses

In summarising the foregoing analysis into a list of strengths and weaknesses, an interesting perspective emerges – that Astra is actively engaged in developing its important strengths and minimising or eliminating its weaknesses.

Strengths

1 Good financial control and a strong financial position.
2 A well organised and efficiently run chain of subsidiary companies.
3 A number of good agreements with other drug firms for joint marketing in particular countries.
4 Very clearly defined objectives and strategies, which are seen to be carried through.
5 Some well established international brands among the product line; these are also among the most profitable, creating strong cash flows for further investment. Long patent lives remaining on some key products.
6 Support of a very loyal workforce.
7 Very strong in R & D, with the finances and resources to maintain and even extend this position, provided the correct policy decisions are taken.
8 Access to all major markets, though indirect in some cases.
9 Strong and skilful marketing organisation.

Weaknesses

1 A large proportion of revenues is generated by products that are out of patent.
2 Much reliance on the static West German market.
3 Little direct experience of the key US market.
4 No international representation at board level.

Strategy options and choice

Because of the developing business strengths of the firm and its strong product portfolio, Astra is faced with a number of strategic alternatives:

1 Going global with the existing product line. Using the joint venture with Merck to gain marketing experience in the US and trying to sell all products to all markets.
2 Going global with an expanded product line. Relying less on research and more on marketing to sell the products of other, research-based companies.
3 Going global with a reduced product line. Concentrating efforts on a smaller number of products to be sold to all markets.

4 Concentration on R & D with all products being sold under licence.
5 Marketing the existing product line to a smaller market, such as northern Europe and Scandinavia.
6 Merging with another large pharmaceutical company to become one of the major global players.
7 Moving into the manufacture and distribution of generic drugs.

Choosing between these various alternatives will be, as much as anything, a function of the mind-set of the top management team – whether to pay most attention to the threats facing the firm and adopt a conservative strategy of diversification, or whether to focus on opportunities and adopt an aggressive strategy of line-of-business concentration coupled with market and new product development.

Because of the existence of substantial environmental threats and the current stage of development of the firm, it is important that Astra does not over-stretch itself. Nevertheless, the preferred strategy ought to be an aggressive, progressive globalisation, but with fewer lines of business to allow efforts to be concentrated in a smaller number of areas. This leads directly to a number of specific proposals, set out below.

Research and development

1 Withdraw from research into infectious diseases. The work of Astra Research Centre could concentrate on diseases of the central nervous system and particularly the successful launch of Roxiam.
2 The Hässle company should be split into two, one company dealing with agents for cardiovascular diseases, in particular Plendril, and the other with agents for gastro-intestinal diseases, especially Losec.
3 Research should remain central to Astra's activities and should not be sacrificed to allow greater spending on marketing. Having a single company dealing with a single therapeutic area will allow specialisation and an improved reputation.

Marketing

1 Astra must work to become less reliant on the markets of Germany and Sweden by increasing its sales in the major markets of the US and Japan. The new products should not be licensed but sold through direct subsidiaries or the joint ventures.
2 To become less dependent on the old drugs which are out of patent, the efforts of sales forces should be concentrated on the new, patent-protected products in each therapeutic area. The old products must not be ignored, but sales will inevitably drop over time.

3 The subsidiaries should be subject to greater control from the product companies in Sweden. As the market becomes increasingly 'global' it will be necessary to have greater coordination centrally. It will also be necessary to employ a small number of marketing personnel within each of the companies and, as with research, they will concentrate on a single therapeutic area.

Human Resources

1 By bringing central marketing within the product companies, Astra will reduce their vulnerability to less committed employees outside Sweden. Efforts should be made, however, to increase employee commitment and greater coordination may help to achieve this.
2 An executive with international experience should be brought in at board level to support the company in the attempts to go global. In addition, a senior marketing executive with experience of the US market should be recruited, if necessary in conjunction with (or from) Merck.

Finance

Astra's long-term agreement with Merck allows that, if Merck's sales of Astra products before 1994 exceed a certain level, Astra may acquire a 50 per cent interest in Merck's US operation related to Astra products. The success of Losec may well give Astra the opportunity to do this and, if so, it should be seized with both hands.

Conclusion

The next ten years are bound to be exciting for Astra. More than most other firms in the world pharmaceutical industry, it has a real opportunity to completely transform its operations and prospects. As Glaxo and SmithKline have done previously, Astra has the chance to ride the potential blockbuster Losec to a position among the leaders of the world drug industry. To seize this opportunity would be a tribute to, and a fulfilment of, the dreams and strategic vision of Ulf Widengren. As company president from 1977 to 1987, he developed Astra from a regional pharmaceutical firm (with diversification into other industries) into a highly international operation tightly concentrated in ethical pharmaceuticals, with growing investments and skills in R & D. The new management team have the opportunity to extend this process and develop a new and ambitious strategic vision for the next ten years. If they fail, Astra will be acquired by a firm with the appropriate vision; even worse, the alternative is that Astra will regress again to become more dependent on its traditional European markets.

CIBA-GEIGY

Company history and development

Ciba-Geigy is an international chemical manufacturing company with its global headquarters in Basle, Switzerland. Since the Middle Ages, Basle has been an important seat of scientific knowledge and a thriving centre of trade and commerce. The company was created in 1970 by the merger of two independent firms, each of which had its own long and distinct tradition. Both Ciba and J.R. Geigy were based in Basle, and both took the decision to embark on the manufacture of synthetic dyestuffs, thereby entering the manufacturing chemical industry, in the same year of 1859.

Ciba developed from a small silk dyeing business owned by Alexander Clavel, based on the manufacture of a new (in 1859) synthetic dye, fuchsin. In 1864 he transferred his operation to the Klybeck site, then outside the town of Basle, which is still occupied by the firm. Over the next thirty years, further synthetic dyes were added to the product line and, in 1889, the company's first pharmaceutical products were presented at the Paris Exhibition. Early drug product lines included antiseptics and antirheumatics, but the firm also diversified into cosmetics, plastics, animal health products, pesticides, photochemicals and electronics.

J.R. Geigy set up shop in Basle in 1758 as a chemist and druggist and the next two generations of his family developed the dyestuffs business to service the booming textile industry. Like Ciba, Geigy started the manufacture of fuchsin in 1859; by the 1930s the firm was deeply involved in textile chemicals, pharmaceuticals and agrochemicals. Perhaps the company's first global brand was DDT, though the triazine selective herbicides were also internationally successful.

In parallel with the product development of the two firms was an intensive programme of market development. For example, Ciba acquired the Clayton Aniline Company in Manchester in 1911 to give the firm its first manufacturing base in the UK; Geigy set up a UK subsidiary in 1920. Following the merger of 1970, aggressive strategies of product and market development were maintained. Today, Ciba-Geigy is highly diversified and highly internationalised, most recently with a move into China. Its principal products are pharmaceuticals, agricultural chemicals, dyestuffs, plastics and additives, photographic chemicals, and a range of consumer products. The company has manufacturing operations in all major markets. The largest subsidiaries and affiliates are in the triad of critical markets – Europe, North America and Japan.

Mission statement

Ciba-Geigy does not publish a formal mission statement for the group as a whole. However, a flavour of the company's philosophy can be had from a statement of corporate principles[10] published by the British subsidiary. It is quoted below in detail because it is very revealing of the internal driving forces within the firm.

Ciba-Geigy is engaged primarily in the field of speciality chemicals and related products and services. Our Company is a subsidiary of Ciba-Geigy Limited, Basle, Switzerland, a publicly owned company, and as such is affiliated with a group of companies engaged in similar activities throughout the world.

Ciba-Geigy believes that business is not simply an end in itself and that it must serve people and society. Its economic success is, however, a prerequisite to the achievement of its aims.

Ciba-Geigy further believes that in its activities it should take due consideration of and harmonise as far as it judges to be possible the interests of the general public and the environment, customers, employees and shareholders.

In this connection we have adopted the following Principles:

The Public and the Environment We will behave as a responsible corporate member of society and will do our best to co-operate in a responsible manner with the appropriate authorities, local and national.

Through our activities, including the utilisation of the worldwide Ciba-Geigy experience and resources available to us, we will contribute to the economic development and well being of our country.

We recognise the need for our involvement in the social problems of our society and accept our social responsibility to participate in efforts to cope with these problems.

We take account of the fact that raw materials, land, water, air and energy are finite resources which must be used carefully and with responsibility.

We take all reasonable measures to ensure that our manufacturing operations and our products have no adverse effects on the environment.

Customers   We will supply products of high quality and at prices which are set, with due regard to all the circumstances, at levels which are competitive.

We will compete vigorously but fairly, and strive to develop confidence in our products through good marketing practices.

We will provide a high standard of customer service in our efforts to maintain customer satisfaction and co-operation with our Company.

Employees   We will strive to create an atmosphere which is conducive at all levels to the effective teamwork which is of great importance for the success of the Company.

We will endeavour to assign jobs, duties and responsibilities in accordance with the capabilities of the individuals concerned and in such a way that each is encouraged to make the best possible personal contribution. Promotions will be made as far as possible from within the Company.

We will define duties and responsibilities throughout the Company, and encourage participation in decision making within the scope of an employee's responsibilities. We will also develop and communicate, as necessary, business objectives and policies, and ensure their implementation.

We remunerate employees fairly on the basis of their assigned jobs, their performance and experience and with due regard to prevailing standards in the industry.

We will progressively provide for the possibility of developing the potential of employees by means of training, education, job rotation and performance appraisal.

Our employees will be provided with appropriate information regarding the activities of the Company and in particular we will ensure that each employee receives all relevant information necessary for the performance of his duties and for an understanding of how these relate to the activities of the Company as a whole.

While respecting the right of the individual to privacy, we recognise our social responsibility to our employees. We treat them fairly and with dignity and provide safe and healthy working conditions as well as schemes designed to afford protection to the employee and his family in case of sickness, old age or death.

Shareholders We intend to maintain and improve our position in our various fields of activity by creative and competitive efforts in research and development, production and marketing.

We will consider entering into new fields of activity, as a result of our own research and development, or in collaboration with third parties, or by acquisition, in order to provide for balanced growth and for the distribution of risk. Fields in which a synergistic effect can be achieved will be preferred.

As a member of the Ciba-Geigy Group and within the framework of its worldwide policies and objectives, our Company has independence of action.

We will, with the means available to us, achieve the short-term and long-term results necessary for the prosperity of the Company.

We will provide our shareholders with adequate information about the Company's operations, plans and objectives.

We will safeguard the Company's property and assets, and will conduct our operations with a high degree of efficiency and care.

Objectives

Ciba-Geigy's long-term objectives could be characterised as follows:

1 Continued development of presence in major markets (EC, US and Japan) and maintain its present status as one of the world's largest pharmaceutical companies.
2 Re-develop the weakening position in the West German market.
3 Development of a sound future R & D strategy.
4 Develop existing specialisation in advanced drug delivery research to become a market leader.
5 Restructuring of functional activities to combat the increase in buyer bargaining power.

Business segments

The pharmaceuticals division of Ciba-Geigy sees itself as performing two principal duties: first, to create efficacious and safe drugs; and, second, to disseminate the necessary information about them. As a result of the first of these, the firm has produced a range of pharmaceutical products in specific fields: cardiovasculars (especially hypertensives), anticoagulants, anti-inflammatories (especially antirheumatics), analgesics, antibiotics, sulphonamides, intestinal antiseptics, psychotropic and neurotropic drugs, pituitary and corticosteroid hormones, sex hormones (including ovulation inhibitors), dermatologicals, and various drugs for use in tropical medicines.

In 1989 the group employed about 92,500 people worldwide, of whom about 24,000 were in the pharmaceuticals division. Since 1985 the employment figure has been growing at about 3.4 per cent per annum, an indicator of the continuing growth of Ciba-Geigy. The company experiences difficulties with skill shortages in its home country, particularly regarding university and polytechnic graduates, the main growth sector within group employment since 1980.

Financial analysis

Ciba-Geigy releases very little operating information regarding the pharmaceuticals division, though the sales pattern is as shown in Table 8.6. By the mid-1980s, drug sales accounted for 30 per cent of the total, and the proportion has remained fairly steady since. Note the successive sales reductions in 1986 and 1987; this was largely due to the great weakening of the US dollar against the Swiss franc. In both years the firm's dollar sales in the US increased at a satisfactory rate.

Table 8.6 Ciba-Geigy sales performance (SFr million)

	1980	*1985*	*1986*	*1987*	*1988*	*1989*
Pharmaceutical sales	3,213	5,596	5,129	4,729	5,168	6,177
Group sales	11,914	18,221	15,955	15,764	17,647	20,608
Pharmaceutical %	27.0	30.7	32.1	30.0	29.3	30.0

The pattern of new capital spending was as shown in Table 8.7. Capital spending on the pharmaceutical division rose very substantially between 1980 and 1985. Since then, not only has the absolute figure of annual new investment in the division fallen by some 18 per cent, but the proportion of group capital expenditure being made within the division has fallen in each successive year, from 28.4 per cent to 14.1 per cent. It is likely that the peak in 1985 was related to the building and equipping of a new R & D facility at Summit, N.J.

Table 8.7 Ciba-Geigy capital spending (SFr million)

	1980	*1985*	*1986*	*1987*	*1988*	*1989*
Pharmaceuticals	147	344	326	262	241	281
Goods	853	1,213	1,232	1,368	1,616	1,987
Pharmaceuticals %	17.2	28.4	26.5	19.2	14.9	14.1

Since 1985 the pharmaceutical division has had great success in its sales efforts in the US market; other promising markets over this period have included the UK, France, Brazil, Canada and Mexico. The importance of the US market to the firm can be seen from the fact that the launch of Voltaren, now the most widely prescribed antirheumatic preparation in the world, in this market led to a 25 per cent increase in Ciba-Geigy's global pharmaceutical turnover over a two-year period.

Activities

Products

The company is well represented in most sectors of the market, and does not have over-much reliance on any one drug, although Voltaren accounted for just under 23 per cent of worldwide sales in 1989. The new range of transdermal patches is becoming more significant, with Nitroderm accounting for sales of around SFr410 million in 1989 and further growth to core, while the newer Estraderm (a transdermal presentation for menopausal conditions) probably produced sales of over SFr150 million. Many other presentations using this technology are in the pipeline. The key ethical products in the portfolio are:

1 Heart disease:

    (a) Beta-blockers such as Trasicor, Slow Trasicor, Trasidrex, Lopresor, Lopresoretic, and Lopresor SR.

    (b) Oral diuretics such as Navidrex, Navidrex-K, Hygroton and Slow-K.

    (c) Vasodilators, such as Apresoline.

    (d) Transderm Nitro is the first application of Ciba's breakthrough patch delivery system, and is used to provide sustained relief from angina pain.

    (e) New anti-clotting drugs are currently being developed to improve existing treatments.

2 Rheumatic and arthritic conditions:
    Voltaren, and Voltaren Retard, are market leaders in anti-arthritic drugs. Voltaren is currently the second biggest anti-arthritis drug, and the seventh biggest drug on the world market.

3 Diseases of the central nervous system:

    (a) Tofranil, Anafranil, Ludiomil, all general purpose antidepressants.

    (b) The difficult condition of major epilepsy has been significantly improved by Tegretol.

(c) Muscular spasticity can be attacked with Lioresal.

4 Menopausal symptoms:

(a) Hormone replacement is the second major use of the transdermal patch.

(b) Estraderm provides up to four days' relief from menopausal symptoms.

5 Bacterial infections:

Tuberculosis treatment has been significantly improved by Rimactane and Rimactazid.

6 Other medical conditions:

(a) Desferal – for the treatment of iron-storage disease and acute iron poisoning.

(b) Lamprene – for the treatment of leprosy.

(c) Metopirone, and Synacthen – to test the functioning of the pituitary gland.

(d) Orimeten – for the treatment of certain types of advanced breast cancer and cancer of the prostate gland.

(e) Symmetrel – for the treatment of Parkinson's disease and influenza.

Ciba-Geigy also has a large number of over-the-counter products, including:

1 Otrivine – nasal spray and drops for treating nasal stuffiness associated with colds. Formulations also exist for hay fever.

2 Mucron and Junior Mucron – nasal decongestants available in tablet and syrup form.

3 Do Do – syrup and tablets to relieve bronchial coughs and breathlessness.

4 Bradosol – used for sore throats.

5 Andursil – for the treatment of heartburn and indigestion.

6 Proflex – for the symptomatic relief of muscular aches and pains.

7 Doan's Backache Pills – self-explanatory use; a well established brand.

8 Lipsyl – the leading brand of lip salve.

9 Tri-Ac – a range of anti-acne preparations.

10 Eurax – for skin irritations such as sunburn.

11 Nupercainal – a local anaesthetic ointment.

12 Librofem – for the relief of menstrual pains.

13 Piz Buin – a very successful range of sun tan creams and preparations.

Much of the ethical product range is for age-related diseases, although the existing R & D programme will probably ensure that this pattern will change in the 1990s. Table 8.8 indicates the degree of change that has occurred in Ciba-Geigy's product portfolio during the 1980s. Over the period 1982–88, Voltaren has developed into a major product for the firm, growing at an average 13.5 per cent per annum. Nitroderm has grown even faster, and the recently introduced Estraderm threatens to out-perform both. The ten top-selling drugs in 1988 accounted for 55.4 per cent of total drug sales in 1988; the corresponding figure for 1982 was 36.4 per cent; the difference represents a measure of how much more focused the Ciba-Geigy portfolio has become over the period.

Table 8.8 Ciba-Geigy's largest-selling pharmaceutical products

Product	Sales (SFr million)		Compound growth % p.a.
	1982	*1988*	
Voltaren	510	1,093	13.5
Lopresor	285	414	6.4
Nitroderm TTS	50	392	40.9
Tegretol	200	334	8.9
Ludiomil	100	146	6.5
Anafranil	62	106	9.4
Oraspor	71	102	6.2
Estraderm TTS	–	99	N/A
Slow-K	155	91	−8.5
Lioresol	54	87	8.3
All other pharmaceuticals	2,596	2,304	−2.0
Total	4,083	5,168	4.0

Source: *Scrip Yearbook* 1985, p.313; 1990, p.309

New products for the early 1990s Some of the more innovative products which Ciba is likely to release on to the market beyond 1989 are shown below. The list confirms the company's diversity in therapeutic areas.

1 *Levoprotilene* (antidepressant). Will help to restore market share lost when Anafranil and Tofranil lost patent protection (Upjohn are rushing to license a very similar product).
2 *Oxacarbamazepine (anti-epileptic).* An improved version of Tegretol, which will shortly lose patent protection; the company claims the new drug is significantly safer and is looking for SFr150 million in the first year. It is thus a major presentation.

3 *Deursil* (dissolves gallstones). Licensed by the FDA for use in the US, and due to be launched there under a licensing agreement. It is likely to be very successful because it avoids the cost, and risk, of surgery; Deursil is a niche product.

4 *Metoros* (beta-blocker). It will be the first transdermal treatment in its therapeutic field, and is likely to be very successful.

5 *Not yet named anti-coagulant.* The company is about to release its first biotechnology drug on to the market, an injectable anticoagulant for use primarily in hospitals; it will displace heparin- and warfarin-based products. It has a much broader margin of safety and will be much easier for staff to administer.

6 *Not yet named anti-asthmatic.* Ciba are presently licensing in Japan a long-acting bronchodilator drug which they hope will take a significant share of Glaxo's Ventolin trade. Sales could be as much as SFr1,000 million per annum after two years.

7 *Not yet named transdermal nicotine patch.* This ethical drug is an aid to giving up smoking. High worldwide sales are expected, as it is a unique product.

New products for the mid-1990s   There are a number of areas in which research is at a less advanced stage. The company is evaluating five novel methods of drug delivery primarily concerned with treating cancer – an area in which the company does not currently have a high profile.

It is also about to embark on Phase III clinical trials with a protease-inhibitor set of biotechnology-derived drugs. These are being tested to treat emphysema, septic shock and arthritic conditions.

The over-the-counter market

Patrick Foster, Cheif Executive Officer of CIBA Consumer Pharma-ceuticals, has outlined the company's wish to double its share of the UK's £250 million over-the-counter market through acquisition, to around 7 per cent.[11] Ciba's UK over-the-counter sales rose fourfold between 1982 and 1986 through a move towards buying existing brands, and a move towards 'drug store' products such as Lypsil and the Piz Buin own-preparation range. Foster says, 'there is only so much you can do within the framework of the law. . . . Slow release gel to replace lotion or ointment, tablet shapes and liquid flavours are all useful ploys, however.' Ciba have also switched prescription-only products to the over-the-counter sector, although it takes time to get official clearance and it is very expensive in marketing costs.

The generics market

There have been widely differing approaches to the threats and opportunities posed by generic drugs. Ciba's Swiss rival Roche has taken the decision to stay out of the generics market. Speaking to *The Wall Street Journal Europe* (March 1987), Roche's Director of Pharmaceuticals Marketing said:

> We have thought about it. But so far Roche has decided that its primary business is new products . . . generics is short term business. We're not in the business to make a quick buck. . . .

For Ciba, the decision to get into generics is seen as a form of insurance. Executive board member Walter von Wartburg has drawn the parallel with the Swiss watch industry, which was backed into a corner by Japanese imitations of a Swiss invention, the electronic watch: 'We came to the conclusion that this is not something you can stay out of.'[12]

Ciba's US generics operation, Geneva Generics Inc, is now one of the top three generic drug manufacturers in the US, with about SFr200 million in annual sales. Ciba also owns a generics company in Holland, the largest European generics market, with an estimated 35 per cent of drug sales. It is official Ciba policy to consider setting up generic subsidiaries elsewhere in Europe when generic sales reach 10 per cent of the national drug market. West Germany is approaching that level with generics at 7 per cent, but Britain, France, Italy and Switzerland are less likely targets because of price controls, low prices or other factors.

Ciba and mergers

Perhaps this is best illustrated by quoting the words of the Ciba-Geigy chairman:[13]

> In attaching so much importance to our own research and development we have made a further important strategic decision, namely to secure the future of our enterprise by our own efforts and not by means of [major] acquisitions. . . . We renew our product mix and achieve growth from inside and not by purchasing growth from outside, in other words by acquisitions; and we mean to go on renewing and growing in the same way.
>
> . . . The price demanded for goodwill in the purchase of businesses and the cost of research and development are so high that even a financial giant cannot afford to pursue both strategies at the same time.

It is, however, worth pointing out that this policy has not precluded Ciba from taking stakes in the two small US biotechnology companies mentioned above. It also has a joint venture with Sandoz in Taiwan, to which we have also already referred.

Research and development

Some commentators think that Ciba has a less promising set of emerging products than Sandoz or Roche.[14] This may be a mistaken and short-term view: the company has a potentially brilliant range of presentations all of which will bear fruit in the late 1990s.

It is generally agreed that there will be in future less return on 'me-too' presentations, as the duplication of research is becoming prohibitive. Ciba is involved in a number of joint ventures with small research companies, the most notable being with Chiron and Alza. Ciba has an 8 per cent stake in Chiron, a Californian biotech company. The two companies own 50 per cent each of Biocine, and are trying to derive medicines for AIDS, herpes, malaria and hepatitis. Biocine is presently undertaking clinical trials for two AIDS treatments, one to kill the virus, one to restore the immuno-function after successful treatment.

Alza, in which Ciba owns a majority stake, specialises in novel delivery mechanisms. It was this joint venture which led to the transdermal patch – Alza invented the patch and Ciba's expertise in plastics enabled it to make and distribute the product. Ciba-Geigy itself is researching eighty-eight new chemical entities, as well as over 100 applications of transdermal delivery.

The research function is widely disseminated around the world: in Canada Ciba is researching ailments of old age; in California it is developing biotechnology; and at Horsham, Sussex, it has the ADDRU (Advanced Drug Delivery Research Unit). Ciba has also opened research facilities in Japan, primarily to break into the Japanese market more quickly. The Swiss head office in Basle is involved in more traditional research, and coordinates all other research. Other points of interest in the R & D function include the following:

1 Ciba-Geigy spent some SFr800 million in 1989, some 13 per cent of sales, putting the firm well within the top ten in the industry. Ciba has, therefore, reached and surpassed the minimum critical mass needed to survive and prosper in the pharmaceutical industry.

2 R & D responsibilities are allocated to 'centres of excellence' (UK, US, Switzerland and India), combined with central management of development.

3 The combined R & D workforce of 4,200 is the third largest in the industry; most are positioned on the development side, where they have become adept at preparation, registration and documentation, and liaison with regulatory bodies.

4 About a third of the present R & D portfolio represents work on products licensed from other companies.

5 Specialisation and experience in ADDR (advanced drug delivery research) have already launched Nitroderm TTS and Estraderm.

Strengths and weaknesses

It is no simple matter to establish a clear picture of Ciba-Geigy's pharmaceutical operations, as the activities of the drugs division are masked by those of the company as a whole. Despite this difficulty, it is still possible to draw the following list of strengths and weaknesses from the foregoing analysis.

Strengths

1 Ciba-Geigy has a marketing organisation and research presence in the major strategic markets: Europe, Japan, and the US.

2 The solid financial base of the group is an important resource for the research-intensive pharmaceutical operation.

3 Voltaren, the company's best-selling product, is perceived as the most effective anti-arthritic agent.

4 Advanced drug delivery research represents a critically important area of specialisation and experience, particularly in transdermal therapeutic systems.

5 The company's reputation and size of sales force in certain therapeutic areas, combined with a large and experienced drug development department efficient in the licensing of drugs, yield a significant competitive advantage.

Weaknesses

1 The portfolio of existing products is mature, with over half of total sales being derived from off-patent drugs.

2 There is growing reliance on the Voltaren group of products as a major source of revenue.

3 For a company of this size, there are few firmly established products in other therapeutic areas.

4 There are some comparative weaknesses in the R & D area: the strategy does not appear to be clearly defined, there are no significant

follow-up drugs, and many of the minor non-innovative R & D outputs will not justify a significant initial marketing spend.

5 Ciba-Geigy seems to be losing relative market share in West Germany, one of its major traditional European markets.

Strategy options and choice

The preceding analysis of Ciba-Geigy's pharmaceutical operations suggests that the firm is likely to follow a defensive strategy orientation in the short term, though, taking into account the aggressively successful nature of some areas of the firm's business activities, it is likely that proactive strategy directions will be followed in the medium term, including vertical and horizontal integration, joint ventures and/or strategic alliances. This, then, suggests some suitable strategic postures for Ciba-Geigy pharmaceuticals:

1 Develop and improve the existing product portfolio in the short term through licensing agreements with smaller, more innovative companies, using the substantial in-house marketing capabilities. Reappraise the current position within each therapeutic area, reallocating resources to successful products, e.g. anti-arthritic and menopausal disorders. Continue rationalisation to achieve a low-cost manufacturing position.

2 Strengthen the research and technological base by accessing external know-how through joint ventures/strategic alliances with smaller research-intensive pharmaceutical companies. In the medium term, backward integration and/or acquisition must be considered a possibility, despite the firm's current antagonism towards mergers.

3 Expansion of the generics subsidiary into other major markets, focusing on new product areas through acquisition or joint venture.

In turn, these broad strategy recommendations lead on to a series of more detailed functional and activity-based strategies which, taken together, may suggest a suitable action plan for the Ciba-Geigy pharmaceutical business.

Research and development

The company is developing an interesting range of products for release throughout the 1990s, but the focus on 'centres of excellence' must be maintained and developed. Ciba's established expertise in ADDR should increasingly be emphasised in all areas. The existing involvement with universities and other external research centres should be increased, together with a focus on the further integration of biotechnology into traditional R & D procedures. The development arm of R & D should be further strengthened to facilitate the quick licensing and launch of new products.

These points give rise to a series of more detailed (and more tentative) suggestions:

1 It is essential that Ciba-Geigy expands research into biotechnology. It is engaged in a number of joint ventures, but there is a distinct possibility that non-drug companies developing the other areas of the field, e.g. food technology, could enter the pharmaceutical industry. As these companies have sufficient capital to effect an entry to the industry, it is important that Ciba-Geigy stay at the forefront of medical biotechnological developments.

2 Research into high-technology delivery systems must continue. The company has a successful range of transdermal delivery products and it is important that new systems are developed to protect Ciba's lead in this field.

3 There should be increased research into the ailments of old age to consolidate the considerable spending that has already been committed in Canada. The effects of demographic changes in the Western and Japanese populations will ensure that this therapeutic market will increase. Ciba-Geigy's strong product portfolio in this market must be augmented with newer bio/high-technological products as soon as possible.

4 Ciba should commit itself to a research programme in China, augmenting the recently commissioned plant in Beijing. There is a historical tradition of natural medicine in China; many of the new chemical entities of the 1940 to 1980 period were the result of research into plant-based remedies and there is likely to be a significant untapped potential for development within Chinese medicine.

5 Another possible move could be for Ciba to enter the diagnostics market, as Abbott (see Chapter 6) has done so successfully. There is an increasing tendency towards earlier detection of disease; a number of recent biotechnology developments have applications in diagnosis. This is a growing market, and Ciba may be foolish to neglect it.

6 Finally, and most tentatively, it may be that Ciba should establish an R & D facility in western Africa to undertake AIDS research, a field in which it has already done some work. In western Africa there is a large indigenous population with the disease, and there would be fewer of the bureaucratic controls that currently slow research in developed countries.

Markets

Ciba-Geigy is well placed in key therapeutic sectors and its research programme should ensure this continues. However, there are opportunities both in geographical terms and in the ethical/proprietary medicines emphasis.

1 *Europe*. The single European market in the 1990s should not pose a major problem for the company. The German government is very cautious about the development of biotechnology. This will probably harm Hoechst and Bayer, and be to Ciba's advantage.

2 *United States*. There is a danger of protectionism becoming US government policy as a reaction to the single European market and US dollar instability. Ciba is well placed in the US market in terms of joint ventures and generics. Greater emphasis should be placed on the large US over-the-counter market in which Ciba-Geigy is not at present a major player.

3 *Japan*. It is important that this market is developed by the company as it is as large as the US market. The Japanese now consume more pills per person than any other nation, giving an opportunity for Ciba-Geigy to develop its over-the-counter trade. Development of the Japanese market will act as a springboard in the other markets of the Pacific Basin.

4 *China*. The Chinese market has huge potential. There will be increasing demand within China for Western medicine, and a market containing a billion potential patients is too large to ignore.

5 *South America*. This is a very unstable market, owing to the budget deficits of the countries in the region. One possibility is for Ciba to open a subsidiary to produce generic medicines: low prices would make them attractive in a region where the branded portfolio of drugs is too expensive.

6 *Africa*. At present, Africa is not a large market, but here again a generic subsidiary could be developed.

7 *Eastern Europe*. It is hard to speculate on the effects of the political changes taking place in the former USSR and its satellites. However, the relatively affluent and open USSR, Polish and Hungarian markets show the most potential. In the first instance, Ciba-Geigy should attempt to develop joint ventures with the state-controlled pharmaceutical industries in these countries. Again, there may be potential for a generic subsidiary to service these markets.

Joint ventures and acquisitions

The company's policy of avoiding take-over battles involving other large pharmaceutical companies is correct; there is little added value to be gained in such moves, and the costs are prohibitive; the resources would be better spent on internal R & D. However, take-overs of smaller companies must not be excluded; there are a number of small firms in the biotechnology and high-technology fields that will be unable to bring their products to the market. Ciba could take them over rather than engage in joint ventures. After all, if these small companies collapsed, the research could fall into the hands of competitors.

For this reason Ciba-Geigy should move to acquire the Chiron Corporation of California at an early date. Chiron has a research programme in biotechnological diagnostic agents in conjunction with Abbott Laboratories; it would be useful to Ciba to have greater access to this programme and this market. If it is unable to take over Chiron then a joint venture with Abbott would protect the AIDS research programme.

Ciba may also wish to consider acquiring, or failing that be looking towards a joint venture with, a medium-size Japanese pharmaceutical firm. This would assist greater penetration of the Japanese market, and might also be of help in the development of a subsidiary in South Korea.

Conclusion

The Ciba-Geigy pharmaceuticals division is reasonably well placed to face the challenges and opportunities of the 1990s. By emphasising innovative research in pharmaceutical substances, and in their delivery systems, the company is likely to maintain (and possibly improve) its position in the world pharmaceutical industry. Its focus is already shifting from the traditional approach of new chemical entities to biotechnology and high-technology delivery systems.

In the past, increased turnover and profits were generated by the expanding market for drugs. This is likely to continue over the 1990s, powered by increasing longevity and the boom in demand for drugs to combat the afflictions of old age. However, in terms of population growth, Ciba-Geigy must not ignore the markets of the developing world if it wishes, in the longer term, to buttress its position at the forefront of the global pharmaceutical industry.

HOECHST GROUP

Company history and development

The firm dates from 1863, when a chemist (Eugene Lucius) and two salesmen (Wilhelm Meister, Lucius' cousin; August Mueller, Lucius' wife's uncle) founded Meister Lucius & Co., on the banks of the river Main in the village of Hoechst – now a suburb of Frankfurt, West Germany. The intention of the three was the manufacture of synthetic dyestuffs, a technology that was sweeping Europe at that time. With a manufacturing workforce of seven, they began making red fuchsin dye (cf. the Ciba and Geigy companies in Switzerland), then the world's most sought-after dye, from a derivative of coal tar. Because of this first product, the firm was given the nickname 'The Red Factory' which still persists locally. The incident that, above all, proved to be the foundation of Hoechst's fortunes occurred when its green aldehyde dye was used to colour a new gown for Empress Eugénie of France, wife of Napoleon III. Instead of appearing blue in the light of the Paris Opera gas lamps, as all previous green dyes had done, the empress's green dress remained a vivid, true green.[15]

Hoechst quickly developed as a world leader in the synthetic dye business, and also diversified into other businesses. In 1883 the firm moved into pharmaceuticals, followed by bulk chemicals (1891), polymers (1913), agricultural chemicals (1916), and high-purity silicon – the key material for the microelectronics industry (1920). By 1925 Hoechst had become one of the three largest German chemical companies and it merged with its two major competitors – Bayer and BASF – to form I. G. Farbenindustrie AG. After World War II this super-corporation was broken up into a number of much smaller operations. However, Hoechst was eventually reconstituted as an independent firm (as were Bayer and BASF) in 1951. Thereafter, the company proceeded on an aggressive development programme; this included rapid inter-nationalisation which culminated in the major US acquisition of the Celanese Corporation in 1986.

In the pharmaceutical business, production began with the analgesic Antipyrin in 1883, followed by the introduction of a diphtheria anti-toxin in 1894. In 1910 Hoechst ushered in the modern age of chemo-therapy with the first 'wonder drug', Salvarsan (see Chapter 1). In the post-World War II era, major developments included penicillin pro-duction (1950), Rastinon for the treatment of some forms of diabetes (1956), the introduction of the diuretic Lasix (1964), the development of Trental, which improves the flow properties of blood in the blood vessels (1972), and the introduction of Claforan (1980) – one of a new generation of antibiotics.

Today, Hoechst is a highly internationalised and widely diversified company based on the chemical industry, though with substantial operations in plant engineering, industrial gases, copiers and cosmetics. The company has major subsidiaries in twelve developed countries, with a much wider network of minor subsidiaries manufacturing and selling Hoechst products in a very large number of countries.

Mission statement

In the 1989 annual report the Chairman of the Management Board, Professor Dr Wolfgang Hilger, noted:[16]

> Within the divisions we shall be forming business units that operate close to the markets and take decisions independently within the framework of jointly agreed strategies. This will produce better cooperation among Hoechst companies throughout the world, as well as speed up the response to market conditions and improve employee motivation.

To supplement this perspective, selected quotations from 'Hoechst – our guiding principles' are worthy of consideration.[17]

Employees:

> We impose exacting demands on ourselves, our skills, our willingness to learn and our commitment to performance. Our financial rewards are commensurate with our own performance and the Company's success.

Research:

> Hoechst develops and manufactures products geared to market requirements. The aim of these products is to meet people's basic needs and improve the quality of life while also safeguarding and raising living standards.

Environmental protection:

> Hoechst believes in acting with far-sightedness and responsibility in matters of safety and environmental protection. These considerations have equal standing with our objective of performing efficiently among international competition.

Objectives

Hoechst's objectives are a very direct development of its mission and closely linked to, and integrated with, its 'Guiding Principles':

1 A worldwide company with an open-minded approach.
2 To continue a successful tradition of scientific and technical progress aimed at improving living standards.
3 To secure a partnership with customers through the market place.
4 To provide shareholders with an appropriate return on their capital.
5 To protect life and the environment.
6 To secure employee commitment and personal development.
7 To provide leadership through consultation.
8 To achieve excellence in all sectors.

Business segments

Hoechst is the third largest chemical company in the world, as well as being one of the largest pharmaceutical firms. The sheer size of the company can be seen from its recent financial performance: group sales for 1989 amounted to DM46 billion and pre-tax profits were over DM4 billion. For reporting purposes, Hoechst groups its operations into six business areas, whose 1989 performance was as shown in Table 8.9.

Turning to the geographical spread of activities, Table 8.10 represents sales and profits derived from each region of the world. Note that, of the above sales total, DM3110 represented inter-company sales, thus

Table 8.9 Hoechst business areas' performance, 1989 (DM million)

Area	Sales	%	Operating profit	%
Chemicals and colour	11,640	25	1,161	29
Fibres plastic film	9,013	20	555	14
Polymers	7,788	17	745	18
Health	8,292	18	947	23
Engineering and technology	6,515	14	489	12
Agriculture	2,650	6	144	4
Total	45,898	100	4,041	100

Table 8.10 Hoechst sales and profits around the world, 1989 (DM million)

Region	Sales	%	Operating profit	%
European Community	30,530	62	2,643	66
Other European countries	1,295	3	89	2
North America	11,946	24	974	24
Latin America	2,180	4	95	2
Africa, Asia, Australasia	3,507	7	240	6
Total	49,458	100	4,041	100

explaining the difference between the sales total by region and the sales total by segment. In terms of profitability, the health sector is clearly pre-eminent, though the 1988 position was less healthy. Also, the dependence on the EC market is very pronounced, with North America also being very important. The geographical analysis does, however, highlight the relatively weak position in the critical third major market, Japan.

Hoechst breaks the health sector into pharmaceuticals – DM7897 million, 95 per cent of health sector sales in 1989 – and cosmetics – DM395 million, 5 per cent of health sector sales. The pharmaceuticals sub-sector includes anti-infectives, cardiovascular drugs, antidiabetics, analgesics, vaso-active preparations, psychotropic drugs, dermatological preparations, synthetic hormones, cytostatic drugs, human plasma derivatives, vaccines, and diagnostic systems. The cosmetics sector includes products sold through selected retail outlets (Marbert), and Jade brand cosmetics and skin-care products; also involved here are Schwartzkopf products for hair and skin care, and hairdresser supplies.

In 1989 Hoechst had 169,295 employees worldwide, 22 per cent of whom were female. R & D employees accounted for 9 per cent of this total, sales and marketing 19 per cent, production and auxiliary plants 53 per cent, administration and other sectors 19 per cent. The company is firmly committed to equal opportunities for men and women, and makes great efforts to help employees combine a job with bringing up their children. Hoechst also places great importance on training; in 1989 over 20,000 took part in advanced training and continuation courses, including a substantial element of computer training.

Financial analysis

Like Ciba-Geigy, Hoechst publishes very little divisional financial data, though the broad pattern is shown in Table 8.11. On average, over the 1980s, pharmaceutical sales grew at a compound rate of 5.8 per cent a year, while total group sales grew at 4.9 per cent per annum. Drugs are now contributing a fairly steady 17 per cent to the Hoechst total.

Table 8.11 Hoechst sales figures, 1980, 1985–89 (DM million)

	1980	1985	1986	1987	1988	1989
Pharmaceutical sales	4,750*	7,055	6,607	6,310	6,951	7,897
Group sales	29,915	42,722	38,012	36,956	40,964	45,898
Pharmaceutical %	15.9	16.5	17.4	17.1	17.0	17.2

* Estimate

Lacking detailed financial data to build a picture of Hoechst's pharmaceutical operations, it is perhaps worth recalling that within the industry Hoechst is regarded as a sort of elder statesman; it is perceived to operate in a very staid and unspectacular manner that is, perhaps, consistent with its traditional German origins. The Hoechst group has good financial control and possesses large financial resources; the pharmaceutical business contributes strongly in this respect and, no doubt, shares in the business strengths that strong finances build.

Activities

Products

As noted above, performance is hardly sparkling, and this is borne out by the data in Table 8.12 which compares Hoechst's ten top-selling drugs in 1988 with the position in 1984. Three drugs (Claforan, Lasix and Novalgin) are shrinking, while a further three (Trental, insulins and Surgam) have fairly high growth rates. As a whole, the top ten products accounted for some 39.8 per cent of total pharmaceutical sales in 1988; in 1984 the top ten (only eight of which were still in the top ten in 1988) accounted for 38.2 per cent of the total. This is a marginal increase in concentration compared to, say, Ciba-Geigy; it implies that the focus of the product portfolio has hardly changed between 1984 and 1988.

Table 8.12 Ten top selling products, 1984 and 1988

Product	Sales (DM million)		Compound growth % p.a.
	1984	*1988*	
Claforan	710	661	−1.8
Trental	285	527	16.6
Lasix	487	385	−5.7
Daonil	250	335	7.6
Novalgin	270	184	−9.1
Rythmodan	142	181	6.3
Surgam	108	155	9.5
Insulins	88	132	10.7
Haemate HS	–	111	N/A
Kybernin HS	–	98	N/A

Source: Scrip Yearbook 1986, p. 301; 1990, p. 322

Another way of looking at the product portfolio is to examine how it has been developed over the last ten years. From the company's perspective, this perhaps gives a fairer view of the dynamic of portfolio development, and it also indicates some of the benefits Hoechst has obtained from its large R & D expenditures in the pharmaceuticals division.

1980 Claforan, a cephalosporin antibiotic, was launched.
Arelix, a diuretic for treating high blood pressure, was under development.
Optisulin, a prolonged action anti-diabetic, was nearing the end of its development cycle.
MMR Vax, an anti-rubella vaccine, was launched in Germany.

1981 Betapressin, a beta-receptor blocker, was launched.
Teceos, a radiodiagnostic agent for skeletal scintigraphy, was launched.
Isoxepac, an anti-rheumatic, was under development.
A herpes vaccine was under development.
Venimmun, an intravenous gamma globulin, was under development.

1982 Euglucon N, an improved oral antidiabetic agent, was launched.
Psyton-Hoechst, an antidepressive/anxiolytic agent, was undergoing clinical trials.
Streptase, a myocardial infarction prevention agent, was under development.
Actosolv, another antithrombolitic, was under development.
Ramipril, an ACE inhibitor, was under development.
Buserelin, an anticancer agent, was under development.

1983 Arelix-RR, a diuretic, was launched.

1984 Cefodizime, a fourth-generation cephalosporin, was under development.
A herpes vaccine was undergoing clinical trials.
Forskolm, a treatment for myocardial insufficiency, was under development.
Betasemid Mild, a treatment for moderate hypertension, was launched.
Aclaplastin, an antibiotic for treating cancer, was launched.

1985 Euglocon N was approved by the FDA and launched in the US.
Trental, a treatment for vascular diseases, was approved and launched in the US.
Cefodizime was undergoing clinical trials.
Buserelin was launched worldwide.

1986 Cytorhodin, an anticancer agent, was undergoing clinical trials.
Tarivid, an antibiotic microlide, was launched in West Germany.

1987 Tarivid was launched in France.
Streptase was launched worldwide.
Propentofyllin, a vasoactive substance, was launched in Japan.
AIDS cooperative research with Bayer AG.
1988 Ramipril was launched worldwide.
Cefpirome, a fourth generation cephalosporin, was launched worldwide.
Hextol, a treatment for cerebral function disorders, was launched worldwide.
1989 Roxit, a gastric ulcer treatment, was registered in West Germany.
Felodipine, an antihypertensive, was launched in West Germany.
Cefodizime ended clinical trials, registration applied for.

Current strategy

The pharmaceutical division faced difficulty from 1985 to 1987, with sales declining from DM7.0 billion to DM6.3 billion. In spite of this, Hoechst continues to increase its capital expenditure in the pharmaceutical division and in 1988 it was approximately DM330 million. Of this, about 55 per cent was invested outside Germany.

Exports from Germany and France have been impaired by a decline in the US dollar. North America now accounts for 12 per cent of pharmaceutical sales. The pharmaceutical sales in 1989 were worth DM7.9 billion; the international spread of these sales is indicated by Table 8.13. In West Germany, the delays in getting marketing approval for new drugs from the regulatory authorities (the most stringent in Europe) and the increasing competition from generics are causing some problems. This has forced Hoechst to launch a comprehensive rationalisation scheme, affecting not only production and marketing but also research and development.

However, Hoechst possesses a wide variety of strengths which have

Table 8.13 Hoechst geographical spread, 1989

Country	% of sales
West Germany	20
Japan	13
France	14
US	12
Italy	9
Other	32

helped maintain its position in the market and will do so in the future. In 1987 the company stated that it was going to concentrate its research effort on diseases and illnesses that are at present untreatable.

Markets

It has been noted that the rate of growth of the pharmaceutical industry is closely linked to the rate of growth of GDP in particular countries; thus the outlook for the world economy is an important determinant of the prospects of the pharmaceutical industry and, in particular, of the prospects of a highly internationalised company like Hoechst. There are two markets which are critical to the firm's future, and these are now briefly reviewed.

First, there is still plenty of opportunity for the Hoechst pharmaceutical business to grow in the US. Its sales level to North America of around DM950 million is still small compared to the total US market size. Apart from being the largest pharmaceutical market, it is also one of the most attractive for commercial development. Although the US government is anxious to contain health care expenditure, it remains one of the fastest-growing markets. Unlike most other markets, there are no pharmaceutical price controls as yet, although the outcome of the Waxman hearings may result in the implementation of price controls.[18] Also, in contrast to Japan, there are no real difficulties in establishing an independent wholly owned operation. Even allowing for the uncertain US economy, the future for Hoechst in North America is bright, buttressed by the Celanese acquisition (1986) and the licence from Boots to bulk manufacture Ibuprofen at the Celanese facility.

However, any downturn in the US economy could be partially balanced (for Hoechst) by the fast growth in the Pacific Rim countries. Currently, the Pacific Basin (excluding Japan) accounts for 17 per cent of world pharmaceutical sales, and is the world's fastest-growing drugs market. The Far East is enjoying real and rapid economic growth at present, with incomes and living standards rising faster than anywhere else in the world. It represents a major new market for Hoechst which should be exploited. However, this may be possible only through joint-venture agreements, owing to the different legal and social pressures on multinationals in these countries.

Joint ventures

One of the obvious strengths of Hoechst has been its willingness to form cooperative ventures, in order to acquire access to skills necessary for the successful commercial exploitation of its own research ideas. An example of this is the cooperation between Hoechst and Polaroid in order to allow the development of measurements from radioactive diagnostic kits. In addition the company is heavily engaged in cooperative research with some of the leading biotechnology research institutes in the world.

The company exploits its wide distribution network by managing the sale and distribution of new pharmaceuticals developed by smaller pharmaceutical companies. In this way the company benefits from the risk taken by these smaller pharmaceutical companies with little, if any, risk to itself. An example is the recent agreement whereby Hoechst will market Astra's new, potentially blockbusting, drug felodipine (Plendril) in West Germany.

Research and development

Hoechst has consistently invested heavily in pharmaceutical research and development, as can be seen from Table 8.14. Hoechst's 1989 expenditure on pharmaceutical R & D represented 44 per cent of total Group R & D expenditure; at around 14 per cent, the firm's investments in research are above the industry norm of 13.5 per cent of sales. The firm tightly coordinates the research efforts of its research centres in Germany, the US, France, Great Britain, Austria, Egypt, India and Japan. In 1987, 30 per cent of the research expenditure went to projects in the company's research facilities outside West Germany. Because of the wide geographical distribution of the research centres, Hoechst is in a good position to respond to regional problems and approach drug development in light of specific market requirements.

Table 8.14 Hoechst investment in R & D, 1985–89 (DM million)

	1985	1986	1987	1988	1989
Total group R&D	2,683	2,138	2,217	2,416	2,621
Health division R&D	972	978	976	1,039	1,153
Health R&D as % of health sales	13.8	14.8	14.5	14.1	13.9

Hoechst, in cooperation with the American biotechnology company Biogen, is working on the development of a vaccine against malaria. This provides a potentially lucrative market, as malaria is endemic in many parts of the Third World which are experiencing rapid economic development. Hoechst is working on the development of new drugs for the following areas: cancer, some forms of heart disease, auto-immune diseases, multiple sclerosis, diabetes, mental illnesses like schizophrenia, Alzheimer's syndrome and AIDS. In the early 1980s, Hoechst recognised that advances in biotechnology were laying the foundation of the future of the pharmaceutical industry. As biotechnological processes, in a simplified form, was the basis of the company's antibiotic production (many of these substances can only be produced by the methods of biotechnology, i.e. fermentation), Hoechst has sought to develop further its expertise in this area. The expertise it had through its Behringwerke subsidiary, whose products were based upon immunological processes, was also of relevance to this area.

Hoechst developed its expertise in the first place by concluding an agreement with the Massachusetts General Hospital in Boston (associated with Harvard University) in 1981 under which Hoechst would finance (at the rate of $5 million per annum) for ten years the research activities of the Molecular Biology Department. Under the terms of the agreement, research topics would be mutually agreed and implemented, and Hoechst would have first say in the exploitation of results. Also, in 1984, Hoechst's French subsidiary Roussel Uclaf established a research institute in genetic engineering in cooperation with CNRS, the French state-run research institute. Finally, in 1985 Hoechst started a cooperative venture with the Georg-Speyer-Haus foundation (Frankfurt), in which the Paul Ehrlich institute is involved, for the development of drugs to combat AIDS. In 1987 Bayer AG entered into this agreement. By funding research in research institutes, and by entering into joint ventures with other pharmaceutical companies, Hoechst spreads both the risk and the expense of such R & D. At the same time the likelihood of success in these programmes is increased owing to the complexity, knowledge and skills range required.

Both the American and French cooperative research projects have already borne fruit in that novel compounds, which constitute new therapies, have been identified and obtained in sufficient purity and quantity to begin clinical trials. The Massachusetts General Hospital managed to produce angiotensin to enable clinical trials concerning its wound-healing attributes to be investigated. The French cooperative effort has resulted in the isolation and identification of two new immunostimulants which are currently undergoing clinical trials for their ability to protect patients who are undergoing cancer chemotherapy from catching infections.

Hoechst's own expertise in biotechnology via the Behringwerke subsidiary has justified the opening of a DM60 million facility in Germany for the production of human insulin from genetically modified bacteria. It has identified a precursor of insulin (diarg insulin) which can be administered intramuscularly to patients, and which is slowly broken down to insulin in the body. This is of major benefit to diabetics, who will now only have to inject once weekly rather than daily. Clinical trials began in 1986 on this compound. In addition Behringwerke began production on a large-scale of erythropoietin, a stimulant of the production of red blood cells, which will be of benefit in the treatment of anaemic patients, particularly those that develop anaemia as a result of dialysis.

Hoechst's present product range covers the following areas: cardiovascular/diuretics, diabetes, hormonal disorders, blood products, antiallergy/inflammatory, the central nervous system, anticancers, antivirals, antibiotics, and hormone disorders. With the exception of 38 per cent of its current drugs Hoechst faces competition from generic drug manufacturers in well over half its current range of pharmaceuticals.

The leading drugs Lasix, Trental and Claforan alone account for approximately 22.5 per cent of Hoechst's pharmaceutical sales. Of the firm's leading drugs, Lasix alone lacks patent protection and is faced with generic competition. The other leading drugs (Claforan and Trental), which were launched in 1979 and 1984 respectively, must be nearing the end of their effective patent lives. This, in conjunction with the apparent worldwide trend for governments to reduce health costs by insisting that generics are prescribed when available, will cause problems for Hoechst unless it continues to develop novel drugs.

As noted above, Hoechst has always invested heavily in pharmaceutical R & D. The importance of the pharmaceutical division to Hoechst can be gauged from the fact that, of the total R & D expenditure of the Hoechst chemical group, the pharmaceutical division has consistently accounted for more than 40 per cent. The results of this consistent heavy expenditure can be seen from the list of new product launches and drugs under development in the previous section. That list was not intended to be comprehensive; its purpose was to illustrate both the range and the relative success of the firm's research effort. In 1987, Hoechst obtained some fifty-five licences for new pharmaceutical preparations in twenty-five countries. In 1988 it had twenty-two new products under review by various licensing authorities, three of which are major therapeutic breakthroughs.[19]

Two of the products launched recently, Ramipril and Streptase, are expected to be leading drugs in their therapeutic categories. Indeed, the clinical trial results of Streptase (anti-heart attack) were thought to be the cause of a £0.07 drop to £4.80 in Beecham's share price; this firm is the current market leader in these thrombolytic products with its drug

Eminase. Streptase is priced much lower than Eminase, and in these cost-conscious days this gives Hoechst a significant competitive advantage.

Ramipril, used for the treatment of hypertension, is expected to generate annual revenues of $45 million in the US by 1992, with 1.4 per cent of the market. The leaders in this field are Squibb and Merck, who were first to launch products of this kind.[20] They are expected to have a more than fifteenfold greater turnover with their respective drugs in this field than Hoechst. This, by itself, indicates the necessity of maintaining an active, innovative R & D programme, as the rewards for those who launch their product first are huge.

Although out of patent protection, Rhythmodan (an anti-arrhythmic) is the most frequently used compound in its therapeutic field and is expected to generate worldwide annual revenues of $100 million by 1991.[21]

The above examples, and the steady stream of new drugs under development, should ensure the continued good performance of the company and keep it within the top ten pharmaceutical companies worldwide in the short to medium term.

Strengths and weaknesses

As with Ciba-Geigy, it is difficult to get an absolutely clear view of Hoechst's strengths and weaknesses. However, some points are fairly clear, and are laid out briefly below.

Strengths

1 The Hoechst pharmaceuticals business is part of the third largest chemical company in the world, and it is one of the world's largest drug firms.
2 It has an excellent international distribution network and a well coordinated international research capability.
3 There is a substantial and continuing investment in biotechnology.
4 There is good access to in-house multi-disciplinary scientific, marketing and management skills.
5 The pharmaceuticals division has proven skills in developing research alliances with other pharmaceutical firms and research institutes.
6 Hoechst has a considerable number of drugs, which represent real therapeutic advances, nearing the completion of the development stage.
7 The Hoechst group is financially sound.

Weaknesses

1 The firm has only a small share of the strategically important US market.

2 Considerably less than half the current drug portfolio has patent protection; this includes a major product, Lasix.

3 Hoechst has only a small pharmaceuticals presence in Japan and South East Asia.

4 Production facilities are based primarily in West Germany and subject to stringent environmental controls. The building of two new genetic engineering facilities at Marburg has been delayed by two years.

Strategy options and choice

Establishing strategic options from the foregoing analysis requires a focus on the strength and stability of Hoechst relative to the pharmaceutical industry as a whole. Matching the pharmaceutical division's strengths and weaknesses with the industry opportunities and threats, outlined earlier in this chapter and in Chapter 5, suggests that it is in a potentially aggressive strategic posture relative to its competitors. The firm is a large and powerful player, enjoying some competitive advantage in an attractive industry. Adopting this general strategic direction would mean a radical change from the apparently conservative strategic approach now being followed. Hoechst should take full advantage of the opportunities that are available to it, and perhaps look for acquisition candidates whose activities are consistent with its own focus, and which would enable it to secure additional revenue and profitability. The specific recommendations which follow have been divided into the short term, and medium term, though, in the case of Hoechst, it is very difficult to distinguish between the two.

Short term

1 Review the conservative strategic posture adopted by the company and move in the direction of a more aggressive strategy consistent with the current competitive advantage possessed by the company.

2 Review the current business strategy of not actively seeking to service the over-the-counter market.

3 Investigate the possibility of forming a strategic alliance with another leading pharmaceutical multinational to focus on shared R & D.

4 Position the company to launch an aggressive attack to secure a profitable niche in the generic drug market, in those therapeutic areas where the patent protection afforded to Hoechst products is due to expire.

5 Review the possibilities of an aggressive posture with respect to those drugs currently produced by competitors under patent protection, on which that protection is due to expire

6 Further market penetration and consolidation is required, particularly in the US and Pacific Basin.

7 It will be necessary to speed up the rate at which Hoechst introduces new drugs on to the market to avoid being beaten at the post, as occurred with the new drug Ramipril. Squibb and Merck beat Hoechst with the ACE inhibitors.

8 Ensure that research and development programmes are marketing-led rather than scientifically driven. The firm must also increase its expertise further in the biotechnological field.

9 Identify the drug requirements specific to the new growth areas of the world, especially South East Asia and the demographic trends in the Western world.

10 Maintain pressure on governments, directly and through trade associations, to extend the patent life granted on pharmaceuticals, owing to the increased time spent in R & D.

Medium term

1 Establish production facilities outside Europe, particularly in South East Asia, where the market demand warrants it.

2 Acquire smaller, highly innovative pharmaceutical and biotechnology companies which may be experiencing cash flow problems due to the expense and time taken for drug development programmes.

3 Concentrate R & D effort on drugs for therapeutic areas which are now inadequately treated or untreated. These areas offer the greatest return if a drug can be developed.

4 Fund further research in universities and research institutes, thereby improving the chances of discovering therapeutically useful new chemical entities.

5 Progressively reduce the cost of drug manufacture by using the expertise present in the company in biotechnology and chemical engineering.

6 Increase the extent to which Hoechst distributes and markets drugs developed by smaller pharmaceutical companies.

7 Maintain and develop strategic alliances with the emerging Japanese pharmaceutical companies.

8 Become a significant force in the over-the-counter market by developing its Cassella subsidiary.

Conclusion

In many ways, the pharmaceutical division of Hoechst is in a similar position to ICI Pharmaceuticals; it is a soundly performing part of a much bigger combine. If Hoechst pharmaceuticals was an independent drugs firm it would probably be concluded that, despite its current profitability and good future potential, the interests of shareholders might be best served by looking for an appropriate merger partner. It is unlikely that the management board of Hoechst will take that path. However, despite its size and past record, this firm must be considered as one of the slumbering (or at least dozing) giants of the pharmaceutical industry. If it is to retain its place as one of the industry leaders it is vital that the correct strategic decisions are made in a timely manner, not only at the level of the pharmaceutical division board but – perhaps more critically – at the top level of the Hoechst group. Failing this, Hoechst's drug business is going to be threatened and surpassed by a number of the more flexible and more focused companies that are now pushing to the forefront of the world pharmaceutical industry.

9 The Japanese pharmaceutical market

THE MARKET

Japan is a relative newcomer to the pharmaceutical industry. Until the beginning of this century, medicines in Japan depended on Chinese herbals, prescribed by oriental physicians. With the arrival of modern Western science around 1900, Japan introduced scientific medicine on a limited scale. Eventually traditional Japanese and Chinese medicines were replaced, but the traditional dealers continued as wholesalers and retailers of imported drugs. Domestic production did not begin until around 1925, but not until long afterwards did Japan establish systems for developing new drugs.

It was in the late 1960s that the indigenous pharmaceutical firms, with much prodding and encouragement from the government, eventually organised themselves to develop new drugs in any meaningful way. They started with the production of antibiotics, including penicillin and streptomycin, though much of the early impetus came from the manufacture of over-the-counter products such as vitamin pills, liver vitalisers and nutritious health aids. In 1961 a government-inspired health insurance scheme was introduced to cover the whole population, and this was extended in 1973 to give free treatment to the elderly.

The output of prescription drugs now represents over 85 per cent of total pharmaceutical production. Imported technology from the West has been critical to the success of new drug introductions in Japan. Drug output has increased from ¥90 billion in 1955 to ¥4 billion billion in 1985, a compound growth rate of about 21 per cent per annum. Despite this success at home, Japanese firms have as yet made relatively little impact in European or North American markets, and exports still account for less than 4 per cent of output. Investments in R & D in the last twenty years have produced many extensions and variations of established pharmaceuticals, but the historical record of producing new chemical entities is poor. Only in the years since 1985 has there been any real evidence that Japanese pharmaceutical firms have developed the high level of expertise needed to produce meaningful new chemical entities. However, as has been the case in many other industries, it is obvious that Japanese firms are climbing this particular learning curve very quickly indeed.

Industry structure

There are about 1,250 drug companies operating in Japan, including 150 subsidiaries of American and European multinationals. In terms of market share, the largest company (Takeda) has just over 10 per cent of the domestic market, which makes the Japanese pharmaceutical industry one of the most fragmented in the world. The small size of such a large number of firms makes it difficult to invest adequately in R & D. Table 9.1 shows the R & D expenditures of Japanese pharmaceutical companies over the period 1975–85. Over this period, expenditures have grown by an average 13.6 per cent per annum, but reaching only 7.04 per cent of sales by 1985. This is significantly lower than the ratios for major competitor nations, and JETRO[1] has a twofold explanation for this:

1 There is a high proportion of drugs made from imports (bulk powder, bulk liquid, bulk products and pelletising materials) which represented 25.5 per cent of output value in 1985.
2 An extremely small amount is spent by many small and medium-size manufacturers on drugs R & D.

Table 9.1 R & D expenditures of the Japanese pharmaceutical industry (¥ billion)

Year	R & D Expenditure	R & D to sales ratio (%)
1975	95.2	4.91
1976	109.5	5.05
1977	120.5	4.84
1978	134.7	5.00
1979	176.9	5.53
1980	189.8	5.45
1981	218.4	5.85
1982	239.8	5.56
1983	289.9	6.59
1984	295.3	6.49
1985	341.9	7.04

Source: JETRO (1987)

By way of comparison, JETRO[2] notes that the average ratio of R & D costs among the eighty-one leading ethical pharmaceutical manufacturers (all members of the Japanese Pharmaceutical Manufacturers Association) was 10.7 per cent in 1985. Foreign firms account for about 20 per cent of the domestic market and are rapidly increasing their presence. The main problem that Japanese firms have in breaking into world markets is that they lack a wide range of exportable drugs; only a few product lines like antibiotics have made any impact in Western markets. This is, of course, exacerbated by lack of access to overseas distribution channels. Therefore, to counter these difficulties, most of the internationalising Japanese firms have entered into licensing agreements with the Western multinational giants; evidence of this trend was noted in Chapters 6, 7 and 8. A significant proportion of prescription drugs sold in Japan are made by Japanese firms under licence from the US or European manufacturers that originally developed them. Since most companies lack overseas distribution networks, the drugs they do export are largely sold by foreign firms under licence.

Since 1985 the emerging Japanese strategy has been to reduce dependence on licensing agreements in favour of strategic alliances, joint ventures and establishing subsidiaries overseas. One important reason is that the ¥5 billion billion home market (only marginally second in size to the US) has now lost much of its appeal. For many years, the domestic industry prospered by producing antibiotics and other drugs that were freely prescribed by doctors and paid for by the Japanese National Health Insurance Plan. Since 1982 the government has slashed the amount it will pay for ethical drugs by over 40 per cent, creating enormous pressures on profitability; hence, Japanese firms are driven to go abroad as local conditions become unattractive.

Production and trade

Table 9.2 shows the aggregate statistics for production and trade in pharmaceuticals over the years 1975–85. It can be seen that, while production grew at a compound rate of 8.4 per cent per annum over the decade, the effect of international trade was marginal. Until 1982 production was growing faster, at about 12 per cent per annum, but thereafter growth dropped off as the government started to adjust drug prices. In 1985 nearly 50 per cent of all production was accounted for by just five therapeutic categories – antibiotics, cardiovasculars, CNS, gastro-intestinals, and metabolics.

Concentration of imports is also high; in 1985, nearly 65 per cent of all

Table 9.2 Production and trade in pharmaceuticals, 1975–85 (¥ million)

Year	Production	Exports	Imports	Balance of Trade
1975	1,792			
1976	2,162	64		
1977	2,458	73		
1978	2,794	68		
1979	3,042	83		
1980	3,482	94	262	(168)
1981	3,679	102	276	(174)
1982	3,980	108	332	(224)
1983	4,032	126	312	(186)
1984	4,027	129	321	(192)
1985	4,002	132	331	(199)

Source: Ministry of Health and Welfare, Ministry of Finance, Customs Statistics, Japan

imports came from three sources – America, West Germany and Switzerland. Exports were less concentrated, with 50 per cent of the total going to five countries – America, West Germany, Taiwan, France and Korea. Note the presence of two significant Far East markets in this list; Japan also exports substantial quantities to China, Australia and Hong Kong.

Japan has a consistent negative balance of payments position in ethical pharmaceuticals of around ¥200 million. Again, this shows a high degree of concentration, with the US regularly accounting for about half the total.

Industry analysis

In terms of the five competitive forces outlined in Chapter 5, the position of the Japanese industry is fairly similar to the world industry as a whole. There are, however, some country-specific factors which have to be evaluated. The main buyer is the government, and this works as an additional barrier to entry (especially for foreign firms), as government policy is to buy from and promote well established Japanese firms. Government policy also restricts new entrants because of excessive bureaucracy involved in securing approval for new drugs.

The intensity of rivalry among existing competitors is generally more severe in Japan because of the intrinsic fragmentation of the domestic industry, because the industry itself has entered a (short-term?) low-growth period since 1982, and because foreign firms want to enter and compete in the Japanese market – almost at any cost – because of its strategic importance to the potential global firm.

As the industry's principal buyer, the Japanese government has been exercising its power throughout most of the 1980s, and has driven prices down to a very marked degree. The bargaining power of suppliers is not very different from the general world situation, but the threat from substitutes may be somewhat higher, owing to the proximity of China (with its alternative approach to human medication) and because of Japan's traditional links with Chinese medicine.

Thus, in summary, entry barriers are more favourable to the existing competitors but three of the other competitive forces – the bargaining power of buyers, threat from substitutes, rivalry – are less favourable. Taking all these together, it must be concluded that the Japanese industry is less attractive than some other major world markets analysed earlier. While this may not be too much of a barrier to foreign multinationals seeking a strategic foothold in the Japanese market, it has certainly become a major factor in motivating many of Japan's larger pharmaceutical firms to seek pastures new in foreign fields – initially through increased exports, subsequently via strategic alliances, joint ventures, wholly owned foreign subsidiaries, and perhaps through major foreign acquisitions in the future.

Opportunities and threats

Apart from the factors reviewed in the foregoing industry analysis, there are few Japan-specific environmental factors which differ markedly from the list of opportunities and threats outlined in Chapter 5. The size and sophistication of the Japanese market together with the rapidly growing standard of living of the Japanese represent a quite definite opportunity area for foreign firms contemplating market entry. For these firms, however, there is a countervailing threat embodied in the very distinct language and cultural barriers presented to incoming firms. Finally, for both domestic and foreign firms, the long-term strength of the yen *vis-à-vis* almost every other currency represents a threat to export activity, and this factor will increase in importance as Japanese and Western firms attempt to access the burgeoning Pacific Rim market from a Japanese base.

In summary, then, the outlook for Japan-based firms is less favourable than for other markets examined in earlier chapters. To assess how this will affect companies in detail, the remainder of this chapter analyses the operations and strategies of three major Japanese firms: Takeda, Fujisawa and Yamanouchi.

TAKEDA CHEMICAL INDUSTRIES LTD

Company history and development

Takeda was founded in 1781, originally as a wholesaler, and started manufacturing its current products only in 1960. The development of comprehensive R & D capabilities over the past three decades has made Takeda by far the largest pharmaceutical company in Japan, and ranked twentieth in the world. It is a diversified company with a strong presence in fine chemicals and animal health products. Manufacturing of pharmaceuticals started by creating a small division at the turn of the century followed, a few years later, by the addition of an export department. Now the company has wholly owned pharmaceutical subsidiaries in the US and West Germany. The US subsidiary markets products for America and Canada, while the West German subsidiary markets in continental Europe and the UK.

Direct presence abroad started in developing countries through joint ventures in Mexico, Taiwan, Thailand, Indonesia, the Philippines and Malaysia. Since the late 1970s emphasis has shifted to industrialised nations through new ventures and licensing agreements in France, West Germany, the US and Italy. The American subsidiary in North Carolina was set up in 1971 to produce vitamin B. Takeda's international approach is flexible, basically expanding through wholly owned subsidiaries, joint ventures and licensing. Management operates autonomously in order to tailor business activities to suit local needs and circumstances.

Mission statements

The firm's published mission statement[3] places great weight on its involvement in the international pharmaceutical industry, though it does have substantial interests in other fields.

Takeda Chemical Industries Ltd is the largest pharmaceutical company in Japan. Founded over two centuries ago, Takeda is a research-based institution with product lines covering every major sector of ethical drugs and various over-the-counter drugs. In addition to pharmaceuticals, Takeda produces fine chemicals, food products and ingredients, chemical products, agricultural chemicals and animal health products.

Takeda is also a leader among Japanese pharmaceutical companies in the international marketplace. The company's many subsidiaries, affiliates and licensees provide Takeda with global R & D and marketing capabilities through a network that spans Japan, Europe, North America and Asia.

Objectives

Again, we can turn to Takeda's own words[4] for an unusually explicit statement of company objectives.

We implemented a five-year plan on April 1, 1987. This plan addresses business challenges in Japan and abroad and steers Takeda towards long-range goals. Building on a technological foundation centred on the biosciences, we will serve global markets. We seek to increase annual net sales to ¥700 billion by 1991 and to ¥1 trillion by 1996. Plans are predicated on three fundamental conditions:

* Continued strengthening of product development capabilities in pharmaceuticals and other operations,
* Vigorous expansion of overseas activities, and
* Full use of our corporate resources in cultivating peripheral markets and markets not necessarily related to pharmaceuticals.

A full commitment of resources backs our determination to fulfil these conditions.

Business in Japan, built around our operations in pharmaceuticals, is the well-spring of the revenues and earnings that fund the expansion of our presence abroad. We further this business through the development of competitive products born of special strengths in basic research. To reinforce the momentum generated by innovative new products and to increase our market share, we will streamline operations to minimize costs and upgrade our marketing efforts.

Business segments

Takeda has substantial distribution strengths in Japan, but it is currently at a disadvantage in other major markets on this key aspect. The firm's products are well regarded in the domestic market, as evidenced by good increases in sales revenues in recent years despite large price reductions enforced by the government. This strong demand for Takeda products in Japan is not reflected in penetration in other markets, which remains relatively weak.

The company has a strong foothold in businesses other than ethical pharmaceuticals. As of April 1990, its business divisions are:

1 Pharmaceutical Division – ethical drugs.
2 Vitamin and Food Division – formed in April 1990 as a combination of Fine Chemicals and Food Products divisions.
3 Healthcare Division – formed in April 1990 to provide a focus in relation to over-the-counter drugs, previously a part of the Pharmaceuticals Division.
4 Agro Division – formed in April 1988 to search for greater synergies in the firm's agriculture-related businesses; it involved combining the Agricultural Chemicals Division and the Animal Health Products Division.
5 Chemical Products Division – a traditional business centred on the manufacture of polyurethanes, organic acids, unsaturated polyester resins, and polyurethane resins.

Remembering, from the above, that one of the three 'fundamental conditions' on which Takeda's plans are predicated is 'full use of our corporate resources in cultivating peripheral markets and markets not necessarily related to pharmaceuticals', it is worth noting at this stage that 65 per cent of all company sales came from pharmaceuticals (including over-the-counter products). Interestingly, a new division has appeared on Takeda's organisation chart called the Environment Products Division, but no details of its activities are available at the time of writing.

It is more difficult to gain any real feeling for the firm's approach to human resource policy, though all the right statements are made in successive annual reports. Recently, the company has launched *Dynamics*, a bi-monthly business communication sheet for staff worldwide. Thus Takeda seems to be feeling the strains which are imposed on corporate culture and human resource policy by increasing internationalisation of operations, and is taking positive steps to counter this.

The firm will have enhanced its international standing amongst the research and scientific community (on whom it critically depends to develop and positively influence the talent within universities which it needs to attract into employment) by entering into collaborative research contracts with the Harvard Medical School and Tulane University in America. The company has also underwritten a Chair at Harvard – the Takeda Professorship in Anatomy and Cellular Biology.

One particular item worth noting here is that the president since 1986, Mr Umemoto, has only been with the firm fourteen years, an unusually short time for a Japanese executive at that level. However, the annual report noted that he had been appointed 'having spent his career in public service, much of it with administrative groups that define some of the essential parameters of our market'.[5]

Financial analysis

Results by segment of activity

Table 9.3 shows Takeda's annual sales for the period 1983–89 broken down over four sectors – pharmaceuticals, vitamin and food products, chemical products and 'agro" (agricultural and animal health) products. Overall, the firm's sales have grown at a compound 4.8 per cent per annum over this period; only pharmaceuticals, at 6.3 per cent per annum, outstripped this average rate of growth. Furthermore, the greatest part of the growth in pharmaceutical sales has occurred in the three-year spell since 1986. Since this is also the period when Takeda's internationalisation programme got fully under way, it is reasonable to assume that rapidly increasing foreign drug sales have powered the company's growth since 1986.

Table 9.3 Takeda performance by segment of activity

Measure	1983	1984	1985	1986	1987	1988	1989
Sales (¥ billion)							
Pharmaceuticals	308.2	308.1	308.1	313.1	336.6	396.5	444.9
Vitamin and food	64.6	63.7	68.2	69.9	69.3	68.8	69.5
Chemical products	93.2	101.2	107.7	109.4	106.4	113.9	119.3
Agro	53.5	57.9	59.8	59.4	59.2	53.7	53.0
Increase on previous year (%)							
Pharmaceuticals	9.6	0.0	0.0	1.6	7.5	17.8	12.2
Vitamin and food	2.7	−1.4	7.1	2.5	−0.9	−0.7	1.0
Chemical products	6.8	8.6	6.4	1.6	−2.7	7.0	4.7
Agro	2.7	8.2	3.3	−0.7	−0.3	−9.3	−1.3
Percentage of total sales							
Pharmaceuticals	59.3	58.0	56.7	56.7	58.9	62.6	64.8
Vitamin and food	12.4	12.0	12.5	12.7	12.1	10.9	10.1
Chemical products	17.9	19.1	19.8	19.8	18.6	18.0	17.4
Agro	10.3	10.9	11.0	10.8	10.4	8.5	7.7

Source: Takeda annual reports and author's estimates

Sales of chemical products have grown steadily since 1983 and this division is now as big as agro, vitamins and food put together. Agro sales grew fairly well up to 1985, but since then have been steadily shrinking year by year. The firm puts this down to less frequent occurrence of rice blight problems (an important market for Takeda), together with adverse government regulations to reduce rice paddy acreage. The vitamin and food business has shown sales increases in some years and decreases in others. Takeda advances a series of explanations for this patchy growth record, but it is likely that the lack of a clear strategic focus for this business has played a part in its relative lack of success.

Figure 9.1 shows graphically how the make-up of Takeda's overall business has changed over the mid and late 1980s. Since 1983 pharmaceutical sales have increased from 59 per cent to 65 per cent of the total, and this rate of change is increasing. In contrast, the other divisions

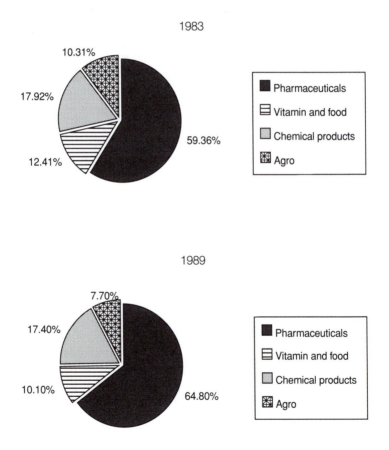

Figure 9.1 Takeda: segment analysis, 1983 and 1989 (per cent) *Source*: Takeda annual reports

have all lost relative size: vitamins and food from 12 per cent to 10 per cent of total sales, chemical products marginally from 18 per cent to 17 per cent, and agro from 10 per cent to 8 per cent. Much of Takeda's overseas sales are accounted for by the pharmaceutical division, especially through TAP Pharmaceuticals – the name given to Takeda's US partnership with Abbott Laboratories. TAP's main success has been in marketing the Lupron group of products in the critically important US market. However, the firm has also had some success in France and Italy, working through local subsidiaries.

However, with the exception of agro products, Takeda's other businesses also have a gradually increasing international element. The firm is the world's second largest producer of bulk vitamins (after Roche of Switzerland). It is developing the US market from a base in Wilmington, North Carolina, where it manufactures vitamins B and C. In food products, too, it is entering the US brewing supplies market with an additive that reduces the quality deterioration of beers. The American market is also the focus for the international activity of the chemical products division. The US subsidiary has set up a technical service in Columbus, Ohio, to meet the needs of Japanese automobile companies manufacturing in North America; this operation provides technical back-up for unsaturated polyester resins for sheet-moulding compounds and polyurethane resin systems.

Financial performance

Takeda's key financial statistics for the seven-year period 1983–89 are shown in Table 9.4. As noted earlier, sales have grown at a compound 4.8 per cent per annum over this period, but operating profit (7.1 per cent per annum) and net income (6.8 per cent per annum) have both grown significantly faster. For both profit parameters, particularly large increases have occurred in the three years since 1986 and, again, it is difficult to avoid the linkage with the increasing internationalisation of Takeda's activities. Another factor has been the firm's success in controlling increases in cost of sales (see Figure 9.2) and this excellent control has allowed R & D expenditures to be increased at a compound 8 per cent per annum without adversely affecting profitability.

It is worth noting that, despite the increases in profitability, the return on shareholders' assets has not grown at all during the 1983–89 period, nor is the absolute figure (8.7 per cent in 1989) very attractive in European or US terms. Japanese shareholders (particularly the large financial institutions) are known to have a different perspective on the risk/return paradigm, and Takeda is a good example of this.

Table 9.4 Takeda financial performance (¥ billion)

Measure	1983	1984	1985	1986	1987	1988	1989
Net sales	519.5	530.9	543.8	551.8	571.5	632.9	686.7
Cost of sales	330.8	340.5	349.5	344.8	350.1	379.7	417.9
Selling, administration,							
etc., expenses	103.7	106.7	111.6	116.6	121.2	131.4	138.2
R & D expenses	28.5	29.8	31.6	33.0	36.3	39.4	45.3
Operating income	56.4	53.9	51.2	57.5	63.8	82.4	85.3
Net income	26.2	24.5	22.2	23.2	28.4	38.0	38.9
Current assets	397.6	429.7	473.9	479.2	544.7	592.0	621.4
Current liabilities	201.9	196.6	228.8	217.4	239.0	264.9	277.7
Working capital	195.7	233.1	245.1	261.8	305.7	327.1	343.7
Fixed assets	86.1	86.5	89.1	89.4	97.6	113.3	123.3
Investments	106.2	109.4	114.5	119.1	121.8	133.3	141.8
Total assets	388.0	429.0	448.7	470.3	525.1	573.7	608.8
Long-term debt	7.3	26.1	24.6	24.6	49.7	54.7	51.0
Shareholders' equity	293.8	312.8	330.1	347.6	347.9	414.2	449.1
Number of							
employees	13,250	13,344	13,378	13,311	13,287	13,547	13,675
As % of sales							
Cost of sales	63.7	64.1	64.3	62.5	61.3	60.0	60.9
Selling, administration,							
etc., expenses	20.0	20.1	20.5	21.1	21.2	20.8	20.1
R & D expenses	5.5	5.6	5.8	6.0	6.4	6.2	6.6
Operating income	10.9	10.2	9.4	10.4	11.2	13.0	12.4
Net income	5.0	4.6	4.1	4.2	5.0	6.0	5.7
Per employee							
(¥ million)							
Sales	39.2	39.8	40.6	41.5	43.0	46.7	50.2
Operating income	4.3	4.0	3.8	4.3	4.8	6.1	6.2
Total assets	29.3	32.1	33.5	35.3	39.5	42.3	44.5
Other ratios							
Asset turnover							
(times)	0.75	0.81	0.83	0.85	0.92	0.91	0.89
Gearing (%)	2.5	8.3	7.5	7.1	13.3	13.2	11.4
Return on							
shareholders' assets							
(%)	8.9	7.8	6.7	6.7	7.6	9.2	8.7

Source: Takeda annual reports

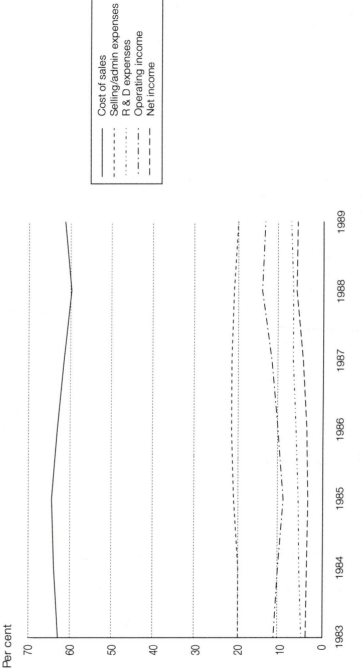

Per cent

Cost of sales
Selling/admin expenses
R & D expenses
Operating income
Net income

1983   1984   1985   1986   1987   1988   1989

Figure 9.2 Takeda: financial performance (as a percentage of sales), 1983–89 *Source:* Takeda annual reports

Because the number of employees has increased only insignificantly between 1983 and 1989, Takeda's employee productivity ratios have performed well; sales per employee have increased from ¥39.2 million in 1983 to ¥50.2 million in 1989 (averaging 4.2 per cent increase per year), operating income per employee from ¥4.3 million to ¥6.2 million (6.6 per cent per annum), and total assets per employee from ¥29.3 million to ¥44.5 million (7.2 per cent per annum).

Activities

Takeda's product portfolio is a wide one, but its most important areas of activity are in cardiovasculars, antibiotics, cancer therapeutics and immunotherapeutics, gastro-intestinals, anti-allergic agents, and metabolic agents. In the last twenty years a large number of useful drugs have emerged from the firm's laboratories, and the tempo of development has noticeably increased in recent times. The following listing is not complete, but gives an indication of the extent and depth of the product portfolio that has been put together by Takeda's own R & D efforts.

1 Morial (molsidomine), a coronary vasodilator, developed in 1972.
2 Lilacillin (sulbenicillin), a penicillin antibiotic, developed in 1972.
3 Eurodin (estazolam), a benzodiazepine hypnotic, developed in 1975.
4 Takesulin (cefsulodin), a cephalosporin antibiotic, developed in 1980.
5 Pansporin (cefistam), a cephalosporin antibiotic, developed in 1980.
6 Prostetin (oxendolone), an agent for benign prostatic hypertrophy, developed in 1981.
7 Hirtonin, an agent for consciousness disturbances, developed in 1981.
8 Bestcall (cefmenoxime), a cephalosporin antibiotic, developed in 1982.
9 Constan (alprazolam), a minor tranquilliser, developed in 1982.
10 Calan (vinpocetine), a cerebral vasodilator, developed in 1983.
11 Lupron (leuprolide acetate), a prostatic anticancer agent, developed in 1985.
12 Avan (idebenone), an agent for improving cerebral metabolism, developed in 1986.
13 Solfa (amlexanox), an anti-allergic, developed in 1987.
14 Maon (spizofurone), an anti-ulcer agent, developed in 1987.
15 Canferon A (recombinant interferon-μ), an agent for multiple myeloma, renal cancer and hepatitis B, developed in 1987.

16 Amasulin (carumonam), a monocyclic B-lactam antibiotic, developed in 1987.

17 Osten (ipriflavone), an anti-osteoporotic agent, developed in 1988.

18 Adecut (angiotensin I-converting enzyme inhibitor), an antihypertensive agent, developed in 1989.

This extensive product development list has led, naturally, to a substantial number of new product launches, especially in the period since 1987. Drug sales have advanced rapidly in Japan and in selected foreign markets. The strategic emphasis now seems to be on expanding overseas markets, especially in developed countries, through all kinds of partnerships, joint ventures and strategic alliances. The successful venture with Abbott Laboratories (TAP Pharmaceuticals) has already been referred to; this dates back to 1977, and was restructured in 1989 to be a more aggressive marketing agent for the Lupron group of products in North America. In 1986 Takeda concluded a contract with Glaxo to collaborate in developing, manufacturing and marketing pharmaceuticals in the UK and the Republic of Ireland.

The over-the-counter market in Japan is also a focus of attention, increasingly so since the government increased its efforts to curtail public expenditure on health care. Takeda's over-the-counter activities have been a separate operating division since April 1989, and the business has been restructured to strengthen over-the-counter marketing and product development.

Takeda has invested in the very latest technology for its main production facilities at Osaka, including automatic formulation and packaging of pharmaceuticals. There are also production facilities in the US and Europe, with the attendant distribution capabilities being developed in each case. The firm has gained experience of overseas production through its vitamins plant in the US; in the case of pharmaceuticals, it seems to have taken care to establish its initial overseas distribution arrangements with major pharmaceutical manufacturers. This kind of arrangement makes it easier to move into overseas production at an appropriate juncture, and this is what has occurred in recent years.

Research and development

Takeda's total expenditure on R & D for 1989 amounted to ¥45.3 billion, a ratio of 6.6 per cent. On the (generous) assumption that all group R & D related to pharmaceuticals, then the ratio was 10.2 per cent of sales. This overestimate is only marginally ahead of the 9.2 per cent average[6] among the top fifteen Japanese pharmaceutical firms, achieved in 1986; it falls well short of the industry norm of 13.5 per cent of sales for large pharmaceutical multinationals. Ethical drugs are the main focus of R & D programmes. The firm has 1,600 staff working on R & D, approximately one in eight of the total workforce. The Central Research Division is the core of Takeda's R & D effort; up to 1987, it comprised eight laboratories and six staff departments, most of which are located at Osaka. Three of the staff departments merit some comment,[7] as their existence and nature throw considerable light on Takeda's approach to, and philosophy of, R & D:

1 A principal role of the Tokyo office is to gather scientific information and to perform liaison activities in the Tokyo area through scientific association with universities, institutes, and government. The Tokyo office aims to contribute to the research planning of Central Research Division by analysing the vast amounts of life science information in the metropolitan area, and by helping researchers gain access to those areas that are of particular interest.

2 The Research Planning and Coordination department is responsible for the overall planning and coordination of the research programmes of the Central Research Division. This department acts as a liaison between CRD and Takeda's operating divisions. It also coordinates the search, selection, scrutiny, and manufacturing process development of drug candidates. RPC also plans and coordinates cooperative research with outside research institutes or pharmaceutical companies in Japan and overseas.

3 The Scientific and Technical Information department gathers scientific books, periodicals and papers from around the world in support of Takeda's R & D; it also analyses and appraises this information for company researchers. Medical and pharmaceutical databases play a key role in computer-aided referencing.

Allowing for the obvious cultural differences between Japanese and US firms, many similarities can be seen comparing this control and coordination system with that of Merck, outlined in Chapter 6.

In March 1987 the R & D partnership between Takeda and Abbott Laboratories was formally reconstituted[8] as the US R & D centre for pharmaceutical products created by Takeda. This unit conducts clinical research in the US, and is responsible for application to the FDA for new drug approvals. In 1988 the firm established the European Research and Development Centre at Frankfurt in West Germany. This facility will carry out development work on new drugs for the European market, and will also coordinate and assist in the R & D activity of Takeda's three joint ventures – in Germany, France, and Italy. This centre is seen as a potential major competitive advantage after the establishment of the single European market[9] (see Chapter 4).

Also in 1988, the Tsukuba Research Laboratories were established in Tokyo to pursue long-term basic research. The initial focus[10] will be the application of genetic and protein engineering to the discovery of bio-active peptides and proteins that relate to and control cell differentiation, growth and ageing. This focus is very much in line with the environmental pressure of a rapidly ageing population that is being forced on the Japanese pharmaceutical industry.

Strengths and weaknesses

Takeda has some very specific strengths, as follows:

1 Financially strong.
2 Market leader in the growing domestic market.
3 Structural foundations in place in Europe and the US.
4 Substantial non-pharmaceutical businesses within the parent group.
5 Strategically alert and competent senior management. Since 1986 the strategic planning function has been strengthened and upgraded.
6 Substantial R & D competence, with a good portfolio of new products.
7 Substantial emphasis from the top on development of information systems using the best technology. This is of value in relation to the managerial coordination task, and also to R & D efforts.

The firm's weaknesses are, perhaps, less obvious and largely related to 'soft' aspects of strategy. However, each of the factors set out below needs to receive particular attention if Takeda wishes to compete in the world pharmaceutical industry on approximately equal terms with existing leaders:

1 Sales force size and capability in Europe and America.
2 While the R & D spend is high in absolute terms, it is well below the benchmark accepted by the firms it is trying to emulate.
3 No lobbying/political influence capability established yet in the US or Europe.
4 The firm is relatively inexperienced in coordinating overseas activities within a global industry.

Strategy options and choice

The international alternative

Takeda has a very clear-cut competitive posture, built primarily upon its financial strength, though its product portfolio has been greatly strengthened in recent years. The main choice is whether to develop this posture aggressively in international markets or conservatively at home, with attendant diversification. The view taken here is that the former approach is the better option. The foregoing analysis, together with the statements Takeda makes in its annual reports, suggests strongly that the firm clearly recognises the key success factors for the pharmaceutical industry, in particular:

1 It is attempting to enhance its R & D capability year by year.
2 It is attempting to build its overseas sales force.
3 It is concerned to protect and enhance its market position in Japan.
4 It recognises the criticality of the speed with which products are processed through the stages between laboratory discovery and reaching the market place, and is investing in developing its effectiveness in this key area, with particular emphasis on international markets.
5 It is seeking to achieve a position where new products can be launched worldwide simultaneously.

To achieve these things, Takeda is prepared to invest heavily, as witnessed by the opening of its European Research Centre, the new research facility at the Tsukuba Science Park, the re-equipping and modernisation of its major production facility at Osaka, and the steady expansion of other production and research facilities in Japan.

Its steps on the road to the development of substantial capabilities in the US and Europe demonstrate a methodical and determined approach to strategic implementation. The approach has been to gain experience of and access to major markets through joint ventures positioned in those markets, ultimately expanding them to encompass development and production in relation to new drugs. It has then established wholly owned regional headquarters to coordinate and control these separate joint ventures. This step-by-step approach, with careful sequencing of activities and avoidance of trying to develop capabilities in big jumps on all fronts simultaneously, is fairly typical of Japanese corporations; it is a phenomenon stemming from deep within the national psyche.

It seems reasonable to expect this approach to continue into the future, with dramatic attempts at acquisition of major players unlikely.

Takeda sees itself in Europe and the US for the long term, and will prefer to develop its sales networks via organic expansion of existing joint ventures. As an indicator of this, in the recent newsletter to employees, the French joint venture reports[11] on its plans for expansion of the sales force by recruitment, and on its plans for increased sales training, and to improve its sales incentive schemes.

Action now required

Takeda has positioned itself well so far in relation to its aims for its overseas activities. It has legal entities established, and has been gaining knowledge and experience of European and US regulatory requirements. It has major R & D centres in both Europe and Japan.

1 It now needs to make moves to expand its European sales force. 'Growing your own" takes time, but the Japanese are likely to see themselves as having time – certainly time enough to expand the sales strengths of these established joint ventures in France, Germany and Italy. The establishment of the European regional head office will bring added push to this process; coordination of international activities must not be allowed to develop on a slow or casual basis.

2 It now needs to build further its capabilities in relation to the regulatory authorities and requirements in Europe.

3 It should perform aggressively in the Japanese market, and take the game to the foreign intruders. It has major competitive advantages in this market over foreign firms, and these should be exploited vigorously – specifically, its strength in distribution, with control of its own pharmaceutical wholesaler, and a large existing sales force. In addition, of course, there are its intimate understanding of Japanese culture, and the way things are done there. Every means of exploiting governmental and regulatory authority relationships should be used to the full.

4 Takeda needs to study closely what competitors are doing in research, because its own spending is below the industry average as a percentage of sales. It may be that it is managing its spending better than more wasteful competitors, but this is something that must be positively ascertained. It may well be that its own R & D investment needs to be expanded even further; the other players are raising the ante. Takeda is strong enough to stay in this game of ever increasing R & D spend if it has to. It is crucial, though, that it now ascertains how strong its R & D is in relation to competitors rather than becoming satisfied by what is already a huge annual investment.

Conclusion

The case of Takeda is fascinating; if it can manage to establish itself as a major player in the world pharmaceutical industry, other Japanese firms will undoubtedly follow. The internationalisation strategy has been set out by the company management and it is being implemented, effectively as far as can be seen. Whether it will be ultimately successful is not, in the final analysis, a matter of strategy but a question of collective management willpower and staying ability.

FUJISAWA PHARMACEUTICAL CO. LTD

Company history and development

Fujisawa originated in 1894 as a private dealership in medicinal herbs. It expanded quickly in the early part of this century, producing basic remedies such as camphor. After the Second World War, Fujisawa continued its fast growth, and specialised in the production of antibiotics, principally using imported technology and pirated formulae, the latter being facilitated by the absence of effective patent law in Japan. Fujisawa was one of the first Japanese pharmaceutical companies to develop cooperative agreements with foreign companies. Amongst such agreements were those to manufacture Irgapyrin, an anti-arthritic drug from Ciba-Geigy, and Xylocaine, licensed from Astra, which it still sells today. One of Fujisawa's earliest self-developed drugs was Trichomycin, an antibiotic used to treat candidiasis and trichomoniasis. Fujisawa's other strength at this time was in vitamin preparations, a major component of the Japanese market. The company continued to grow in the 1950s and 1960s, aided by the introduction of National Health Insurance (NHI) by the government. It further developed its international associations through linkages with Delagrange and Fisons, and attempted to increase exports, which had previously been at a low level. In 1971, the introduction of its version of an injectable cephalosporin, Cefalozin, a third–generation antibiotic, gave it a drug that was highly desirable in the US market, and led to a joint venture in that country with SmithKline Beckman (SKB) in 1977. There was also a reciprocal agreement with SKB to sell drugs such as Tagamet in Japan. More recently, Fujisawa has attempted to directly market its drugs in Europe and the US, in an attempt to combat difficult trading conditions in Japan.

Mission statement

The following statement is derived principally from successive annual reports of the company. In contrast to many Japanese firms, there is little florid language in these reports, and almost no reference to the welfare of its staff, hence the absence of any mention of this below.

Fujisawa has responded, and will continue to respond, to the concern for health care by providing quality products, which it considers its social responsibility.

Fujisawa's emphasis is on R & D, in which it sees itself as a leading company. To this end, ethical drugs are the main focus of the company's strategy, and future growth in sales and profits will depend on the investment made in this area.

It is Fujisawa's resolve to grow into an international organisation, and to this end it vigorously promotes many international activities, including joint ventures, equity participations, and licensing arrangements.

Objectives

Fujisawa is very open about the objectives it needs to achieve in its all-out drive for globalisation by the end of the century. The programme is called 'Frontier 21", and calls for:[12]

1 The establishment of full-fledged, independent operations in four strategic regions: Japan, the US, Europe, Asia.
2 Annual sales of ¥700 billion by 2001, making Fujisawa one of the world's top twenty drug firms.
3 Half of all sales to be made outside Japan by 2001.
4 Twenty per cent of corporate sales in non-ethical drugs 2001.
5 As an interim stage, domestic sales of ¥300 billion and foreign sales of ¥100 billion by 1995.

Business segments

Fujisawa's current strategy has been broadly in line with the sentiments expressed in the mission statement. There have been significant developments in its international expansion programme recently. In 1987 Fujisawa SmithKline in the US became a wholly owned subsidiary, and during last year Lyphomed, a manufacturer of generic drugs in which Fujisawa had been gradually increasing its equity stake throughout the 1980s, was taken over. Since the end of financial year 1989 there has been a major reorganisation of activity in the US, and a holding company has been set up with three divisions. The major operating division consists of Fujisawa Pharmaceutical Company, (Fujisawa SmithKline renamed) Lyphomed, and a clinical research centre based at Bethesda, conveniently located in the same town as the FDA. In Europe, equity participation in Klinge Pharma GmbH has been gradually increased to 74 per cent, and Klinge's activities have been consolidated into the accounts. Klinge has a manufacturing facility in Ireland. Fujisawa also has a clinical research centre based in London, and smaller affiliates in Italy and Holland. An International Development Group has been established in Japan to coordinate overseas product development.

Owing to adverse market conditions in Japan, Fujisawa has increased sales promotion, and attempted to decrease the costs of production. It would, however, be fair to say that these are not the critical areas of its current strategy.

Finally a brief mention ought to be made of Fujisawa's other operating divisions away from ethical drugs. The company is involved in medical equipment and supplies, consumer products (including some over-the-counter drugs) and chemical and animal health products. These each have some synergy with the main focus of Fujisawa's activity, and whilst all are targeted for growth, they do not appear to be diverting substantial funds away from ethical drug development.

The principal assumptions on which the above strategy is based are sound, i.e. that in order to boost profits in the long term the company needs to invest heavily in R & D, capitalising on its current strengths and considering high-growth product areas, and that it needs to make money away from Japan.

Financial analysis

Results by segment of activity

For the purposes of this analysis, Fujisawa's sales have been classified into four segments, as shown in Table 9.5. Over the ten year period 1981–90, overall sales have grown at the compound rate of 4.1 per cent per annum. The figure for the ethical drugs segment is 4.9 per cent per annum and would have been significantly higher had it not been for the poor years 1985 and 1986 when government price cuts and other restrictions had maximum impact on the firm's domestic sales. Since the crisis year of 1986, ethical sales have grown at an average 7.8 per cent per annum. Both the over-the-counter sector and the chemicals and animal health products have remained fairly stable in size throughout the 1980 though when inflation is taken into account it is likely that there have been significant volume losses here. The medical equipment and supplies sector has lost sales at the average rate of 2.3 per cent per annum throughout the decade; so, including the inflation factor, there have been large volume losses in this sector, probably between 30 per cent and 40 per cent. The sum total of all these fluctuations has been that the segment proportion of sales has changed a great deal since 1981. Ethical drugs

Table 9.5 Fujisawa results by segment of activity

Measure	1981	1986	1987	1988	1989	1990
Sales (¥ billion)						
Ethical drugs	131.8	149.7	153.1	170.2	198.4	202.2
Medical equipment and supplies	4.0	3.3	3.4	3.8	3.0	3.2
Consumer products (OTC)	12.1	8.6	9.2	10.2	11.3	11.6
Chemicals and animal health	12.7	11.9	11.2	11.0	12.2	13.2
Total exports	5.9	11.6	10.7	11.8	10.6	15.5
Increase on previous year (%)						
Ethical drugs		−13.9	2.3	11.2	16.6	1.9
Medical equipment and supplies		−13.2	3.0	11.8	−21.1	6.7
Consumer products (OTC)		−25.2	7.0	10.9	10.8	2.7
Chemicals and animal health		−24.2	−5.9	−1.8	10.9	8.2
Total exports						
Proportion of total sales (%)						
Ethical drugs	82.1	86.3	86.5	87.2	88.2	87.8
Medical equipment and supplies	2.5	1.9	1.9	1.9	1.3	1.4
Consumer products (OTC)	7.5	5.0	5.2	5.2	5.0	5.0
Chemicals and animal health	7.9	6.9	6.3	5.6	5.4	5.7
Total exports	4	7	6	6	5	7
Indexed sales						
Ethical drugs	100	114	116	129	151	153
Medical equipment and supplies	100	83	86	96	76	81
Consumer products (OTC)	100	71	76	84	93	96
Chemicals and animal health	100	94	88	87	96	104
Total exports	100	195	180	199	178	261

Source: Fujisawa annual reports and author's estimates
Note: OTC, over-the-counter

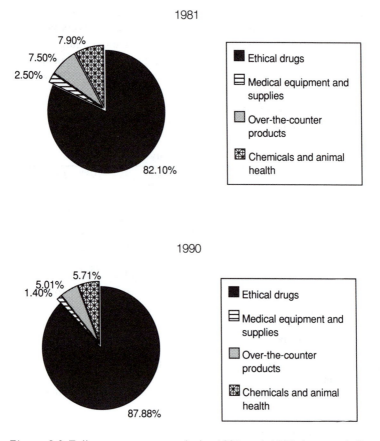

Figure 9.3 Fujisawa: segment analysis, 1981 and 1990 (per cent) *Source*: Fujisawa annual reports

have increased from 82 per cent of total sales to 88 per cent over the decade, while all other sectors have suffered reductions: medical equipment and supplies from 2 per cent to 1 per cent, over-the-counter products from 8 per cent to 5 per cent, chemicals and animal health products from 8 per cent to 6 per cent. This is shown graphically in Figure 9.3.

Note that total exports (all segments) have increased at a compound rate of 11.2 per cent per annum since 1981 (Table 9.5), which is a much higher rate than for any individual segment. Good though this figure is, it understates the process of internationalisation that has been going on within Fujisawa as a growing proportion of foreign sales are now manufactured abroad rather than exported from Japan.

Results by therapeutic category

Fujisawa did not publish a breakdown of ethical sales for the year 1981, so Table 9.6 has 1982 as the base year. At the beginning of the 1980s the antibiotics and biologicals category accounted for over half the firm's ethical revenues, but cash sales fell steeply and consistently till 1987. Since then, some sales gains have been made in this sector mainly owing to the contribution of a new product (Cefspan). The category which includes the nervous system, sensory organs and anti-allergic drugs followed a similar pattern, declining steeply until 1986, then putting on some good growth. Again, this was due to a series of new product launches, including Ridaura (an anti-arthritic agent) in 1987, Gramalil (a drug for the treatment of psychomotor disturbances of the aged) also in 1987, and Alnert (for the treatment of neurological symptoms of cerebrovascular disease) in 1988.

Sales of vitamins and other metabolic drugs increased steadily through 1986, then took a spectacular jump due to a large sales increase

Table 9.6 Fujisawa results by therapeutic category

Measure	1982	1986	1987	1988	1989	1990
Sales (¥ billion)						
Antibiotics and biologicals	76.7	57.2	52.4	58.4	65.8	67.0
Digestive system drugs	21.1	44.8	43.8	44.2	49.0	45.8
Nervous, sensory,						
anti-allergic	32.7	20.2	22.7	32.9	39.5	40.3
CVs and respiratory system	6.2	15.4	18.3	18.9	27.6	29.8
Vitamins, metabolics	7.3	10.6	14.7	14.7	14.5	13.3
Others	5.9	1.5	1.2	1.1	2.1	6.1
Increase on previous year (%)						
Antibiotics and biologicals		−14.9	−8.4	11.5	12.7	1.8
Digestive system drugs		−11.3	−2.2	0.9	10.9	−6.5
Nervous, sensory,						
anti-allergic		−36.3	12.4	44.9	20.1	2.0
CVs and respiratory system		8.5	18.8	3.3	46.0	8.0
Vitamins, metabolics		27.7	38.7	0.0	−1.4	−8.3
Others		−21.1	−20.0	−8.3	90.0	190.5
Proportion of total sales (%)						
Antibiotics and biologicals	51.2	38.2	34.2	34.3	33.1	33.1
Digestive system drugs	14.1	29.9	28.6	26.0	24.7	22.6
Nervous, sensory, anti-allergic	21.8	13.5	14.8	19.3	19.9	19.9
CVs and respiratory system	4.1	10.3	12.0	11.1	13.9	14.7
Vitamins, metabolics	4.9	7.1	9.6	8.6	7.3	6.6
Others	3.9	1.0	0.8	0.6	1.1	3.0

Source: Fujisawa annual reports and author's estimates

for One-alpha (an active vitamin D_3 preparation) and the launch of the new product Urokinase. The therapeutic category which includes digestive system drugs has had a 'scenic railway' profile over the 1980s, starting with a huge sales increase in 1983 (due to the launch of Tagamet, sold under licence from SmithKline), taking a nasty dip in the mid-1980s (due to price controls and the launch of the competitive product Zantac in Japan), followed by an upturn in 1989 (increased sales of Tagamet due to extended indications), and another decline in 1990 (tight competition in the H_2-blocker market leading to reduced sales of Dogmatyl).

It is the cardiovascular and respiratory system category, which has been the star therapeutic category for Fujisawa during the 1980s, registering a spectacular compound growth figure of 19.1 per cent per annum over the period. This was due to good performance by a range of products including Seloken – a B_1-receptor blocker used for the treatment of hypertension, angina pectoris and arrhythmia, Mucosolvan – an expectorant with a unique pharmacological effect, and Nivadil – a new calcium channel blocker launched as an antihypertensive agent in 1989.

Again, the sum total of these changes has led to a radical alteration in the therapeutic category make-up of sales, as shown in Figure 9.4. Instead of being heavily dependent on one therapeutic category, as it was in 1982, Fujisawa now has a much more balanced portfolio, with four major therapeutic sectors and two minor ones. This is a particularly important change of profile for a firm with such ambitiously stated internationalisation objectives.

Financial performance

Fujisawa's financial statistics for the 1980s are shown in Table 9.7. Perhaps the most obvious feature of this analysis is the persistent, year-by-year decline in both operating income and net income. For both parameters 1986 represented the nadir, with a minor recovery in 1988 being followed by further decline in 1989 and 1990. The company has stressed the negative effects of government price cuts and other regulation in the home market, and this has certainly had an effect. Further analysis indicates that other factors may also be at work.

Figure 9.5 illustrates some important parameters as a proportion of sales. There must be concern at the high level of cost of goods sold through the mid-1980s. The company points proudly to the fact that this variable has been reduced in the last three years, but does not stress that almost all the gains made here have been swallowed up by increasing

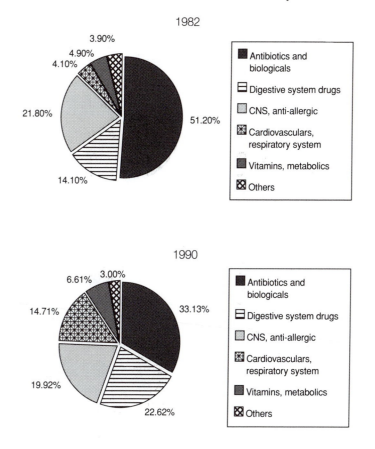

Figure 9.4 Fujisawa: sub-segment analysis, 1982 and 1990 (per cent) *Source*: Fujisawa annual reports

selling, general and administrative expenses. Figure 9.4 also shows that the firm has been making determined efforts to increase R & D expenditure, but these efforts must be severely limited by profitability constraints.

Other parameters in Table 9.7 also gave rise to some concern. Current liabilities took a massive jump of over ¥90 million, largely accounted for by a new issue of commercial paper with interest principally at 7.17 per cent per annum. This short-term loan of ¥60 million is at an interest rate nearly 3 per cent higher than Fujisawa was paying for short term money in 1989. Similarly, the gearing ratio has increased to the very high (for the pharmaceutical industry) rate of

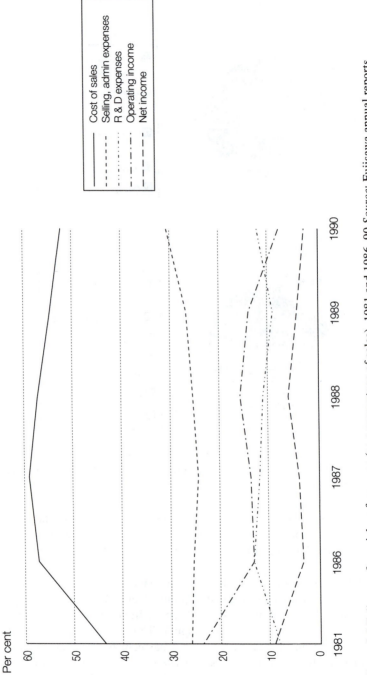

Per cent

Cost of sales
Selling, admin expenses
R & D expenses
Operating income
Net income

1981   1986   1987   1988   1989   1990

Figure 9.5 Fujisawa: financial performance (as a percentage of sales), 1981 and 1986–90 *Source*: Fujisawa annual reports

Table 9.7 Fujisawa financial performance (¥ million)

Measure	1981	1986	1987	1988	1989	1990
Sales	160,551	173,629	176,889	195,158	224,929	230,201
Cost of goods sold	71,202	100,147	105,332	112,792	123,360	120,200
Selling, general, admin.	42,465	42,732	42,096	49,771	61,649	70,846
R & D expenses	13,457	20,089	19,514	20,157	21,789	26,596
Operating income	38,674	20,322	21,483	31,894	31,122	19,692
Net income	15,604	4,510	5,672	11,020	8,741	6,131
Current liabilities	58,647	79,677	86,465	90,979	99,361	191,756
Current assets	113,724	187,721	194,444	230,548	241,724	309,611
Working capital	55,077	108,044	107,979	139,569	142,363	117,855
Fixed assets	30,143	40,988	42,295	44,721	47,325	60,691
Investments	34,239	45,636	70,995	63,941	65,167	38,716
Other assets	6,218	8,816	9,800	7,160	16,336	110,708
Total assets	125,677	203,484	231,069	255,391	271,191	327,970
Long term debt	1,376	22,225	42,153	51,375	49,874	83,301
As % of sales						
Cost of goods sold	44.3	57.7	59.5	57.8	54.8	52.2
Selling, general, admin.	26.4	24.6	23.8	25.5	27.4	30.8
R & D expenses	8.4	11.6	11.0	10.3	9.7	11.6
Operating income	24.1	11.7	12.1	16.3	13.8	8.6
Net income	9.7	2.6	3.2	5.6	3.9	2.7
Other ratios						
Total asset turnover (times)	1.3	0.9	0.8	0.8	0.8	0.7
Return on shareholders' assets (%)	30.8	10.0	9.3	12.5	11.5	6.0
Gearing ratio (%)	1.1	10.9	18.2	20.1	18.4	25.4

Source: Fujisawa annual reports and author's estimates

25.4 per cent. Again the jump in the latest year is largely accounted for by a bank loan due 1997 payable in US dollars at the London Interbank Offering Rate. No doubt Fujisawa would argue that these funds are needed for the international expansion programme, but this factor does increase the pressure for the internationalisation process to pay dividends quickly.

Activities

Antibiotics

Overall, this therapeutic category rivals cardiovascular drugs as the biggest worldwide drug market. Competition is intense at the sub-sectoral level, and Japanese companies are traditionally very strong here. The category accounts for the biggest single slice of Fujisawa's turnover, but is gradually declining in importance. The firm is particularly strong in cephalosporins, a slow-growth drug category used mainly in hospitals for fighting infections. The main products are Cefamezin and Epocelin, which are injectables, and Cefspan, which is an oral cephalosporin. The first two are older products that have been hit by NHI price cuts and are in medium-term decline in Japan. Cefspan was introduced in 1987, and sales continue to grow. All three of these drugs have been successfully exported to the US (Cefspan through a licensing agreement with American Cyanamid), so the NHI cuts have become less critical.

Fujisawa has the third-generation cephalosporin Cefzon already filed as a new drug application, and it should be launched in 1991. The main sub-sectoral competition is from Shionogi (Kefral and Keflex), with Sankyo's Banan also being an important competitor as it has been less affected by recent price cuts.

Digestive system drugs

This is another intensely competitive market worldwide, though it is less fragmented than antibiotics at sub-sectoral level. Drugs in this category are mainly used to treat ulcers. This has been an important sector for Fujisawa throughout the 1980s. The firm has been marketing SmithKline's Tagamet in Japan under licence, and has done so very successfully. However, the merger between SmithKline and Beecham probably means that the new combine is likely to 'go it alone" in Japan, and the agreement may be dissolved. In any case, Tagamet loses its patent protection in Japan in 1992, and this will result in intense generic competition.

However, Fujisawa appears to have a ready replacement for this gap in Omepral (omeprazole, licensed from Astra, who market the drug as Losec). If the Fujisawa sales force can achieve effective switching to Omepral, it will boost sales and profits substantially. It will not be affected by the NHI price cuts as it is a new drug, due to be launched in Japan in late 1990.

Fujisawa has also had some success with its own product Dogmatyl, with the more specialist product, coded FK176, in Phase II development; this product is an anticholinergic agent with antispasmodic properties.

The main competition in this sector is Glaxo's Zantac, marketed in Japan by Sankyo, and Yamanouchi's Gaster.

CNS, sensory organ, and anti-allergic drugs

This is a peculiar grouping of products, specific to Fujisawa, and it has accounted for a steady 20 per cent of ethical sales in the last three years. In CNS, two specialised drugs have recently been introduced: Gramalil, for treating psychomotor disorders, cerebral arteriosclerosis, and dyskinesia; and Alnert, a treatment for neurological symptoms associated with cerebrovascular disease. Nivadil is in Phase III trials for new indications with regard to cerebrovascular complaints. It is difficult to detail competition in this sub-sector as individual drugs have very specific therapeutic effects.

In anti-allergy drugs, Fujisawa has been successful with Intal, licensed from Fisons; new indications and formulations (e.g. aerosol) have prolonged the life cycle of this product. The product coded FK021 is currently in Phase II trials in Japan; it is an orally active anti-allergic agent for treating asthma and other allergic diseases. Competition in this area is intense, with the most active opposition coming from Glaxo's Ventolin and Becotide, and Sandoz's Zaditen.

Cardiovascular and respiratory drugs

The cardiovascular area is a major growth node for Fujisawa, and has become very prominent in the firm's portfolio. The company markets the beta-blocker Seloken jointly with Astra; an improved version of this drug, used for treating hypertension and angina patients, is under development. Nivadil (see above) is a newer calcium antagonist anti-hypertensive drug, and sold well (over ¥5 million) in the first year after launch. However, the market is saturated with competitive products (Yamanouchi's Perdipine, Takeda/Bayer's Adalat), and further R & D advances will be needed if Fujisawa is to maintain or improve its position in this field. The firm is clearly aware of this, as it has Cibenol (an anti-arrhythmic agent), FK409 (an anti-angina product), and FK664 (a cardiotonic) at various stages of development.

Mucosolvan is the only prominent drug Fujisawa has in the respiratory category. It is an expectorant which sold well for a few years, but is now in a static position. It appears that research in this area has been wound down.

Immunological drugs

Fujisawa has some potential blockbusters in this category. FK506 is an immunosuppressant that has shown signs of being much more effective than cyclosporin in organ transplants and as a therapy for auto-immune diseases. Unlike the former, the market for auto-immune diseases is potentially huge, and the only significant competitor at the moment is Sandoz's Sandimmun.

FK565 is an immunostimulant with significant potential as a treatment for AIDS and possibly also as an anticancer. Again, the potential markets for this product are clearly huge.

Cancer therapies

In addition to FK565, Fujisawa is researching several other potentially significant anticancer drugs. Rubratin is coming to the market as an anti-tumour agent, and its most significant competitor will be Sankyo's ageing blockbuster Krestin, which has worldwide sales of ¥50 billion. FK435, developed originally by Fujisawa's German subsidiary Klinge, is in Phase II trials as a potential treatment for breast cancer. FK973 is a product in the early stages of development as a possible remedy for solid tumours and leukaemia.

Research and development

As was seen in Table 9.7, Fujisawa has increased its R & D investments from 8.4 per cent of sales in 1981 to 11.6 per cent in 1990. Assuming that all this expenditure is on ethical drugs, the proportion rises to 13.2 per cent which is very close to the industry norm of 13.5 per cent. The major research facilities are at Osaka and Tsukuba (Tokyo), and employ around 1,400 staff. As indicated above, the priority areas of research are infectious disease, cardiovascular disorders, allergy and inflammation, cancer, and gastro-intestinal disorders. In addition, innovative R & D approaches are also being used in the fields of biotechnology, neuroscience and immunology.

Clinical research centres have been established in the UK (1985) and in the US (1990). Also in Europe, the West German subsidiary Klinge has its own free-standing R & D facility. In order to coordinate the work at these centres, Fujisawa has established the International Development Group within its R & D organisation. The IDG assumes the role of planning development programmes outside Japan for products with real potential, and also of fulfilling various requirements for the development, registration, and production of drugs.[13] In addition, a twice-yearly international development conference is held in Japan to encourage active information exchanges. These are all brave efforts at coordinating dispersed R & D activity, particularly for a newly internationalising pharmaceutical firm, but they do not yet compare well with the measures taken by the industry leaders (cf. Merck, Chapter 6).

Strengths and weaknesses

Strengths

1 Fujisawa has a demonstrable commitment to establishing an international presence. Marketing, R & D and manufacturing are all now set up in each major market, plus facilities in Korea and Taiwan.
2 The current product portfolio is strong, and R & D programmes seem to be highly effective. There is a steady stream of new products in attractive competitive areas, plus the promise of innovation in unexploited therapies with substantial potential.
3 There is a proven ability to pick winners in products licensed for the Japanese market. The good links which have been built up with major overseas companies will facilitate the achievement of foreign growth targets.

Weaknesses

1 There is some doubt about the stringency of the firm's financial controls and the nature of financial management.
2 There is little or no marketing experience in two new product areas currently under promising development – immunology and cancer.
3 There remains a fairly heavy reliance on the slow-growth antibiotics market in Japan.
4 There must be a general concern regarding future Japanese licensing arrangements, as major European and American firms reassess their positions and operational strategies for the Japanese market.
5 Some doubt must exist regarding Fujisawa's ability to coordinate dispersed facilities and activities as the process of internationalisation proceeds.

Strategy options and choice

Conceptually, at least, a number of alternatives are open to Fujisawa:

1 Retrenchment and concentration on the Japanese home market.
2 Diversification at home into the over-the-counter market or household goods.

3 Continuing the current strategy of development at home and abroad by organic growth coupled with small acquisitions.

4 Attempting to take over a large company in one of the major overseas markets to gain instant market share.

5 Consider a friendly merger or formal strategic alliance over and above current licensing agreements, e.g. pooling R & D knowledge.

The majority of the above strategic options are available to Fujisawa. Several can be discounted because they represent the opposite of current strategy, which, as discussed earlier, is fundamentally sound, given the exigencies of the Japanese pharmaceutical industry. Fujisawa certainly has sufficient credibility to finance a bid for at least a medium-sized player in the US or Europe. That it has not done so is probably due to the style of management in the company. Whilst it is heavily committed to the need for excellence in R & D, fundamentally Fujisawa is relatively conservative and does not take exceptional risks. The pharmaceutical industry has enough general risk for most companies not to seek to add to it; this is one of the reasons the industry remains fragmented, and why few major mergers have taken place. The current Fujisawa strategy must be adjudged fundamentally sound. Once the decision had been made to internationalise in order to enhance profitability, few other routes could have been followed.

The company should certainly consider any acquisitions that present themselves in the industry. However, it is not in trouble commercially or in terms of an absence of new products coming on stream, so it does not need to merge. Perhaps the firm should be looking to reduce its exposure to the possibility of Astra or its other partners in Japan setting up their own sales forces; Fujisawa could consider buying equity in such companies, possibly on a reciprocal basis. The company is not shy of raising finance through equity, and the Japanese system encourages cross-holdings domestically, so this might prove a way of maintaining such 'supplier" links on an international basis.

As a broad objective in the long term, Fujisawa should aim to increase substantially the profits generated from abroad as a percentage of total profit. As much as 25 per cent of total profits should be achievable within the next five years, provided at least one of Fujisawa's new drugs proves successful in foreign markets.

Financial strategy

Apart from the few warning signals sounded above, there is little room for major criticism of Fujisawa's financial strategy unless extravagant growth rates are required; this latter, of course, is simply not in the company's nature. Improvements in Fujisawa's financial position will come principally from successful products, and no amount of financial manipulation will alter that.

There is some scope to improve gross profit by manufacturing certain products away from Japan, in lower-cost environments, and re-importing them. Without details this is unquantifiable, and it may not generate sufficient income to justify itself, but the plants in Taiwan and Korea could be used, particularly if certain drugs were under serious threat from generics.

Marketing strategy

Following evaluation of the product portfolio and its foreign sales potential, steps should be taken to ensure there are sufficient staff to ensure effective launches in the US and Europe. A drug launch is critical to the eventual success of the product, and although marketing needs are specific to individual countries, Japanese-style productivity could be highly desirable.

Consideration should be given in the longer term to increasing sales of over-the-counter products in Japan, and ultimately in other markets, in order to maximise profit on out-of-patent drugs.

On-going market research is essential in order that R & D is led by the customer's requirements, and not pushed by pure research abilities and interests.

R & D strategy

Fujisawa must continue to direct research at growing therapeutic markets, and R & D expenditure must be increased as a percentage of sales when justified by increasing profitability in order to maintain the flow of new ideas. Further efforts should be made (cf. Takeda) to build strong links with outside basic research establishments. Finally, further detailed consideration must be given to the potential of biotechnology, given the company's expertise in fermentation techniques.

Conclusion

Fujisawa has passed the point of no return in its internationalisation strategy, and must now push this approach to (and beyond?) the limits of its own corporate culture. In the end, success or failure will rest on how quickly the firm can develop the necessary expertise in coordinating dispersed international facilities.

YAMANOUCHI PHARMACEUTICAL CO. LTD

Company history and development

Yamanouchi is about one-third the size of Takeda in terms of sales, and about one-half in asset values; it is ranked seventh within the Japanese pharmaceutical industry. It was founded in 1923 under the name of Yamanouchi Yakuhin Shokai Ltd, but changed its name to the present one in 1940. It was not until 1968 that it completed its first manufacturing plant in Tokyo, diversifying from the wholesale business. The firm's primary activities include research, manufacturing and marketing ethical and over-the-counter drugs and, to a much smaller extent, the manufacture of veterinary medicines, medical instruments and foodstuffs. The over-the-counter drug division was only established in 1984, and is still very small.

Like Takeda, Yamanouchi has built its overseas presence through joint ventures and partnership with European and US firms. In 1983 a long-term technical agreement with Eli Lilly was concluded; in the same year a joint venture with the Sterling drug company was established. In 1986 wholly owned subsidiaries were set up in the Netherlands and Ireland. The Tokyo-based export department is augmented by offices opened in London, Frankfurt and New York. In Japan the firm has four large plants, a research laboratory, and a distribution centre.

Early in 1988 Yamanouchi bought a 77 per cent shareholding in Shaklee Japan KK as a diversification into direct marketing of nutritional, household and personal care products. About a month later, the firm acquired a controlling interest in the parent Shaklee Corporation, a US firm involved in nutritional supplements, food products and roses. This represents a considerable diversification for Yamanouchi, both in terms of product line and geographical markets served. Shaklee was founded in 1946 by Dr Forrest C. Shaklee and quickly developed into an international provider of nutritional, household, and personal care products; additionally, it sells water purification systems through independent sales representatives. The firm is based in San Francisco and sells its products in the US, Canada, Japan, Taiwan, Malaysia and Singapore. It has a subsidiary, the Bear Creek Corporation, which is the largest US direct mail marketer of gift fruits, rose plants and other gardening products. The acquisition was a friendly one, and the Shaklee management have joined their company within Yamanouchi.

Mission statement

Having just made a major diversifying acquisition, the Yamanouchi management are probably now engaged in hammering out a new mission statement, but the 'profile' published in 1990[14] throws some light on current thinking:

Yamanouchi Pharmaceutical Co. Ltd is one of Japan's leading pharmaceutical companies. The Company researches, manufactures and markets a wide array of ethical and over-the-counter drugs renowned for their safety and efficacy.

Yamanouchi's expanding research network covers Japan, Europe, and the United States and local production and clinical development gives it a strong presence overseas.

The new members of the Yamanouchi Group, Shaklee Corporation – including Shaklee US, Shaklee Canada, and Bear Creek Corporation – and Shaklee Japan, major providers of nutritional supplements and other products, help make Yamanouchi a multinational enterprise with comprehensive health care capabilities.

Objectives

Perhaps more than any other pharmaceutical firm surveyed in this book, Yamanouchi is firmly focused on one overarching objective, first clearly enunciated by company president Shigeo Morioka,[15] and repeated frequently since:

The ultimate goal of our global strategy is to have profitable independent operations abroad that contribute to the steady growth of the Company and to the health and well-being of humankind.

Business segments

Until the acquisition of Shaklee, Yamanouchi was very firmly based in the ethical pharmaceutical industry, with around 95 per cent of its sales in that category throughout the 1980s. In 1984, probably as a response to the Japanese government's increasing pressure on drug prices, Yamanouchi made some definite moves to formalise its diversification plans. The over-the-counter range was augmented and the Proprietary, Cosmetic and Veterinary Products Department was set up. Further support came in 1985 with the establishment of the Consumer Products Research Laboratories, designed to assist the expansion of the over-the-counter business. An impressive list of product launches followed these organisational and investment moves:

1984 Launch of Spirulina-μ a diet supplement balanced with protein and B-group vitamins.

1985 Introduction of Gines, a natural vitamin E preparation.
Transfer of the ethical product Codecillin Cough Syrup to over-the-counter.

1986 Launch of Cakonal, a liquid cold remedy that does not encourage sleepiness.

1987 Launch of Guinness Gold, a health drink that counteracts fatigue by restoring essential nutrients to the body.
Introduction of Kyupap, a salve-coated antiphlogistic patch for the treatment of contusions, sprains and stiff shoulders.

1988 Introduction of Cleanmate Suppository, a new haemorrhoid preparation.
Introduction of Chuoko Pap, an anti-inflammatory poultice.
Introduction of Halt Kaze Pap, a poultice applied to the chest or neck for treating cold symptoms.

1989 Launch of Makiron Repellent Spray, an insect repellent.
Launch of Nemutol, a product designed to counter drowsiness.

1990 Introduction of Bionathul, a medicated cosmetic cream to protect the skin against ultraviolet light.

Such a list of new product launches, including a significant number of new market sectors, suggests strongly that Yamanouchi sees the over-the-counter market as an important source of future profits, and also that it has the requisite R & D skills to match and support its market ambitions.

Also starting in 1984, the firm made a determined effort to develop a range of diagnostic reagents and equipment. For a few years thereafter there was quite an active programme of product launches, but it would seem that this sector has not lived up to early expectations, as very little has been heard of it since 1987. Perhaps Shaklee's experience in this area will help Yamanouchi rediscover its attraction to the sector.

Financial analysis

Geographical spread

Yamanouchi does not release details of sales made in particular countries, but a glance at Table 9.8 will confirm that exports have grown very rapidly indeed over the 1980s; in fact, the annual compound growth figure was 26.8 per cent, very impressive by any standard. Note that the export figure includes exports from the Irish factory as well as from Japan.

Table 9.8 Yamanouchi results by segment of activity

Measure	1980	1985	1986	1987	1988	1990
Sales (¥ billion)						
Ethical drugs	76.6	117.9	140.6	164.1	185.1	200.4
Nutritional products						44.1
Food, etc.						19.1
Total exports	2.4	8.2	11.1	15.6	17.4	20.4
Increase on previous year (%)						
Ethical drugs	11.7	9.7	19.3	16.7	12.8	8.3
Nutritional products						
Food, etc.						
Total exports		46.4	35.4	40.5	11.5	17.2
Proportion of total sales (%)						
Ethical drugs	100.0	100.0	100.0	100.0	100.0	76.0
Nutritional products						16.7
Food, etc.						7.2
Total exports	3.1	7.0	7.9	9.5	9.4	7.7

Source: Yamanouchi annual reports and author's estimates
Note: Yamanouchi's 1989 fiscal year consisted of only three months in order to facilitate a change of year-ending to 31 March. 1990 was a twelve-month fiscal year. 1989 has also been omitted above and from Tables 9.9 and 9.10

The firm's geographical spread can be further assessed from the fact that several of its products have gained worldwide acceptance, e.g.

1 Gaster is licensed to Merck and is now sold in eighty-eight countries.
2 Perdipine is marketed in forty-four countries by various firms, including Syntex and Sandoz.
3 Yamatetan is sold in twelve countries.
4 Josamycin is offered in forty countries, including the People's Republic of China, where it is soon to be manufactured at eight plants.

In addition, ¥97.5 billion of overseas sales were made by overseas licence-holders of Yamanouchi-developed drugs. Taken together, these moves represent a reasonable degree of success for Yamanouchi's internationalisation strategy during the 1980s.

Results by segment of activity

Until 1990 Yamanouchi described its sales as being 'pharmaceuticals'. The acquisition of Shaklee in 1989 has changed the picture quite radically (see Figure 9.6); instead of being 100 per cent pharma-

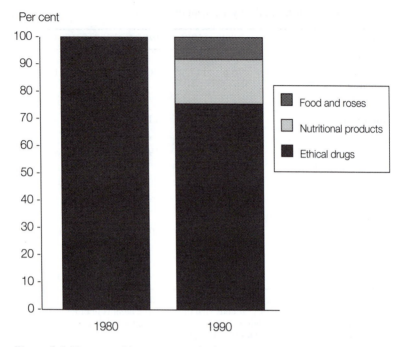

Figure 9.6 Yamanouchi: segment analysis (as a percentage of sales), 1980 and 1990 *Source*: Yamanouchi annual reports

ceuticals, the firm's sales now include 16.7 per cent of nutritional products and 7.2 per cent of food and roses. The substantial addition of Shaklee's sales, provided they continue to be profitable, will greatly assist in spreading Yamanouchi's overall risk away from complete dependence on the drugs market.

Results by therapeutic category

Table 9.9 gives a breakdown of Yamanouchi's pharmaceutical sales by therapeutic category. Bearing in mind that Yamanouchi's total drug sales grew at a compound rate of 11 per cent per annum over the 1980s, the performance within some of the sub-sectors is worthy of comment. The star performer by a long way was the digestive system category, which grew at an average rate of 35 per cent in each year of the decade. Most of the growth came in the explosive period between 1985 and 1988 when Gaster was launched so successfully. By 1990 the annual growth had shaded off considerably, though the product is the top selling H_2 antagonist in Japan, with about one-third of all sales.

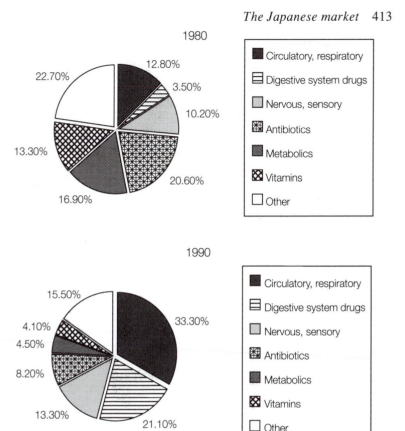

Figure 9.7 Yamanouchi: sub-segment analysis, 1980 and 1990 *Source*: Yamanounchi annual reports

twenty two consolidated subsidiaries and Shaklee's high marketing expenses for nutritional supplements. Accepting this at face value, it must still be observed that selling, general and administrative expenses represent a potential cost-control problem for Yamanouchi.

The excellence of the firm's financial control is also evidenced by the very large increases (average 26 per cent per annum) throughout the decade in working capital. Long-term debt has also risen rapidly, again more so in 1990 to fund the major acquisition. Despite this, gearing was only 34.4 per cent in 1990. While this is higher than Fujisawa, and three times the level of Takeda, it does represent a post-acquisition situation together with a successful and aggressively implemented programme of internationalisation. With Yamanouchi's record of financial control, this should not be a problem, either short or long-term.

Table 9.10 Yamanouchi financial performance (¥ million)

Measure	1980	1985	1986	1987	1988	1990
Sales	76,601	117,933	140,574	164,054	185,176	263,630
Cost of goods sold	34,169	51,291	57,329	57,471	61,208	75,770
Selling, general, admin.	28,092	46,628	54,209	60,799	69,618	120,511
R & D expenses	6,962	12,279	15,103	16,057	17,119	22,189
Operating income	15,337	23,283	34,298	51,092	63,799	74,965
Net income	5,556	7,360	10,484	16,746	22,497	31,871
Current liabilities	27,863	38,873	48,735	58,123	63,894	88,534
Current assets	62,273	157,432	175,155	214,802	267,417	374,249
Working capital	34,410	118,559	126,420	156,679	203,523	285,715
Fixed assets	8,860	23,066	23,397	25,253	26,481	66,009
Investments	9,532	12,347	13,287	25,657	35,597	42,138
Other assets						72,186
Total assets	52,802	153,972	163,104	207,589	265,601	466,048
Long term debt	1,584	29,885	27,718	49,629	77,087	160,469
Shareholders' equity	38,089	107,587	118,578	138,854	161,991	259,807
As % of sales						
Cost of goods sold	44.6	43.5	40.8	35.0	33.1	28.7
Selling, general, admin.	36.7	39.5	38.6	37.1	37.6	45.7
R & D expenses	9.1	10.4	10.7	9.8	9.2	8.4
Operating income	20.0	19.7	24.4	31.1	34.5	28.4
Net income	7.3	6.2	7.5	10.2	12.1	12.1
Other ratios						
Total asset turnover (times)	1.5	0.8	0.9	0.8	0.7	0.6
Return on shareholders' assets (%)	40.3	21.6	28.9	36.8	39.4	28.9
Gearing ratio %	3.0	19.4	17.0	23.9	29.0	34.4

Source: Yamanouchi annual reports and author's estimates

Activities

Gastro-intestinals

Yamanouchi's star product here is Gaster (famotidine), a treatment for
duodenal and gastric ulcers. It was launched in mid-1985, and recorded
sales of ¥5.6 billion in its first five months. The explosive growth that
followed brought sales of ¥19.2 billion in 1986, ¥31.6 billion in 1987,
¥39.2 billion in 1988 and ¥40.5 billion (estimate) in 1989. The product
is now being manufactured in bulk form at the firm's new factory in
Ireland. The output is being exported to Japan, to European markets and
to the US.

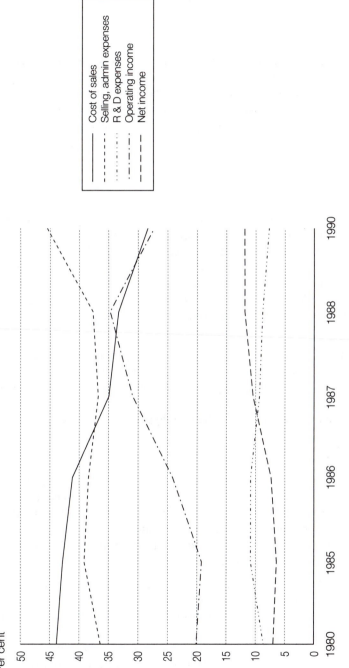

Per cent

Cost of sales
Selling, admin expenses
R & D expenses
Operating income
Net income

Figure 9.8 Yamanouchi: financial performance (as a percentage of sales), 1980 and 1985–90 *Source*: Yamanouchi annual reports

CNS

The main driving force in this category has been Elen (indeloxazine), a Yamanouchi-developed product which treats the symptoms of mental disorders associated with cerebrovascular damage. It is thus an appropriate drug to aim at any market where the proportion of elderly people is growing. This includes Japan and every other developed country. Elen was launched in the first quarter of 1988 and recorded sales of ¥12.5 billion in its first nine months. In fiscal 1990 it posted sales of ¥21.7 billion, a startling increase of almost 75 per cent.

Cardiovasculars

Perdipine (nicardipine) has become Japan's leading calcium antagonist for treating hypertension and disorders of cerebral circulation. It was launched in 1981 and by 1984 was recording sales of ¥23 billion. Two product extensions have been added: Perdipine LA (the long-acting version) and an injectable formulation. Taken together, the Perdipine range recorded 1990 sales of ¥40 billion. Like Gaster and Elen, Perdipine was developed in Yamanouchi's own laboratories. Other products in this category include:

1 Pronon (propafenone), an anti-arrhythmic agent licensed from Petrik, a West German firm, and launched in Japan in mid-1989.
2 Frandol, a circulatory drug for the treatment of angina pectoris, with sales of ¥14.5 billion in 1990.
3 Lowgan, a beta-blocker for treating hypertension, launched in 1988.

Antibiotics

This was Yamanouchi's traditional area of strength till 1982, when it was overtaken by the cardiovascular category. This segment has been particularly badly hit by intensifying competition in the domestic market and by the government's price cutting policy. Despite this, it still turns in acceptable sales and profits for Yamanouchi. There are three principal products here:

1 Yamatetan, a long-acting third-generation cephamycin antibiotic; 1990 sales were about ¥7 billion.
2 Suncefal, a long-acting cephalosporin, with 1990 sales of about ¥4 billion.
3 Josamycin, a microlide antibiotic; this was Yamanouchi's first truly international product, but is now on the decline; in 1990 it recorded sales of about ¥5 billion.

Other products

1 Euglucon, an oral antidiabetic, with 1990 sales of ¥3.7 billion.

2 Norditropen (somatropin), developed by Novo Nordisk; it is a biosynthetic human growth hormone dependent on recombinant genetic technology; it was launched in 1989 and was well received on the Japanese market.

3 Yamanouchi also markets Novo Nordisk's full range of insulin preparations and glucogen in Japan.

4 Lentinan, an anti-cancer agent, launched in 1986, and recording 1990 sales of about ¥5 billion.

Research and development

Over the last ten years, Yamanouchi's R & D expenditures have varied between 9.1 per cent and 10.7 per cent of sales. While this is still a long way short of the 13.5 per cent benchmark accepted by the leading pharmaceutical multinationals, whose company Yamanouchi is so anxious to join, the firm is certainly among Japan's most research-intensive drug companies. However, size of expenditure is only one measure; the other critical factor is the effectiveness of the expenditure. Yamanouchi scores highly here, as witness the constant stream of high-selling drugs that emerged from its laboratories throughout the 1980s. Nevertheless, the firm still seems intent on increasing its R & D investments. In 1990 its expenditure was up by 30 per cent; measured against pharmaceutical sales, this comes to 11.1 per cent of sales – the highest figure ever recorded by Yamanouchi.

The company's total R & D workforce amounts to some 800, or about 20 per cent of all employees. There are three medicinal research laboratories and two devoted to biomedical research, all in Japan. Four of these facilities are in Tokyo; the fifth is on the Tsukuba Science Park, north-east of Tokyo, where Takeda and Fujisawa are also located. These facilities are all linked by a highly advanced teleconferencing system, which is one way Yamanouchi attempts to overcome the problems of coordinating research carried out at dispersed centres. Supporting these are a number of applied pharmacology and development laboratories, and product development laboratories.

In its drive to internationalise operations, Yamanouchi has not neglected R & D. Near Oxford, England, the firm employs twenty five R & D scientists in the newly established Yamanouchi Research Institute (UK). Under active investigation is the setting up of a parallel facility in the US. The UK unit will focus on basic research in cell biology; further joint work in biotechnology will be carried out by

Yamanouchi with T Cell Sciences Inc, Microgenics Corporation, and Geritech Inc of the US, and with Innogenetics SA of Belgium. Finally, the firm has agreed to participate in a wide range of joint research with the Chinese Academy of Sciences in the People's Republic of China. As of August 1990 Yamanouchi had thirteen important drugs at the clinical stage (or later) of development in Japan (see Table 9.11).[16] It takes little analysis to conclude that Yamanouchi sees its future in the pharmaceutical industry as leadership contenders in the cardiovascular and CNS therapeutic segments.

Table 9.11 Yamanouchi drugs at the clinical stage of development, August 1990, in order of proximity to market launch

Drug	Stage	Description
Emilace	Filed	Major tranquilliser
Hypoca	Filed	Antihypertensive (calcium antagonist)
Sepan	Filed	Heart failure treatment (β_1 selective partial antagonist)
Cartonic	Filed	Heart failure treatment
Anexate	Filed	Benzodiazepine antagonist
YM12617	Phase III	Dysuria treatment (alpha-blocker)
YM14673	Phase III	Brain activator
YM170	Phase III	Muscle relaxant
YM881	Phase II	Anticancer agent
YM018	Phase II	Heart failure treatment
YM175	Phase I	Osteoporosis treatment
YM435	Phase I	Circulatory insufficiency treatment
YM044	Phase I	Penem-type antibiotic

Strengths and weaknesses

Strengths

1 The management team is strong, as evidenced by the impressive performance throughout the 1980s.
2 The firm is established in the world's second largest market, with a good financial base, and strong financial control.
3 R & D expenditure is high, as is R & D productivity, and the range of products is good in growing industry sectors.
4 New, efficient production plants in Japan, Taiwan and Ireland.
5 The firm also has subsidiaries in West Germany and Britain, and – through its acquisition of Shaklee – a major presence in America.
6 It has excellent collaborative experience, which has brought access to distribution channels as an added bonus.

Weaknesses

1 Yamanouchi is small by world standards, and even relatively so by Japanese standards.
2 While the product line is good, it is also narrow.
3 R & D expenditure is still significantly below the international industry norm of 13.5 per cent of sales.
4 The firm is still over-dependent on the Japanese market, where government policies constantly drive down profits.
5 The over-the-counter diversification is still very small.

STRATEGY OPTIONS AND CHOICE

Emerging from the foregoing analysis is a list of seven fairly stark (though mainly attractive) choices for Yamanouchi:

1 The company can continue to do what is does best.
2 Enter overseas markets and vigorously promote products either under its own name or via an established company in that market.
3 Buy an overseas manufacturer in a related field.
4 Buy an overseas manufacturer in a different field as a further diversification.
5 Establish a pharmaceuticals joint venture in the US.
6 Establish a pharmaceuticals joint venture in Europe.
7 Enter the Chinese drug market.

Option 1. By continuing to do what it has done best in the past, the company is only 'playing safe'. It will continue to be profitable over the next decade, but after that will have lost any competitive advantage. Also, owing to its size, if still successful it will be taken over either by one of the other Japanese firms or, more likely, by an overseas competitor.

Option 2. The Japanese market is reaching saturation. Profit margins are falling as the government continues to cut costs. The exchange rate of the yen is making foreign products cheap, and Yamanouchi's products expensive overseas. To continue to increase sales, the company must be operating in the larger world market, but it must be done in a way that fits best with its company culture. Marketing via an established company would give it instant access to the markets. This would also enable it to exchange research technology and possibly lead to greater collaboration.

Options 3 and 4. The company has already bought Shaklee in the US. It could utilise this experience and some of its financial resources to make another acquistion. This should be in a different product line, while still being in a growing market.

Options 5 and 6. Establishing a joint venture is the firm's best opportunity of increasing its power base quickly in the drug industry. This will reduce overheads still further through shared expenses. Yamanouchi is technologically advanced in its own field, so it can approach other companies from a position of advantage. The US is a candidate market for this option because it is the world's largest. Europe is a candidate market because of the wide variety of pharmaceutical firms based there, and because of the potential of the single European market after 1992; it is also on the doorstep of Eastern Europe.

Option 7. The Chinese market is a large market, with a broadly similar cultural background. Also, many of Japan's pharmaceutical companies have had previous experience of the alternative medicines found in China. The possibility of exchanging production techniques and product know-how is a live one.

Strategy recommendation. The company has excellent products but only some are marketed abroad, and in some markets. To remain competitive in the long term, Yamanouchi must increase market share to provide future funds. For this reason it should adopt option 2 in the short term and enter markets where it it currently not represented, and increase sales and product offerings in those foreign markets where it is already represented. For this reason, it should be looking to more licensing and sales deals. This will also decrease reliance on the domestic market in Japan. Since it has no sales network in most countries, licensing is possibly the best alternative.

Yamanouchi should give consideration to further concentric diversification. Shaklee came with an associated pattern of international distribution channels, which Yamanouchi could use to develop the marketing of its existing over-the-counter range, especially in the US.

The firm has already set up a plant in Ireland, and it should be looking to expand its European presence. To exploit this huge market and the opportunity for entry into Eastern Europe, Yamanouchi should seek to form a joint venture with a European pharmaceuticals firm.

The Chinese market will be difficult even for Yamanouchi to penetrate. However, the company should be actively looking for a joint collaborative research/manufacturing venture to act as a 'loss leader' in the short term, for the eventual rewards accruing to the early movers will be massive.

Conclusion

Yamanouchi has some excellent products, with more about to come on stream – but it is over-concentrated in one market. This limits its potential, and the firm has correctly diagnosed internationalisation as the only realistic grand strategy. Yamanouchi is a market leader rather than a market follower, and this should largely dictate its future course of action. However, the basic choice is stark – expand aggressively into foreign markets or be absorbed into a Western pharmaceutical multi-national looking for a substantial foothold in the strategically important Japanese market.

10 Towards the millennium

In 1977 Barrie James[1] made a number of predictions concerning the development of the multinational pharmaceutical industry up to 1990. While, inevitably, a number of these predictions did not come to pass, a surprisingly high proportion were fairly accurate – surprise arising because this is a notoriously difficult industry to predict. For example, he was fairly close to the mark with the following scenarios about the 1980s:

1 Governments and private health care systems were expected to continue and increase downward pressure on prices.
2 Small multinationals and exporters were expected to adopt marketing and licensing arrangements in an increasingly concentrated search for a cost-effective approach to new market and/or new product development.
3 Concentration of the industry would increase, owing to increased cost pressures on less financially sound firms. Such merger activity would be nationally based in countries (e.g. France) where indigenous companies were encouraged to dominate the home market, whilst cross-border mergers would decrease in importance for already internationalised firms (save those based in Germany or Japan).
4 Therapeutic area concentration was expected to increase, owing to economic pressures, and this would inevitably lead to increased multinational dominance of the affected sectors.
5 Smaller pharmaceutical firms would attempt to assure access to new products by collaborating nationally and internationally with other small and medium-size firms.
6 Economic pressures would result in the virtual elimination of fringe R & D activities in favour of research in a limited number of areas of major epidemiological importance.

7 Internal company controls on the effectiveness of R & D expenditure were expected to increase; but still the rate of innovation would fall below the rate of the 1945–75 era.

8 Multinationals were expected to accelerate the decentralisation of R & D activities on an international scale to offset delays in new product registration brought about by the increasingly stringent demands of particular national regulatory agencies. In addition, many new drugs would be marginal therapeutic advances because of increased regulation.

9 Basic pharmaceutical research would become increasingly concentrated within a smaller number of major multinationals, with universities and government research agencies also holding an important place.

10 The high visibility of the pharmaceutical industry would bring greatly increased pressure on prices and profits as governments strove to maximise the returns from public expenditure on health care services.

11 Despite noises to the contrary, no developed country would be prepared to nationalise its pharmaceutical industry, though protectionist or nationalist tendencies would bring this result in some less developed countries.

12 A general evening-up in the level of regulatory control was expected to take place in developed countries, but with little harmonisation save in supranational trading blocs like the EC.

13 It was forecast that pharmaceutical firms would underestimate intelligent public opposition to their interests and would thus fall in public esteem, being unable – individually or through national associations – to deflect the negative impact of this rise in consumerism.

14 Pharmaceutical multinationals would be less able to implement individual market pricing policies owing to supranational bodies like the EC; price controls would be reinforced by physician prescribing restraints and the increasing availability of adequate generic substitutes.

15 Developed countries were expected to place increasing restraints on the promotional methods used by pharmaceutical firms, though intense competitive pressures would tend to force upward the effectiveness of promotional expenditures.

In retrospect, of course, it may seem that some of the above outcomes were fairly obvious, but any honest observer of the world pharmaceutical industry will remember that the future was not quite so clear in

1977. As the foregoing pages of this book have indicated, the economic and political imperatives driving many of James's predictions are still working themselves through the world pharmaceutical industry. Despite the difficulties of prognostication, it is hard to avoid the temptation of looking forward to the end of the century to examine the possible futures in the drug industry's collective crystal ball.

THE INDUSTRY

Without any shadow of doubt, the key to the future growth and prosperity of the pharmaceutical industry will be the effectiveness of massive investments in R & D; such has always been the case, and no alternative broad scenario can be envisaged. As James noted above, economic pressures drive the industry, and rising R & D costs represent the most intense of these; R & D is also the driving force which is most likely to encourage, even compel, increasing concentration in the industry. It has been suggested[2] that this tendency towards concentration may be ameliorated, even reversed, by either of two considerations. The first is technical, whereby leading-edge advances in the understanding of biological systems yield an R & D competitive advantage not dependent on economies of scale, thus boosting the chances of the medium-size drug firm and the new entrants. The second is political, and envisages regulating authorities in a shift towards benefit maximisation. The resulting de-emphasis on risk-avoidance would again mean that large firms would lose certain economics of scale and reverse the move towards higher concentration. The first of these considerations, as of 1990, shows some signs of realisation; the second is, as yet, ephemeral.

The US pharmaceutical industry

The US market is the honeypot towards which all international players in the world pharmaceutical industry are attracted. It is still the world's largest market, with least price control, and with the highest rates of profitability; but perhaps the end of the good days is in sight. Competition will increase as global firms identify new user markets for existing products and/or new products for existing markets. Generic drug sales will increase because of the pressure of health maintenance organisations, and because of the ever-tightening squeeze on public expenditure. It is difficult to see how this scenario will yield attractive prospects for the future, but the perspective of the major industry members may be refreshingly different in that, for me, they are taking a larger view. Predictions for the twenty-first century seem to be based on a new epoch of discovery and development where the focus will be on the causes of disease rather than just the symptoms. Clearly, R & D investments will have a key role to play here, though increasing innovation cycles will put merger pressures on smaller firms, e.g. Sterling's acquisition by Kodak, AHP's acquisition of A.H. Robins. The industry is also focusing on the medical problems of ageing and meeting the challenge of developing drugs to treat and prevent new diseases such as AIDS, as well as long-standing ones such as cancer. The development of new drug delivery systems will also become important; these systems will be designed to influence the way in which active medicinal agents get to where they are needed in the body.

For the future, it seems that sales will not be greatly affected by purely economic forces, though repatriation to the US of internationally earned profits may become more problematic if the dollar appreciates relative to other major currencies. The industry can expect to be under continued political pressure in the US as far as pricing and regulation are concerned. This will not be affected by changes in the political ideology of government, as Democrats seem to appreciate as much as Republicans that government-funded health care operations need to be efficient. Given the large profits earned by pharmaceutical firms, they will inevitably be regarded as an easy target. Biotechnology is undoubtedly the biggest technological question faced by the US industry. Major breakthroughs from this direction could have dramatic consequences, such as lowering entry barriers, which could create downward pressure on industry profits. It is thus clear that major drug firms must remain at the forefront of this technology in order to take advantage of breakthroughs rather than be victims of them.

The UK pharmaceutical industry

The UK industry is unlikely to avoid increasing government safety regulations and price restrictions because of government obsession with safety and cost containment on drugs supplied to the NHS. However, as the industry continues to contribute substantially to Britain's foreign exchange position, the government is likely to provide continuing preferential treatment to British-based pharmaceutical manufacturers regarding return on capital, with the side effect of boosting R & D expenditure within the UK. Owing to the high costs of R & D, research efforts are more likely to be concentrated in areas of growing and future potential markets, following, for example, well established demographic trends. In the UK this is likely to mean concentration on diseases affecting the older sector of the population. Also, British R & D will most likely concentrate on the diseases most common in the 'triad' of Western Europe, Japan and the US – the regions which provide the largest and most profitable share of the global market. Thus, despite the erosion of historic profitability, the industry will still remain one of the most profitable in the manufacturing sector because of the high demand for health care products.

Intensified regulation will further exacerbate the already fierce competition in the ethical drugs sector. Individual firms will strive to have their drugs put and kept on the NHS 'white' prescription list and will fight on quality, effectiveness and price. Since the overall effect of NHS activity is to depress prices, the outcome will clearly benefit companies in a cost leadership position. Profit erosion and escalating R & D costs will bring differential pressures to bear on the UK industry; large firms which can afford the capital investment will be able to take that route to cost control and profit stability, leading to further concentration of the prescription pharmaceuticals sector in the hands of fewer companies. Increasingly, smaller firms will have to concentrate on the proprietary or over-the-counter market, which will thus experience more intense rivalry. This tendency will be aggravated by the fact that entry barriers to the over-the-counter sector will be much lower than those to the ethical sector, and so more over-the-counter entrants will emerge. Furthermore, since the risk of failure is so high in ethicals, while concurrently offering a high potential rate of return, the need for flexible and effective strategy processes within the industry becomes imperative. The ability of any individual firm to mobilise its resources effectively will determine its success in surviving an increasingly turbulent environment. The clear need is to map industry changes, to reorganise to meet the market challenges and competitive moves, and evolve a superior competitive strategy.

The European pharmaceutical industry

The continental European drug industry falls into two parts: that within the EC (covered in detail in Chapter 4), and the non-EC bloc. For the EC, the most important environmental factor is the single market legislation which was planned to be fully implemented by 31 December 1992. In all likelihood, a single integrated European pharmaceutical market will not be created by 1 January 1993 but will evolve slowly by the selective enforcement of various articles of the Treaty of Rome relating to competition policy, and by selective enforcement of the directives discussed in Chapter 4. This evolutionary process to, and the creation of, a single integrated European drugs market will result in significant changes in the structure of both the industry and the market and in the relative relationships of the various elements both within and between the industry and the market. Perhaps the greatest danger in the creation of a single European market is the risk of the development of 'Fortress Europe'. In order to avoid the possibility of being refused access to the EC market both the Swiss and the US pharmaceutical multinationals are increasing their presence within the bloc. A manufacturing base is a prerequisite if there is any risk of 'Fortress Europe' developing and a viable presence in any major market can only stem from a strong local manufacturing base. However, the development of 'Fortress Europe' would also seriously injure the European pharmaceutical industry, as it might be refused access to non-EC markets.

On the assumption that the aims of 1992 are eventually achieved, they should create a better climate in which a much-needed industry restructuring can be implemented. At the very least, there is likely to be a significant shake-out of the smaller, and even some of the larger, companies in the peripheral areas of the EC such as Spain, Portugal and Greece. Here, increased competition is likely to force many of the smaller companies out of business, while some of the larger ones could be soft acquisition targets. It is likely that the restructuring of the industry will leave surviving only those firms which have a global perspective, a strong product spread across important therapeutic sub-sectors, solid R & D, technological (particularly biological) strengths and leadership in the higher value-added areas. However, the impact of the single market from a pan-European domestic viewpoint may be negligible overall and, on balance, may even be beneficial. It will create a European pharmaceutical industry that is more viable though smaller in terms of members, and it will be more efficient and more internationally competitive. However, should the Japanese pharmaceutical industry, which is currently showing signs of expansionary activity outside Japan (see Chapter 9), set up facilities in Europe, then the nature and extent of any industry restructuring would be greatly magnified.

In the non-EC sector, perhaps the most interesting segment is the Nordic market (Denmark is also in the EC). Here, despite a singular mix of socio-environmental factors and government control, a number of success stories can be posted. In Norway, for example, two firms in particular have carved themselves out substantial niche markets and have gained international recognition in their chosen fields. Nycomed has carved itself an international niche market based on its expertise and investment in contrast diagnosis; internationalisation has been rapid, and exports now account for over 85 per cent of sales. Apothekernes Laboratorium has become the leading world producer of Bacitracin, which it sells mostly in bulk for veterinary purposes; its special expertise is biotechnical production with special application to antibiotic fermentation processes.

Astra dominates the Swedish domestic market (see Chapter 8) but the second firm, Pharmacia, is represented in about 130 countries and is one of the world's leading suppliers of analytical systems for biotechnology and bio-research. Two Danish firms, Novo and Nordisk Gentofte, have invested heavily in biogenetic engineering and hormones; between them, they have over 50 per cent of the world insulin market. Thus, while there is not a conspicuous Nordic pharmaceutical industry as there is a UK, US or Japanese industry, the area does contribute significantly to the world health products markets. Differentiation is the favoured generic strategy which enables even relatively small firms, through the development and application of selective expertise, to become major players – and even leaders – in world markets. With the fast-rising use of biotechnology throughout the industry, and with the commitment and expertise that Nordic innovators have shown towards this new tool, there is every reason to suppose that the Nordic pharmaceutical industry will progress and expand its share of world markets.

The Japanese pharmaceutical industry

The pharmaceutical industry in Japan is still, relatively speaking, in its infancy but is developing steadily. It could be argued that, this far, industry fragmentation has retarded growth. Many firms are small, rendering meaningful R & D investments difficult or impossible. Long-term survival of these firms will be difficult without amalgamations or alliances, because foreign firms are overcoming entry barriers despite price controls and high taxes. In the last fifteen years, total Japanese investment in drug R & D has increased enormously and this has had a positive effect on the number of new drugs and approvals. However, many of these products do not yet meet the regulatory requirements in other developed countries, and so the Japanese industry lacks a sufficient volume of exportable products.

Despite its problems, the Japanese pharmaceutical industry will continue to grow at a much faster rate than its European and US counterparts with the impetus of huge investments in plant and automated equipment, and a continuous flow of higher-level innovations. Joint research with Western firms and institutions will continue until the Japanese are self-reliant. As in the US, biotechnology will be a major competitive weapon, particularly in the cancer area. Major breakthroughs in this area will see Japan develop into a key player in the international pharmaceutical industry.

THE COMPANIES

Having looked at the future scenarios from the perspective of the industry, we can now repeat the process from the point of view of the individual players analysed in Chapters 6–9. For each company, a preferred future strategy was set out, and a synthesis of these might yield some classification of the broad strategic thrusts open to major players over the next ten years.

First, there is fairly natural grouping of three firms sharing very similar structural characteristics; ICI, Ciba-Geigy and Hoechst all have very substantial international pharmaceutical businesses which are part of much larger (and generally successful) chemical manufacturing corporations. Earlier analysis also showed that their future strategic needs also had some commonalities:

1 Less than normal need to diversify pharmaceutical operations, as the business risk of the parent corporation is already well spread; this allows the respective pharmaceutical divisions to concentrate strongly on core areas of technical and market expertise.
2 An increasingly pressing need to achieve true global marketing capability; this could be achieved organically in the case of all three firms, but it would be slow and expensive by this route. By far the quicker and less expensive route would be through the development of permanent joint ventures or strategic alliances, particularly with substantial Japanese and US partners.
3 A similar, though possibly less obvious, need to expand the ideas and creativity base of already excellent though highly focused R & D activities. Specifically, there is a need to tap the research expertise of small, dynamic firms and/or institutional research laboratories by a variety of methods including joint ventures, strategic alliances, subcontracted work, purchase of new-molecule licences, sponsored work, and acquisition.
4 Finally, a less obvious commonality is the strategic and overall bargaining power of each of these businesses within its respective parent–subsidiary relationship. The point was made in Chapter 7 that the bargaining power of the subsidiary depends to a very large extent on a substantial reliance of the parent on the subsidiary for

contributions to corporation profitability. Currently, all three pharmaceutical divisions contribute well, but not excessively to the overall well-being of the respective parents; and because the parents are relatively well balanced in terms of business risk and market coverage, it is unlikely that any of these three firms will be involved in major acquisitions in the coming decade. By a similar token, it could be argued that the parents are unlikely to dispose of pharmaceutical divisions. However, the case of third-party predators has to be considered and, in this respect, overall corporate size and power offer the best protection. Thus, in this group of three firms, Hoechst is most likely to reach the end of the decade in something resembling its present form and structure, and ICI is the least likely.

Looking for a second natural grouping, attention is drawn immediately to the three Japanese firms: Takeda, Fujisawa and Yamanouchi. At first sight, these would seem to have important characteristics in common, including country and culture of origin, importance of the domestic market, and degree of internationalisation.

It takes little more than a glance at the earlier strategic analysis to sunder this supposedly 'natural grouping'. Yamanouchi's growth record over the 1980s has been significantly more impressive in terms of several important parameters, and cannot be considered as a constituent of a grouping which includes Takeda and Fujisawa. These two firms do share a number of strategic commonalities, including:

1 There is a need to focus attention on achieving a defensible position in strategically important foreign markets, and perhaps Fujisawa could learn something from Takeda's approach to the US market through its link with Abbott. Both companies urgently need to establish strong trading and manufacturing bases in Europe, especially in view of the 1992 single market legislation and the industry fears about 'Fortress Europe'.

2 Both firms have a requirement to improve performance significantly in the home market, where they are in danger of losing substantial ground to domestic and foreign competitors. That said, each has a good market share and a well developed system of distribution, both of which factors would be highly attractive to a foreign firm wishing to make an acquisition in order to improve its global position in the critical triad of strategically important markets.

3 Both firms urgently need to increase the rate of growth of R & D expenditure in order to increase the flow of innovations, especially those which are globally acceptable and can be successfully launched throughout the triad. At the same time, both firms are hampered in

doing this by financial constraints; these constraints are, in turn, a function of over-reliance on a domestic market where the government has controlled prices strictly in recent years, and even forced them down on occasion. Thus the tight vicious circle: internationalisation promises higher profitability, but is held back for lack of funding due to a low degree of internationalisation.

Among the other firms in our sample of twelve, it could be argued that Pfizer may be part of a natural grouping with Takeda and Fujisawa. During the 1980s it became a great deal more dependent on its domestic market for increases in sales volume. Conversely it lost ground significantly in Europe and even more so in Asia. Like Fujisawa, Pfizer has greatly boosted its R & D spending since 1985, but the fruits of these investments in terms of an increased flow of innovatory products is not yet in evidence. However, the case for grouping Pfizer with Takeda and Fujisawa must be suspended for further judgement below.

The third clearly demarcated group is a small one, consisting of only two firms – Astra and Glaxo. The commonalities between the two are almost uncanny, the only major difference being a time shift of approximately seven years between the respective development cycles (with Glaxo ahead). Both were diversified and then concentrated on ethical pharmaceuticals; both were essentially regional, then developed a global perspective; both were guided into and through explosive growth phases by a chief executive of outstanding calibre; and both have had blockbusters in the anti-ulcer therapeutic area. In terms of future strategy recommendations, the commonalities are fewer but significant:

1 The need to focus research on areas where there is some likelihood of developing new blockbusters to replace current anti-ulcer products when they reach the decline stage of the product life cycle
2 The need to establish strong operating bases in each of the strategically important triad of markets while the firms are on a rising curve of optimism and profitability, in order to develop into truly global entities.
3 The need to find a working solution to the strategic conundrum of whether to diversify into related products and markets, or to stick with earlier decisions to concentrate on pharmaceuticals, with all the attendant risks and benefits.

Both Astra and Glaxo have the enormous benefit of huge positive cash flows from blockbusting drugs which can be used to develop the firms into possibly the first truly global firms in the world pharmaceutical industry. The executives who started the process – Widengren and Girolami respectively – have now passed the leader's baton on to the next generation of management. If either Astra or Glaxo falters, loses focus or fails to develop successful innovatory products, the fate of SmithKline – a forerunner of the potential global firm – awaits.

Thus, we are left with four firms – Merck, Abbott, Wellcome and Yamanouchi – and the question: do these comprise a homogeneous strategic group within the industry? We might also enquire whether Pfizer more likely belongs with this group than with Takeda and Fujisawa. There is a big difference in the size of these firms: Merck is among the world's largest pharmaceutical firms (as is Pfizer), Abbott and Wellcome are middle-range drug firms, and Yamanouchi is among the smallest of the international firms in the industry (though fast-growing); the national bases of the three firms are spread over the triad of strategically important markets; and their main therapeutic sub-groups and market dispositions show many dissimilarities. Again, however, we must look at commonalities in future strategy orientation if we are to establish a basis for grouping these firms together; thus we find:

1 The need to milk 'cash cow' products relentlessly to provide cash flows for future strategic development projects.
2 The need to focus intensively on a strategy of product innovation in order to maintain and advance favourable positions developed during the 1980s. In the case of Abbott there is a further decision to be made – to concentrate this innovatory activity outwith its pharmaceutical business or to allow its drugs division to share in it in an attempt to regain its former leading position.
3 The requirement to maintain the internationalisation thrust of the 1980s and expand it where necessary, particularly in terms of the triad of strategically important markets – Japan, the US and Europe.

Two points should be made here: first, it is still not entirely clear whether Pfizer fits with this group or with that containing Takeda and Fujisawa; second, this fourth grouping of companies is fairly weak, and it would be helpful if some further classification evidence could be advanced. Accordingly, the performance records of nine of the firms – excluding those which are general chemical manufacturers – were re-scrutinised using the basic data set out in Chapters 6–9. Table 10.1 contains data for the compound growth rate of four variables over the 1980s – corporate sales, corporate R & D expenditures, corporate net income after taxation, and pharmaceutical sales. Figure 10.1 shows the plot of sales growth against R & D growth; there is a visually clear grouping of Merck, Abbott, Wellcome and Yamanouchi – and Pfizer is not obviously part of this group, being more comfortably classified with Takeda and Fujisawa. In the top right-hand corner of Figure 10.1 Astra and Glaxo comprise a fairly clearly separated group. Figure 10.2 plots sales growth against net income growth and again yields a classification of the same three groups of firms as Figure 10.1. R & D growth is plotted against growth of pharmaceutical sales in Figure 10.3. Again, the same three groups emerge, though the exact classification of Pfizer is more problematical; even here, however, it can be argued that Pfizer should be classified with Takeda and Fujisawa, as its drug sales growth (8.5 per cent per annum) is less than half that of the top-performing firm on this parameter (Glaxo), while Merck, Abbott, Wellcome and Yamanouchi are all above this level. Finally, applying the data of Table 10.1 to statistical cluster analysis yields the same three groupings of firms as appear in Figures 10.1–3.

Table 10.1 Compound annual growth rates during the 1980s (%)

Company	Corporate sales	Corporate R & D	Corporate after-tax income	Drug sales
Merck	10.2	13.8	15.3	11.4
Abbott	11.4	20.0	16.7	10.0
Pfizer	7.1	14.1	11.5	8.5
Glaxo	16.7	29.1	33.0	18.7
Wellcome	12.7	17.5	22.0	11.7
Astra	15.8	17.4	33.4	16.0
Takeda	4.8	8.0	6.8	6.3
Fujisawa	4.1	7.9	−9.9	4.9
Yamanouchi	13.2	12.3	19.1	10.1

Source: Derived from various annual reports and accounts

Thus, we have established a case for classifying the twelve companies analysed in Chapters 6–9 as in Table 10.2.

Table 10.2 Classification of the companies whose cases have been studied, according to likely future and strategy

Group 1	Group 2	Group 3	Group 4
Astra	Merck	Pfizer	Hoechst
Glaxo	Abbott	Takeda	Ciba-Geigy
	Wellcome	Fujisawa	ICI
	Yamanouchi		

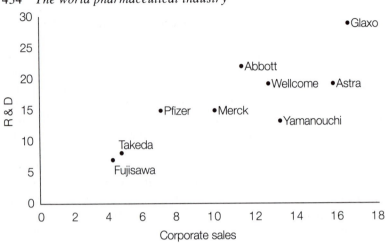

Figure 10.1 The growth rate of corporate sales *v.* R & D during the 1980s: annual increase (per cent) *Source*: Company annual reports

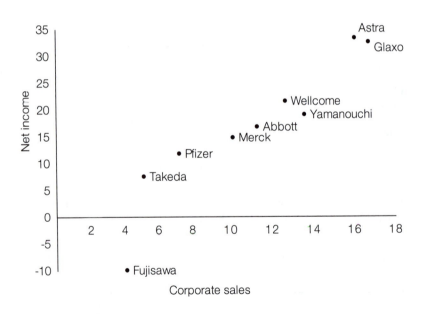

Figure 10.2 The growth rate of corporate sales *v.* net income during the 1980s: annual increase (per cent) *Source*: Company annual reports

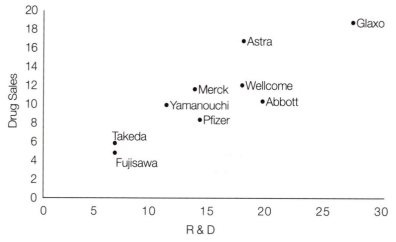

Figure 10.3 The growth rate of R & D *v.* drug sales during the 1980s: annual increase (per cent) *Source*: Company annual reports

RESEARCH AND DEVELOPMENT

It has been repeatedly stressed throughout this book that the product innovation process is critical to establishing a sustainable competitive advantage in the pharmaceutical industry. As international firms come to put more and more emphasis on the outputs of R & D, so attention is focused on the key role of R & D inputs. Chapter 3 stressed the need of pharmaceutical firms dealing in international markets to internationalise R & D, and this will be an important facet of sustaining competitive advantage throughout the 1990s, and beyond.

A recent study[3] has indicated that there are twelve determinants which are critical to the decision to locate a pharmaceutical R & D facility in a foreign country; in descending order of importance, they are:

1 The strategic importance of the firm's physical presence in a particular country.
2 The existence of efficient patent law.
3 A high existing stock of scientists, technologists and engineers.
4 A high level of competitors' R & D activity in a particular country.
5 The excellence of the tertiary education system.
6 Helpful regulations for new drug development.
7 High growth potential of a country's drug market.
8 Host government empathy with the pharmaceutical industry.
9 High consumption of pharmaceuticals in a particular country.

10 High number of new drugs developed in a particular country.
11 The existence of sympathetic drug safety regulations.
12 The existence of high technical expertise in research-specific areas in a particular country.

Each of these factors is deemed to have positive effect on a country's chances of being selected by a pharmaceutical firm as the location for a new R & D facility. This decision is an important one for the country involved because it creates a relatively large number of high-quality, long-lived jobs which can have important multiplier effects on local economies; because the presence of foreign drug multinationals leads to a considerably lower drug import bill; and because the presence of these firms also stimulates local companies to much higher levels of efficiency.

In the study referred to above, the twelve major locational determinants were modelled for six 'target' countries – the US, UK, Germany, France, Italy, Japan. Perceptions of the twelve determinants were gathered by personal interview with fourteen US pharmaceutical multinationals and eight of European origin. The purpose of the model is to determine existing overall perceptions of the locational desirability of the six target countries for a new pharmaceutical R & D facility, and to examine the strategic and policy consequences of changes in these perceptions.

The first notable result of this data analysis is that US pharmaceutical firms appear to be significantly more ethnocentric in perception when facing the foreign R & D locational decision. This conclusion emerged from the finding that, taking the US as the standard for comparison, all other target countries are more attractive to European than to US firms as potential R & D locations. While this may not be too surprising initially in that four of the target countries are European, it has to be borne in mind that, overall, the US market is more attractive to European firms than the individual home markets for the establishment of new R & D facilities.

Another interesting result is derived from these aggregate data, ranking the target countries in order of preference for a foreign R & D facility. The only difference between European and US firms is that the latter rank the UK above Germany while the former put Germany ahead. This is a mark of the esteem in which the UK is still held by US pharmaceutical multinationals as a location for foreign R & D facilities, borne out by the large proportion of existing foreign units which are currently based in the UK.

The core result stemming from analysis of the locational model was the aggregate order of preference, as expressed by the twenty-two pharmaceutical multinationals who participated in the research, of the six target countries as preferred locations for a future R & D facility. Thus, in descending order of suitability:

1 US.
2 Germany.
3 UK.
4 Japan.
5 France.
6 Italy.

Germany rated only marginally above the UK, and these countries could be considered to be in equal second place; there was a significant difference between the other rankings. Discussion with respondents suggested that, up to around 1981–82, the UK was a clear second choice after the US but, in recent years, Germany and Japan have become more favoured as foreign R & D locations. Thus, because of the tight grouping of Germany, the UK and Japan – and because of the relatively large gaps above and below this grouping – the perceptions of these three countries were subjected to sensitivity analysis. The underlying assumption was that feasible combinations of changes in host government policy and pharmaceutical multinational strategy could cause changes in the relative order within this grouping, but not outwith it. The main results of this sensitivity analysis were:

1 Provided the governments of the UK and Germany do nothing to weaken their position as preferential locations for foreign pharmaceutical R & D, there is no combination of the key determinants that the Japanese government can manipulate which would allow Japan to overtake either the UK or Germany in the rankings shown above.

2 For the UK, the position is more complicated. Policy changes by the UK government which improved the perceptions of pharmaceutical multinationals in respect of at least six of the twelve key determinants (while leaving the others unaffected) would rank the UK clearly ahead of Germany. However, policy changes which produced a negative effect on at least six of the twelve key determinants would have the effect of ranking the UK statistically significantly behind Germany (a change from the current marginal position). Only by adopting policy changes which had a negative effect on all the key determinants could the UK fall significantly behind Japan.

3 Again, in the case of Germany, only a negative movement in all key determinants ranks Germany significantly behind Japan. In general,

setting six of the key determinants high (or low) while keeping the others constant has the effect of setting Germany significantly above (below) the UK. Of particular importance here is the set of four determinants: efficient patent law, new drug regulations, drug safety regulations and government empathy. The model manipulations showed that improving perceptions of this group of determinants increased the likelihood of Germany being preferred to the UK as a site for a foreign pharmaceutical R & D facility; a negative movement in these determinants had the opposite effect.

Strategy responses of pharmaceutical multinationals

Strategy options for pharmaceutical multinationals do not flow easily from the study of a model constructed on the interplay of location-specific factors, but two points can be noted. First, it seems likely from the above analysis that there is a wide range of perceptions of the international pharmaceutical marketplace as represented by the six target countries. As to whether this difference is based on variations in national culture, commercial culture, industrial culture, corporate culture or history, it is not possible to state any definitive view here. However, the differences are likely to have a powerful effect on the response of the pharmaceutical multinationals to change (or lack of change) in host government attitudes towards the industry. If the firms do respond differently, it is unlikely that the responses will all be optimum in respect of any particular country. It is likely that any particular firm will have a perspective of the international market place that differs (perhaps markedly) from the industry norm; the nature of, and reasons for, any such variation should be a matter of considerable interest to corporate management, as it might be the basis of a welcome competitive advantage or a potentially crippling disadvantage.

Second, the analysis indicated quite clearly that particular changes in the locational determinants can have a marked effect on the desirability of a country as a preferred R & D site. Pharmaceutical multinationals showed by the high response to the 'government empathy' determinant that they are aware of the key role the host government can play. They also indicated by the very low response to a 'pro-industry pressure group' determinant that they have little confidence in the ability of manufacturers' associations and other pro-industry groups to have a positive effect on host government policy response. There is clearly a case here, either for firms taking up this lobbying role individually and in an effective manner, or for gathering the resources and talents into manufacturers' associations, to do so on an industry-wide basis. The benefits would be felt not only in the case of new foreign R & D units, but also in the operation of existing R & D facilities.

Policy responses by governments of potential host countries

On a global level, the US government can be satisfied that for the foreseeable future, and barring any major policy changes, it will be the host of first preference for footloose pharmaceutical R & D investment. Equally, the governments of France and Italy can feel relaxed about their low positions in the ranking; they will not change quickly or easily. Certainly, France may continue to secure a modicum of inward pharmaceutical R & D investment by threat, pressure and draconian regulation, but the chances of a foreign drug multinational voluntarily setting up a laboratory either there or in Italy seem remote.

Of course, any government – whether or not in one of the target countries – should be particularly aware of the importance of the twelve key determinants to pharmaceutical multinationals, especially if it harbours any hope of attracting inward R & D investment. Some of these variables can be manipulated directly and individually by the government. With others, it may be a case of assessing carefully what the host country has to offer by way of resource infrastructure and ensuring that potential inward investors are made fully aware of it.

At the country level, it comes as something of a surprise that the model manipulation offered so little in the way of policy response to Japan, to increase the likelihood of attracting inward R & D investment from pharmaceutical multinationals. The reason for this, of course, may be a matter of the assumptions used to build the model, and the algorithm used for the sensitivity analysis. However, if – and this is just as likely – it hinges on the barrier presented by the initial gap as shown by the model between Japan and the UK, then this does illustrate graphically the problems confronted by policy-makers there. It also underlines the magnitude of the gulf between Japan and France, and between the US and the rest of the world.

The most specific comments are to be made about Germany and the UK, as the sensitivity analysis showed a number of possible rank change permutations for these countries. Partly, this was a function of the closeness of their positions by the standard model ranking, but an analysis of the permutations showed some interesting dissimilarities. First, the 'determinant score' for Germany varied over a wider range than that for the UK during the sensitivity analysis. Second, this relative instability was underlined by greater propensity shown by

Germany to change rank (both upwards and downwards) with the various model manipulations. Third, there was some evidence that, while the group of determinants including efficient patent law and the three drug regulatory factors was relatively more important than the other groups for moving Germany's ranking up and down (also true of Japan), there was no pre-eminent group of determinants in the case of the UK. In general, though this must obviously be a tentative conclusion, the UK performed more robustly in the sensitivity analysis than might have been suggested by criticism from respondents during the research. It seems that in matters of locational preference for international R & D facilities the UK has an underlying structural attractiveness which has not yet been totally eroded by negative government response to the drug industry.

Finally, it should be noted from the sensitivity analysis that successful policy response does not necessarily entail governments attempting to improve all the key determinants simultaneously. Obviously, in the case of all three countries which were subjected to the sensitivity analysis, where all three groups of determinants were raised to the highest level or reduced to the lowest, this had the expected effect on the rank order. However, in six of the cases where a country moved up the rank order, one of the groups was held static; in one case, two groups were held constant; and in two cases, one of the groups was actually reduced to the low value. Similarly, in one of the cases of rank reduction, one of the groups had been raised to the high level. The lesson for governments seems clear. Policy response to pharmaceutical R & D activities is not a case of crudely pushing all the determinants in one direction or another. That is impossible, or at least inadvisable, in a balanced and pluralist society where there is great competition for limited resources, especially those controlled by governments. Rather, it is clearly possible, and certainly advisable, to fine-tune policy response by manipulating combinations of the determinants in both directions to achieve both the desired industrial result and the desired economy of resource.

MERGERS AND ACQUISITIONS

Merger and acquisition activity has been referred to constantly throughout this book; it has been a much-used strategy in the past for quickly increasing firm size, markets covered, and product line. It is becoming a valuable strategy for spreading the R & D base, in terms of both inputs and outputs, and this is likely to be the case increasingly during the 1990s. The intention here is not to evaluate pharmaceutical mergers and acquisitions *per se* (that is the subject of another book), but to assess the position with regard to the medium-term future of the industry. To do this, the recent major merger between Beecham and SmithKline will be used as a case example.

According to one observer,[4] both SmithKline and Beecham had been long-time acquisition targets owing to declining performance; the only surprise was that agreed merger was the method chosen for the marriage. At the time of the merger, SmithKline was in the less favourable position, having many internal weaknesses and facing many external threats. Beecham had some useful internal strengths, including an improving financial position and a consistent product development record. In contrast, the merged company (SKB) appears to be in a much more favourable position. As a major player within the industry (world No. 3 in ethicals) in terms of sales and marketing resources, it is theoretically in a position to take advantage of the opportunities that exist internationally. The nub of this is SKB's ability to meet the pharmaceutical industry's key success factors – the ability to bring new products to market and the ability to maximise their sales. In particular, the increased sales force in all major markets will allow the firm to increase penetration of drugs like Tagamet which have been losing out to competitors (Zantac, Losec). Beecham's lack of marketing/R & D presence in the US and Japan will be overcome, and SmithKline will be strengthened in Western Europe. Beecham's strength in product development will complement SK's strength in more basic long-term research. If the future R & D programme is properly focused, the facility to ensure a steady flow of patentable products will quickly develop. With one of the largest sales forces in the industry, SKB will have an advantage in pursuing economies of scale and maximising the sales potential of its launched products.

There are, however, some downside risks. First, the merger draws together two different country and company cultures. Failure to harmonise these cultures effectively (e.g. through suitable leadership and structural alterations) could result in an introverted atmosphere, thus diverting energies from competing in the market place. Culture change is a long-term process and the company must be aware of this. Second, a weak financial position resulting from the merger will diminish SKB's ability to buy-in new products and technologies. The high financial gearing, in conjunction with a slowing of sales growth, could have a negative effect on margins. High operating gearing (high fixed costs are a peculiarity of the industry) will keep up this pressure on profit margins. Third, although merging has brought an overall broadening of the profit profile, SKB still faces a situation in which all its principal products (78 per cent of sales volume), excluding Augmentin, are in maturity or decline. Fourth, leadership is critical in this situation; Bob Bauman has made an impressive start, but the demands on his abilities will be huge.

Thus, SKB's medium term objectives are likely to include:

1 Sell non-core activities to generate cash and reduce debt.
2 Use new corporate strengths in negotiating licences and exchanges to enhance the effectiveness of the sales force, to offset the maturity of the current portfolio, and to improve the product profile in the longer term.
3 Merge the sales forces and R & D activity quickly and effectively to achieve economies of scale rapidly.
4 Focus selling efforts on new medicines such as Eminase.
5 Focus R & D on the speedy development of products for strategically important markets, with special attention to medicines for the elderly and drugs in novel areas.
6 Proactively search for opportunities to move drugs such as Tagamet into the over-the-counter sector of major markets.

Of course, whether SKB manages to achieve these objectives and eventually emerges as a prime mover (as well as being a major player) in the world pharmaceutical industry will depend much more on the complicated interplay of competitive factors which have figured so largely in this book than it will on any internal activities.

PROGNOSIS

Following the example of Barrie James noted at the beginning of this chapter, it seems right to end this book by putting forward a number of clearly stated forecasts for the period up to the end of the century; doing this also avoids the temptation to end with a series of pompous and meaningless statements about the social value of the industry, the benefit of market-driven solutions, and the blessings of the capitalist system. Accordingly, the following are prognostications for the world pharmaceutical industry for the year 2000.

1 Despite government efforts to the contrary, the world pharmaceutical industry will continue to grow faster than output as a whole.
2 Despite economic and regulatory pressures, shareholders in firms within the industry will continue to receive above-average returns on investment.
3 A spate of acquisition activity will see the industry further con-

centrated, and the number of significant research-intensive pharmaceutical multinationals within the world industry will drop to under twenty.

4 Smaller firms will resort to strategic alliances, backed by leading-edge use of management information technology, to achieve significant R & D breakthroughs.

5 There will be explosive growth in the sales of drugs for diseases of the post-industrial society; developing-country problems will still be a relatively ignored area.

6 The European market will become the biggest single driving force within the world pharmaceutical industry.

7 The UK will lose out to Germany as a preferred location for multinational R & D.

8 The Japanese firms will not come to dominate this industry; they will still be followers rather than leaders.

9 Glaxo, Merck and SKB will be world leaders.

10 Astra, Wellcome and Yamanouchi will be strong contenders in the second echelon.

11 Pfizer, Takeda, Fujisawa and ICI will be under different ownership.

12 The pharmaceutical businesses of Abbott, Hoechst and Ciba-Geigy will become relatively less important to the parent corporations.

Notes

1 The development of the world pharmaceutical industry

1 Breckon, W. (1972), *The Drug Makers*, Eyre Methuen, London.
2 *The Economist*, 1 September 1984.
3 *The Economist*, 19 May 1984.
4 Pradhan, S.B. (1983), *International Pharmaceutical Marketing*, Quorum Books, Westport, Conn.
5 Pradhan, op. cit.
6 Chew, R., Teeling-Smith, G. and Wells, N. (1985), *Pharmaceuticals in Seven Nations*, Office of Health Economics, London.
7 Reekie, W.D. and Weber, M.H. (1979), *Profits, Politics and Drugs*, Macmillan, London.
8 Estimate given in Annual Report (1985) of the Association of the British Pharmaceutical Industry, London.
9 Rigoni, R., Griffiths, A. and Laing, W. (1985), *Pharmaceutical Multinationals: Polemics, Perceptions and Paradoxes*, Wiley, Chichester.
10 Chew *et al.*, op. cit.
11 Reekie, W.D. (1975), *The Economics of the Pharmaceutical Industry*, Macmillan, London.
12 NEDO (1972), *Focus on Pharmaceuticals*, HMSO, London.
13 Mund, V.N. (1969), 'The Return on Investment of the Innovative Pharmaceutical Firm', in Joseph E. Cooper (ed.), *The Economics of Drug Innovation*, The American University, Washington, D.C.
14 Schwartzmann, D. (1976), *Innovation in the Pharmaceutical Industry*, Johns Hopkins University Press, Baltimore.
15 Schnee, J.E. (1978), 'International Shifts in Innovative Activity: the Case of Pharmaceuticals', *Columbia Journal of World Business*, spring 1978, pp. 112–21.
16 Clymer, H.A. (1970), 'The Changing Costs of Pharmaceutical Innovation', in Joseph E. Cooper (ed.), *The Economics of Drug Innovation,* The American University, Washington, D.C.
17 Schwartzmann, op. cit.
18 NEDO (1986), *A New Focus on Pharmaceuticals*, HMSO, London.
19 OECD (1977), *Impact of Multinational Enterprises on National Scientific and Technical Capacities: Pharmaceutical Industry*, OECD, Paris.
20 Comanor, W.S. (1965), 'Research and Technical Change in the Pharma-

ceutical Industry', *Review of Economics and Statistics* 47, pp. 182–90.
Grabowski, H. (1968), 'Determinants of Industrial Research and Development: A Study of the Chemical, Drug and Petroleum Industries', *Journal of Political Economy* 76 (2), pp. 292–306. Reekie, W.D. (1969), 'Location and Relative Efficiency of Research and Development in the Pharmaceutical Industry', *Business Ratios*, London. Monopolies Commission (1972), *Beecham Group Ltd and Glaxo Group Ltd; The Boots Co. Ltd and Glaxo Group Ltd: a Report on the Proposed Mergers*, H.C. 341, London.
21 Angilley, A.S. (1973), 'Returns to Scale in Research in the Ethical Pharmaceutical Industry: Some Further Empirical Evidence', *Journal of Industrial Economics* 22 (2), pp. 81–93.
22 NEDO, (1972) op. cit.
23 Dunning, J.H., Pearce, R.D., Cantwell, J. and Casson, M. (1987), *'Global Research Strategy and International Competitiveness'*, proposal for ESRC research grant.
24 Cited in Reekie (1975), op. cit.
25 Schwartzmann, op. cit.
26 United Nations Centre on Transnational Corporations (UNCTC) (1979), *Transnational Corporations and the Pharmaceutical Industry*, UNCTC, New York.
27 Walker, H.D. (1971), *Market Power and Price Levels in the Ethical Drugs Industry*, Indiana University Press, Indianapolis.
28 Schwartzmann, op. cit.
29 Chew *et al.*, op. cit.
30 Wilkinson, A. (1983), 'Technology - an Increasingly Dominant Factor in Corporate Strategy', *R & D Management*, 13 (4), pp. 245–59.
31 NEDO, (1986), op. cit.
32 Gereffi, G., (1983), *The Pharmaceutical Industry and Dependency on the Third World*, Princeton University Press, Princeton.
33 UNCTC, op. cit.

2 Applying multinational theory to the world pharmaceutical industry

1 Young, S. (1986), 'Scottish Multinationals and the Scottish Economy', Conference Proceedings, *Scotland and the Multinationals*, Institute for Research on Multinationals and Strathclyde International Business Unit, Glasgow.
2 An excellent description of the Heckscher–Ohlin theory is given in: F.R., Root, F. R. (1978), *International Trade and Investment*, South Western Publishing, Cincinnati, chapter 2.
3 Leontief, W. (1953), 'Domestic Production and Foreign Trade: the American Capital Position Re-examined', *Proceedings of the American Philosophical Society* 97 (September), pp. 332–49.
4 Posner, M. (1961), 'International Trade and Technical Change', *Oxford Economic Papers* 13 (October), pp. 323–41.
5 Linder, S.B. (1961), *An Essay on Trade Transformation*, Wiley, New York.
6 Cited in Wells (1972), *The Product Life Cycle and International Trade*, Harvard University Press, Boston, Mass.

7 Cited in Hood, N. and Young, S., (1979), *The Economics of Multinational Enterprise*, Longman, London, chapter 4.
8 Root, F.R. (1978), *International Trade and Investment*, South Western Publishing, Cincinnati.
9 Hymer, S. (1960), 'The International Operations of National Firms: a Study of Direct Investment', doctoral dissertation, Massachusetts Institute of Technology.
10 Kindleberger, C.P. (1969), *American Business Abroad: Six Lectures on Direct Investment*, Yale University Press, New Haven.
11 Knickerbocker, F.T. (1973), *Oligopolistic Reaction and the Multinational Enterprise*, Harvard University Press, Boston.
12 Aliber, R. (1970), 'A Theory of Direct Foreign Investment', in C.P. Kindleberger (ed.), *The International Corporation: a Symposium*, MIT Press, Cambridge, Mass.
13 Coase, R.H. (1937), 'The Nature of the Firm', *Economica* 4 (November).
14 Buckley, P.J. and Casson, M. (1976), *The Future of the Multinational Enterprise*, Macmillan, London.
15 Dunning, J.H. and Rugman, A.M. (1985), 'The Influence of Hymer's Dissertation on the Theory of Foreign Direct Investment', *American Economic Review*, May 1985.
16 Giddy, I.H. (1978), 'The Demise of the Product Life Cycle Model in International Business Theory', *Columbia Journal of World Business* 23 (1), pp. 90–7.
17 Magee, S.P. (1981), *The Appropriability Theory of Multinational Corporation Behaviour*, University of Reading Discussion Papers in International Investment and Business Studies 51.
18 Southard, F.A., Jr. (1931), cited in Casson, ed., op.cit.
19 Dunning, J.H. (1958), *American Investment in British Manufacturing Industry*, Allen & Unwin, London.
20 Hood and Young (1979), op. cit.
21 Ronstadt, R. (1977), *Research and Development Abroad by US Multinationals*, Praeger, New York.
22 Lall, S. (1979), 'The International Allocation of Research Activity by US Multinationals', *Oxford Bulletin of Economics and Statistics* 41, pp. 313–32.
23 Vernon, R. (1966), 'International Investment and International Trade in the Product Cycle', *Quarterly Journal of Economics* 80 (May), pp. 190–207.
24 Wells, L.T., Jr. (ed. 1972), *The Product Life Cycle and International Trade*, Harvard University Press, Boston.
25 Root (1978), op. cit.
26 Rugman, A.M. (1980), 'Internalisation as a General Theory of Foreign Direct Investment: A Reappraisal of the Literature', *Weltwirtschaftliches, Archiv* 116 (2), pp. 365–79.
27 Vernon, R. (1977), *Storm over the Multinationals*, Harvard University Press, Cambridge, Mass.
28 Giddy (1978), op. cit.
29 Magee, S.P. (1977), 'Multinational Corporations, Industry Technology Cycle and Development', *Journal of World Trade Law* 11, pp. 297–321.
30 Nelson (1962), cited in Magee (1977), op. cit.

31 Dunning, J.H. (1973), *The Location of International Firms in an Enlarged EEC: An Exploratory Paper*, Manchester Statistical Society.
32 Hirsch, S. (1976), 'An International Trade and Investment Theory of the Firm', *Oxford Economic Papers* 28, pp. 258–70.
33 Dunning, J.H. (1977), 'Trade Location of Economic Activity and the Multinational Enterprise: A Search for an Eclectic Approach', in B. Ohlin, P.O. Hesselborn and P.M. Wijkman (eds), *The International Allocation of Economic Activity* , Macmillan, London.

3 Applying technology theory to the world pharmaceutical industry

1 Green, K.M. and Morphet, C. (1977), *Research and Technology as Economic Activities*, Butterworth, London.
2 Green and Morphet, (1977), op. cit.
3 Green and Morphet, (1977), op. cit.
4 Green and Morphet, (1977), op. cit.
5 Green and Morphet, (1977), op. cit.
6 National Science Foundation (1976), *Research and Development in Industry*, NSF Report No. 76–322, Washington D.C.
7 National Science Foundation (1976), op. cit.
8 Schmookler, J. (1962), 'Determinants of Inventive Activity', *American Economic Review*, Proceedings 52 (May), pp. 165–76.
9 Schumpeter, J.A. (1950), *Capitalism, Socialism and Democracy*, Harper & Row, New York.
10 Hamberg, D. (1964), 'Size of Firm, Oligopoly and Research: the Evidence', *Canadian Journal of Economics and Political Science* 15 (February), pp. 62–75.
11 Scherer, F.M. (1965), 'Size of Firm, Oligopoly and Research: a Comment', *Canadian Journal of Economics and Political Science* 16 (May), pp. 256–67.
12 Johannison, B. and Lindstrom, C. (1971), 'Firm Size and Inventive Activity', *Swedish Journal of Economics* 73 (4), pp. 427–42.
13 Comanor, W.S. and Scherer, F.M. (1969), 'Patent Statistics as a Measure of Technical Change', *Journal of Political Economy* 77 (May–June), pp. 392–98.
14 Rosenberg, J.B. (1976), 'Research and Market Share: A Reappraisal of the Schumpeter Hypothesis', *Journal of Industrial Economics* 25 (2), pp. 101–12.
15 Shrieves, R.E. (1978), 'Market Structure and Innovation', *Journal of Industrial Economics* 26 (4), pp. 329–47.
16 Soete, L.L.G. (1979), 'Firm Size and Inventive Activity', *European Economic Review* 12, pp. 319–40.
17 Anglemar, R. (1985), 'Market Structure and Research Intensity in High-Technological-Opportunity Industries', *Journal of Industrial Economics* 34 (1), pp. 69–79.
18 Roberts, E.B. (1977), 'Generating Effective Corporate Innovation', *Technology Review*, October–November.
19 Gerstenfeld, A. and Sumiyoshi, K. (1980), 'The Management of Innovation

in Japan – Seven Forces that Make the Difference', *Research Management* (January), pp. 30–4.

20 Bartell, M. (1984), 'Innovation and the Canadian Experience', *Columbia Journal of World Business* (winter), pp. 88–91.

21 Chakrabarti, A.K., Feinman, S. and Fuentivilla, W. (1982), 'The Cross-National Comparison of Patterns of Industrial Innovations', *Columbia Journal of World Business* (fall), pp. 33–9.

22 Ferdows, K. and Rosenbloom, R.S. (1981), 'Technology Policy and Economic Development: Perspectives for Asia in the 1980s', *Columbia Journal of World Business* (summer), pp. 36–46.

23 Shrivastava, P. (1984), 'Technological Innovation in Developing Countries', *Columbia Journal of World Business* (winter), pp. 23–29.

24 Franko, L.G. (1987), 'Multinationals: the End of US Dominance', *Harvard Business Review* 56 (6), pp. 93–101.

25 Mansefield, E. (1974), 'Technology and Technological Change', in J.H. Dunning (ed.), *Economic Analysis and Multinational Enterprise*, Allen & Unwin, London.

26 Mansefield (1974), op. cit.

27 Hood, N. and Young, S. (1981), 'British Policy and Inward Direct Investment', *Journal of World Trade Law* 15 (3), pp. 231–50.

28 Caves, R.E. (1982), *Multinational Enterprise and Economic Analysis*, Cambridge University Press, Cambridge and New York.

29 Organisation for Economic Co-operation and Development (OECD) (1980), *Impact of Multinational Enterprises on National Scientific and Technological Capacities* (Analytical Report), OECD, Paris.

30 Contractor, F.J. and Sagafi-Nejad, T. (1981), 'International Technology Transfer', *Journal of International Business Studies* 12 (2), pp. 113–36.

31 Baranson, J. (1970), 'Technology Transfer through the International Firm', *American Economic Review* 60, pp. 435–48.

32 Jeannet, J.P. and Liander, B. (1978), 'Some Patterns in the Transfer of Technology within Multinational Corporations', *Journal of International Business Studies* 9 (3), pp. 108–18.

33 Gold, B. (1975), 'Alternative Strategies for Advancing a Company's Technology', *Research Management* 18 (4), p. 24.

34 Mansefield, E., Rapoport, J., Romeo, A., Wagner, S. and Beardsley, G. (1977), 'Social and Private Rates of Return from Industrial Innovations', *Quarterly Journal of Economics* 91 (2), pp. 221–40.

35 Yaprak, A. (1984), 'National Patterns of Research and Development: Implications for International Trade Theory', *Proceedings of the European International Business Association* December, 1.

36 Nason, II.K. (1979), 'The Environment for Industrial Innovation in the United States', in A. Gerstenfeld and R. Brainard (eds), *Technical Innovation: Government/Industry Co-operation*, Wiley, New York.

37 Mansefield, E., Romeo, A. and Wagner, S. (1978), 'Foreign Trade and US Research and Development', *Review of Economics and Statistics* pp. 49–57.

38 Yaprak (1984), op. cit.

39 *The Economist*, 7 April 1984.

4 The single European market and the pharmaceutical industry

1 White Paper, *Completing the Internal Market* (1985), Com(85) 310 final, Commission of the European Communities, Brussels.
2 *Blueprint for Europe: The Views of the UK Pharmaceutical Industry on the Single European Market in 1992*, Association of the British Pharmaceutical Industry, London.
3 Directorate General for Economic and Financial Affairs (1989), *The Economics of 1992:An Assessment of the Potential Economic Effects of Completing the Internal Market of the European Community*, Commission of the European Communities, Brussels.
4 *The Rules Governing Medicinal Products for Human Use in the European Community*, 1 (1989), Commission of the European Communities, Brussels.
5 Shearson Lehman Hutton (1989), *A Controversial Vision of the Future: Challenges Posed by Pharmaceutical Deregulation*, London.
6 Economists Advisory Group, (1988), *The 'Cost of Non-Europe' in the Pharmaceutical Industry*, Commission of the European Communities, Brussels.
7 Com (88) 143, March 1988, Commission of the European Communities, Brussels.
8 Report from the Commission to the Council on the Activities of the Committee for Proprietary Medicinal Products, Press Release, 1P (88) 190, 1988.
9 *Memorandum on the Future System for the Authorisation of Medicinal Products in the European Community* (April 1989), Commission of the European Communities, Brussels.
10 National Office of Animal Health (1989), *Veterinary Medicinal Products, Comments on European Documentation 4228/89 – Com (88) 779*, National Office of Animal Health, London.
11 *Guidelines on the Quality, Safety and Efficacy of Medicinal Products for Human Use*, 3 (1989), Commission of the European Communities, Brussels.
12 Economists Advisory Group (1988), op. cit.
13 Economists Advisory Group (1988), op. cit.
14 Economists Advisory Group (1988), op. cit.
15 Shearson Lehman Hutton (1989), op. cit.
16 de Wolf, P. (1988), *The Pharmaceutical Industry: Structure, Intervention and Competitive Strength*, European Industry Structure.
17 Economists Advisory Group (1988), op. cit.
18 Economists Advisory Group (1988), op. cit.
19 *Scrip* 1419, 9 June 1989, pp. 1–5.

5 The competitive environment of the world pharmaceutical industry

1 Porter, M.E. (1980), *Competitive Strategy*, Free Press, New York, p. xiii.
2 Porter (1980), op. cit., p. 3.
3 *Scrip* 1302, 22 April 1988, pp. 18–20.
4 *Scrip* 1297/8, 6/8 April 1988, p. 20.

5 Novo Annual Report, 1987.
6 Porter (1980), op. cit., p. 25.
7 Porter (1980), op. cit., p. 26.
8 Porter, M.E. (1985), *Competitive Advantage*, Free Press, New York, pp. 279–80.
9 Porter (1985), op. cit., p. 292.
10 Porter (1980), op. cit., p. 24.
11 Porter (1980), op. cit., pp. 18–21.
12 Porter (1980), op. cit., p. 6.
13 Porter (1980), op. cit., p. 35.

6 The US pharmaceutical market

1 *Scrip Yearbook* (1990), PJB Publications, Richmond, Surrey, p. 13.
2 *Scrip Yearbook* (1990), op. cit., p. 13.
3 *Scrip Yearbook* (1990), op. cit., pp. 17–20.
4 Quoted in *Scrip* 1420 (1989), p. 14.
5 Merck & Co. Inc, Annual Report 1989, p. 3.
6 Merck & Co. Inc, Annual Report 1989, p. 78.
7 Much of the remainder of this section is developed from an interview with Mr Stanley J. Fidelman, Senior Vice President Planning and Development, Merck Sharp & Dohme Research Laboratories, Rahway, New Jersey.
8 Abbott Laboratories, Annual Report 1989, p. 1.
9 Abbott Laboratories, Annual Report 1989, p. 13.
10 Abbott Laboratories, Annual Report 1975, p. 4.
11 Abbott Laboratories, Annual Report 1989, p. 2.
12 Abbott Laboratories, Annual Report 1989, p. 7.
13 Much of the remainder of this section is developed from an interview with Dr Robert S. Janicki, Vice-President Pharmaceutical Products Research and Development, Abbott Laboratories, North Chicago, Ilinois.
14 Pfizer Inc, Annual Report 1989, p. 2.
15 'Pharmaceuticals in the 1990s', James Capel & Co., Research Document, London, 1990.

7 The British pharmaceutical market

1 NEDO (1986), *A New Focus on Pharmaceuticals*, HMSO, London, pp. 1–9.
2 Chew, Robert (1988), *The Pharmaceutical Industry and the Nation's Health*, ABPI, London, p. 3.
3 Chew (1988), op. cit., p. 3.
4 Glaxo, Annual Report and Accounts 1990, p. 11.
5 Chew (1988), op. cit., p. 8.
6 Association of the British Pharmaceutical Industry (1989), Annual Report 1988–89, p. 12.
7 ABPI (1989); this section leans heavily on a review of UK pharmaceutical R & D carried out by the ABPI in 1988 and reported in op. cit., pp. 21–3.
8 Glaxo, *Key Facts* 1988, pp. 1 and 6.
9 Glaxo, Annual Report and Accounts 1990, p. 6.

10 ICI, Annual Report and Accounts 1989, inside front cover.
11 ICI, Annual Report and Accounts 1989, p. 17.
12 Wellcome, Annual Report and Accounts 1990, p. 2.
13 Wellcome, Annual Report and Accounts 1990, pp. 10–11.

8 The European pharmaceutical market

1 ABPI (1988), *Blueprint for Europe; the views of the UK Pharmaceutical Industry on the Single European Market in 1992*, ABPI, London.
2 *Scrip Yearbook* 1990, p. 24.
3 Directorate General of Economic and Financial Affairs (1989), *The economics of 1992: an Assessment of the Potential Economic Effects of completing the Internal Market of the European Community*. Commission of the European Communities.
4 'Drug Patent Life Erosion may Damage Industry Health', *European Chemical News*, 1992 review, May 1989, pp. 52–4.
5 *Scrip Yearbook* 1988.
6 Economists Advisory Group (1988), *The Cost of Non-Europe in the Pharmaceutical Industry*, Economists Advisory Group, London.
7 Economists Advisory Group (1988), op. cit.
8 Shearson Lehman Hutton (1989), *A Controversial Vision of the Future: Challenges posed by Pharmaceutical Deregulation*, Report by Shearson Lehman Hutton, London .
9 *Scrip* 1427, 7 July 1989, pp. 4–7.
10 Ciba-Geigy PLC (1986), 'The Corporate Principles of Ciba-Geigy in the United Kingdom'.
11 Interview with *Marketing*, April 1987.
12 Walter von Wartburg, quoted in the February 1989 edition of the Ciba-Geigy *Journal*.
13 Address of Chairman Dr Alex Krauer to the Ciba-Geigy Ltd Annual General Meeting, 4 May 1988.
14 See, for example, the *Financial Times*, 17 November 1988.
15 Quoted in *Pronounced Success: America and Hoechst, 1953–1978*, published by American Hoechst Corporation, p. 8.
16 Hoechst AG Annual Report 1989, p. 2.
17 Quoted in Hoechst AG Annual Report 1989, pp. 10, 12, 14.
18 *Scrip* 1274, 1988, p. 22.
19 *Financial Times*, 25 October 1988, p. 15.
20 *Scrip* 1234, 1988, p. 15.
21 *Scrip Yearbook* 1988, p. 64.

9 The Japanese pharmaceutical market

1 'Your Market in Japan: Pharmaceuticals', *JETRO*, March 1987, p. 14.
2 *JETRO*, op. cit., p. 14
3 Takeda, Annual Report, 1989, inside front cover.
4 Takeda, Annual Report, 1987, p. 3.
5 Takeda, Annual Report, 1986, p. 4.

6 Takeda, Annual Report, 1989, p. 19.
7 'Central Research Division' (1988), published by Takeda Chemical Industries Ltd.
8 Takeda, Annual Report, 1989, p. 6.
9 Takeda, Annual Report, 1989, p. 7.
10 Takeda, Annual Report, 1989, p. 6.
11 *Dynamics*, No. 1, April 1990, published by Takeda Chemical Industries.
12 Fujisawa, Annual Report, 1990, p. 4.
13 Fujisawa, Annual Report, 1990, p. 10.
14 Yamanouchi, Annual Report, 1990, inside front cover.
15 Yamanouchi, Annual Report, 1985, p. 4.
16 Yamanouchi, Annual Report, 1990, p. 16.

10 Towards the millennium

1 James, Barrie G. (1977), *The Future of the Multinational Pharmaceutical Industry to 1990*, Associated Business Programmes, London.
2 Rigoni, R., Griffiths, A. and Laing, W. (1985), *Pharmaceutical Multinationals: Polemics, Perceptions and Paradoxes*, Institute for Research into Multinationals, Geneva.
3 Taggart, J.H. (1988), 'Strategic Determinants of the Foreign R & D Locational Decision: the Case of the International Pharmaceutical Industry', Ph.D. thesis, University of Strathclyde, Glasgow.
4 Blackhurst, C. (1989), 'In Search of the Global Prescription', *Sunday Times*, 30 April 1989, p. D11.

Index

Abbokinase 200
Abbott, Wallace C. 185
Abbott Alkaloid Company 185; *see also* Abbott Laboratories
Abbott Laboratories 2, 37, 185–206, 432, 443; business segments 187–9; Ciba-Geigy and Chiron 355; company history and development 185–6; financial analysis 189–97, 433–5; geographical spread 189–91; mission statement 186; objectives 186–7; performance 194–7, 433–5; products and competition 24, 197–200; R & D 201–4; segmental analysis 191–4; strategic position 32, 35, 36, 37, 38; strategy options/choice 205–6; strengths 204; and Takeda 386; weaknesses 204; *see also* Takeda-Abbott Pharmaceuticals
absolute advantage 43, 46
Aclaplastin 361
acquisitions 440–2; Abbott 205; Ciba-Geigy 355; German companies 111; Hoechst 369; ICI 286; MNCs and technology 80; Pfizer 229, 230, 230–1; prognosis 442–3; Wellcome 315; Yamanouchi 406, 419–20; *see also* mergers
Actifed 235, 308
Activase 200
Actosolv 361
acupuncture 140
Adecut 385

advanced drug delivery research (ADDR) 350, 351, 352
Africa 353; Abbott's market 189–91; Ciba-Geigy's market 354; Glaxo's market 245, 246–7, 248–9; Pfizer's market 212–14
ageing population 156, 353
aggressive strategies 368, 369, 389
agricultural products 210; Takeda 378, 379–81; *see also* animal health products
AIDS drugs/research 425; Ciba-Geigy 350, 353; Hoechst 362, 365; Wellcome 288, 307
Aldomet 163, 174
Allen and Hanburys Ltd 240
Alnert 395, 401
alternative medicines 139
Alza 350
Alzheimer's disease 87, 156
Amasulin 385
American Home Products 24, 32, 34, 35, 37, 38
Amersham International 238
anaesthetics: Astra and local 324, 328, 329, 330, 334; ICI 277
Anafranil 345, 347
analgesics 167, 168, 169
Andursil 346
Anexate 418
Anglemar, R. 74
aniline purple 1
animal health products: Fujisawa 392, 393–4; Merck 163, 180; Pfizer 210; *see also* agricultural products